Networks of Privilege in the Middle East

Networks of Privilege in the Middle East: The Politics of Economic Reform Revisited

Edited by

Steven Heydemann

palgrave
macmillan

NETWORKS OF PRIVILEGE IN THE MIDDLE EAST
© Steven Heydemann, 2004.

First published 2004 by
PALGRAVE MACMILLAN™
175 Fifth Avenue, New York, N.Y. 10010 and
Houndmills, Basingstoke, Hampshire, England RG21 6XS
Companies and representatives throughout the world

PALGRAVE MACMILLAN is the global academic imprint of the Palgrave Macmillan division of St. Martin's Press, LLC and of Palgrave Macmillan Ltd. Macmillan® is a registered trademark in the United States, United Kingdom and other countries. Palgrave is a registered trademark in the European Union and other countries.

ISBN 1–4039–6352–5 hardback

Library of Congress Cataloging-in-Publication Data
Networks of privilege in the Middle East / edited by Steven Heydemann.
        p. cm.
    Includes bibliographical references and index.
    ISBN 1–4039–6352–5 (cloth: alk. paper)
        1. Business and politics—Arab countries—Case studies.
    2. Elite (Social sciences)—Arab countries—Case studies.
    I. Heydemann, Steven.

JQ1850.A91N48 2004
330.956—dc22   2004044257

A catalogue record for this book is available from the British Library.

Design by Newgen Imaging Systems (P) Ltd., Chennai, India.

First edition: August 2004
10 9 8 7 6 5 4 3 2 1

Printed in the United States of America.

Contents

Acknowledgments

This volume is the product of a collaborative research project sponsored by the Mediterranean Program of the Robert Schuman Center of the European University Institute. Participants in the working group were selected through an open competition that drew more than 50 applications. Beginning in December 1999, participants took part in three workshops at the European University Institute where drafts of papers were presented, discussed, and—in the intervals between meetings—revised. Some participants in the group also took part in two thematic conversations held at the 2001 and 2002 meetings of the Middle East Studies Association, in San Francisco and Washington, respectively. Final revisions were completed in 2002–2003.

The origins of this project, however, are almost entirely the result of serendipity. Working at home one day in 1998, I received an e-mail from Yves Meny, then Director of the Robert Schuman Center and now President of the European University Institute. The e-mail invited me to submit a proposal to a competition for funding to direct a research working group. It noted, rather sternly, that if my proposal were selected I might be required to travel to Florence from time to time to take part in workshops and to give presentations about the project at EUI's request. It took about nine seconds to conclude that this was a condition I could live with and prepared a proposal for a working group on the role of informal networks in the politics of economic reform in the Middle East, a topic I had been moving toward for some time in my work on economic reform in Syria. I e-mailed it in and, some six weeks later, through means no less mysterious than those surrounding the original invitation, was informed that my proposal had been approved.

Thus began a collaboration that ends, formally, with the publication of this volume. But my connection to the EUI has been important for reasons that go well beyond this project. Not least, it afforded me the privilege of working at the Robert Schuman Center and getting to know Yves Meny for the remarkable scholar and administrator he is—a description that is equally applicable to Helen Wallace, his successor as the Schuman Center's director. It offered to me and other participants in the working group a chance to take part in the activities of EUI's Mediterranean Program, and to benefit from the professionalism, support, and exceptional competence of its staff, especially Imco Brouwer and his assistant Anne-Charlotte Svantesson. I am also deeply grateful for the support and assistance of Filipa di Sousa, who has the unenviable task of helping EUI's visiting scholars to cope with the bureaucratic and other demands of daily life in Italy. Valerie Amiraux, who served with Imco Brouwer as co-scientific secretary of the Mediterranean Program, became a good friend and an invaluable source of information about EUI, Florence, and Italy.

The project also gave me the chance to work with and get to know a remarkable group of scholars. Participants in the project represented diverse disciplines, approaches, and intellectual concerns. Some were well established in their careers, others just starting out. They work in a variety of national and institutional settings, including the United States, Turkey, Italy, France, England, and Germany. Yet they all brought to this project a deep commitment to and insightful engagement with the issues at stake in our collective endeavor. I am grateful to all of them, including those who took part in and helped shape our discussions at one stage or another but whose essays do not appear in this volume. Two such participants deserve particular recognition: Ayse Bugra and Bryan Daves. Our editor at Palgrave, David Pervin, occupies a different but no less important position in the collaboration that this volume represents, not least in finding readers whose anonymous comments helped to guide us in revising these chapters. We were also fortunate to benefit from the sometimes sharp critique of two anonymous reviewers who assessed our papers at an earlier stage. At Georgetown, Alan Treat, a graduate student in the School of Foreign Service, performed wonders as multilingual copy editor, bibliographer, and grammarian. As in all my own endeavors, however, the collaboration and support for which I am most thankful is that of my wife, Gail David, and my daughters, Sarah David Heydemann and Julia David Heydemann, to whom I dedicate this volume.

INTRODUCTION

Networks of Privilege: Rethinking the Politics of Economic Reform in the Middle East

Steven Heydemann

airness. A level playing field. Accountability. These remain the elusive but sought after ends of a massive effort to change institutions, organizations, and practices on a global scale, transforming inward-looking, inefficient, and corrupt economic arrangements and policies into market-oriented economies that create incentives for individuals and firms to invest, save, trade, and work. Arguably, this wide-scale movement to strengthen markets, and to create them where they did not previously exist, has led to significant improvements in macroeconomic performance. Broad trends over the past two decades suggest that where economic reforms have taken hold, investment and employment rise, trade expands, and economic growth rates increase. The social and economic disruptions associated with economic reform are far from trivial. In many early reformers, criticism of market-based development strategies is becoming more visible. Yet the longer-term, macroeconomic benefits of liberalizing an economy are often seen as sufficiently compelling to justify the short-run costs.

Nonetheless, the experience of reform also makes clear just how intangible the aims of fairness, accountability, and transparency remain. Without exception, economic reform programs either reproduce or create anew arrangements that give a privileged few unequal access to the benefits of new economic policies. Whether this happens by intent, as progressive critics of economic liberalization programs allege, or through politically motivated distortions of the reform process, economic liberalization and reform have everywhere been accompanied by the persistence or restructuring, if not deepening, of practices that they were intended to overcome. One practice stands out in this regard as especially resistant to reform: the pursuit of rents, an activity broadly understood as nonproductive or directly counterproductive efforts to capture "excess" profit by creating or exploiting government regulation to avoid competition.

Despite the intent of reformers to reduce or eliminate rent seeking, and to increase transparency and accountability, economic reform and the pursuit of rents go hand in hand.[1] Certainly, the effects of reform on rent seeking vary from place to place, as do the effects of rent seeking on economic performance. Nonetheless, it would not be inappropriate to describe economic reform as a process that, among other things, reorganizes the structures and practices of rent seeking through which some economic actors will capture a disproportionate share of the benefits of new economic policies.

The chapters in this volume present the efforts of a diverse, international group of scholars to shed light on the politics that have shaped the experience of economic reform in the Middle East. However, our interests are less generic than this implies. The intent of the chapters is not to provide an overview of reform processes and their (all too visible) limits in the Middle East. Our aim, instead, is to account for variation and patterns in the outcome of economic liberalization programs where outcomes, for our purposes, are defined in terms of (a) shifts in the policies and institutions that regulate extraction and distribution (fiscal policy and the domain of fiscality more broadly), and (b) shifts in the organization of politically mediated economic arrangements, notably but not exclusively the organization of rent seeking and other networks that mobilize to influence the form and content of new economic policies and exploit new regulatory environments created by policy reform. This is the focus of the research presented in chapters by Cammett, Haddad, Leenders, Sfakianakis, Wils, and Wurzel. The following chapters also investigate the strategic uses of reform and reform discourses by incumbents and economic elites to advance their political interests, focusing on fiscal policy as a domain in which these strategies have been especially important. This is the concern of chapters by Cassarino, Hibou, and Kienle.

These chapters, in other words, use a range of approaches to explain variation and patterns in the organization and reorganization of what might be called "networks of privilege" during and after economic reform in a select set of Middle East cases. We do not examine every country in the region. In fact, some cases are the subject of more than one chapter to bring different perspectives to bear on a single experience of reform. Wurzel, Sfakianakis, and Kienle offer quite different accounts of how networks functioned in the course of economic reform in Egypt, and how reforms in turn affected networks of economic privilege. Overall, however, these chapters explore whether and how the organization of economic privilege before reform, in particular the organization of state–business relations, explains the outcome of reform programs themselves, including the ways in which economic privilege is (politically) reorganized as a result of reform. They seek to account for outcomes in which the results of reform could not easily be predicted by the structure of interests prior to reform, and to identify the factors that produce variation in the outcomes of reform across a universe of cases that are, in many ways, quite similar in the organization of their political economies and in the kind of economic reform programs they have experienced.

Moreover, we approach this task with the understanding that "reform" in the Arab Middle East falls short of an ideal-typical transition from state to market. In the region studied here, policy reform has been partial and selective, at best. This reality has led some observers to question whether reform is an appropriate characterization of the shifts that have taken place in Middle East political economies over the past ten to twenty years.[2] And, needless to say, whether economic reform has happened in the Middle East has obvious and important implications for this volume. Not least, it has a direct bearing on our claim that existing frameworks do not adequately explain the politics of economic reform in these, and perhaps other, cases. If regional experiences don't qualify as reform in a meaningful sense, surely this claim must be invalid. Why, after all, should theories of economic reform be expected to account for processes that, whatever we might call them, do not meet some minimally accepted definition of that process?

These are appropriate concerns. Yet it would be wrong to view our cases as outliers whose experiences place them beyond the scope of the literature on economic reform. The relevant question in determining the analytic standing of our cases isn't whether they satisfy an ideal-typical conception of reform, but where they can be situated on a spectrum ranging from no reform to full reform and, more important, whether they can be situated far enough along that spectrum to exhibit the kinds of political and social processes that bring our cases within the compass of existing theoretical frameworks. The issue is not whether economic policy reform in the Middle East resembles that in Chile or the Czech Republic, but whether it generated the kinds of politics that permit comparison between Middle East cases and those that are situated further down the spectrum of reform experiences. As the chapters that follow demonstrate, this is clearly the case.

What the authors in this volume argue, therefore, is that despite the limits of economic reform in the Middle East, and despite ongoing debates about whether and how much the economies of the region have changed, we find ample evidence that local actors experience shifts in economic policy as consequential to their interests, and as a meaningful basis for political mobilization. These dynamics have tended to be concentrated within sectoral or policy-specific domains that become relatively bounded "islands of reform." This phenomenon is evident, for example, in Cammett's case of bargaining over regulations that affect textile exports in Morocco, the dynamics of tax reform in Jordan discussed by Wils, and the privatization of state-owned enterprises in Egypt that are covered by Wurzel. Certainly, the politics of economic reform are as pervasive, volatile, and diffuse in the Middle East as in other developing regions, constituting a central element of public life. However, the strategic interactions of most interest for this volume appear most powerfully within what are often described as "policy domains," spaces within which delimited sets of actors actively engage in shaping the outcomes of struggles over policy making.[3] Within those domains we find the kinds of distributional politics that are in keeping with those that accompany economic reform anywhere. On these grounds, the experiences discussed in the following chapters can not only be considered to fall within the ambit of the literature on the politics of economic reform, but to challenge that literature in ways we hope will be seen as productive.

If our agenda is thus more limited than trying to account for reform outcomes in the Middle East in general, it is nonetheless ambitious. We hope to explain how reform is shaped by, and in turn helps to reorganize, the structures and practices through which select actors capture, politically, positions of economic privilege, and why a largely similar process applied to similar political economies has exhibited a range of outcomes in how this reorganization of privilege has occurred. Where do we begin in constructing such an explanation? In general terms, the chapters in this volume focus on three factors. First, they explore from a variety of perspectives how institutional and regulatory arrangements mold structures of economic privilege and organize rent-seeking arrangements in the pre-reform period, with a particular interest in state–business relations. Second, they assess how structures of economic privilege and the organization of rent seeking affect the bargaining and negotiation that accompany institutional and regulatory reform. Third, they examine the impact of this bargaining on the design of new regulatory regimes and institutions, and thus on the structure of rent-seeking opportunities and other forms of politically mediated economic exchange in the period after reform. Collectively, evaluating these three factors makes it possible to identify whether there exist correlations among them that explain not only why economic liberalization—fiscal policy reform in particular—reproduces or creates new possibilities for politically privileged economic actors to collude in capturing the benefits of reform, but also to explain how these possibilities are organized, and why they differ in significant ways across cases.

The rationale for adopting this particular approach—highlighting the importance of formal and informal networks in bargaining over policy reform—rests on three claims that need to be made explicit. One is that processes of reform in the Middle East (and elsewhere) exhibit hybrid characteristics, take place through forms of bargaining and negotiation, and produce outcomes that do not fit well within existing theoretical frameworks. The second claim is that closing gaps between existing theories and what we see happening on the ground is critical to the development of an adequate explanation of the politics of economic reform in the Middle East, and to a satisfactory account of why reforms look the way they do, that is to say, partial, uneven, and selective.

In addition, hidden not so deeply within this project is a third claim: that the dynamics we observe are not unique to the Middle East but have implications that extend beyond a single region. In particular, as I develop in more detail below, these cases suggest, with some reservations, the benefit of adopting network-based forms of analysis in accounting for the politics of economic reform. In this sense, the experience of economic reform in the Middle East points us toward larger theoretical concerns about agency in the process of reform; and about the relationship among actors, institutions, and networks. It challenges existing accounts of the politics of economic reform by unpacking the basic unit of agency—distributional coalitions—that is central to research in the comparative political economy of reform. It also brings into closer, and I hope more productive, contact the more fully socialized approaches to institutional formation and change that have emerged within economic sociology and the material–rationalist accounts that tend to prevail in economics and parts of comparative politics. The volume thus holds out potential for generating approaches that could change the way we think about the politics of economic reform not only in the Middle East cases discussed here, but more broadly. I develop these points further in subsequent sections of this introduction, focusing in particular on the logic underlying the view that network approaches can advance our research on the politics and political economy of economic reform.

Policy Reform and the Reorganization of Rent Seeking

What is it, then, about the dynamics of economic reform in the Middle East for which we do not yet have an adequate explanation? Of the many possible answers to this question, this volume is organized around one in particular. As indicated earlier, our starting point is the simple and perhaps even self-evident proposition that in the Middle East, as in other settings, economic liberalization is a process that reorganizes opportunities for rent seeking.[4] I do not claim that this is the only thing economic liberalization does. Certainly, economic policy reform has had quite wide-ranging consequences, even in the Middle East where heterodox reform strategies dominate, and the Washington Consensus has a weak foothold. Yet everywhere economic reforms have been introduced in the Middle East (and elsewhere) some privileged economic actors have been effective in preserving their positions from the presumed consequences of the transition from state to semi-market economies. Wherever reforms have been implemented, they have produced outcomes that continue to provide significant opportunities for privileged economic actors, old or new, to collaborate in capturing the gains that can be extracted from a particular set of regulatory arrangements and economic institutions.

What these chapters all take as central questions, therefore, is how a given configuration of privileged economic actors mobilize in response to shifts in economic institutions and regulations, to preserve if not enhance their access to politically mediated economic resources; why some "winners" seem more adept than others at doing so, and how shifts in economic policy do or do not create space for the organization of politically mediated forms of economic privilege. Our intent is to develop a better understanding of how such actors and the networks through which they often mobilize politically both shape economic reforms and how shifts in economic policy, in turn, reshape the organization of rent-seeking opportunities that they wish to exploit; to identify the variables that account for the specific ways in which economic reforms reorganize rent-seeking opportunities in specific cases; to explain patterns and variation in outcomes across cases in the Middle East; and to develop explanations that will permit us (though we do not do so in this volume) to test our models against the experiences of economic reform beyond the Middle East.

Situating the Volume Theoretically

Following sections of this introduction "situate" this volume in two distinct ways. The first, presented here, focuses on where these chapters fit in a larger literature on the political economy of economic policy reform. It addresses where we think current frameworks fall short, and why they do so. The second, developed in the subsequent section, suggests a strategy for responding to gaps in existing models, by more closely integrating network approaches into research on the politics of economic reform.

Over the past two decades, a dense literature has grown up around efforts to explain the politics that shape economic liberalization programs. Throughout this period, the role of privileged actors—their impact on reform processes and the effects reform has on them—has received particular attention, for good reasons. For many analysts, these actors are believed to hold the fate of reform in their hands. This power, whether real or not, has accorded them a special place in the literature on reform—and not necessarily a place of honor. In its earliest phases, this literature tended to assume that economic policy reform would (appropriately) disrupt and destabilize existing political coalitions and displace the privileged economic actors that circulated within them.[5] Economic reform, it was argued, depoliticized access to resources,[6] causing those who benefited from privileged economic positions to become losers in the more competitive environments created by economic reform.[7] Indeed, the breakup of privileged economic networks was viewed as critical for the success of reform.[8] Managing this process, building coalitions of winners and excluding losers from undermining new policies, was seen as central to the political dynamics of economic reforms.[9]

For much of the 1980s and well into the 1990s, international financial institutions such as the World Bank and International Monetary Fund viewed pre-reform economic networks as an obstacle that had to be overcome to ensure the success of new economic policies.[10] Creating the conditions for growth required dismantling economic arrangements that served the interests of political power holders, and replacing them with arrangements that reflected the "logic of economics."[11] In this view, liberalization was seen as causing a shift from cronyism, patronage, and rent seeking to transparency, accountability, and well-defined property rights.

Moreover, because it threatened the position of entrenched interest groups, liberalization was perceived to carry tremendous political risks. Those who benefited most from pre-reform economic arrangements were expected to mobilize in opposition to reform. This opposition not only jeopardized the success of reform, it threatened overall political and social stability. To avoid such an outcome, researchers worked to identify strategies for managing reform that minimize the political risks associated with dramatic changes in the organization of an economy.[12]

This view of how liberalization works shaped much of the early thinking about the politics of economic reform in a huge range of cases. Outside the Middle East, it has been applied to such cases as Indonesia, Kenya, and Japan, among many others. Within the Middle East, it has been used to explain the dynamics of economic policy reform in Egypt, Turkey, Jordan, Syria, Tunisia, and Morocco. It would, in fact, be hard to overestimate the influence of this perspective on first-generation theories of how economic policy reform operates. The idea that economic reform represents the replacement of political logics by economic logics as the basis for policy making was a touchstone of comparative political economy for much of the 1980s and well into the 1990s.

Yet the actual experience of reform has raised important questions about the accuracy of these assumptions. In fact, as a number of scholars have pointed out, pre-reform economic networks have proven to be quite resilient. Both in the Middle East and elsewhere, privileged economic actors have been effective in preserving their positions from the presumed consequences of economic liberalization. Even when policy reforms are designed to increase transparency and eliminate opportunities for rent seeking, such actors continue to dominate important arenas of economic exchange. This is true of the experience of privatization in Russia, which transferred public assets to Soviet-era managers at huge discounts to their true value;[13] of Israel, where privatization has enhanced the economic position of dominant business families and reduced competition;[14] of privatization in Latin America;[15] and of reform in Arab states such as Egypt, Tunisia, Jordan, and Morocco where pre-reform business and political elites occupy privileged positions within newly liberalized sectors of the economy.[16] Even where economic liberalization improves economic performance, strengthens markets, and broadens the boundaries of economic inclusion (which, according to the World Bank, is happening in Egypt and Morocco) we find that privileged economic networks capture a disproportionate share of the benefits of reform.

Moreover, if all processes of reform in the Middle East seem alike in providing opportunities for "networks of privilege" to survive, there are clear and significant variations in the political processes through which structures of rent seeking are reorganized. We find meaningful variation in the extent to which patterns of economic inclusion and exclusion are transformed, and in the degree to which pre-reform networks are forced to adapt, adjust, or regroup in the face of new economic policies. In some cases, such as Jordan, Lebanon, and Morocco, private business interests may exert meaningful weight in shaping reform outcomes, as indicated by Wils, Leenders, and Cammett (chapters 4, 5, and 8). In others, such as Syria, they may be almost entirely excluded from policy making even though peak business elites benefit disproportionally from economic liberalization, as Haddad demonstrates quite clearly (chapter 1). In yet others, such as Egypt and Tunisia, the peak business elites occupy more ambiguous positions in the reform process, as shown by Sfakianakis, Hibou, and Cassarino (chapters 2, 6, and 7).

Moreover, the influence of international financial institutions (IFIs) and foreign investors varies across cases in defining reform agendas and ensuring local compliance once reforms have been enacted, ranging from high levels of interaction between IFIs and local policy-makers (in cases such as Egypt, Tunisia, Morocco, and Jordan) to the almost complete insulation of local actors from the influence of IFIs (again, Syria is an illustrative case). Moreover, organized labor and other interest groups vary in their reactions to reform, and in the strategies they adopt to resist or exploit it,[17] while bureaucrats and politicians vary in their responsiveness to pressures for reform and their commitment to liberalization.

Rent Seeking as Normal Politics?

These diverse reform outcomes have provoked a range of reactions from interested parties, including efforts by the World Bank and other IFIs to develop strategies for overcoming what are now widely seen as shortcomings in earlier reform efforts.[18] Nonetheless, for some researchers, the persistence and reorganization of rent-seeking arrangements after reform is neither unanticipated nor, necessarily, unintended. Thus, if the old school Washington Consensus perspective might consider our starting point—economic reform as a process that reorganizes opportunities for rent seeking—to be undesirable and theoretically controversial, other approaches are more likely to view the persistence of rent seeking as the predictable result of conditions in which economic policy is driven by private rather than public interests. To situate this volume effectively, it is important to establish how the chapters here respond to the challenges posed by this work.

Perhaps the most significant challenges to this volume can be found in the claims of scholars who write on rent-seeking behavior and on predatory and developmental states, including the work of economists ranging from James Buchanan, Mancur Olson, Anne Krueger, Gary Becker, Alice Amsden, and Douglass North; to political scientists and sociologists including Margaret Levy, David Waldner, Stephan Haggard, Robert Kaufman, John Waterbury, Thomas Callaghy, Robert Bates, Barbara Geddes, Miles Kahler, Joan Nelson, and Peter Evans, among many others. While I do not wish capriciously to lump together methodological approaches as different as various forms of new institutionalism, rational choice theories of predatory rule, and public choice economics—much less arbitrarily draw connections between them and critics of public choice such as Evans, Boyer and Hollingsworth, or Kahler—the wide-ranging literatures I refer to share certain minimum assumptions.[19]

Most centrally, arguments about developmental success or failure tend to share the view that where property rights are not clearly specified; or where state institutions lack particular kinds of qualities (embedded autonomy, for

Evans; the capacity to function as a neutral third party, in North's work; or the capacity to manage the transition to markets, in Kahler's case); or where the time horizon of state elites is too short to permit them to view investment in development as a matter of self-interest (as in Olson's more recent work[20]) the result will be the capture of the state and its policy-making apparatus by coalitions of public and private actors who then use their positions to extract from the economy the maximum possible amount of resources.

Further, as Olson, Callaghy, Haggard, Bates, and Evans have all demonstrated in different contexts, once such rent-seeking networks control the state apparatus, they resist or undermine reforms that might jeopardize their privileged economic positions. Dani Rodrik makes this familiar case with respect to trade reform: "from the perspective of policy makers, the pure reshuffling of income must be counted as a political cost. In politics, rents and revenues that accrue on a regular basis create entitlements. Whether viewed as desirable or not, taking income away from one group is rarely easy for a politician to accomplish."[21]

It is worth noting that whether public and private interests are compatible—that is, whether certain forms of rent seeking are consistent with economic development or necessarily lead to destructive forms of predation—is not as clear as some of the above-named scholars might believe, North and Olson in particular. Amsden's description of corruption, bribery, and rent seeking in her account of developmental success in Korea exhibits a number of similarities to Bates's description of bribery, corruption, and rent seeking in his account of developmental failure in Africa.[22] More recently, research on rent seeking and development in Asia has worked toward a more articulated understanding of when such activity is or is not developmentally productive.[23] It is also worth noting that whether it is seen as developmentally productive or not, much of this literature locates the origins and persistence of rent seeking not among a powerful class of entrepreneurs that dominates state institutions (the starting point of much dependency literature), but among strategic state elites responding to the requirements of short-term political survival. Capitalists are more often policy takers in this literature than they are policy makers.[24] Nonetheless, the core point remains. In Evans's terms, the embeddedness of a state bureaucracy in networks of private capital "will degenerate into a super-cartel, aimed, like all cartels, at protecting its members from changes in the status quo."[25]

This view of the negative relationship between rent seeking and reform is being qualified in useful ways, but it nonetheless poses a meaningful challenge for this volume. It suggests that we are focusing on a well-understood phenomenon and, as a result, that the extent of our contribution will be to apply the insights of existing literatures to a broader range of cases. Even if this were so, and the chapters in this volume went no further than to test these literatures against the dynamics of bargaining over reform in Middle East cases, both the disciplines and the field of Middle East studies would benefit. My sense, however, is that the volume does more than this, contributing to three ongoing debates within the broad field of comparative political economy. First, the volume provides the basis for moving toward more systematic explanations of how predation and economic efficiency interact, and reinforce the view that the relationship is more varied than is often assumed in the literature on economic reform. We know that in some cases, Korea for instance, these practices were consistent with high growth. We know that in others, such as tropical Africa, they were not. Similarly, we know that in some cases, such as Kenya, Russia, and Indonesia the prevalence and power of rent-seeking networks has impeded possibilities for economic reform, while in others such as Egypt, Morocco, and Tunisia such networks have posed more limited obstacles to reform. Yet to date we do not have good systematic explanations of the specific conditions under which rent-seeking networks disrupt reform, promote reform, or are neutral in their impact on economic policy change.[26] This volume sheds light on such questions and thus brings us closer to such systematic explanations.

Second, as indicated earlier, the experiences of Middle East states complicate claims about the negative correlation between rent seeking on one hand, and the capacity to liberalize economic policy and improve economic performance, on the other. They open up the possibility that rent seeking may be a condition for, rather than an obstacle to, "market-rational" shifts in the organization of a political economy. A number of hypotheses suggest why this might be the case. One is that policy makers might preserve privileged economic arrangements to induce compliance with reforms that, in general, broaden the scope of markets and of economic inclusion even if they do so imperfectly. The structure of such inducements will, obviously, differ depending on their targets. With respect to business, this might mean that reformers use their control of access to rents as inducements they can provide to business elites, in the form of side payments, in exchange for their willingness to invest under new rules and thus increase the likelihood of improvements in overall economic performance. With respect to labor, this might imply that policy makers structure reforms in ways that preserve the privileged access of workers to public resources, whether in the form of employment guarantees for public sector workers, the maintenance of corporatist labor institutions, or a commitment to sustain certain levels of welfare expenditure in the national budget.

A second hypothesis is simply that rent-seeking skills may well be portable across policy regimes; those who are most adept at rent seeking before reform will have an acquired advantage—in personal ties, information, expertise—in securing privileged access to new arenas of rent seeking created as a result of reform. A third is that policy makers seeking to establish a coalition in support of reforms may use their regulatory authority in a way that creates new alliances among rent seekers whose interests were previously at odds. In other words, economic reform is not simply a process in which pre-reform networks bargain with policy makers over the terms of new economic arrangements on the basis of fixed and predetermined interests. Reform is also *constitutive* of new networks, distributive coalitions, and political alliances. As a result, policy makers may exploit their regulatory authority to induce, through the distribution of economic privileges, the formation of coalitions and networks that will enhance the overall prospects for reforms to move forward. And new rent-seeking networks may emerge from the bottom up as social groups organize to exploit the possibility reforms offer for securing new or additional access to state resources.

These hypotheses suggest the possibility that there exists a positive-sum relationship between rent seeking, capacity for reform, and improved economic performance—under some conditions. They also highlight a problem that brings us to the third major debate these chapters engage: the question of agency in the politics of economic policy reform. They underscore that actors in the reform process do not fit neatly within the conventional categories to which they typically are assigned. While researchers tend to invest categories such as worker and capitalist with their own agency and autonomy—predicting responses to reform, for example, based on an individual's presumed identity as a worker, capitalist, or technocrat—one of the implications of our focus on networks is precisely that the boundaries of these categories are porous, flexible, and often ambiguous, including, notably, the boundary between the categories of public and private.

This claim includes but goes beyond the observation that categories should not be permitted to obscure the diversity of interests of those they lump together. We take as a given that the interests of capitalists, like those of workers, bureaucrats, IFIs, or politicians will inevitably be fragmented and will inevitably produce conflict as well as collaboration. Rather, our claim is that networks disrupt, undermine, and cut across the categories that appear regularly in the research literature as the principal agents of reform. Networks permit the formation of unexpected coalitions of actors. They promote patterns of bargaining and interaction that appear counterintuitive based on a less flexible reading of the categories that actors are presumed to occupy.

Networks, in other words, contribute to environments in which policy reforms take shape as regulatory hybrids, compromise formulas, half-measures, and unwieldy amalgams of seemingly conflicting interests.[27]

Two implications follow, though of different kinds. First, any effort to develop a systematic explanation of reform outcomes based on how relations among a given set of actors are configured must come to terms with the presence of such crosscutting networks and the messy policy environments to which they contribute.[28] Second, a better-theorized approach to the role of networks in reorganizing structures of rent seeking may force us to rethink how we conceptualize the messy policy environments that define the reform process almost everywhere in the developing world. In other words, by constructing our independent variables as agents who are not bounded by their position within fixed categories, we will almost inevitably be forced to rethink the bargaining and politics through which our dependent variable—reform outcomes—are produced.

Reform as a Social Process: Networks and the Problem of Agency

As research on the political economy of economic reform has developed, it has moved through three broad phases or "generations" of work, summarized in table 0.1. Like any taxonomy, this one no doubt fails to do justice to the complexity and variety of the thing it classifies. My purpose, however, is precisely to simplify and sharpen distinctions and elaborate on why it makes sense to bring network analysis more centrally into research on the politics of economic reform—not as a synonym for informality or corruption (since much rent-seeking activity is entirely legal), but as an alternative way to conceptualize how we think about actors, agency, causality, and the nature of economic reform as a *social process*. In brief, and I elaborate in the following, this volume resides a bit uneasily within what I would define as a third generation of work on the politics of economic reform, adopting some of its premises but challenging others.

For the purposes of this volume, a useful way to think about generations of research on the political economy of economic reform is to organize them in terms of three main attributes: (1) who the relevant *actors* are and how their *interests* are conceived; (2) what the *process* of reform is about; and (3) what kind of *outcome* is expected. I've added to this a fourth category, what each of these generations (or research programs) felt needed to be explained—in other words, what each one takes as a core analytic problem to be solved.

14

Table 0.1 Mapping generations of research on the politics of economic reform

Generations	Actors	Process	Outcome	To be explained
First	Reformers versus distributive coalitions	Deregulation	Markets	Conditions that promote or obstruct movement from state to market
	Interests of "winners" and "losers" largely fixed by their position in pre-reform political economy	State shrinking State withdrawal	Forms of economic liberalization	Strategies of coalition management
Second	Reformers versus distributive coalitions	Deregulation	Semi-markets	Patterns and variation in hybrid market forms
	Interests of "winners" and "losers" largely fixed by their position in pre-reform political economy	State shrinking State withdrawal	Partial, "incomplete," or even dysfunctional forms of economic liberalization	Redistributive consequences of partial reform, including how "winners take all"

Third	Reformers versus distributive coalitions Interests of "winners" and "losers" largely fixed by their positions in pre-reform political economy	Reregulation	Reorganization of state capacity Reorganization of state–market relations	Patterns and variation in reregulation Redistributive consequences of reregulation
Our project	Reformers and other actors embedded in networks that reflect complexity of interests Distributive coalitions coexist with other modes for organizing bargaining among actors	Reregulation Reorganization of structures of rent seeking	Reorganization of state capacity Reorganization of state–market relations Shifts in the organization and possibly, though not necessarily, in the distribution of rents	Conditions that determine modes of bargaining over reform: when networks matter and when they don't Redistributive consequences of reform Patterns and variation in reregulation and the reorganization of rent-seeking arrangements

What stands out right away in table 0.1 is that much of the movement from one generation of literature to another has taken place through shifts in the way we think about process, outcomes, and the resulting analytic problems on which we need to focus. Actors, on the other hand, have been conceptualized in much more static terms. In table 1.1, this shows up as shifts in the content of cells in the column on the right and moves left with each generation of work. Thus, we have moved from what might be called a "Washington Consensus" view of reform in the late 1980s and early 1990s, to a "Neoinstitutional" approach of the mid-1990s to what might be called the "Reregulation" approach of the last couple of years. These generations are not neatly bounded, discrete approaches that progress cleanly from one to another. Nor does the arrival of one signal the disappearance of its predecessor. Nonetheless, there are important differences.

First-generation work on reform, heavily influenced by the theories (and neoorthodox politics) of public choice theory (via Olson, Tollison, Tullock, Riker, and many others), conceptualized the state largely as a problem—a source of regulation and thus distortion in the efficiency of markets—to be overcome by diminishing it. If, as Beker asserts, "participants in the political sector" are as narrowly self-seeking as their private sector counterparts, than the assumption that economic policy reform will create environments in which rent seeking and the pursuit of economic privilege are overcome is highly questionable.[29] Indeed, Michel's "iron law of oligarchy" might well be rephrased as an iron law of rent seeking: where there is regulation, there is rent seeking, and where there is rent seeking, there is inefficiency. On this logic, the possibility for developmentally effective forms of regulation, or for variation in the effects of rent seeking on economic performance, essentially disappear. The most productive approach to economic reform, in this case, becomes a straightforward process of "state shrinking," the transfer of assets and functions from state to market. The biggest obstacle to success is the presence of interests that organize in the form of distributional coalitions to defend their privileges.

In this work, which has been largely superceded (not least because it proved an unreliable guide to the design and management of reform programs),[30] institutions were pushed to the background out of a neoorthodox conviction in the naturalness of markets. The aim of reform was simply to get the prices right, ensuring that as few distortions as possible could arise. Reform outcomes hinged, most centrally, on the capacity of reformers to overcome the efforts of "winners" who would organize to resist the loss of rents. As Eggertsson notes:

> The interest-group theory of government has supplied important insights, but it has weaknesses that are particularly apparent in many of its applications in the rent-seeking literature. The theory does not make clear

what the state is, except presumably an aggregate of competing interest groups who somehow reach an equilibrium in the political market. Yet in much of the rent-seeking writings there seems to be a presumption that the state will somehow supply output-maximizing property rights if only special interest groups can be contained. This is evident in Olson's (1982) famous book, *The Rise and Decline of Nations*, which is perhaps the best known manifestation of the rent-seeking literature.[31]

This negative image of interests and of the role of distributional coalitions is pervasive in first-generation work on economic reform. It has spilled over into subsequent work, which continued to view interests as an impediment to an idealized notion of economic efficiency.

In the second generation a positive view of institutions reemerges, along with an appreciation of the link between state capacity and the ability of reformers to construct and consolidate market-supporting institutions. This has obvious and important implications for how reform is defined, for the sorts of tensions associated with it, and for the analytic issues it raises. It provided the basis for a powerful critique of neoliberal development theory by scholars as diverse as Peter Evans, Colin Leys, and Robert Bates. For this generation of work (which is ongoing) the question is not about state withdrawal, but about state transformation—reshaping state capacity to promote market-supporting forms of intervention and regulation. The state may well shrink, but it remains centrally involved in the production and maintenance of markets. The 2002 World Development Report, *Building Institutions for Markets*, is a good example of sophisticated second-generation work.[32]

However, though the state, institutions, and regulation are central to this generation of research the process of reform itself is still conceptualized largely in neoliberal terms. In particular, markets are viewed not simply as apolitical, but as domains in which politics need to be held at bay if reform is to be effective. The rationality of markets is conceived of as distinct from, and incommensurate with, the logic of interest-group politics. Thus the emphasis in work such as Waterbury's on "change teams," on insulation and delegation, or in Evans's work on how embeddedness must nonetheless preserve the autonomy of the bureaucracy from politics for a developmental state to come about. Outcomes in which "winners take all," to use Hellman's term, are cast as dysfunctional distortions of the reform process.

The conclusion of this literature is not that the underlying conceptions of markets or of reform as a process should be changed, but that new strategies are needed for managing interest groups in ways that prevent some actors from capturing (privatizing) its benefits. Partly for this reason, we see the focus of the literature shift in recent years to what the World Bank now calls "second-generation reforms," and to what kinds of polities, presidential or parliamentary, are most likely to give politicians the autonomy to manage markets unconstrained, or minimally constrained, by the logic of politics.

In third-generation research, reflected in the work of Snyder, Schamis, and others, conceptions of both process and outcome have changed. Markets are now conceptualized as political, reform has been recast as a process of reregulation, and questions of insulation or delegation have moved to the background, if they are present at all.[33] Certainly, the understanding remains that reform outcomes differ in their effects on economic productivity and growth, but the idea of markets as a domain that can plausibly be isolated from the logic of politics is no longer viable. Political logics infuse markets no less than they do other domains of life, and economic policy reform is an inherently political process. Questions about how to ensure the "integrity" of a reform process, about evaluating success or failure by the extent to which interests are kept at arms length, become less meaningful. Here too, institutions matter. As in second-generation work a core interest of this research is how institutional forms affect the politics and distributional consequences of various processes through which economic policies are renegotiated. Although institutions tend to be conceptualized in terms that second-generation work would find familiar (heavily influenced by Douglass C. North and new economic institutionalism), the process of reform no longer carries with it the neoliberal assumptions of earlier work.

Each shift from one generation of research to another has produced movement toward a richer, more fully theorized account of economic reform as a social as well as political process. From this taxonomy, moreover, the elements that this volume shares with third-generation work become clearer. The chapters in this volume share a sense of markets as politically constructed and maintained. They view reform as a negotiated process of reregulation that is shaped by the interaction of political and economic interests, including, notably, the interest of incumbents in remaining in power. They share a concern with the redistributive consequences of reform, while giving more weight to the effects of reregulation in the reorganization of rent seeking than is common in third-generation literature.[34] The chapters also share, to varying degrees, a concern with institutions and how institutional forms affect the bargaining and conflicts that define the reregulation and determine its outcomes.

At the same time, one category has changed very little in the movement from one generation of work to another: actors and how they are conceptualized. With few exceptions the political economy literature defines actors in similar terms, taking interest groups, notably distributive coalitions, as the unit of agency. Underlying this reliance on distributive coalitions is the (reasonable) commitment of most in political economy to some notion of rationality and methodological individualism.[35] However, the reliance on distributive coalitions as a near hegemonic category for theorizing about the organization of interests is problematic. This is not to say that each generation of work conceptualizes actors in precisely the same way. First- and second-generation work tend to view group interests with a negative bias, as a source of market distortions via rent seeking. Third-generation work focuses more on the distributional consequences of group interests with less concern for whether these distort an ideal or maximally efficient allocation of resources.[36]

Starting with rationalist assumptions about interests and the role of distributive coalitions as the key unit of agency, it becomes possible to construct a variety of deductive hypotheses about the politics of reform as a struggle among actors who (usually but not always) get assigned to one of two binary categories: winners or losers. Shared interests among those allocated to one or another category provides the basis for distributive coalitions to form—though as we know and as the literature recognizes (much of the time), collective-action problems are not resolved quite this easily. It is often argued, for example, that losers organize more readily than winners because the certainty of losing is a more potent source of mobilization than the possibility of winning, though Synder and others have challenged this view quite effectively. Still, outcomes of reform are believed to be dependent, in part, on the skill with which politicians manage coalitions and in part on the relative power of coalitions. Institutions come into play at almost every stage, especially in second- and third-generation literatures. They shape the organization of interests, influence opportunities for coalition formation, affect the strategies of winners and losers, and partly determine whether new policies and practices can be consolidated.

Thus, public choice work on rent seeking (first generation), Waterbury's book on public enterprise reform (second generation), and Snyder's work on reregulation (third generation) are all explicit in adopting distributional coalitions as their core units of agency. Haggard and Webb also note, in *Voting for Reform*, the widespread use in work on policy making, including the politics of economic policy reform, of a "simple" interest-based model.

The most common approach to policymaking in democracies—both among academics and nonspecialists—is to focus on the role of interest groups. The model is a simple one. Policy reform has distributive consequences for different groups, which organize to protect their incomes and rents. Politicians respond to constituent pressures because they seek to remain in office, and they exchange policy distortions for political support. The fate of reform thus hinges on the political balance of power between the winners and losers in the reform effort.[37]

While the model as they describe it is indeed simple, it should not be underestimated. Interest-based models and the concept of distributional coalitions are quite powerful analytically. They capture important elements of reality and as Cammett's essay in this volume shows (chapter 8) can lead us to interesting and counterintuitive findings. Indeed, this volume is more a critical extension of earlier work rather than an outright rejection of it. In some important respects, these chapters are responding to gaps that the literature itself has acknowledged but not resolved. For instance, in their introduction to *The Politics of Economic Adjustment*, Haggard and Kaufman include an important discussion of challenges to interest-group-based models.

Summarizing the chapters in their volume, Haggard and Kaufman note that while they use "interests as their main point of departure," they also "raise serious questions about the ability to explain economic policy by reference to distributional outcomes and group interests alone." They elaborate in ways that are worth quoting. Their comment is useful in framing the questions that this volume focuses on and why they matter, as well as moving us toward a justification for our interest in network-based approaches.

> One limit on societal explanations . . . concerns the ubiquity of collective action problems. The political power of economic actors depends on their capacity to organize, but organization does not follow from shared economic interests alone. Compared to those who gain from the status quo, the diffuse beneficiaries of reforms may have substantial difficulty organizing, particularly when the gains from the policy reform are ambiguous and uncertain.
>
> An equally important set of limitations on interest group analysis concerns the problem of deriving interests from a group's position in the economy. *The ambiguity of groups' policy interests stem from a number of different sources. . . . [I]ndividuals and groups occupy a number of positions in the economic structure simultaneously, and may well have a variety of other identifications such as religious or ethnic ones that cut across their economic interests.* Incomes are affected through a variety of channels . . . Moreover, the distributional consequences of policy are highly sensitive to [a number of factors.] It may therefore be difficult for groups to calculate the costs and benefits of reform or to weigh the tradeoffs between short-term losses and longer-term gains. [Emphasis added]

These concerns are far from trivial, but Haggard and Kaufman go on to add a couple more. First, they note, interests are dynamic, not static—they change in response to policy shifts at an earlier point in time. This is consistent with my view of reform as constitutive of interests. Distributional analyses frequently assume that actors' interests are fixed, and thus can't accommodate the sequencing effects of reforms that play out over time. Yet what Haggard and Kaufman consider the most "damaging limitation" of interest-based models, the one we engage most directly, "concerns the mechanisms through which interests are translated into policy outputs... Most coalitional models of politics rest on very simple aggregation rules, or simple decision-making mechanisms such as lobbying, voting, or pure capture of office. The essays in [their] volume concur that the influence of social groups is a more complex function of the way legal and institutional setting provide or limit opportunities for influence."[38] These are critical problems that raise important questions about the adequacy of interest-based accounts. Such approaches don't acknowledge the multiplicity of forms that political influence can take. They allocate interests to actors based on a rigid and narrow conception of the positions they occupy in an economy, and thus fail to take into account the socially embedded, plural, and hybrid quality of interests, or what this means for the politics of economic policy-making and policy reform.

Does it matter that we misread or oversimplify actors' interests and how they are expressed politically? I would argue it does, for both analytic and empirical reasons. For instance, how would such approaches contend with the problem confronted in Cammett's case, in which the positions of winners and losers are destablized in the process of bargaining over economic policy reform, along lines that do not reflect a simple reading of their interests or political influence? Could a more narrowly interest-based account explain Tunisian strategies for exploiting reform to restructure systems of privilege as discussed by Hibou or Cassarino? How well would it account for the shifts in the relationship between business and state relations in the cases covered by Haddad, Sfakianakis, and Wils, or for the difficulties Kienle raises in determining where agency should be located in his case, Egypt, despite the willingness of most observers unproblematically to assume that it rests with a small economic superelite? Based on these kinds of experiences, my sense is that narrowly interest-based approaches provide fewer insights into the dynamics that most interest us in the politics of economic reform than we might wish. It conveys a partial and in some respects distorted image of the process of economic restructuring, reregulation, and the reorganization of politically mediated forms of economic privilege.

Nonetheless, despite the acknowledgment that they are problematic in their conception of actors and how they organize, surprisingly little has been done about it. The problems have been recognized for some time, their implications are serious, but they have been largely ignored.[39] In fact, the concerns expressed by Haggard and Kaufman have largely been set aside by subsequent research. Certainly this is the case in literature that adopts a strategic-rationality approach to the political economy of reform, where the emphasis has not been on actors and agency, but on developing new conceptions of reform as a process, its outcomes, and what it is that needs to be explained (in other words, the second, third, and fourth columns in table 0.1).

Moreover, these concerns have faded at a time when the gap between narrow, interest-based conceptions of actors and the conditions to which they are being applied has grown wider and more problematic. Research programs have developed more complex models of economic reform. Processes of reform themselves have exhibited trajectories that earlier models might not have predicted. Not least, research on reform long ago moved beyond the electoral democracies in which interest-based models originated into authoritarian settings, like those in the Middle East, where they are not so readily applicable. Much has changed, in other words, both empirically and analytically, but our conception of actors has not kept pace.

This, in my view, is where the current volume can help to fill a gap. Research on the political economy of reform has come a long way. It has moved from the somewhat stilted approaches of the first-generation literature to the much richer views embodied in third-generation work. One of our aims is to push the boundaries of third-generation work even further by developing new conceptualizations of actors. Our contribution, or one of them, is to develop and test approaches for studying the politics of economic reform that provide a more complex understanding of actors, identities, interests, and how these are expressed politically. The authors in this volume are especially well suited to make this contribution because they have all carried out the extensive fieldwork that is essential for the construction of more fully socialized and hybrid conceptions of agency.

In other words, we are trying to move beyond the notion that interests express themselves politically in one generic form, the distributional coalition. We are trying to move beyond the binary categorization of actors as winners or losers, recognizing that such labels don't begin to capture the range of possible relationships that define how actors experience the process of economic reform; are inadequate in providing a way to understand actors' interests; and thus operate with a partial sense (as reflected in table 0.1) of what the process of reform is about and what needs to be explained.

The important question, of course, is: how do we do this? What kind of analytic tools can we adopt, adapt, or create that reflect a more complex conception of actors, interests, and politics, and ultimately give us a more adequate account of the process of economic policy reform? As I suggest here, one plausible strategy concerns the integration of network approaches into work on the political economy of economic reform.

The Role of Networks

There are, of course, all kinds of ways to tell more complex stories about the world. Why networks? In large part network approaches are appealing conceptually because they express an understanding of economic behavior as both social and political. They move us toward an alternative to the current reliance on distributive coalitions as the sole meaningful units of agency. I am not alone in viewing network analysis in this light. In fact, one strand of network theory in economic sociology grew out of a critique not terribly dissimilar to the one I make of the literature on the political economy of reform. As Granovetter and Swedberg stress:

> Economic action is socially situated and cannot be explained by reference to individual motives alone. It is embedded in ongoing networks of personal relationships rather than being carried out by atomised actors. By *network* we mean a regular set of contacts of similar social connections among individuals or groups. An action by a member of a network is *embedded*, because it is expressed in interaction with other people. The network approach helps avoid not only the conceptual trap of atomized actors but also theories that point to technology, the structure of ownership, or culture as the exclusive explanation of economic events.[40]

This observation is at the core of the emergence of economic sociology as a field, and of the development of network analysis as an alternative to the materialist conceptions of behavior associated with mainstream economics and new institutional economics (NIE). And while the tension between network analysis, with its socialized conception of economic behavior, and rational choice or new institutionalist approaches that view behavior in terms of means–ends efficiency, have been seen as an obstacle to their integration, there are few intrinsic reasons for not doing so (for example, see Mustafa Emirbayer and Jeff Goodwin, "Network Analysis, Culture, and the Problem of Agency," *American Journal of Sociology* 99, no. 6 [1994]: 1411–1454).

Economic sociology criticizes mainstream economics for promoting an atomistic vision of actors as narrowly self-seeking, yet it doesn't reject the notion of rationality or the idea that actors have and pursue interests. It simply (though importantly) recognizes the embeddedness of individuals in a social context—rooted in a particular historical experience—that is integral to the formation and expression of identity, interests, behavior, and the meaning of rationality.[41] No less important is the extent to which network approaches permit us to accommodate questions of power and resource disparities in explaining outcomes in ways that efficiency-based NIE literature, including parts of North's work, neglects.

Thus, network analysis pushes us toward (or back to) a Weberian or Durkheimian (and to some extent Polanyian) conception of an economy as a social domain. It moves *relationships* to the foreground as units of agency. It does not *ex ante* constrain the number and variety of networks in which any given individual might be embedded: families, ethnic groups; professional associations; sporting clubs, alumni groups, religious associations, and others. Instead, it permits us to understand why certain kinds of networks may be more effective in capturing resources than others under specific conditions, but less so when those conditions change—even though the identity of an actor as a businessman, worker, or bureaucrat, remains constant.

We thus have a starting point for a conception of interest in which actors are not one-dimensional products of their position in a system of production or some other set of deductive categories, but multidimensional social beings whose interests can be unpacked through the inductive study of the social contexts that shape their lives and political opportunity structures. This is not to say that every relationship is equivalent. Networks vary, and some of the most interesting issues to pursue have to do with explaining how networks vary in the kinds of mobilization they facilitate, in their flexibility and durability.[42] Still, by using network approaches we can get at this complexity and explore relationships that cut across what otherwise appear as institutional (state–society), juridical (public–private), or class (worker–manager) boundaries that other approaches tend to take as given.

However, this notion of complex, socialized agents whose interests are, in part, constituted through processes of bargaining, needs to be qualified. First, it doesn't mean that networks are fluid amalgams that spontaneously form and dissolve. The idea of embeddedness cuts against the idea of actors as free agents, able to choose unilaterally their social positions, opportunities, and interests. Indeed, within the social networks' literature, networks are understood as structures and constraints. For instance, Wasserman and Galaskiewicz note:

> instead of analyzing individual behaviors, attitudes, and beliefs, social network analysis focuses its attention on social entities or actors in inter-action with one another and on *how those interactions constitute a frame-work or structure that can be studied and analyzed in its own right.* [Emphasis added][43]

Similarly, if even more emphatically, a recent introduction to the subject stresses that social network theory "analyses *overall relations* in an inductive attempt to identify behaviour patterns and the groups or social strata that correlate with those patterns. Then it sorts out the pertinent groups *a posteriori* and *identifies the concrete constraints of structure on behaviour at the same time as it uncovers constraints on structure from group interactions.*"[44]

Both accounts acknowledge that "actors" can take a variety of forms and may not always be individuals. They may be firms, associations, or unions. The real point, however, is that "networks" are not synonymous with any kind of informal connection, ad hoc mode of exchange, or corruption. They are, as the literature reminds us, embedded, and their embeddedness gives them structural attributes and the causal (or constraining) force we associate with structures in general.

At the same time, this notion of networks as tangible units of agency raises other kinds of issues, notably: Which particular networks are of interest to us in this volume? Given the kinds of data to which these authors had access, can we make productive use of data-intensive network approaches? Can we resolve the very relevant issues that Kienle raises in chapter 9 about causality, selecting among alternative explanations, and so on. What does it mean for these chapters to focus on relationships as units of agency?

Fortunately, the answer to the first of these questions is straightforward. Without wishing to seem flip, the kinds of networks we are interested in are the ones that matter with respect to the outcomes we are trying to explain. In the network analysis literature, going back to the early 1980s, we find the notion of *policy domains* as defining a particular kind of analytic space. According to the authors of one recent study a policy domain has the following characteristics:

> A policy domain consists only of actors having common interests in certain types of public policies (but not identical preferences) who must take one another into account in their efforts to influence those policy decisions.

Every domain encompasses a diversity of controversial policy matters and numerous claimant groups and public authorities, each seeking in varying degrees to influence the ultimate decisions about matters of importance to them and to their constituencies. Burstein (1991) argued that each policy domain also develops a logically coherent substantive or functional basis for framing its policies and that its participants usually construct a common culture about how society does and should work.[45]

Elements of this definition may be more or less appropriate for the cases included here. Certainly, policy domains can be expected to take different forms in advanced industrial democracies than they do in the late-developing states of the Middle East. For instance, the authors of *Comparing Policy Networks* view policy domains as autonomous, with important implications for the degree of specialization we can expect among networks within any given domain. I suspect that policy domains are far more interconnected in the Middle East, reflecting the density of elites, their concentration in positions of power, and the interlocking relationships that bind them to one another. Still, we have adapted the idea, not uncritically, to suit our purposes.

With these caveats in mind, the relevant "policy domain" for this volume is fiscal policy reform, or fiscality more broadly. The networks of interest to us are those that have a direct stake in the outcomes of fiscal policy reform. To narrow it down even further, the networks of immediate interest to us are the ones that mobilize to influence the outcome of fiscal policy reforms, recognizing that some actors or networks who have an interest may not mobilize (for reasons that may be worthwhile exploring in their own right). It is true, of course, that chapters encompass a range of policy domains, from privatization to reform of trade policy to more general conceptions of economic reform as an overarching instance of a policy macro-domain. However, there are some important elements of coherence that run throughout. One, as I noted earlier, is the extent to which chapters reflect the general orientation of third-generation work on the politics of economic reform, in particular, a concern with the redistributive consequences of reform and the notion of reform as a process of reregulation that provides ample scope for the reassertion and reorganization of economic privilege. A second is our shared commitment to more complex notions of actors, interests, and agency than is typical in work on reform, including third-generation work. A third is our general interest in networks (units of agency, structured relationships of different kinds) that cut across one particular boundary: the boundary separating the nominally private from the nominally public.

Finally, there is also a useful degree of consistency in the way network approaches are used to guide research, again, not uncritically, throughout the volume. For many, impressions of network analysis have been shaped by one component of such work: the technical forms of micro-level modeling that require data that are largely beyond the reach of those who study Middle East cases. What comes to mind in thinking about network analysis are techniques that use detailed inductive data to locate the positions of individuals within social networks and produce spatial maps of network forms as the starting point for understanding how variation in network forms affect outcomes. However, and without getting into a definitional debate about what constitutes network analysis, these are not the only models available to us. Nor is micro-level modeling of social ties the only kind of work that "qualifies" as network analysis. For instance, Wasserman and Galaskiewicz go to some length to point out the value of network models for linking micro and macro levels of analysis.

> ... a central item on the network agenda is to bridge the gap between the micro- and the macro-order. ... One way that network analysis provides a "bridge" between the micro- and macro-orders is that successive levels are "embedded" in one another. Individual relational ties are the crucial components of dyads; dyads constitute triads; triads are contained in higher order subgraphs; and all are embedded in complete networks. The network itself is often embedded in a larger institutional context (whether social, political, economic, epidemiological, or whatever); further even the institutional order is embedded in myriad networks that connect to other institutional sectors in a national and international context. The beauty of network analysis is that it allows a researcher to tie together so many interdependent parts that constitute micro- and macro-social orders.[46]

Granovetter and Swedberg make a similar claim about the capacity of an economic sociology that is rooted in network analysis to shed light on macro-level questions, especially concerning institutional formation, maintenance, and transformation. And the breadth of work that is often used as examples of network analysis is in fact broader than a narrow definition of the approach might suggest. In other words, we have to be careful not to conflate the methodological commitments that define network analysis, which the authors here share, with one but only one of the *techniques* through which those commitments have been operationalized. The methodological commitments are consistent with a wide range of applications, and can be operationalized across different levels of analysis. While there is certainly a strong "scientistic" bent among some network analysts, the core commitments that underlie it are methodologically pluralist.[47]

This doesn't fully address the questions that Kienle poses in chapter 9 about how we can tell, definitively, when agents operating through specific network ties cause a particular outcome, but it helps us refine them in ways that may bring solutions closer to hand. In pushing researchers to be clear about the causal role of networks, Kienle was expressing, appropriately, the concern that researchers who work on the Middle East don't have the kinds of data that permit productive use of network approaches. My response is that data needs are not given, but are a byproduct of the particular kinds of techniques that scholars use. By my reckoning, Cammett, Hibou, Sfakianakis, Wils, and others here do indeed possess the data they need to advance the aim of reconceptualizing actors, interests, and units of agency. The issue isn't whether they can satisfy the demands of spatial modeling techniques, but whether they have been attentive to the standards of evidence required to support the particular kinds of causal claims they are making. All things being equal we might prefer that we had more fine-grained data to work with concerning the social positions of actors. But not having this data only means that we need to make use of approaches consistent with the level of data we do have, and apply to them the appropriate standards of evidence. We can't make causal claims of the sort that require micro-level spatial mapping of social networks, but this is only a problem if we pretended we could.

What this volume has tried to do, therefore, is to begin a process of rethinking the politics of economic reform based on a more complex, fully socialized conception of actors, one that looks beyond their formal position in a political economy to take the hybrid and multiplex construction of interests into account. While these chapters represent initial and in some respects tentative moves in this direction, we hope they will be seen as useful contributions to a larger reconception of the politics of economic reform.

Notes

1. Recently, a new research literature has begun to develop a more nuanced understanding of rent seeking and its effects on development, and to address the interactions of rent seeking, "re-regulation, and economic restructuring. For example, see Timothy Mitchell, *Rule of Experts: Egypt, Techno-Politics, Modernity* (Berkeley: University of California Press, 2002).
2. On the other hand, there is also a literature that views the political economies of the region as dominated by neoliberal policies associated with international financial institutions and their supporters (see Mitchell, *Rule of Experts*).
3. See David Knoke, Franz Urban Pappi, Jeffrey Broadbent, and Yutaka Tsujinaka, *Comparing Policy Networks: Labor Politics in the U.S., Germany, and Japan* (New York: Cambridge University Press, 1996).

4. By rent seeking I am referring here to any activity directed toward the pursuit of politically mediated economic gains.

5. See, e.g., Ilya Harik, "Privatization: The Issue, the Prospects, and the Fears," in Ilya Harik and Denis J. Sullivan, eds., *Privatization and Liberalization in the Middle East* (Bloomington: Indiana University Press, 1992), 1–23.

6. *World Development Report, 1996: From Plan to Market* (New York: Oxford University Press, 1996), 22, makes the (dubious) claim that liberalization depoliticizes access to resources. This view is also expressed in Volker Perthes, "The Syrian Private Commercial and Industrial Sectors and the State," *International Journal of Middle East Studies* 24, no. 2 (May 1992): 207–230.

7. As one recent study emphasizes, "it is commonly argued that losses from economic reform are concentrated among specific groups—namely, those who were privileged or subsidized by the previous status quo..." Joel S. Hellman, "Winners Take All: The Politics of Partial Reform in Postcommunist Transitions," *World Politics* 50, no. 2 (January 1998): 206.

8. My use of the term "network" is drawn from recent work in network theory in sociology, in which units of analysis cut across what are typically recognized as institutional or juridical boundaries. Networks of business and state actors who collaborate to manage access to economic benefits—disregarding their formal juridical separation into private and public actors—are a prominent example of this phenomenon. Much of the literature on the political economy of liberalization presents an image of state and private actors as existing on opposite sides of a boundary. This project takes into account that they often are interconnected in ways that overwhelm the idea that they represent distinct and coherent categories of actors. See Walter W. Powell, "Neither Market Nor Hierarchy: Network Forms of Organization," *Research in Organizational Behavior* 12 (1990): 295–336.

9. The importance of managing groups of winners and losers to ensure a winning coalition in support of reform is the theme of John Waterbury, "The Political Economy of Economic Adjustment and Reform," in Joan M. Nelson, ed., *Fragile Coalitions: The Politics of Economic Adjustment* (Washington, DC: Overseas Development Institute, 1989), 39–56.

10. The gap between the Bank's theory of what liberalization is supposed to accomplish and what it actually does is painfully apparent in *From Plan to Market*, 13. After pointing to the achievements of liberalization experiences in some 26 countries in transition, the report acknowledges that these countries have not adequately reformed the critical areas of tax administration, public administration, fiscal controls, or legal institutions, and that they are "plagued" by serious conflicts of interest.

11. On the tension between the logic of politics and the logic of economics, see Thomas Callaghy, "Lost Between State and Market: The Politics of Economic Adjustment in Ghana, Zambia, and Nigeria," in Joan M. Nelson, ed., *Economic Crisis and Policy Choice: The Politics of Adjustment in the Third World* (Princeton: Princeton University Press, 1990), 257–319.

12. One common strategy is delegation—shifting responsibility for economic policy-making to technocrats insulated from political pressure. A second involves strategies of coalition management to balance the political influence of either winners or losers. For an "exclude the winners" approach, see Hellman, "Winners Take All." For an approach more concerned about the political impact of losers, see John Waterbury, "The Political Management of Economic Adjustment and Reform," in Joan M. Nelson, ed., *Fragile Coalitions: The Politics of Economic Adjustment* (New Brunswick: Transaction Books, 1989), 39–56.

13. See Ira W. Lieberman and John Nellis, eds., *Russia: Creating Private Enterprise and Efficient Markets*, Studies of Economies in Transformation Series No. 15 (Washington, DC: The World Bank, 1995). See also, Steven L. Solnick, *Stealing the State: Control and Collapse in Soviet Institutions* (Cambridge: Harvard University Press, 1998). Michael McFaul estimates that "insiders—that is, Soviet-era enterprise directors, in cahoots with trade-union officials loyal to them—gained controlling shares at three-quarters of all large enterprises." "Russia Needs True Reform, Not Higher Taxes," *New York Times*, August 4, 1998.

14. For a recent account describing Israel's privatization program as having increased the concentration of share ownership among a small economic elite and reduced competition, see Judy Dempsey, "Doubts Exist Over Benefits of Sales," *Financial Times*, sec. 2, March 26, 1998.

15. Luigi Manzetti, *Privatization South American Style* (New York: Oxford University Press, 2000).

16. Note that the World Bank regards Morocco, Tunisia, and Jordan as examples of successful, if incomplete, reform. See Nemat Shafik et al., eds., *Claiming the Future: Choosing Prosperity in the Middle East* (Washington, DC: The World Bank, 1995). On the experience of economic reform in the Middle East, see Henri Barkey, ed., *The Politics of Economic Reform in the Middle East* (New York: St. Martin's Press, 1992); Nemat Shafik, ed., *Economic Challenges Facing Middle Eastern and North African Countries: Alternative Futures* (New York: St. Martin's Press, 1998); Christian Morrisson, *Adjustment and Equity in Morocco* (Paris: Development Centre of the Organization for Economic Co-operation and Development, 1991); and Iliya Harik, *Economic Policy Reform in Egypt* (Gainesville, FL: University Press of Florida, 1997).

17. This variation in labor's response to reform is a central theme in Marsha Posusney, *Labor and the State in Egypt: Workers, Unions, and Economic Restructuring, 1952–1996* (New York: Columbia University Press, 1997).

18. Anne O. Kreuger, ed., *Economic Policy Reform: The Second Stage* (Chicago: University of Chicago Press, 2000).

19. See Evans, *Embedded Autonomy: States and Industrial Transformation* (Princeton, NJ: Princeton University Press, 1995); Robert Boyer and J. Rogers Hollingsworth, eds., *Contemporary Capitalism: The Embeddedness of Institutions* (New York: Cambridge University Press, 1997); Miles Kahler, "Orthodoxy and Its Alternatives: Explaining Approaches to Stabilization and Adjustment," in

Joan M. Nelson, ed., *Economic Crisis and Policy Choice: The Politics of Adjustment in the Third World* (Princeton: Princeton University Press, 1990), 33–61.

20. Along these lines, see Mancur Olson, "Why Poor Economic Policies Must Promote Corruption: Lessons from the East for All Countries," in Mario Baldassarri, Luigi Paganetto, and Edmund S. Phelps, eds., *Institutions and Economic Organization in the Advanced Economies* (New York: St. Martin's Press, 1998), 9–51.

21. Dani Rodrik, "The Rush to Free Trade in the Developing World: Why So Late? Why Now? Will It Last?" in Federico Sturzenegger and Mariano Tommasi, eds., *The Political Economy of Reform* (Cambridge: MIT Press, 1998), 209–239.

22. Alice Amsden, *Asia's Next Giant: South Korea and Late Industrialization* (New York: Oxford University Press, 1989); and Robert H. Bates, *Markets and States in Tropical Africa: The Political Basis of Agricultural Policies* (Berkeley: University of California Press, 1981). Interestingly (if a bit of a digression), for Amsden financial liberalization is a tool that state elites use to discipline industrialists who threaten to exit from the privileged economic arrangements in which they are embedded. Although Peter Evans relies heavily on Amsden for his own account of Korea in *Embedded Autonomy*, he seems not to realize how powerfully Amsden's argument challenges his claims about the impact of developmental success on state autonomy. Evans argues that success creates new possibilities for industrialists to develop alliances with multinationals, and thus undermines the capacity of autonomous states to manage economic growth. He tells us that developmental states become their own "gravediggers." Amsden, on the other hand, argues that industrialists prefer embeddedness, view market liberalization as a threat, and that state elites will manipulate industrialists' fear of competition to preserve their control over economic decision-making.

23. See Mushtaq H. Khan and K. S. Jomo, eds., *Rents, Rent-Seeking and Economic Development: Theory and Evidence in Asia* (Cambridge: Cambridge University Press, 2000).

24. This is certainly the view, e.g., in John Waterbury, *Exposed to Innumerable Delusions: Public Enterprise and State Power in Egypt, India, Mexico, and Turkey* (New York: Cambridge University Press, 1993).

25. Peter Evans, *Embedded Autonomy: States and Industrial Transformation* (Princeton: Princeton University Press, 1995), 58.

26. For example, there is a widely held view that the size of the state is negatively correlated with economic performance, based on the assumption that large bureaucracies create greater possibilities for predatory and rent-seeking behaviors. However, as one author has recently argued regarding Africa: "with respect to larger bureaucracies being associated with lagging national incomes, the inverse comes closer to the truth." Arthur A. Goldsmith, "Africa's Overgrown State Reconsidered: Bureaucracy and Economic Growth," *World Politics* 51 (July 1999): 520–546.

27. Within the Middle East, which is not the only region characterized by such outcomes, this is reflected in Béatrice Hibou, "From Privatising the Economy to Privatising the State: An Analysis of the Continual Formation of the State," in

Hibou, ed., *Privatising the State* (London, Hurst, and New York: Columbia University Press, 2004), 1–46; and Dieter Weiss and Ulrich Wurzel, *The Economics and Politics of Transition to an Open Market Economy: Egypt* (Paris: Development Centre of the OECD, 1998).

28. I use the term "messy" here in a technical sense, to refer to environments characterized by a high number of interactions over time among a large set of actors. On messy research agendas, see Peter Evans and John D. Stephens, "Studying Development Since the Sixties: The Emergence of a New Comparative Political Economy," *Theory and Society* 17 (1988): 713–745.

29. Gary Becker, "Political Competition Among Interest Groups," in Jason F. Shogren, ed., *The Political Economy of Government Regulation* (Boston: Kluwer Academic Publishers, 1989), 16. See also Becker, "A Theory of Competition Among Pressure Groups for Political Influence," *The Quarterly Journal of Economics* 98 (1983): 371–400.

30. For instance, see Anne Kreuger, ed., *Economic Policy Reform: The Second Stage* (Chicago: University of Chicago Press, 2000).

31. Thrainn Eggertsson, *Economic Behavior and Institutions* (New York: Cambridge University Press, 1990), 279.

32. *Building Institutions* includes a section on "Norms and Networks," conflating the two and calling them both informal institutions. The concern to extend neoinstitutional economic modes of analysis to norms and networks is interesting and in some ways productive. In other ways, however, it seems a bit limiting. More on this later.

33. In her politicized view of markets, there's a sense in which Chaudhry's book falls into this generation of literature as well. See K. A. Chaudhry, *The Price of Wealth: Economies and Institutions in the Middle East* (Ithaca: Cornell University Press, 1997).

34. For a kick (well, it's not that much fun), check out the following website for the newsletter of a very poorly named movement to reform economics: post-autistic economics: www.paecon.net.

35. The commitment to rationality is nonproblematic when rationality is understood not in the reductionist terms that very few scholars now accept, but in a thicker sense that is now quite widely accepted. This latter view takes adequate account of such issues as altruism, self-sacrifice, and emotion, as well as the implications for rationality of incomplete information, the influence of norms, institutions, and ideas (culture) as constraints on individual behavior, and so on. This is not to say that the nature of rationality is a settled problem, only that we can use the concept without worrying about adopting the baggage associated with earlier conceptions.

36. One way to think about this is the trade-off between growth and equity in the allocation of resources and in definitions of efficiency. For first-generation work, there is a clear preference for arrangements that privilege growth over equity. Thus, bargaining over redistribution of resources is seen as a key source of

distortion in an economy. For third-generation work, the trade-off is less clear-cut. In some cases, equity may be preferable to growth, and the politics of defining and allocating resources in pursuit of equity become a legitimate means for determining how economic arrangements will be organized.

37. Stephan Haggard and Steven B. Webb, "Introduction," in Haggard and Webb, eds., *Voting for Reform: Democracy, Political Liberalization, and Economic Adjustment* (New York: Oxford University Press, 1994), 8. The link between democracy and interest-group models is explicit, and poses questions about exporting such models to nondemocracies that are relevant and important. They have been dealt with to some degree in the literature, but are beyond the scope of this work.

38. All of the text quoted is from Stephan Haggard and Robert R. Kaufman, "Institutions and Economic Adjustment," in Haggard and Kaufman, eds., *The Politics of Economic Adjustment: International Constraints, Distributive Conflicts, and the State* (Princeton: Princeton University Press, 1992), 27–28. It is striking how little impact this very insightful and self-reflective critique—now a decade old—has had on subsequent research.

39. I am open to alternative views of the literature, including the possibility that the problems I have identified here have in fact been dealt with in the literature. I do not believe so, but am open to persuasion.

40. Mark Granovetter and Richard Swedberg, "Introduction," in Granovetter and Swedberg, eds., *The Sociology of Economic Life* (Colorado: Westview Press, 1992), 9.

41. This tension between the "undersocialized" view of individuals in economics and the tendency of some economic sociologists to construct "oversocialized" views has received a fair amount of attention. See Mark Granovetter, "Problems of Explanation in Economic Sociology," in Nitin Nohria and Robert G. Eccles, eds., *Networks and Organizations: Structure, Form, Action* (Cambridge: Harvard Business School Press, 1992), 23–56.

42. For instance, networks based on extended families may be harder to mobilize for tightly defined purposes, but easier to discipline. On the other hand, networks of members in a professional association may be easier to mobilize around an issue with clear financial consequences for the profession, but harder to discipline. These kinds of distinctions matter in understanding variation in network efficacy, among other things.

43. Stanley Wasserman and Joseph Galaskiewicz, eds., *Advances in Social Network Analysis: Research in the Social and Behavioral Sciences* (California: Sage, 1994), xii.

44. Alain Degenne and Michel Forse, *Introducing Social Networks* (London: Sage, 1999), 2–3. For me, the emphasis here on the *inductive* foundations of network analysis is another reason the approaches are useful for the kind of data-rich projects that are represented in the working group.

45. David Knoke, Franz Urban Pappi, Jeffrey Broadbent, and Yutaka Tsujinaka, *Comparing Policy Networks: Labor Politics in the U.S., Germany, and Japan* (New York: Cambridge University Press, 1996), 9.

46. Wasserman and Galaskiewicz, *Advances in Social Network Analysis*, xiii.
47. This is true of Wellman and Berkowitz, eds., *Social Structures: A Network Approach* (New York: Cambridge University Press, 1988), despite the inclusion of several chapters that don't lend themselves to formalization. I wonder, though, whether the linkage of economic sociology and network analysis, which postdates the chapters in Wellman and Berkowitz, reflect the methodological opening up of an approach that had previously been largely formal in its orientation.

PART 1

State–Business Networks and the
Politics of Economic Reform

CHAPTER 1

The Formation and Development of Economic Networks in Syria: Implications for Economic and Fiscal Reforms, 1986–2000

Bassam Haddad

The Social, Economic, and Political Context of Exclusionary Networks

In virtually all developing countries,[1] and beyond,[2] relations between the state and business have taken the form of economic or policy networks that may or may not operate through formal institutions. Though networks are ubiquitous in nearly all settings where state and business cooperate, their impact on economic growth and development can be more or less detrimental or positive depending on the conditions of their emergence, their internal dynamics, and their relation to the broader institutional and social context.[3] This chapter posits that the effects of the maturing economic networks—combining capitalists and bureaucrats—in Syria in the late 1980s became extant in the economic, regulatory, and fiscal policy reforms of the late 1980s and the 1990s. The foreign exchange crisis of 1986 marks the acceleration of economic networks' consolidation and influence, albeit at an informal level, until 1991 when these networks hijacked the official institutional expression of the "private sector" under the rubric of the government's reform policy, that is, *al-ta`adudiyya al-iqtisadiyya* (economic pluralism). The role of privileged economic networks[4] in bringing about economic and fiscal change can be analyzed by examining the institutional and social context within which these networks emerge and on which their sustenance rests. Although the impact of such networks has been largely limited to middle- and lower-range policies, their ability to bypass or manipulate laws and regulations has significantly widened their reach and allowed them, intentionally or inadvertently, to shape general developmental change in idiosyncratic ways that were detrimental to economic productivity.[5] These economic downturns were not desired or intended by the state, the business community, or the network participants who represent the primary beneficiaries from the reform process. Economic decline was in large part a result of rampant rent seeking and rent allocation that was almost totally unchecked on the one hand, and misdirected by a widely penetrated and incoherent bureaucracy on the other.[6] The proximity of these networks to, and overlap with, decision-making bodies made rent seeking and rent allocation an extremely efficient process during the post-1986 reforms. What, then, is the source of these networks' endurance, and why did they emerge in the first place?

Networks and Institutions: Why Do Economic Networks Emerge?

Pervasive and powerful economic networks combining webs of bureaucrats and capitalists have been prominent features of political economies in transition from a centralized arrangement to a more decentralized and not necessarily market-oriented one.[7] In this sense, networks do not "replace" existing institutions, but they operate side by side as shadow forms of organization that are largely responsible for the dramatic growth of shadow economies so pervasive in reforming states, from Russia to Egypt. Though economic networks are ubiquitous, the context in which they emerge shapes their nature, dynamics, and development. Why, for example, did the Syrian regime resort to networking with business elites rather than formally extending or reforming its own economic institutions after the "Corrective Movement" in the 1970s. Why did the regime avoid "opening" the door to all possible investors and generate opportunities amenable to exploitation across the entire business community?

In the case of Syria, networks did not precede state or market, however limited the latter, nor were they merely the product of economically inefficient institutions. They emerged within existing states and markets as a means for state elites and business partners to secure extraordinary benefits that neither could obtain under formal state–business arrangements.

However, the motives for each party differed: state elites were looking for security, first and foremost, and business partners were looking for profits that could not be obtained under the constraints imposed on the private sector as a whole. Without examining the institutional and social context in which state elites and business actors were operating, the development of pervasive, informal, and selective relations between state and business remains incomprehensible.

The institutional context in which these networks emerged is the dilution or unraveling of a "populist-authoritarian" system, whereby the distributive commitments of populist-authoritarian states begin to give way to populist demobilization and alliance shuffling in favor of excluded business actors. Although ideological constraints related to distributive commitments and the exclusion of business from the state's corporatist structure proved surmountable in the case of populist-authoritarian regimes like Egypt, the challenge remains one of security for cases such as Syria.[8] The lack of trust between the regime and the business community, based on deep-seated historical antagonism, has prevented the state elite in Syria from pursuing rapprochement with business à la Egypt: the Syrian regime could neither dissolve its ruling Ba`th Party (as the Egyptian regime did with the Arab Socialist Union) nor replace it with a new one (such as Egypt's National Democratic Party) that is institutionally and ideologically more amenable to the official incorporation of business interests. The Syrian political elite had reasons to fear a resurgence of the traditional business community, despite their institutionally weakened position since the 1963 Ba`th takeover. According to Heydemann,

> [t]he union [UAR] educated this generation of radical reformers about the resilience of the private sector, the intensity of business opposition to social reform, and the strategies capitalists could employ to undermine the radical restructuring of Syria's political economy. . . . The union experience became its [the Ba`th's] touchstone and its antimodel, the crucible within which many elements of the Ba`th's political repertoire took shape.[9]

By 1970, the socio-institutional context made rational some informal networking in the service of capital accumulation and security. It also prevented the regime from disciplining or safely mobilizing the business community as a whole. As a result, the official institutions of the business community were further suppressed and contained at the expense of collective collaboration and efficiency. Ironically, it is these emerging informal state–business networks that developed an interest in rejuvenating business associations after the late 1980s, particularly in 1991, when reform measures were formally formulated and implemented as such.

Because networks take on a life of their own as alternative mechanisms of association, their conditions of emergence are not the sole reason for their development and consolidation.[10] In the Syrian case they were also fostered by a political crisis of waning legitimacy and attendant institutional atrophy. The conflict between the state and the Islamists in the 1970s and early 1980s was in many ways spurred by the perceived lack of legitimacy of the regime, both political and economic, from the perspective of excluded traditional sectors and most small businesses in the traditional urban *suq* (traditional market of manufacturers and artisans). The state–opposition showdown between 1979 and 1982 catalyzed selective rapprochement between the state and business in the form of informal networks.[11] The civil unrest—very much tied to the power of the then weakened traditional business classes—accelerated the formation and consolidation of economic networks as a safe-guarding strategy (i.e., state elites would try to create a business elite in their own image and would themselves become even more heavily involved in business).

The Genesis of Economic Networks in Syria

As part of the regime's retrenching strategy after Asad's 1970 coup, top elites took the initiative in bringing back into the political economic equation part of the business community. Unable to officially incorporate the business community as a whole for security concerns, state elites embarked on the creation and development of informal ties with particular established and ascending business actors. More broadly, we witness the formation of key economic networks in the mid- to late-1970s, comprising top state officials (including military, security, and bureaucratic personnel), select business actors, and para-official actors connected to the regime mainly through familial and communal, but also through professional ties (e.g., former teachers, doctors, engineers). (See table 1.1.) What is significant here is that, early on, these networks included state actors that had little or no business history/experience in the professional sense and were thus more dependent on their proximity to the state for "staying in business." Also included in these networks are lay individuals that have largely been catapulted by state officials from various professional and blue-collar backgrounds into the business world during the investment boom of the mid-1970s[12] and, later, through mixed-sector ventures, smuggling, black-marketeering, and cronyism. These actors were

Table 1.1   Patterns of state–business relations: networks, rent, and economic change

Nature of business incorporation	State–business relations in Syria: development periods		
	1970–1990 informal		1991 onward formal
	1970–1977	1978–1986	(1987–2000)
Character of state–business relations	Rapprochement	Selective cooperation	Fragmented collusion
Type of economic reform	Controlled liberalization	Selective liberalization	Circumscribed liberalization
State's role	Producer	Midwife (creating private wealth)	Rent guarantor (of Rentierism)
Rent opportunities	Public investments/ purchases/ contracts with foreign agents	Mixed-sector ventures smuggling/ black market USSR debt repayment	Tailored reregulation (imports/exports), investment law #10 USSR D/R, black market
Formation/ consolidation of economic networks	(Consolidation) within the state	(Formation) between state and private sector	(Consolidation) within economic networks
Formal business incorporation	—	—	Chambers of commerce/industry Guidance Committee Parliament (1991)

seen by the regime as the most loyal, because they had few or no options compared to formerly more established and trained business actors drawn from the ranks of the old, but culturally vigorous bourgeoisie.[13] By the same token, the adversarial state–business legacy left an evident imprint on emerging state–business networks, not least because of the communal as well as the socioeconomic differences between the political elite and capitalists in the pre-populist periods (1946–1958 and 1961–1963). Institutionalized as they became after 1970,[14] such differences reinforced the narrowness of the ruling coalition at the top rungs, and rendered the regime vulnerable by reducing its capacity for incorporating/absorbing social forces without being overtaken by them. Hence, the pattern of incorporation the state pursued was to include similarly vulnerable individuals and groups—ones that generally lacked strong social bases of support.

Sustained by a particular configuration of factors and interest,[15] this situation of mutual dependence within state–business networks shaped their development and consolidation throughout the 1970s, 1980s, and 1990s. (See table 1.1.) Mutual vulnerability fostered the conditions for collusive relations between state and business and, by the mid-1990s, produced collectively costly outcomes, socially, administratively, and economically. The operating dynamic has been the organization and reorganization of rent-seeking opportunities in the context of protracted economic liberalization. Exacerbating collusive state–business relations is the fact that a growing number among the political, military, and bureaucratic elite including, later, their offspring, went into business either directly or through protégés in the 1970s, but more vigorously in the 1980s and 1990s. The fusion of the roles of public decision-maker and capitalist in the hands of officials and para-officials has had a tremendous impact on the nature of the economic decision-making process in its formulation and implementation phases, especially before and after liberalization agendas began to appear.

Notably, state–business networks did not acquire a formal expression until the early 1990s when the government implicitly proclaimed a shift in its economic policy and development strategy, one that gave recognition to and conferred legitimacy on the developmental role of the hitherto admonished private sector. Not only did these rent-seeking networks survive this shift, they actually participated in shaping it and in shaping the ensuing process of liberalization, if not by totally hijacking it then by circumscribing further the limits of economic liberalization by diverting resources from collective to private targets. The unintended effect of these particularist policies was a deep economic slump beginning in 1994. By the end of the 1990s, a serious liquidity crisis led to the dramatic shrinking of rent opportunities. Throughout the period of economic downturn, the logic of rent-seeking economic networks collided with the broader political logic of regime maintenance: the developmental cost of rent seeking began to outweigh the benefits of instrumental reform as a regime maintenance strategy. Record lows in economic productivity and public/private investments were evidenced by potentially destabilizing widespread unemployment—reaching 20–25 percent by nearly all nongovernment estimates in 2000.[16] Such notable downturns sounded serious alarm signals to the regime, especially in the absence of new oil finds as an alternative source of state revenue, as was the case in 1991.[17]

Despite competition for shrinking rent opportunities within economic networks in the late 1990s, individuals[18] involved—especially private actors—found common cause in coming together among calls for the overhaul of the entire economic system from the larger business community and the (re)emerging civil society. Opportunities for alternative social alliance-making that involve the reorganization, if not dissolution, of these networks coincided with the succession struggle and were tainted by it. Until Asad's death in June 2000, the economy was at a standstill but was poised to undergo some change in the medium run. Entrenched economic networks were able to survive yet another challenging transition. Forming the nexus of continued state–business collusion, these economic networks represent an important research area and an explanatory variable in the study of both the politics of economic change and limits of state–business collusion in periods of economic liberalization.

Characteristics of Economic Networks: A Summary

Based on the foregoing discussion, the operative attributes of emerging networks can be summarized as follows:

1. They are strategic in nature (as opposed to organic) and largely responsive to security concerns, that is, they are interest based—"interest" here is defined broadly, encompassing economic, social, and political interests—and instrumentally formed. Empirically, network members have come and gone based on security and other concerns, revealing the loose bonds that exist between them. Relations within networks are based on calculative trust[19] (see section on networks and institutions).

2. They include civil (public officials and private citizens) and military elements. (See figure 1.1 on the "Sectoral and Institutional Sources of Economic Networks Members.")

3. They are cross-sectarian (including Sunnis, Shi`is, `Alawis, and some Christians).

4. Internally, they are informally organized in a pyramidical structure with the military/security service component at the top (possessing decisional and coercive power), a bureaucratic component (possessing administrative power/keys), and a private component (possessing capital and/or entrepreneurial skills of sorts). Externally, the combinations of such networks are organized along the lines of prominent power centers in the top leadership, the military, the bureaucracy, and the

44

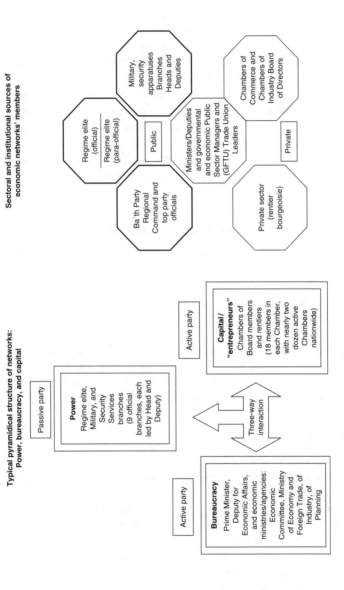

Figure 1.1 Structure and source of economic networks.

party. (See figure 1.1 on the "Typical Pyramidal Structure of Networks: Power, Bureaucracy, and Capital.")

5. These network structures are characterized by modularity, that is, made up of various relational parts that can be exchanged, interchanged, and/or taken out altogether, without affecting the structure of the network as a whole. The most stable component of these networks, however, is related to the top leadership and all coercive apparatuses. The bureaucratic/ministerial component follows. The private component of these networks is most substitutable, particularly those businessmen that were the beneficiaries of the shady deals and partnerships of the 1980s. These businessmen tend to have the least legitimacy vis-à-vis the public and thus are most vulnerable to replacement or forced defection.

6. The networks' connections to institutions are sporadic, inconsistent, and usually irrelevant since informal connections to power centers suffice for bypassing institutional authority.

One caveat should be kept in mind. While it is evident that these networks are ostensibly headed by military and bureaucratic officials, they are by no means always run by them. As both private and public members of these networks accumulate more capital, their bargaining power increases and they become more attuned to the market, where the criteria for leadership differs from those of the state. Policy or economic outcomes, therefore, reflect a subtle form of intra-network bargaining and negotiation, where the capital and skills of private business balance the decisional power of network members in officialdom. The institutional context has so far shaped the development of this subtle form of conflict between the state and "private" capital.

Networks, Trust, and Institutions

The institutions that brought the state and business together after 1991 demonstrate the prevalence of the tendency to preserve particularist gains, either by eroding the operations of such institutions, or through the production of policies tailored to fit members of this alliance. More significantly for our purposes, it is evident that in the Syrian case these institutions represent the organizational expression of maturing economic networks seeking both to secure and to legitimize past, present, and future gains. The principal linking institution, or the Guidance Committee, is the only governmental body with official private sector representation, where state, capital, and labor[20] come together primarily to approve, ignore, or disapprove suggestions and requests made by private sector or trade union members. But its role is viewed as, at best, vague, and reactionary. The Guidance Committee aborts the role of the legislature because it also exercises that role in a roundabout way, as when it decided to raise the exchange rate of the customs dollar—an indirect infringement of the constitution. At best, the Guidance Committee acquired the role of an ambulance, but one that arrives only after the bleeding is well under way.[21]

Although some bargaining takes place during Guidance Committee meetings, most occurs informally, behind closed doors, as it did between 1986 and 1991.[22] Alternatively, bargaining is not always necessary, as decision makers sitting on the committee are themselves involved in common business ventures. The former prime minister, Mahmoud al-Zu`bi,[23] and the former deputy prime minister for Economic Affairs, Salim Yassin,[24] were heavily involved in public–private economic networks whose businesses extended from commerce to light (though protected) manufacturing.[25] A favorable tax policy or selective implementation thereof, was in their own interest as much as it was in the interest of members of these networks.[26]

Private sector representative institutions such as the Chambers of Commerce and Industry were also rejuvenated in the mid-to-late 1980s, just when economic networks began to consolidate. These institutions constitute the funneling bodies in which identification, initiation, and/or recruitment of potential collaborators occurs. Negotiation and bargaining within these institutions and between them and the government do take place, but on a very limited scale and often concerning the most banal of issues (e.g., what time to close the market in the afternoon during the summer!). Generally, the Chambers are not (yet) taken seriously as representative institutions by prominent members of the business community. As one businessman noted,

> the Chamber of Commerce has approximately 50,000 members, but less than 9,000 actually vote. Why do they join if they don't vote, given that these Chambers are supposed to serve their interests? Also, artisans are registered with both the Chamber of Industry and the Artisans Cooperatives Union. There is no separation between industrialists, professionals, and artisans. . . . There are sectors that are not represented and sectors that are represented more than once. . . . My business [auto dealer] is not represented. There are a thousand reasons why people join or avoid the Chambers.[27]

However, the Chambers are latent arenas of mobilization where, for good or ill, businessmen come together. There, in the Chambers, private sector power centers are lured, co-opted, or manipulated by the regime—or they play their cards right, exploit their capital, and penetrate the regime elite and state institutions alike. Alternatively, the chambers represent the strategic arena for those who wish to carve out independent space in preparation for the coming stages of Syria's liberalization or turmoil.[28] The former tendency represents that of the rentier bourgeoisie, that is, network members, and the latter that of the recalcitrant old bourgeoisie and the new but largely independent business people.[29] At any rate, powerful members of the Chambers are usually openly associated with the security services or high-ranking regime officials, making the reach of the networks quite deep and debilitating for collective action on the part of any of the Chambers across Syria.

Institutions and Economic Reforms

Institutions can be conceptualized as forms of organization and rules that are intended to serve a given purpose.[30] Whether they serve that purpose or not depends on a larger set of factors that are far more complex than the will and the intention of the powers that be. Nonetheless, the raison d'etre for the emergence of institutions at the time of their establishment can be gleaned from the interests of dominant actors as well as from the rules that govern the institutions, officially and in practice. The manner in which economic institutions were established or rejuvenated in Syria in the late 1980s, along with the rules of participation, inclusion, and operations that pervade them, reflect the interests of those actors that stood to benefit from the impending formalization of reforms.[31] Three factors marked the initial intent behind the establishment/rejuvenation of economic institutions in Syria: (a) access to influence, (b) function, and (c) top–down nature of rules (e.g., for electing board members, granting licenses, etc.).

Only those parties that the regime favored were able to have access to positions of influence within new economic institutions. Access alone was necessary but insufficient for pressing demands: only what is called "subsidized access" (i.e., access supported by strong elements within the regime) could guarantee that the actors' demands would be heard and, often, satisfied in one form or another. The function of these institutions, as with the Guidance Committee, was not to aggregate the interests and demands of the business community for the purpose of formulating positive-sum policies (policies that are within everyone's reach and that, therefore, may benefit both business actors and the economy as a whole). Instead, their function was to circumscribe decision making by limiting it to a small set of actors and, subsequently, manage the demands and preferences of these actors, not in accordance with what serves the economy, but rather in accordance with what serves whom (i.e., what demands/policies must be adopted because of the weight of the actors and their partners pressing for them).

Finally, these are essentially top–down institutions that are governed wholly by regime, not business, rules. The implications are immense. First, these are not genuinely representative institutions despite the fact that they do represent the interests of some business actors. These institutions take the part for the whole, that is, they consider the interests of affiliated actors as representative of the interests of all those in their sector or line of business. This myopia creates a short circuit vis-à-vis information gathering and exchange (i.e., the information loop) and undercuts the credibility of even the most mundane policies because such policies do not figure among the preferences of the larger business community or are viewed as part of the prioritization of rival actors. Thus, independent business actors do not support them, and, in some cases, elect not to take advantage of them for fear of losing their independence or injuring their reputation among their allies/partners.[32]

Moreover, the manner in which board members of the Chambers of Commerce and Industry are elected further diminishes the credibility of these institutions. For instance, in the Chamber of Industry in Damascus, as is the case with other influential Chambers of both Commerce and Industry elsewhere, the distribution of pro-regime and independent board members is predetermined by the regime. In the Damascus Chamber, "6 out of the 18 board members are appointed by the government. The election for the remaining twelve is real and clean."[33] Nonetheless, according to a number of independent board members in Damascus and Aleppo, where the Chambers are most powerful, the pressure that is exercised by regime officials and their protégés within the Chambers has invariably been more than sufficient to ensure that Chamber presidents are either "men of the regime" (*rijaal al-nithaam*) or men beholden to the regime. It is thus important to examine the process of (s)election of the Chambers' board members, since they are the ones who elect the Chambers' presidents who are represented on the Guidance Committee and are able to weigh in on its decisions with their own and their allies' demands. Hence, the connection between representative business institutions such as the Chambers and institutions such as the Guidance Committee ostensibly link the state with business interests. In reality, such "representative" institutions and "linking" institutions are not only engineered to serve the interests of exclusionary state–business networks, they are also intended to maintain high barriers to entry for "outsiders" lest rent opportunities become further divided or, worse still, erode.

Trust and Institutions: Institutional Dead Ends

Lack of trust between the regime and the business community (based on political as well as social antagonism) produced exclusionary business institutions that were neither representative of the business community nor responsive to the interests of independent businessmen. Instead, they reflected the interests of the increasingly influential networks of capitalists and bureaucrats, networks that served as the launching grounds for rejuvenating old institutions and creating new ones. Furthermore, the intra-network dynamics within these institutions produced unintended consequences that included the undermining of the ability of the state to steer the economy, notwithstanding retrospective sanctioning and *ex post facto* disciplinary actions.

This pattern of exclusionary institutions, itself conditioned by structural variables, has sustained the lack of trust between the regime and the business community while producing what can be called calculative or encapsulated trust between the regime and select business actors. Calculative or encapsulated trust emerges between parties that share short-term interests, and thus, their cooperation is delimited by short-term goals. For an economy to grow in a sustained manner, long-term investments are necessary. In the continued absence of trust between the state and the business community, as well as the "encapsulated" or "calculative" trust that emerges between bureaucrats and select capitalists, the time horizons of investors and their partners are severely shortened, resulting in the promotion of short-term ventures that produce little, if any, added value. This benefits a few parties immensely at the expense of providing collective benefits (e.g., by protecting inefficient manufacturers or monopoly traders, prices of respective products/commodities rise beyond their local, regional, and international market value).

Unintended Consequences of Mistrust Within Institutions

Assume two parties/actors, A and B, both represent a group or individuals within a group. Party A represents individuals within the regime who are willing to cooperate with private partners and party B represents private individuals willing to cooperate with the regime. Assume that both parties cooperate because they need each other, not because they trust each other. Party A seeks capital and entrepreneurship that they do not possess and party B seeks the opportunities and protection that are selectively available to individuals willing to cooperate with party A. A third assumption is that, ultimately, party A must act collectively to achieve its highest goal (i.e., state security) and party B can achieve its highest goal (i.e., profit) either as individual actors or as a collective. The question is, *at what point do institutions based on calculative mistrust between bargaining partners produce unintended outcomes for the parties involved, especially for the stronger party?*

Mistrust between parties within institutions at the point of their inception is likely to be an outcome of bargaining processes that predate their emergence. Depending on the changes in the conditions under which prior bargaining took place, mistrust within institutions is either increased or reduced.

If mistrust between parties predates the emergence of institutions—understood here as a set of rules—the rules of these institutions are likely to reflect the interests of the more powerful parties. Power differentials are one key factor in determining the dynamics of network relations as well as the individual behavior of actors within institutions.[34] When trust is not an issue between two parties that are asymmetric in terms of their power differentials, the stronger party is likely to have more leverage and is thus able to exact higher distributional gains from cooperation, at least initially. Power differentials can be defined as a function of breakdown values (i.e., the party that has a greater set of alternatives available to it in case of noncooperation is invariably the one with greater power and greater leverage). Since some parties would be more affected by noncooperation, they are likely to seek cooperation in the short and medium run even if their gains are reduced in the process. Thus, the weaker parties (in the Syrian case, private businessmen) cooperate not because they trust the rules of the game or their more powerful partners (among the political elite), but rather, they cooperate because they are able to exact higher distributional gains through cooperation than they would in the case of noncooperation. This calculus holds irrespective of the fact that the more powerful party benefits disproportionately. When mistrust between parties is an issue, what changes is not so much the behavior of individual actors—since all actors will continue to serve their interests—but the type of cooperation that takes place: cooperation in a low-trust system of networks does not involve the kind of open information exchange and reciprocity that is necessary for formulating productive long-term economic policies. Instead, the hoarding of information by the regime and the withholding of information by private actors produce short-term, tailored policies that benefit both parties as individuals at the expense of state coffers, the business community as a whole, the consumer, and the hospitability of the investment climate. Thus, the entire economy suffers. But that is not all. Unintended consequences related to the increase in business power in general end up delimiting the regime's choices for an exit that sustains its security.

Practical Implications of Institutional Dead Ends

Over time, unintended consequences may result as the weaker parties (B) accumulate distributional gains and broaden their alternatives, thus changing breakdown values. At that point, cooperation becomes more strained. However, changes in breakdown values under conditions of sustained mistrust at the macro level between the regime and the business community, relative international insulation, and external sources of state income—such as those existing in Syria—are not sufficient to terminate cooperation. Changes in breakdown values do, however, affect the bargaining that takes place between both parties and the extent to which each party, especially the weaker one, is able to press for advantageous cooperative formulas. The improved bargaining power of the private members of economic networks is a result of tailored policies that were formulated in the late 1980s and early 1990s. By 1995, however, the cumulative effect of tailored policies, combined with decreasing confidence of local and foreign investors vis-à-vis Law #10, have literally brought the economy to a halt. Because of their increasing wealth and decreasing vulnerability to unfavorable cooperation, the mistrusted capitalists—though members of the same networks—stand to benefit from bargaining with the regime. At the same time, the regime is seeking an exit from economic stagnation and decline that has brought economic growth to negative figures for consecutive years. But the regime's choices are rather limited: it is neither able to give more concessions to network members because it would be doing so at a higher risk, nor is it able to broaden the political game to involve hitherto excluded actors, both domestically and internationally (since that would further undermine its decisional autonomy, as Syrian elites observed in the Egyptian case in the 1990s). The most secure exit from the perspective of the regime, then, is to crack down on these networks, reorganize them to the extent it can, and further constrict the largest distributional gains to smaller circles of regime loyalists. This process halts the development even of exclusionary institutions and leads to the reorganization of latent interests in the business community. Crises of succession in contexts such as those that Syria has witnessed since 1998—when former president, Asad, began explicitly preparing his son Bashar to be his successor—can accelerate the process immensely by creating a split between those who stand to gain from the impending succession and those whose fortune is yet to be determined under the new rule. In Syria, this is manifested in the split between the old guard and supporters of Bashar al-Asad. Depending on who benefits disproportionately from existing networks (in the Syrian case, it was the old guard or regime hard-liners) the succession crisis pits relative reformers (the new leadership) against

hard-liners. In Syria, the regime hard-liners (the old guard) aligned themselves with the private network members with stronger ties to the business
community, and the soft-liners (the new leadership) opted for diverting the
most lucrative rent opportunities to a small number of individuals with high
proximity to the family of the president. This latter group had been securing
various posts within the government and the military and security apparatuses since 1998. Furthermore, it has been recruiting new, younger, and more
dynamic cadres who were not previously affiliated with the dominant
economic networks.

The end result as of the time of writing is an institutional gridlock that
has put on hold much of the plans for economic opening because of the risks
involved even in further reorganization of rent-seeking networks. The institutional dead-end was a creation of the regime, which since the 1980s boxed
itself in when it helped to consolidate informal economic networks that
monopolized most distributional gains from subsequent processes and
policies of economic change. It is noteworthy that even within exclusionary
networks, private sector members were deprived of the instruments and
information they would need to lend more credibility to their alliance with
the state bourgeoisie. Once more, the social mistrust between the regime and
the business community as a whole permeated the regime's own networks.
However, this did not occur at the expense of the alliance between the state
elite and the select business actors within: it occurred at the expense of the
health of the economy.

In sum, the exclusionary pattern of state intervention in the context of
regime–business mistrust produced unintended consequences within the networks themselves. The unintended consequences involve an unfavorable shift
in breakdown values between the regime and its private sector partners (i.e., a
shift that puts the regime at a relational disadvantage). A correlate has been
a halt in investment both from within and without economic networks after
1995. Politically, these factors have dramatically reduced the regime's room for
institutional maneuvering. From the perspective of the most significant
faction of the state elite, their immediate private partners within economic
networks became less trustworthy: their bargaining power increased without
a concomitant deepening of the alliance. The larger business community
remained both excluded and, thus, hostile to the regime as a whole. On the
other hand, labor had nothing (left) to offer the regime, except passive silence.
Only a decisive shift to democracy would revive support among the silent
majority, an unlikely prospect in the foreseeable future. Finally, the regime's
historic opponents, the Islamists, remain a non-option for alliance making.
Given this stalemate, the regime has only the external sphere as an exit.

But even relations with the European Community that included plans for conditional cooperation have fallen through because of the regime's slow pace of reform and its handling of human rights issues domestically.[35] This institutional dead-end has also chipped away at the capacity of the state to extract resources from an increasingly impoverished population and labor force, leaving the regime even more dependent on the international prices of oil (constituting upward of 65 percent of the state's foreign exchange revenue)[36] and residual aid from Arab Gulf countries.

Such institutional dead-ends are dialectically related to network dynamics: lack of trust among network members shortens time horizons for investors within the networks and without; this leads to particularly nonproductive and short-term investment patterns, and to the subsequent formulation of short-term tailored policies. These factors combine to influence general economic performance in a detrimental manner. In the meantime, network members who are private sector actors accumulate capital and improve their bargaining power vis-à-vis their partners in officialdom, thus making it more difficult for the regime willingly to give more concessions. This differential between the individual and institutional levels of analysis gets played out in the intra-network dynamics where both businessmen and "bureaucrats" act as individuals before the (unintended) effects prompt a regime response.

The Impact of Economic Networks on Fiscal Change, 1986–2000

This section constitutes a brief and focused case study on the impact of economic networks on fiscal change in Syria. Fiscal change is part of the general economic change Syria has witnessed since 1986. But as revealed here, fiscal change and change in fiscal policy is not the same thing in Syria: general fiscal policy need not change to accommodate the interests of powerful networks. Members of these networks are able to benefit from tax and other exemptions tacked onto other reform measures, the most important of which are discussed in the introduction. In a country where tax evasion (SP 50 billion worth) amounts to three times the tax income, official fiscal policy is hardly a measure of any influence.[37] Thus, it is more important to examine actual fiscal change (i.e., from where the fiscal revenue of the state comes) than fiscal policy reform (i.e., new fiscal legislation/measures).

The impact of economic networks on economic and fiscal policies in Syria is evident both in the economic statistics and in the decline in living standards of the majority of Syrians.[38] The focus on fiscal policy is not meant to deflect attention from other areas. On the contrary, it is meant to demonstrate how the influence of these economic networks has decisively crept into the crucial developmental areas of budgeting, tax laws, and associated regulations. The outcome of states' expenditure policies in any given society is a window into both what is considered socially and politically important/necessary to decision makers (irrespective of the source) and what the medium- to long-term economic future of that society is likely to be. Though the examination of fiscal policy ought not to be isolated from the examination of other areas that impinge on the economy, here it is considered as an indicator that reveals the priorities of the government and how these priorities are formed and executed.

The Empirical Record of Fiscal Change in Syria After 1986: The General Budget

The manner in which the budget is prepared is tailored to avoid pointing out explicitly the beneficiaries or holding any particular party accountable, except of course the state in the abstract. Four cautionary points on how the budget is prepared and what it represents guide this research effort:

- The budget is released six or seven months into the year in which it should take effect. By that time,[39] its effectiveness is dramatically diminished, especially with regard to investment spending.
- Most crucial budgetary decisions are handled by the Ba`th Party leadership and not the government officials entrusted with preparing the budget—hence, the prevalence of the mysterious categories of "other expenditures" and "various expenditures" that amount to 25 percent of the budget.[40] In effect, administrative officials in the economic institutions, that is, those who are supposed to prepare the budget, "have become administrative employees that execute ministerial and *non*-ministerial orders."[41]
- The administrative nature of setting exchange rates allows for selecting different exchange rates for different purposes (e.g., imports, Central Bank loans, customs duties, and exports).[42] This leads to severe economic distortions and renders much of the data in the budget misleading, especially with regard to what are referred to as "achievements" in the Ministry of Finance.
- Although the budget takes into account the regional distribution of the Syrian population, it does so in an unscientific manner: allocations do not reflect year-to-year changes in the regions/populations concerned.[43] The reason is the near-total absence of studies that calculate the effects of

previous budgets on the various regions and population groups/segments (e.g., by region, cost of living, income, age, and sex).

These reasons indicate why the figures of the general budget in Syria are either unreliable on a number of issues or must undergo an informed filtering process before they begin to approximate reality.[44] Nonetheless, the reasons for the lack of credibility of the budget are instructive. They reveal two important points: first, they demonstrate why it is important in most cases to look elsewhere for indicators on public spending and wealth distribution and, second, they begin to tell us where to look. In other words, they tell us to look for those benefiting from the manner in which the budget is prepared. Not incidentally, these are the beneficiaries of vast tax exemptions and their associates in officialdom, and thus, they usually do not contribute much to its revenues (i.e., to the treasury).

Hence, when examining the government's accounts of revenues and expenditures, it is important to note the difference between the nominal conception of budget deficits or surpluses on the one hand and the real social and economic outcomes and effects on the other. According to most critical economists (i.e., not "state intellectuals" beholden to the regime's rhetoric), the methods by which the budget is drafted, and by which the process itself is politicized, tell us much more than the nominal surpluses "achieved" and deficits incurred[45] as well as allow us to better assess the source of shifts in the allocation of public resources.

Shifts in Expenditures, Extraction, and Allocation of Resources

In the Syrian case, it is prudent to start with general figures that reveal broad and readily ascertainable shifts in the distribution of wealth since the 1970s, but more clearly since 1986. The quadrupling of the net domestic product (NDP) at factor cost (1995 fixed prices) has been met with a mere 46 percent increase in per capita income.[46] Evidently, rapid population growth accounts for some of this discrepancy, but not most of it, as the very poor distribution of wealth makes clear. In fact, even according to official Syrian statistics, per capita income at the end of the 1990s was much lower than that of the early 1980s, when the Syrian economy had already suffered sharp downturns partly as a result of the drying up of Arab aid after the oil boom period in the 1970s.[47] Moreover, the distribution of actual per capita income reveals that less than half of that amount goes to the Syrian individual, as evident in the dramatic drop in living standards of most Syrians in the 1990s.[48] The question is: where is the money going?

In response to economic crisis pressures and the growing influence of crony relations in the mid-1980s, the government started to reduce the quantity of goods and services that were subsidized[49] and increased the prices of various subsidized products to "turn governmental institutions from a state of loss to a state of profit."[50] The ways in which the government went about doing so had devastating long-term consequences in both social and macroeconomic terms. Most significantly, for instance, hiking up the price of formerly subsidized crops and especially wheat in the late 1980s caused the government to borrow from the central bank to cover the costs.[51] Such borrowing served to increase inflation and impose an indirect tax on the Syrian population, which was faced with higher prices all around for the same products. Noteworthy here is that the hike in prices was not accompanied by a proportional hike in salaries, forcing most Syrians to borrow, work more, or, in most cases, reduce their already low living standards.[52] Table 1.2 illustrates the near-steady reduction in government subsidies.

It is evident that the numeric figure representing the sum of indirect taxes minus public subsidies has risen dramatically since 1986, after being in the

Table 1.2   Indirect taxes + reduction in subsidies

Year	Sum of indirect taxes + reduction in subsidies in million SP*
1985	(−919)
1986	190
1987	5,359
1988	9,149
1989	13,961
1990	13,745
1991	20,532
1992	29,405
1993	40,811
1994	53,047
1995	61,004
1996	51,413
1997	54,961

*`Arif Dalila, "The General Budget Deficit and Methods for Its Treatment," Paper No. 9, 1999 Conference Series (Damascus: Economic Sciences Association, April 20, 1999), 279.

negative in 1985 (when the amount of subsidies was larger than that of indirect taxes),[53] that is, ordinary people are being taxed more and the products they purchase are subsidized less. This situation was caused primarily by keeping wages down while strengthening the mechanisms of tax collection, especially vis-à-vis public sector and lower-income salaried workers.[54] Almost yearly since 1992, the Ministry of Finance has announced budget surpluses[55] drawn from a 30 percent increase in tax collection over projected figures. It fails to announce that, at the same time, government spending on public investment is slashed 25–40 percent while current account spending on matters such as personal luxury commodities exceeds projected figures.[56]

Simultaneously, as discussed later, tax exemptions for a plethora of new commercial activities after 1991 denied the treasury a substantial increase in tax revenue and ended up benefiting a select few who were poised to take advantage of tax loopholes and exemptions.[57] A larger discrepancy lies in the unusual correlation between dramatic increases in domestic public revenues and a dramatic decline in overall economic growth after 1994. According to conventional economic principles, increases in domestic public revenues usually accompany positive, not negative, economic growth rates. In the Syrian case, and based on other statistics on taxation surveyed in this section, this also means that a substantial amount of the accumulated wealth in Syria was/is neither taxed nor recorded. Thus, the wealthy accumulate more untaxed wealth, while the government cuts subsidies, leaving the middle and working classes to pick up the tab by way of strict tax collection measures and rampant inflation caused by central bank loans that finance deficit spending on administratively hiked prices.

All the while, segments of the population in the lower rungs of the economic ladder are being taxed on subsistence income and not surplus income. According to conventional economic principles, taxes should be drawn from income surplus. In Syria, wages continue to be far lower than the value of labor power, or far lower than the cost of living.[58] True, the tax burden in Syria continues to be less than half of what is it in most other countries, that is, 13–15 percent as opposed to 20–30 percent,[59] but, upon inspection, that reflects a serious imbalance in terms of the segments being taxed, not the actual tax burden across the board. The budget does not reveal such imbalance. The reason is not simply administrative; it is political through and through, and can be traced to the increasing power of economic networks beginning in 1986, when the budget replaced the principal mechanism of central planning, the five-year plans.[60]

Other Measures Related to Fiscality: Lending and Foreign
Exchange "Policies"/Decisions

The effectiveness of fiscal policy is intimately related to lending and currency exchange policies. However, there is no such thing as an official lending policy in Syria. As of the end of 2000, the banks, ironically, do not provide most of the necessary banking functions for the purpose of investments and loans, let alone the pressing need of the Syrian banking system for a serious overhaul.[61] Lending decisions or policies are usually exegetically administered by officials in various ministries, especially the Ministry of the Economy and Foreign Trade and the Ministry of Finance. On the other hand, the second and last official currency exchange policy in Syria was drafted in 1981,[62] and thus both lending and foreign exchange policies are subject to administrative orders and "necessities." These "necessities" have increasingly reflected the interests of what can be called big business since the mid-1980s, but more visibly since 1991 when Syria took a more explicit, if not decisive, turn vis-à-vis central planning and, ostensibly, toward a more market-oriented economy. Ultimately, the stasis in currency exchange policy served as a powerful mechanism for raising barriers to entry into big business and for monitoring existing members of economic networks who might develop dissident views.

Similarly, since 1991, bank lending practices across the board—from the Central Bank to the agricultural, commercial, public lending, and real estate banks—have increasingly shifted from developmental investments toward short-term commercial activity. For one thing, the Industrial Bank has been effectively frozen by virtue of its limited financial resources. Even these limited financial resources were borrowed by sources that are "exempt" from paying their loans by virtue of the political weight of their associates.[63] According to bank officers, such unpaid loans have not appeared as delinquent in the bank's reports once the loans have been made.

A more general—though less readily ascertainable in official statistics— illustration of networks' influence on economic and fiscal decisions, if not policies, is the actual target and lending pattern of the Central Bank of Syria and its sectoral branches. Those analysts searching for official mechanisms by which lending practices are handled would look to no avail. Because the Central Bank and its sectoral branches are subject to state control and because, for instance, cabinet ministers and the prime minister are themselves silent business partners (not so silent in some cases), lending decisions can be implemented by administrative fiat once a sum of money is earmarked for investment projects.[64] However, what is notable here is that the policy-making process involves the vocal business partners of officials sitting on the boards of Chambers of Commerce and Industry throughout the country. They have access to pivotal state–business linking institutions such as the Guidance Committee.

Nonetheless, much can be deduced through cross-referencing and informed inference regarding lending practices that are intimately related to the general budget. Between 1991 and 1998, the sum of money borrowed from the Agricultural Bank and the Commercial Bank of Syria doubled, while the sum of borrowed money remained largely the same during that period in the industrial and other sectors (for *both* the public and private sectors). Between December 31, 1991 and June 30, 1998, the amount of money borrowed from the commercial, agricultural, and industrial branches changed respectively in the following manner: SP 71.4 to 156.7 billion, 12 to 28 billion, and 5.9 to 5.07 billion.[65] The import of this lending pattern for the matter at hand is twofold. First, the state-owned and -controlled banks are lending more money (on easy terms, with no guarantees or collateral) to the less productive and notoriously more corrupt commercial sectors where rent-seeking networks are lodged. Second, though these figures apply to both public and private sectors, it is evident that the commercial *private* sector, in both agriculture and trade, is the primary beneficiary: 98 percent of the agricultural sector has historically been in private hands and the commercial sector became predominantly private after 1987, but especially after 1991 when the private sector encroached heavily on external trade. These latter sectors were the dominant private sectors in the pre-reform period of the 1970s and 1980s, when economic networks were formed; hence, the decisional and policy influence of pre-reform economic networks on economic and fiscal reform policies. This clout or preferential treatment reinforces the contention that not only have these networks survived and benefited from reform, they have also played a significant role through institutional and informal avenues in influencing the form and content, if not pace, of economic reform patterns.

Also related to the general budget is the issue of administratively set exchange rates, which represents another area from which economic networks have benefited and worked to perpetuate even as other areas of the economy were undergoing piecemeal liberalization. The year 1986, or the year of the most serious foreign exchange crisis in Syria, created a foreign exchange "obsession" among leading policy-makers as well as prominent business people with accumulating foreign currency, irrespective of the means, the source, or developmental consequences of controlling foreign exchange. The Commercial Bank, for instance, had by the end of 1998 a frozen account of more than $5.5 billion in Swiss banks, presumably a reflection of the deep sense of insecurity that the 1986 crisis created vis-à-vis foreign exchange.[66] This amount has effectively been denied for domestic investment purposes. Nonetheless, the government continues to sell for hard currency various public sector products to domestic buyers. At the same time, there is a penalty according to Decree 24 of up to a 15-year prison sentence for dealing with hard currency, alongside a myriad of intricate regulations that independently allow for partial dealing with such currency. Thus, various public–private economic networks are benefiting from such "obsession"[67] while the government, including members of the most powerful of these networks, are satisfying their security concerns by reserving the legal right to crack down on those who "must violate the law" to do business, to survive: "only the government has the right to violate the law or force citizens to violate the law so it can selectively persecute them for the violation according to the law!"[68] To avoid the regulatory mess, and the consequential perils, most investors have refrained from investments that would require extensive foreign exchange dealings and most Syrians have their foreign exchange accounts in neighboring countries[69] or in Europe and the United States. Free trade zones and whole cities in both Egypt and the UAE are replete with Syrian investors who are not willing to risk doing business inside Syria because of the various restrictions on dealing with foreign exchange, let alone other monumental bureaucratic hurdles.[70] Most observers estimate the amount of expatriate capital at more than $60 billion.[71] In sum, lending and foreign exchange policies or "decisions" have led to capital flight and provided a disincentive to productive investments, denying the treasury the benefit of both taxes and interest rates. This situation, which could be slowly reversed by the authorities, is sustained because of the rent-seeking benefits that accrue to members of powerful economic networks, including those that have not yet (at the time of writing) repaid their loans from the Central Bank's sectoral branches.

Tax Policy: The Significance of Tax Exemptions

A marked impact of the past two decades of economic change in Syria is the redistribution of wealth from lower income groups to higher income groups. The redistribution does not occur solely as a result of business pressure nor is it a reflection of *dirigisme*. In fact, this is where the analytical utility of the notion of economic networks becomes evident: for neither is the regime interested in polarizing society (no established regime resting on even a modicum of populist legitimacy would have this as its explicit goal), nor is the business community as a whole interested or able to act collectively, much less to do so for the benefit of some sectors at the expense of others. Economic networks of capitalists and bureaucrats (often fused) in less developed countries (LDCs) help explain the particularist turn away from both the state and the business community as corporate interests. Notably, this diversion of resources has at times undermined the regime as a social force, leading to the freezing of reform measures vis-à-vis high-range economic policies after the commercial boom of the early 1990s. The area of tax law reform and tax exemptions is instructive. The fiscally consequential record of tax and customs duties exemptions is discussed before analyzing the mechanisms through which economic networks influence the implementation and interpretation of tax regulations, if not reform.[72] Though we are interested in changes that occurred after 1986, some regulatory changes have their roots in legislation prior to that year:

1. The 1972 legislative decree 84 regarding duty-free areas exempted all foreign products from all kinds of taxes and customs duties.[73]

2. The 1986 legislative decree #10 exempts stock-holding companies in the agricultural sector from all kinds of taxation and customs duties provided that products are not sold on the local market. This included all factors of production and vehicles imported for "business" purposes.[74]

3. The 1991 law #10 exempted projects in manufacturing, agriculture, and transportation (and other sectors) from paying income tax for seven years, including tax and customs duties on all related imports.

4. The 1985 decision #186 exempts projects in the tourism sector (providing first- or world-class service) from all kinds of taxes and customs duties for seven years and eternally exempts 50 percent of profits from taxation (this includes all necessary imports). The decision was extended to restaurants and bars. This decision is an example of illegal tax exemption. Because it is issued by the executive branch rather than the legislative branch, this decision is a violation of section 81 of the Syrian constitution, which forbids the modification or creation of a tax except through legislative authority.[75]

Most of these exemptions are associated with essentially nonproductive ventures and do not distinguish between a cement factory and a nightclub. This is a result of the increasing pressures of economic networks immersed in legal as well as under the table trade transactions and, at the same time, reflects the type of economic operations that the state is willing to cede to the private sector. In other words, it is not a reflection of the broad-based business community, but a response to lobbying of economic networks in the Guidance Committee, networks that stand to benefit from the ability to circumvent or ignore the letter of law.[76] Hence, their satisfaction after 1991 and the marked reduction, on the part of powerful beneficiaries, in terms of both efforts and heavy demand to open up the economy in the mid-1990s.[77] The situation changed in the late 1990s, of course, when privileges became less and less economically rewarding as a result of economic downturns and fierce competition from the maturing offspring of entrenched officials.

The empirical record of change in tax policies and decisions supports two conclusions: first, as Syrian economist Raslan Khadour put it, "tax exemptions became a tool for the distribution of poverty instead of being a tool for the distribution of wealth,"[78] since the mid-1980s. Second, tax exemptions are essentially methods for administratively sanctioned tax evasion brought about by deliberately vague tax law regulations and modifications. These regulations, which became more explicitly pro-big business as the 1980s came to a close, are the outcome of various forms of "bargaining" or collusion, either informally or in the institutions that link state and business.[79]

Economic Networks: Domains of Influence

Thus, a principal mechanism by which wealth is redistributed from lower income groups to higher income groups in Syria is found in the realm of taxation, which, in most LDCs, should be divided into formulation of the actual laws and regulations and their implementation. The reason for distinguishing between the formulation and implementation of tax policy is simply that in the absence of the rule of law, the letter of the law becomes a tool that is subject to exegetical use by the powers that be.[80] More specifically, to the extent that the powers that be are able to selectively set aside, or overstep, the rule of law, it becomes more pressing for researchers to focus on implementation rather than on actual tax policies—the latter, in any case, are themselves socially and economically problematic. The lack of separation of powers becomes a crucial factor. Syria is an instructive case in this regard, where the near-literal fusion of the legislative and the judicial branches into that of the executive, and where monitoring and "accountability committees" are firmly under the control of the prime minister.[81] Under such conditions, which have their own causes of emergence, tax policy formulation and implementation is subject to various systemic and social pressures. And, contra Kienle's critique in this volume (chapter 9), it would be a mistake to dismiss the influence of economic networks when we are not able to ascertain all the links in tracing the causal chain between networks and "policy reform." In fact, the impact of economic networks on *economic policy reform* understates their power simply because, comparatively, there have not been *reform policies* to speak of in Syria (virtually none of significance between 1994 and 2000). But members of these networks are handsomely, some say "criminally,"[82] enriching themselves. Members of these networks have not been keenly interested in *policy reform* as such because the existing policy environment does not constitute a barrier for them. Moreover, many members of these networks have accumulated a large portion of their capital by transgressing laws and regulations that no one else can without incurring a high risk under current policy conditions. Why change the rules when you are the only one who can bend them to your benefit, and why make long-term investments when rent seeking in quick-profit commercial activity brings more capital?

In the Syrian case, where the core of the tax law has not been modified since 1949, implementation processes for both the original letter of the law and the myriad of added regulations of the legal and illegal variety[83] become more important than the actual tax laws or broader policies. This is evident in the areas of direct taxes and customs duties, where the actual state revenue from these categories is but a fraction of what it is supposed to be according to both imports figures and even declared incomes that have already been partly exempted from taxation.[84] In 1992, for instance, the ratio of taxes to GDP was 6.53 percent, by far the lowest among Arab and most other countries.[85] Yet, lower-income groups pay their taxes fully, almost to the last penny in the case of public sector workers. By contrast, the government collected $300 million in taxes from the private sector while the private sector contributes to 60 percent of GDP. This translates into an average tax burden of 3 percent of private sector declared income.[86]

Notes on Fiscal Change in Syria: The Importance of Middle-Range Policies

The tenor of this case study is simple, and it applies to both fiscal and regulatory change: whereas the Syrian regime is able to control what can be termed guiding or high-range economic policies/decisions, on which economic networks have little effect, it is unable[87] or unwilling[88] to meddle with most middle- and lower-range policies/decisions that are indeed subject to ample pressure and veto power from powerful economic networks, especially in commerce and tourism. Here, for instance, high-range policies refer to general matters such as the actual tax law and divisions into income brackets, while middle-range policies refer to the numerous regulations and exemptions that are tacked onto existing laws. Lower-range policies refer to issue areas that are pertinent to specific activities or commodities and are usually subject to change without explicit referral to, or approval by, institutional authorities. In an economy dominated by small-scale ventures, even if run by "big-business," and where manufacturing is restricted to consumer, not capital goods, influence over middle- and lower-range policies is what most business sectors/interest groups—particularly those in dominant economic networks—are interested in, not least when it comes to tax laws. Hence, the increasing importance in Syria of middle-range economic institutions such as the Guidance Committee (officially titled the Committee for the Guidance of Imports, Exports, and Consumption) at the expense of the more traditional and centralized Economic Committee. Often labeled the "Tailoring Committee," the Guidance Committee has become since the early 1990s the sole economic institution on which the private sector is represented. While the Chambers were considered the institutional expression of the private sector as a whole in the 1990s, the Guidance Committee became the institutional expression of privileged economic networks, despite its stated function as the institution that aggregates and responds to the interests of the private sector, the public sector, the GFTU (General Federation of Trade Unions), and the party.

As discussed earlier, because of the factor of mistrust, the relational dynamics within these institutions have produced unintended consequences that were detrimental to the health of the economy. This is occurring today well beyond the realm of fiscal policy, but other areas are even more difficult to research at this point, for example, the oil sector. The price that the Syrian economy has paid for transgressions and unintended consequences is extremely high, but remains within bounds that can be tolerated by the regime, for the time being. It is questionable how long the Syrian leadership can afford to subordinate the interests of the state to the security of the regime. All indicators since Hafiz al-Asad's death—including the further circumscription of reform benefits—point to the contention that this is not the appropriate question. Rather, one should ask whether the Syrian regime is able to get out of the social and institutional deadlock in which it has been lodging itself for nearly four decades.

Concluding Comments

Using Syria as a case of a low-trust system between state and business, this chapter has identified the institutional and social conditions that gave rise to economic networks between "bureaucrats" and "capitalists," and traced the impact of these conditions on the intra-network dynamics and, in turn, on fiscal policy change. The relationship between state–business historical legacies and emerging networks is quite complex, as it involves a social history, an institutional history, and various levels of strategic interactions. Key among these is the relationship between trust, networks, institutions, and economic performance. It is often difficult to disentangle these variables in practice. More important is the task of understanding how they relate to one another on the one hand, and how they themselves can always be traced to structural and strategic variables that shape them—that is, external rents, and the economy's relative insulation both domestically and internationally. In the Syrian case, a particular legacy of adversarial state–business relations generated deep-seated suspicion between "bureaucrats" and capitalists. This social antagonism considerably diminished trust between them, leading to the creation of selective informal networks between officials and business-men. These networks prospered through backdoor deals, semi-legal or illegal. Their internal dynamics were marked by calculative trust, informed by the larger social setting. The institutions these networks spawned were colored by calculative trust as well, leading to various unintended consequences in policy formulation and economic performance as individual interests clashed with regime interests. Calculative trust within networks shortened time horizons, and severely diminished transparency and information exchange, crucial elements for formulating sound economic policies. Ensuing economic activity and change took on a predictable nonproductive turn and reflected the interest of entrenched economic networks.

The case of Syria compels researchers to probe the concept of networks in order to understand political–economic outcomes that cannot be explained adequately by either state-centered or society-centered approaches that focus on statist logic, classes, or particular corporatist interests. Moreover, the Syrian case clearly supports the contention that a dialectical approach to network analysis is crucial for understanding the formation and development of networks. Specifically, the Syrian case confirms two assumptions posited by David Marsh and Martin Smith, authors of the dialectical model:[89] first, that the "broader structural context affects both the network structure and the resources that actors have to utilize within the network," and that "network interaction and bargaining reflects a combination of the actor's resources, the actor's skill, the network structure and the policy interac-tion."[90] Hence, the ability of the politically impotent private business partners to wield significant influence within economic networks. One con-tribution from the Syrian case is the importance of the security dimension as an additional incentive of intra-network cooperation, which often rises over and above that of short-term individual economic interest. Whereas network members collaborate to increase profits, for instance, in the case that Marsh and Smith discuss,[91] network members in Syria cooperate also to survive, either in the political sense from the perspective of the political elite, or in the economic *and* political sense from the perspective of their private business partners. The alliance between the Damascene bourgeoisie and the state against the rising militant Islamist opposition in the late 1970s and early 1980s is a clear and trend-setting case in point. The current retrenchment of network members in the face of the reemerging civil society's calls for fundamental economic reforms is another testament. Another important contribution from the Syrian case is the importance of unintended outcomes as a product of network interaction. Hence, the contention that neither the state nor the business community is guiding economic change. And though networks benefit from rent seeking, the constellation of unintended policy outcomes has run the economy into the ground since the mid-1990s. According to Marsh and Smith, "policy outcomes are the product of the interaction between agents and structures, not merely the sum of the effect of structure and agents."[92] Thus, the less coordination there is within and between institutions, and the less actors are constrained by institutional authority, which is the case in Syria, the more unintended the outcomes.

Notes

1. On economic or policy networks, or alternatively, on distributional coalitions, see Andrew W. Buck, "Networks of Governance and Privatization: A View from Provincial Russia," in Diane E. Davis, ed., *Political Power and Social Theory* (JAI Press: Stamford, CT, 1999) and Hector E. Schamis, "Distributional Coalitions and the Politics of Economic Reform in Latin America," *World Politics* 51 (January 1999): 236–268.
2. See for instance, Edward H. Lorenz, "Neither Friends nor Strangers: Informal Networks of Subcontracting in French Industry," in Diego Gambetta, ed., *Trust: Making and Breaking Cooperative Relations* (New York: Basil Blackwell, 1988), 194–210; and Philippe C. Schmitter and Wolfgang Streeck, "Community, Market, State and Associations? The Prospective Contribution of Interest Governance to Social Order," in Graham Thompson, Jennifer Frances, Rosalind Levacic, and Jeremy Mitchell, eds., *Markets, Hierarchies, and Networks: The Coordination of Social Life* (London: Sage Publications, 1991), 227–241.
3. For an introduction to network analysis, see David Knoke and James H. Kuklinski, "Network Analysis: Basic Concepts," in Graham Thompson, Jennifer Frances, Rosalind Levacic, and Jeremy Mitchell, eds., *Markets, Hierarchies, and*

Networks: The Coordination of Social Life (London: Sage Publications, 1991), 173–182. For empirically grounded research on network analysis, see Paul Dimaggio, "Nadel's Paradox Revisited: Relational and Cultural Aspects of Organizational Structure," in Robert G. Eccles and Nitin Nohria, eds., *Networks and Organizations: Structure, Form, and Action* (Boston: Harvard Business School Press, 1992), 118–142; and Mustafa Emirbayer and Jeff Goodwin, "Network Analysis, Culture, and the Problem Agency," *American Journal of Sociology* 99, no. 6 (1994): 1411–1454.

4. Economic networks in Syria refer to what generically could be called big business. Although one might find wealthy Syrians who are not associated with these networks, seldom can one find powerful *and* continuously active businessmen who are not part of these networks.

5. Signs of economic stagnation beginning in the mid-1990s include an overall drop in production; a rise in unemployment to unprecedented levels; the shrinking of foreign investments; a drop in real wages, purchasing power, and aggregate demand; the closure of some enterprises established under law #10; and finally, the stockpiling of goods in factories and at retail stores. See *Statistical Abstract 1998*, "National Accounts," (Damascus: Central Bureau of Statistics, 1998), chap. 16, 503–563. For more information on indicators regarding Syria's economic stagnation in the late 1990s, see *Syria: Country Profile 1998, 1999*, and *2000* (London: Economist Intelligence Unit).

6. To be sure, economic networks did not cause economic decline, but exacerbated inefficiency in an economy with a declining productivity since the early 1980s, despite numeric growth in the late 1980s. For more on the causes of economic decline in the 1980s and 1990s and on the artificial growth in the late 1980s, see this author's "The Political Dynamics of Economic Liberalization in Populist-Authoritarian Regimes: Administrative Disintegration, Social Polarization, and Economic Stagnation in Syria, 1986–2000," conference paper, First Mediterranean Social and Political Research Meeting, March 2000, European University Institute, Florence, Italy.

7. Such networks exist in normal or non-transitional periods and usually do survive such periods. What is peculiar, however, are the conditions for rent seeking in transitional/reform periods—blurry/contradictory laws and regulations; increased power of discretion given to middle- and lower-range policy makers and regulators while the domain of economic activity expands considerably; the proliferation of new and bigger contracts with foreign companies; the further weakening of institutions and agencies that monitor and adjudicate either by virtue of their incapacity to keep pace with or track of rapid and non-transparent reregulation, or by virtue of their muting by the powers that be.

8. See Raymond Hinnebusch, "Democratization in the Middle East: The Evidence from the Syrian Case," in Gerd Nonneman, ed., *Political and Economic Liberalization: Dynamics and Linkages in Comparative Perspective* (London: Lynne Rienner Publishers, 1996), 163–164.

9. See Steven Heydemann, *Authoritarianism in Syria: Institutions and Social Conflict, 1946–1970* (Ithaca, NY: Cornell University Press, 1999), 85.

10. See David Marsh and Martin Smith, "Understanding Policy Networks: Towards a Dialectical Approach," in which they emphasize the dialectical interaction between network and context, in *Political Studies* 48 (2000): 421.

11. See Hanna Batatu, *Syria's Peasantry, the Descendants of Its Lesser Rural Notables, and Their Politics* (Princeton, NJ: Princeton University Press, 1999), 208.

12. See Volker Perthes, *The Political Economy of Syria Under Asad* (London: I.B. Tauris, 1998), 49–53.

13. For more on generic criteria regarding the reliability of network partners, see Dimaggio, "Nadel's Paradox," 118–142.

14. This occurred in the 1970s through various election and selection processes that benefited individuals primarily from rural backgrounds, but increasingly from `Alawi backgrounds as the decade drew to a close. In many ways, such rural, secular, and sectarian favoritism—always a means, not an end in Syrian politics hitherto—had fueled the growing urban, Sunni, petite bourgeois dissatisfaction with the regime. For more information on the regional, socioeconomic, communal, and sectarian causes for the confrontation between the state and the Islamists between the late 1970s and 1982, see Raymond A. Hinnebusch, *Authoritarian Power and State Formation in Ba`thist Syria: Army, Party and Peasant* (Boulder: Westview Press, 1990), chap. 9.

15. These factors include the relative insulation of Syria from external economic actors; the sectoral distribution/organization of the business community, which is not conducive to collective action; the structure of state revenue, which includes large sums of capital inflow from rent; the lack of administrative autonomy/coherence of state institutions; the socially narrow nature of the leadership; and the balance of social forces, which include an extremist opposition that is feared by both the regime and big business.

16. See *Syria: Country Profile 2000* (London: EIU). For investment figures, see *Statistical Abstract 2000*, "National Accounts."

17. See Steven Heydemann, "Taxation Without Representation," in Ellis Goldberg and Joel Migdal, eds., *Rules and Rights in the Middle East* (University of Washington Press, 1993).

18. These individuals—who shall remain anonymous—have connections with the old bourgeoisie. As the succession crisis intensified, they became more eager to distance themselves temporarily from the regime.

19. Oliver Williamson, "Calculativeness, Trust, and Economic Organization," *Journal of Law and Economics* 36 (April 1993): 453–502.

20. Since 1985, labor representatives have become little more than mouthpieces for the government. Author interview with Dr. Nabil Marzouq, an academic consultant at the GFTU, Damascus, April 21, 1999.

21. This view is very much shared across the board among Syrian businessmen. Few, however, are willing to go on record with such depictions. Ihsan Sanqar has said

as much in his parliamentary commentaries and proposals. Author interview with Ihsan Sanqar, Damascus, December 29, 1998.

22. Business members from the Chambers of Commerce or Industry that are "not in favor," or are outside the crony networks, do occasionally attend and make requests, but such requests are limited and, usually, insignificant. When I asked a prominent member in an Aleppo Chamber, who had sat on some of the meetings, about the progress of the Guidance Committee's role since 1991, he replied, "Yes, a year ago 'we' permitted the export of donkeys to Kuwait." Interview, Aleppo, March 4, 1999.

23. Mahmoud al-Zo`bi was accused of corruption and later committed suicide in the spring of 2000. See the weekly *al-Wasat*, no. 437 (June 12–18, 2000): 12.

24. Salim Yassin was also found to be involved in corruption and has been under house arrest since the end of spring 2000. See ibid.

25. Various informal interviews with former officials at the Industrial Bank and the Commercial Bank of Syria validate this commonly known fact; Damascus, March–April 1999. Although such partnerships are not always formal (i.e., the names of officials do not always appear on contracts), their involvement in running businesses and securing accounts and foreign exchange is evident to bank personalities and to other business partners who know well who is behind various exemptions and protected products.

26. As noted in note 25, both men were placed under house arrest when their economic ventures began to collide with the political interests of the top rung of elites in early 2000. Contrary to official rhetoric, their arrests had much more to do with the then-impending succession crisis.

27. Author interview with Ihsan Sanqar, Damascus, December 29, 1998.

28. Parliament member and prominent industrialist Riad Saif is a prime example of such personalities.

29. Usually, independent businessmen can accumulate only so much capital before they become subject to harassment and/or attempts at co-optation.

30. This conceptualization captures the common denominator among various schools of thought on the emergence of institutions. The difference rests on the actual purpose. More pertinent to this study is the sociopolitical factor that motivated the concerned elites. This does not mean that transaction costs were not considered, as the new institutional economists (NIE) would advance. Simply, transaction costs are determined based on a more sociological and historical calculation that involves a number of social, economic, and political factors. These factors have been the subject of preceding chapters. Thus, an eclectic approach that combines historical, sociological, and rational choice institutionalism serves this study best. As the following makes more apparent, the task is to discern when the logic of consequences dominates behavior (i.e., the basis of rational choice new institutionalism) and when the logic of appropriateness dominates behavior (i.e., the basis of historical and sociological new institutionalism). See Elinor Ostrom, "Rational Choice Theory and Institutional Analysis: Toward Complementarity,"

American Political Science Review 85, no. 1 (March 1991): 238–243; and Peter A. Hall and Rosemary C. R. Taylor, "Political Science and the Three Institutionalisms," *Political Studies* 44 (1996): 936–957. For transaction cost institutionalism, see Douglass C. North, *Institutions, Institutional Change and Economic Performance* (Cambridge: Cambridge University Press, 1990).

31. Actual economic reforms, which began in 1986, preceded their officially pro-claimed variety in Syria. Economic reform as an official policy—defined by a minimal acknowledgment by the government for a need to liberalize the eco-nomic system—was not pronounced until 1991, when the government rejuve-nated what came to be known as "economic pluralism" (*al-ta`addudiyya al-iqtisadiyya*). This term, used extensively in official statements by Hafiz al-Asad upon his assumption of power in 1970, refers primarily to the actualization of the complementary formula that brings together the public, private, and mixed sectors under the service of the "national economy" (*al-iqtisad al-watani*). For a review of such early statements, which are repeated in nearly every speech or printed text on economic change, see the yearly reports by the Chambers of Commerce and Industry in Damascus and Aleppo, and President Hafiz al-Asad's inauguration speeches in 1992 and 1999. Also, see (virtually all) papers on the topic of economic reform presented at the ESA since 1991, Tuesday Lectures at ESA, *Nadawat al-Thulathâ, al-Jam`iyyah al-Iqtisaadiyyah* (Damascus: Economic Sciences Association, 1991–2001). Even papers by otherwise critical writers and economists have adopted one dimension or another of the "*ta`addudiyya*" dis-course. See, for instance, papers by Marzouq, Nabulsi, and Khadour, from 1996 to 2000. It is noteworthy that the power of the economic pluralism discourse rests in the fact that parts of it (e.g., division of labor between the public and the private sector) coincide with progressive economic thought worldwide in the 1990s, albeit only in form. Thus, repeating some of its tenets (e.g., that the pub-lic and the private sector ought to complement each other) may be intended to reflect the conditions of sound economic policy, but the unintended outcome, especially when particular vocabulary is used (e.g., *al-iqtisad al-watani*), is to reinforce Asad's discourse.

32. One prominent independent businessman notes the following when asked about new opportunities presented by new regulations in 1999: "I would not exploit such opportunities. I may accumulate financial capital on a deal or two, but I may lose respect among my peers." Interview with Ihsan Sanqar, Damascus, April 13, 1999.

33. Interview with Riad Saif, former board member at the Damascus Chamber of Industry and a two-term member of parliament since 1991. At the time of writ-ing, Saif has been sentenced to five years in prison because of his civil-society activism and outspoken criticism of government policies (see *al-Hayat*, April 5, 2002); author interview, Damascus, December 22, 1998.

34. See Henry Farrell and Jack Knight, "Trust, Institutions, and Institutional Evolution: Industrial Districts and the Social Capital Hypothesis," unpublished paper, 2001.

35. See Sami Moubayed, "EU Projects Stall in Syria," and "Vimpex Pulls Technicians from Syria: Working Conditions Were 'Unbelievable,'" in the Lebanese newspaper *Daily Star*, July 2, 2001 and September 17, 2001, respectively. Also see "Syria's Economy Opens to Regional Opportunities," in *The Daily Star*, September 6, 2001.

36. See `Izz al-Din Juni, "Oil, the Lifeblood of Development and Industrialization in Syria: World Prices Substantially Influence Oil Exports," in the Syrian weekly *al-Iqtisadiyyah* 27 (December 30, 2001).

37. See Samar Izmishli, "Syria: The Amount of Tax Evasion Equals Three Times the Revenues, and Weakens the Capacity of the State to Spend on Health, Education, and Services," *al-Hayat*, March 26, 2001.

38. See the 1997 and 1998 reports of the Central Bureau of Statistics in Syria and `Arif Dalila, "The General Budget Deficit and Methods for Its Treatment" [`Ajz al-Muwazana al-`Amma wa Subul Mu`alajatihi], Paper No. 9, 1999 Conference Series (Damascus: Economic Sciences Association, April 20, 1999).

39. This has become a part of conventional knowledge in Syria to the point where most Syrians generally disregard the budget's contents. Economists, however, insist on pointing out the social and economic implications of such (deliberate) delinquency in various public forums and, in the late 1990s, in the state-run press. The ESA's annual lectures are one site where prominent economists bring this issue to the fore. See the 1999 collection of ESA's Tuesday Lecture Series.

40. See Dalila, "The General Budget Deficit," 282.

41. Ibid., 284. Emphasis mine.

42. See Perthes, "The Political Economy of Syria under Asad," 56. Perthes states that, "from 1991, the government also began to calculate *certain* budgetary items and public-sector imports and exports on the basis of the neighboring countries' rate." Emphasis mine.

43. See Dalila, "The General Budget," 275.

44. Dalila cites five principal reasons that account for the unreliability of the budget: the budget adopts a lower exchange rate for the U.S. dollar; the largest portion of the supply deficit is excluded from the budget; there are revenues and expenditures that are not accounted for in the budget; the budget does not refer to the revenues and expenditures of local administrations; and the budget ignores some crucial factors, such as dramatic drops in oil prices. See Dalila, "The General Budget," 289.

45. Ibid., 269.

46. Outspoken Syrian economists estimate that at the end of the 1990s nearly all the national income "goes to the hands of five percent of the Syrian people," with a quickly declining middle class and widespread poverty on the horizon. Among other statistics presented in this paper, see *al-Hayat*, October 1, 2000, 4.

47. See *Statistical Abstract* 1998, 526–527. Per capita NDP at factor cost dropped from SP 43,450 in 1980 to SP 3,310 in 1997.

48. The Syrian government does not release such statistics, but independent Syrian economists estimate that average Syrians are making much less today than they

did in the 1960s when NDP was even lower. This has been recorded in various interviews conducted by the author in 1998–2000. For instance, according to the 1997 budget alone, if we calculate the difference between increased extraction measures and expected fiscal revenues (that generally target lower income salaried workers) and decreased government spending, we find that the living standard of the general population has dropped by 15% in one year. See Dalila, "The General Budget Deficit," 284.

49. It is notable that the government could do so only if decision makers were confident that there existed an alternative on the supply end; i.e., the very same economic networks that supplied the Syrian domestic markets with consumer goods that the government was unable to provide or unwilling to subsidize in the early 1980s, when a severe shortage economy took hold.

50. See Dalila, "The General Budget Deficit," 278.

51. See `Arif Dalila, "The Public Sector and Its Role in Development" [al-Qita`al-`Amm wa Dawrahu fi al-Tanmiya], Paper No. 3, 1986 Conference Series (Damascus: Economic Sciences Association, 1986).

52. See Dalila, "The General Budget Deficit," 278.

53. Ibid.

54. This includes the belated collection of taxes from delinquent sources. By the time these accounts were paid, inflation had gobbled the initial real value of taxes due. Ibid., 284.

55. There are several key sources for "nominal" budget surpluses. One major structuring source is the fact that investment budgets are not executed until the sixth or seventh month into the respective year. Another serious source is that, by administrative orders, the budget leaves out most figures under the category of supply deficits and, at the same time, inflates the category of "other revenues," which are in essence numeric price differentials that reflect the rise in inflation rates (i.e., inflation here can be considered a form of indirect taxes on the majority of the population). Ibid.

56. See article on Syria's economic troubles, in the Communist Party publication, al-Sha`b, by `Arif Dalila, March 1999.

57. Investment Law #10 of 1991 allowed for both legal and illegal maneuvering around tax laws by virtue of the generous tax exemptions that it provided as well as other distinctions that were henceforth abused by the majority of investors. See the section on Tax Exemptions later for more detail.

58. See Dalila, "The General Budget Deficit," 281.

59. See Raslan Khadour, "Tax and Customs Exemption Policy," Buhuth Iqtisadiyya `Arabiyya, June 1996.

60. One way to understand the decline of authority of the five-year plans, as well as of the Regional Conferences, is to contrast the content of the last five-year plan and the resolutions of the eighth and last conference held to date with the actual measures that the government adopted in response to the 1986 crisis. While the Regional Command conference and the five-year plan focused on the importance

of the public sector's control and monopoly over imports and agricultural inputs respectively, the measures adopted expanded the role of the private sector in foreign trade and industry and allowed it to encroach on the import and distribution monopoly of the public sector in various economic spheres. See the reports of the eighth Regional Command Conference [*Taqarir wa Muqarrarat al-Muátamar al-Qutri al-Thamin*] (Damascus, 1985) as compared with the actual measures described by Sukkar in "The Crisis of 1986 and Syria's Plan for Reform," in Eberhard Kienle, ed., *Contemporary Syria: Liberalization Between Cold War and Cold Peace* (London: I.B. Taurus, 1997), 32–36.

61. Most critically, state-owned banks do not enjoy any significant measure of autonomy to conduct banking functions, nor does the Central Bank have available to it the traditional banking policy tools that are intended to direct savings and investments. Interview with Dr. Amr Lutfi at the Faculty of Economics, February 1999, Aleppo University, Aleppo. See also articles on the state of the Syrian banking system in the ESA's 1999 Lecture Series.

62. See Dalila, "The General Budget Deficit," 285.

63. Interview with a high-level official at the Industrial Bank in Damascus, May 1999. The names of these individuals are well known to the interested Syrian public, and they include such tycoons as Saáib Nahhas and the recently cast out of favor Anwar al-`Aqqad, both of whom borrowed money to invest in projects under law #10 of 1991. It is noteworthy that despite the large amounts borrowed by more than ten prominent businessmen (each amounting to more than SP 100 million, and some more than SP 200 million), they are borrowed at interest rates lower than those at which public-sector workers borrow from the Public Lending Bank to cover their basic living expenses. The latter loans are collected "to the last drop."

64. The operating mechanism for implementing such lending practices varies from a nonpolicy related letter from a top cabinet official to a simple telephone call. In fact, if there is a system of checks and balances, it works in a more detrimental direction. According to a number of employees (mostly former ones) in the Commercial, Agricultural, and Industrial Banks, permission to grant a loan with no collateral to a particular business partner is sometimes rivaled by a similar loan grant to another partner. As one former employee put it, "they say, 'this way, we are equal.'" These individuals shall remain unnamed.

65. See the 1998 Central Bank of Syria report for a more "muffled" version of these figures. The cited figures were obtained in an interview with a former official at the Commercial Bank of Syria; Damascus, April 1999. Another strikingly similar set of figures were obtained in an interview with an academic who has access to "ministerial papers" that broke down Central Bank figures on lending patterns; Damascus, June 1990. These individuals are to remain anonymous.

66. Interview with former employee at the Commercial Bank of Syria. Also see, Dalila, "The General Budget Deficit," 286.

67. Two of the most extensive hard currency black market networks (i.e., networks of individuals who have a political cover for providing foreign exchange to satisfy domestic demands) are run out of Latakia and Aleppo, and are partners in some of the most powerful economic networks in Syria. These networks, both business and black market ones, have an interest in perpetuating the hard currency short-age situation as the latter benefit directly from speculative exchange deals and the former get a better exchange rate than the rest of the less, or not, well-connected businessmen.

68. See Dalila, "The General Budget Deficit," 287.

69. A number of banks in Lebanon, beginning in the early 1990s, conduct a sub-stantial portion of their business with Syrian investors who are free to travel back and forth for their banking needs. Interviews with two assistant bank managers in Beirut, February–April 1999. It was requested that the names of the banks not be disclosed. Lebanese banks' employees and consultants have begun to provide "special" services to Syrian investors by driving across the border, collecting deposits, and returning to Lebanon to credit their respective accounts. As a par-ticipant observer, the author has been on one such trip in which a Lebanese bank employee meeting informally with traders in the traditional Suq al-Hamidiyyah of Damascus conducted such a transaction. Two important facts stand out: first, nearly all of such Syrian "depositors" do not document such transactions, that is, no papers are signed by either party for fear of reprisal and, second, those bank employees who shuttle back and forth carry special passes (*khatt `askari,* or mil-itary line) that allows them to bypass heavy traffic and meticulous searching (often excavating) at the border. Such passes are handed out only by official permission from the Syrian government or those who influence the respective agency.

70. Interview with a Syrian businessman residing in Dubai, who was on one of his six yearly visits to see his family in Damascus, June 2000.

71. See Leonard Robinson, "Elite Cohesion, Regime Succession and Political Instability in Syria," *Middle East Policy* 5, no. 4 (January 1998).

72. For an updated account, see Muhammad al-Jlailati, "The Syrian Tax System and Avenues for Its Reform" [*al-Nizam al-Daribi al-Suri wa-Ittijahat Islahihi*], Paper No. 7, 2000 Conference Series (Damascus: Economic Sciences Association, March 2, 1999).

73. Ibid.

74. See Khadour, "Tax and Customs," 94.

75. Ibid.

76. Beneficiaries of exemptions, most often part of powerful public–private eco-nomic networks, use(d) their import privilege to satisfy the local market. Moreover, the goods and services provided by projects that benefit from these exemptions are provided at relatively high costs and prices, rendering them non-conducive to exports—an essential part of the conditions of any project under Investment Law #10.

77. A most notable example is the opposition in 1995 of three major business tycoons to the creation of a stock market for agricultural products. These tycoons ran the joint-sector agricultural establishments and were able to freely set the prices of such stocks at a level higher than their market value. Interview with a former official at the Commercial Bank of Syria, December 1998.

78. See Khadour, "Tax and Customs," 108–109.

79. Interview with an Aleppan economist who occasionally sits in on Guidance Committee meetings as a consultant for one of the chambers of industry, Aleppo, February 1999. According to him, many of the explicit decisions at the meetings seem superficial, but certain "requests" are put on the discussion table as ones that would "encourage us to invest," if not attract Arab or even foreign money. Such requests are not explicitly decided upon in reference to those who made the requests—trade unions and party representatives attending would not have this kind of responsiveness!—but they are subsequently decided upon and end up being quite responsive to particular individuals' needs.

80. See the empirical record earlier, which shows how exemptions were abused for purposes not related to exempted investment. The contradictory legal environment in Syria (let alone the notorious category of verbal decrees and decisions issued and reversed regularly by the minister of the Economy and Foreign Trade and through the prime minister's office) makes virtually all major business transactions both legal and illegal at the same time. In other words, the rule of law is replaced by the role of law in sustaining a particular form of economic activity with its attendant winners. The best way to explain this situation is to borrow the example of a popular industrialist: "our situation is like being in a room with one open door that has a 'no exit' sign on it and a guard standing by. If you get out, which you must do to survive, you have violated the law. It is up to the 'officials' (al-masáulin) to apply the law or not." This legal context was made possible by the accumulation of laws and regulations, some of which extend to Ottoman times. It creates a ituation in which, for all intents and purposes, the law becomes an arbitrary tool controlled by the regime and its junior partners in their definition and enforcement of barriers to entry into the network of beneficiaries. Riad Saif (Syrian industrialist, parliament member, and board member in the Damascus Chamber of Industry), Goethe Institute Lecture Series, Damascus, April 4, 1999.

81. See Raslan Khadour, "The Economic Effects of Administrative Corruption" [al-Athar al-igtisadiyya lil-fasad al-idari], Paper no. 2, 1999 Conference Series (Damascus: Economic Sciences Association, February 23, 1999).

82. In ESA symposia, what are called the "new bourgeoisie" are often referred to as "criminals, robbing the public." More outspoken critics, such as Dalila, do not shy away from openly associating them with "partners" in the government. Author's notes from ESA's 1999 Conference Series, al-Markaz al-'Arabi al-Thaqafi, Damascus, February–May 1999.

83. For instance, the constitution states that no tax is to be imposed or exempted without undergoing a legal process, which, in most cases, involves ratification by

the legislature; however, several tax exemptions have been decreed by politicians, including decision 186 (1985) issued by the prime minister to exempt all investors in first- and second-class tourism projects from all kinds of taxes, customs, and municipal and financial duties. See Khadour, "Tax and Customs."

84. For various figures on both customs duties and direct taxes revenue, see figures drawn from Khadour, "Tax and Customs," 87–114, and Dalila, "The General Budget Deficit."

85. See Khadour, "Tax and Customs," 103.

86. See `Arif Dalila, "Issues in the General Budget," a news column in *al-Hayat*, March 2001.

87. The state's institutional capacity with regard to economic issues at the end of the 1980s became dismal, leading to various problems including fragmentation of policy making and contradictory regulations. See, for instance, *Tishrin*, May 22, 1997, where six ministries provide through their press staff contradictory answers to the simple question of what agency/organizational body is supposed to monitor exports. Also, in more than one instance at the ESA lectures, audience members would suggest that "we need to pick up our legal and regulatory framework and throw it in the trash;" 1999 ESA lecture series, Damascus, February–May 1999.

88. The unwillingness of the regime refers here to the fact that, in the 1990s, regime officials themselves were benefiting from both a lopsided tax "system" and their ability "legally" to maximize rent under existing conditions.

89. See Marsh and Smith, "Understanding Policy Networks."

90. Ibid., 9–10.

91. The authors discuss "The Agricultural Policy Network in Britain since the 1930s." It is important to note that in the case of Late Developing Countries, certainly in Syria, speaking of networks often refers to networks that operate across most if not all policy areas. In the example here, and others abound in the case of advanced capitalist countries, policy networks are often differentiated by sector.

92. See Marsh and Smith, "Understanding Policy Networks," 11.

CHAPTER 2

The Whales of the Nile: Networks, Businessmen, and Bureaucrats During the Era of Privatization in Egypt

John Sfakianakis

S ocial science has long been concerned with the way individuals organize
themselves and how they influence or help bring about a certain social
structure. Networks are an important component to economic life,
both in a developed economic setting or a reforming and developing economy. An understanding of how networks operate in a specific politico-
economic environment is telling of how certain bonds of affiliation, that are
often informal in nature and character, act as "lubricants for getting things
done" and of how order and meaning in social life is maintained.[1] The role
of networks in economic life and particularly during the era of belated economic reform in Egypt and other parts of the Middle East is crucial to an
understanding of the reformist project and its outcome.

Networks are defined in a variety of ways but I have tried to remain within
the interpretive boundaries of socio-anthropology. A network is a regular set
of contacts of similar social connections among individuals or groups. Actors
are not just self-seeking animals but are also embedded in structures of economic life that construct and express common interests. Viewed in this way
those that prosper are those who are able to develop multiple ties with nonre-
dundant contacts that include families, professional associations, sporting

clubs, political parties, alumni groups, social clubs, and so forth.[2] The guiding notion behind the application of a network approach to economic reform is to understand *why* and *how* certain kinds of networks are more effective in capturing resources than others under certain reform conditions. Social network literature makes that point quite clearly by studying actors in interaction with one another and how those interactions constitute a framework or structure that can be studied and analyzed.[3]

The arguments that are put forward in this essay are based on participant observation research conducted among members of the business elite of Egypt in the 1990s. The interviews cited here are drawn from field research that was carried out for more than three years as part of a doctoral thesis on state–business relations in Egypt in the 1990s.

This essay examines the process of economic reform since the early 1990s and shows how that process created opportunities for particular actors located both inside and outside the state. Specifically, I examine the impact of reforms on three groups of actors: (1) state officials involved in the implementation of reform policies; (2) former bureaucrats who were recent entrants into the private sector; and (3) the established business elite. My argument, at the most general level, is that reforms created the possibility for the creation of new networks that linked state officials and former bureaucrats, and permitted them to capture the benefits of privatization, often at the expense of more established business actors.

Offering a different perspective than that by Ulrich Wurzel (chapter 3), this essay argues that Egypt's reform process, and particularly the privatization experience since the 1990s, offers insights not only into the dynamics of existing, pre-reform economic networks, but about the role of policy reform in network creation. Economic policy reforms in the 1990s provided space for new networks to emerge in an institutional and social environment that had long sustained privileged ties between business and state. In this sense, state–business relations in this period operated on two distinct but interconnected levels. On one hand, businessmen acted to preserve the collective good represented by an environment of crony capitalism that favored the presence of privileged economic networks. On the other, they competed, often aggressively, to insert their particular networks into channels of rent seeking that were being altered by policy reforms. This sometimes entailed the reshaping of networks to incorporate actors best positioned to compete effectively for rents created by the reregulation of the Egyptian economy. The interplay of these two levels of action, the complementarities and tensions that they exhibited, offer a useful framework for understanding the broader politics of economic reform in Egypt.

Some 32 businessmen comprised the established business elite of Egypt, with a large majority engaged mainly in import-substitution. This elite sector flourished behind barriers of protection, was largely uncompetitive in the international market, and existed in large part due to rent-seeking operations that became more pronounced in the 1990s as the Egyptian economy expanded. Many of these businessmen were importers and agents, and benefited from a selective regime of high tariffs in the 1990s. Privatization offered an opportunity for these import-oriented rent seekers to sustain, if not enlarge, their business interests against those of exporters who were unable to organize effective and powerful networks to support their cause. By preventing the system from becoming more competitive and more transparent, even as it underwent a partial and selective process of economic reform, these businessmen sustained their privileged access to information, links with well-positioned bureaucrats, and economic opportunities. By maintaining the system of privilege between certain businessmen and the state the former created a system in which it was extremely difficult for other, less-well-connected, businessman to penetrate the ranks of the 32. Hence, another reason for creating a network among elite businessmen was to raise the barriers to entry for nonelite businessmen.

Having said this, however, networks did not operate at all times during the process of reform, or rather, *intra-elite networks* were sometimes subordinate to *crosscutting networks* that linked elites to state decision-makers who had the authority to award public contracts. When large-scale public construction contracts were up for grabs, businessmen used their personal networks with bureaucrats, rather than intra-elite networks, to advance their individual interests and win new business deals. Yet it was this system of cooperation and competition among overlapping networks that both linked elites but also cut across the public and private sectors that was reorganized in the process of economic reform and privatization. Policy shifts gave rise to an assortment of network opportunities, of three kinds: within the state, between state officials and their former colleagues who had entered the world of private business, and among those former bureaucrats aspiring to enter the business elite. More established elite businessmen were sometimes participants in these new networks but were sometimes excluded from them. Thus, privatization on its own did not help the more established businessmen to augment their wealth in the 1990s: elite businessmen in Egypt were not catapulted into positions of vast wealth as a result of privatization as happened in Russia under Boris Yeltsin. By the time privatization began to take off in Egypt these elite businessmen had already established important business niches and developed links with the state to sustain them. Where privatization played a very important accumulative role was among the acting and former members of the bureaucracy.

Thus, whatever the arguments are about the limits of reform in Egypt it is clear that certain policies were maintained and others adopted that gave rise to a new set of business actors. Whatever misgivings we might have about the way privatization was implemented, the government did begin a process of selling its assets in 1993. The process was uneven and often ambivalent. Yet it nonetheless created opportunities for former bureaucrats to establish powerful networks of privilege that benefited themselves and occasionally to compete with established private sector elites. At times, these newer business interests were able to turn public monopolies into private monopolies. At other times they colluded in purchasing parts of privatized companies. Overall, however, a new set of powerful business actors created a set of networks or fortified previous ones that they could exploit to their own advantage.

The existence of powerful business networks and proximity between businessmen and bureaucrats should not lead us to assume that whatever was privatized was merely shared between bureaucrats and cronies, or that existing networks were simply brought into play as mechanisms of resource allocation and control. During privatization, certain networks came into play at various points to secure the transition of a system that previously supported public monopolies to a new system that now supported private monopolies and oligopolies. The use of networks by privileged businessmen and former bureaucrats allowed them to become the "whales" or *hitan* of the country in the 1990s, a popular Egyptian term describing the very wealthy.

The point to stress in this chapter is that the existence of cronyism does not in and of itself determine how networks will become organized, which ones will be activated under particular conditions, or how effectively they will respond to new opportunities—in this case the opportunities resulting from a process of economic reform. Accounts of economic reform that assume continuity in the composition of privileged economic networks, presume that the presence of networks on its own can account for the dynamics of policy change, or fail to appreciate the extent to which reforms are constitutive of interests and of network opportunities, are missing important parts of the story. Without an array of networks, cronies would not have been able to gain access to the state. Yet within this context there was ample room for reforms to bring about the reorganization and recomposition of business networks.

The Businessmen

As Wasserman and Galaskiewicz note, "instead of analyzing individual behaviors, attitudes, and beliefs, social network analysis focuses its attention on social entities or actors in interaction with one another and on how those interactions constitute a framework or structure that can be studied and analyzed in its own right."[4] Network analysis looks at economic action as socially situated behavior that cannot be explained by reference to individual motives alone.[5] As Granovetter and Swedberg stress, networks represent a "regular set of contacts of similar social connections among individuals or groups."[6] With these as starting points, one can explore a defining characteristic of economic networks in Egypt: the preponderance of informality. These frameworks allow us to define networks as mechanisms by which individuals organize and regulate their interests beyond the available formal structures. Such networks emerge to pursue common interests or, in this case, to obstruct reforms that would impose rules of transparency, regulation, and accountability. By focusing on networks I look at *which* network has privileged access to patronage and resources and *how* it secures them. In this way the work of Burt is employed, searching to find not only the networks that benefit in particular policy settings but also how certain structural arrangements generate benefits and opportunities for certain networks.[7]

In the same spirit, this essay does not merely focus on those networks that benefited during the era of reform in the 1990s in Egypt but also examines aspects of the macroeconomic field that helped particular networks to prosper. I have to account, in particular, for the persistence of the particular networks that were the beneficiaries of the reform project of the 1990s. At the crux of network persistence are the informal mechanisms that are coordinated, in a systemic way, to facilitate "interdependent flows of resources [and] reciprocal lines of communication."[8] Not surprisingly, however, the importance of informal mechanisms does not discount the possibility of business elites employing formal channels to gain access to patronage. If anything, networks are able to affect regulatory, market, and resource allocation outcomes due to the flexibility with which they exploit both formal and informal channels.

In order to better understand the reorganization of business networks in Egypt we need to take stock of their standing in relation to that of the state and the regime. As I indicated earlier, businessmen who benefited from the reform project of the 1990s owe their rise into the elite both to the crony ties that linked them to the regime and to their ability to establish multiple networks among themselves. Yet first and foremost, business success was safeguarded as a result of the networks these businessmen had with the state. Crosscutting networks that linked current and former bureaucrats were created to safeguard the privileged position of rising elites in the business landscape of Egypt. These network ties were needed precisely because the regime was fairly autonomous in managing the crony system that increasingly characterized state–business relations during the 1990s and in bending this system to advance its own interests, above all its interest in regime incumbency. The cultivation and enrichment of new business networks served the regime's purposes by supplementing other elements of its ruling coalition, including senior bureaucrats located more squarely within the public sector and the elite of the military/security apparatus. The maintenance of the business elite was also safeguarded because businessmen provided extra-salary handouts to bureaucrats and politicians.

In the early 1990s, these arrangements did not signal the emergence of new business networks capable of asserting their interests in relations with the regime. During these years, businessmen remained dependent on the regime for access to privilege. However, as businessmen became financially powerful by the mid-1990s they begin to form networks that ensured their continued access to resources and increased their own autonomy vis-à-vis the state. Although the regime played an instrumental role in establishing a system of crony business ties that defined the structure of the political economy in the 1990s, elite businessmen gradually appropriated that structure and used it to secure positions of economic privilege. However, their growing influence in economic matters did not extend into the political arena. The political landscape continued to be dominated by the regime, with businessmen serving as clients of the political elite.

These networks drew strength from the crony system that benefited those already in close proximity to the regime. Although the style in which influence was carried out by elite businessmen was individualist and atomistic, they pushed the system in similar directions and thus engaged in uncoordinated collective action that worked to secure the maintenance of the monopolistic structure of business. Not only did business cronies oppose transparency and anticorruption efforts, they also resisted any change in the political landscape of Egypt that might have brought about a new regime structure. Even when a new competition law was drawn up in the late 1990s it was far from the doorsteps of parliament and the corridors of the presidential palace. Preserving low levels of transparency was not merely a goal of political actors resisting the imprecations of international institutions, it was also an elite business affair. More broadly, the belatedness of economic reform and liberalization in Egypt since the 1990s was not merely the product of an autonomous state, but was also the work of business networks that were able to prevent change and limit competition by exogenous business elite interests that could encroach on their business empires.

Networks and Privatization

Privatization in Egypt should be viewed as a process of bargaining between different networks of privilege. It is correct to assume, at least at the initial phase of the reform project during the early 1990s, that the most powerful networks "opposing" or "supporting" privatization were located within the state. Some preferred a more radical and immediate process of state divestiture and others, including Mubarak, advocated a more gradual approach. Quite clearly, it was the latter group that prevailed since the early 1990s. Nevertheless, privatization created new opportunities within the state for those who were well connected enough to take advantage of the sale of public assets.

The reform experience of the 1990s at large and the privatization process in particular, was not immune from bargaining and back room deals involving different businessmen and other interests. At times, fierce challenges took place, with elite businessmen confronting each other. At other junctures former bureaucrats confronted powerful businessmen. Indeed, the privatization of the 1990s was a fascinating period to observe because it brought to the fore different networks with divergent views about the nature of power and the economy and the boundaries or lack thereof of the public and private domains. It also brought to the fore some of those actors that were operating with the help of state actors and who themselves were former well-placed bureaucrats. The state bourgeoisie did get involved in the process of privatization but on a smaller scale. Aside from the businessmen it was mainly former bureaucrats who kept their ties to the state bureaucracy and developed parallel ties with the business elite that enabled them to reach new heights of wealth.

At the outset of the reform epoch, in the early 1990s, the degree to which the dominant regime networks were willing to accept a complete set of economic reforms that would have led to a substantial part of the state withdrawing from the economy was unclear. The various methods that were used to privatize state-owned companies, proved to be an important indicator of the debates that were taking place within the ranks of the state, and disprove a static view of privatization in Egypt. I argue here that there has to be a separation between the different stages of the reform process in Egypt to categorize the different networks and alliances that took place as the process of privatization unfolded. This type of ongoing conflict and shifting alliances is not a uniquely Egyptian phenomenon. Through the work of David Stark and Laszlo Bruszt on East Central Europe and Luigi Manzetti on Latin America, we know that privatization everywhere is a process that is far from a *fait accompli*, and is, instead, a project of discord and reconfiguration.[9]

The first phase of reform in the early 1990s are best described as years of "reform realization" through a process that was guided and directed by the president, Hosni Mubarak. The state was quite well insulated from societal pressures in its initial decision to embark on a reform project during this period. Although opposition to reform was evident to those within the ranks of the regime, it did not crystallize in the shape of an elite network. The "reform realization" period was followed by a phase of "reform stabilization" between 1991 and 1993. During both of these phases, two camps faced one another: on one side was the "apprehensive" group and on the other were the "reformers." The former were circumspect about the entire economic reform project, whereas the latter believed in the necessity of restructuring the economy and reforming some important parts of the economy, changes long advocated by the World Bank and the International Monetary Fund (IMF). The latter group was principally concerned with the poor fiscal situation of the state, yet beyond its general endorsement of reform there was little sense of a time frame, or detailed conception of a development project that would bring together different actors in support of economic reform. In many ways, the management of the economy did not change fundamentally during this period, which incapacitated the reform project. Trial and error was the preferred avenue of the 1990s instead of decisive and coherent reform policies.

Importantly, the initial phase of reforms did not immediately give rise to a set of new business networks. Over time, however, the business elite of Egypt became more attuned to the reform project, which it understood would affect the way business was conducted. And it was only later, during the second phase of reform, that new business elites secured more regular access to the spoils of privatization as a result of their own decisiveness in establishing powerful networks.

The wealth that these businessmen amassed over the course of the decade could not have been accumulated without their crony ties to the state, as mentioned earlier. As such, their fortunes depended on an economic system that rewarded those closest to the state and not necessarily the most innovative or efficient. And not surprisingly, this type of accumulation benefited state officials as well as bureaucrats-turned-businessmen. Privatizing the state became a process by which wealth was generated for both. Thus, especially in the period after 1993, a different type of bargaining and competition took place in which a "new money" network featured more prominently. The composition of this network was a hybrid, and included both high state officials that had developed important accumulative and investment interests in Egyptian business, as well as those emanating from the ranks of the business elite. These groups formed an alliance not only because some had joint investment projects in the formal sector of the economy, but also because business was conducted on the basis of the transfer of contracts in return for money. This interdependency among the actors of the "new money" network did indeed give rise to a "winner take all" mentality. Actors within that network were willing to create impediments, delay the process of reform, or restructure it in such a way, as Joel Hellman pointed out, so as to "preserve [their] gains by maintaining the imbalances of partial reform over time."[10] For a variety of reasons, therefore, Egypt's privatization process did not instigate what Stark and Bruszt call the "marketization" of the economy.[11]

Going After the Spoils of Privatization

My intent in this section is not to give an account of the factors that led to the privatization project in Egypt or to present a detailed chronology of what was privatized throughout the past decade. Instead, I show the ways in which the Egyptian privatization experiment brought competing interests and networks to the fore. My core argument focuses on two related variables. First, I argue that the privatization process in Egypt was politically managed to maintain an active role for the state in the economy. The pace was not defined by the networks of opposition or by the pressure of international institutions, but by the political calculations of the incumbent political elite. In this way, the Egyptian privatization experiment did not differ from what Manzetti described in the case of Latin America in the 1980s:

> The policy response to the debt crisis of the 1980s was usually tentative and tried invariably to avoid an economic adjustment program that encountered the opposition of powerful lobbies (like those sectors of the business community that benefited from high import barriers and generous state contracts and subsidies, labor, the military, and the government bureaucracy). Although decision-makers saw the need for a fiscal adjustment through government reform, market deregulation, and privatization, they also believed that the political cost of these reforms was too high. A "politics as usual" approach ensued, based upon incremental changes whose palliative nature did not address the distribution of political power and economic resources, which was at the core of the crisis.[12]

Thus, while the Egyptian government had overseen the sale of 29 percent of state-owned enterprises by 2000,[13] privatization did not change the nature of political power. Incumbency was maintained by the Mubarak regime not by its embrace of political pluralism and norms of accountability. On the contrary, it was maintained through the allocation of economic patronage—distributive in character—and by restrictive authoritarianism that allowed hands-on control of the political opposition and of electoral institutions. However, "politics as usual" does not, on its own, provide an adequate explanation of the process of reform in Egypt during the 1990s. A second variable was also at work, a "Winners Take All" dynamic. As defined by Hellman, the limits of reform in post-communist countries was the result of "actors [who] can hardly be classified as short-term net losers in the overall reform process. On the contrary, they were its earliest and biggest winners. The net winners did not oppose the initiation of the reform process, nor have they sought a full-scale reversal of reform. Instead, they have frequently attempted to block specific advances in the reform process that threaten to eliminate the special advantages and market distortions upon which their own early reform gains were based." In Egypt, new crosscutting public–private networks linking bureaucrats and businessmen behaved in similar ways to capture for themselves the benefits of the early stages of reform.

The Business Whales

During the 1990s, a new set of inter-network alliances emerged in Egypt to exploit an environment of cronyism and capture the benefits of partial reform, especially in services and tourism. These new moneymaking ventures are not proof that liberalization was taking shape in Egypt. On the contrary, these new moneymaking ventures directly involved, in a new way, the role of the state. A good example is the Egyptian mobile-phone sector, which is neither properly regulated nor properly liberalized. Instead, the phone system has been preserved as a deliberalized duopoly. On the one hand, the state has allowed the operation of two mobile phone licenses since 1997, and despite apparent competition between the two companies—MobiNil and Click—the sector has not been adequately regulated. The state, on the other hand, is beginning a process of deliberalization by allowing itself the possibility to become the prospective third cellular service provider. In other words, the state is still uncertain whether to perpetuate its role as investor/producer or as regulator. This process of mixed competition and deliberalization has been closely followed by certain networks, which became the beneficiaries of economic change as well as of the process of privatization.

Another good example of a monopolized market is the production of alcohol. The privatization of Al-Ahram beverages (ABC) in 1997 to the Luxor Group was hailed as a privatization success story by the Egyptian government and investment banks. Previous attempts to privatize, as in the case of the producers of Egypt's famous Stella beer, were both complicated and lacking in transparency. ABC was among those public sector companies that were consistently profitable. Prior to privatization, ABC had gross margins of some 60 percent, with net profit in 1996 reaching LE 41.3 million. In addition, in 1996 ABC was LE 96 million cash rich and was one of the few public sector companies that despite poor quality-control standards, was consistently debt free.[14] At the helm of the Luxor Group were the Zayat brothers, led by Ahmed Zayat, well connected with financiers from his days in Wall Street, as well as with the political elite. Prior to Zayat the government made several attempts through both international and local investors to sell ABC to no avail. Heineken, the company that founded ABC in 1897, was approached in the early 1990s but the talks failed. In June 1996 an Initial Public Offering (IPO) of 30 percent of the shares was launched but the issue was only one-third subscribed. Prior to and again after the failed IPO the government of Egypt approached two elite businessmen for a majority stake in the company but both declined.

Forming a powerful consortium of former bureaucrats, elite businessmen, and public sector companies does not guarantee that bids will be successful. In 1996, a bid for ABC (70 percent of the company) was made by a consortium of the Egyptian Finance Company, led by real estate developer Farid Saad, and Al-Ahly for Development & Investment, the first venture capital company formed in Egypt in 1995, which was led by the former minister of tourism Fouad Sultan but included in its ranks the state-owned National Bank of Egypt, as well as two elite businessmen, Mohamed Nosseir and Mohamed Ragab, as well as another well-known businessman, Youssef Ramsis Atteya. The consortium made a bid of LE 400 million for ABC, which was rejected by the government as too low.

However, Zayat reached an agreement about the way the Luxor Group would pay the government for its acquisition, which demonstrated ingenuity on the part of Ahmed Zayat. Initially, ABC shares were floated in the London Stock Exchange (LSE) during Egypt's first Global Depository Receipt (GDR). The Luxor Group acquired 74.9 percent of ABC's shares at LE 68.5 per shares. The Group then sold the shares in the form of GDRs on the LSE in February 1997. Each share was split into two, with each half being sold at LE 52.5. Within three months the Luxor Group made a 36 percent net profit from the issue of the GDRs and then in February the group paid the Egyptian government the LE 231 million for ABC.

Zayat agreed with the government to build a new greenfield brewery at El Obour city, 40 km east of Cairo, in return for a ten-year tax exemption. Only Nile Brewery, owned by three elite businessmen Hani Rizk, Mohamed Nosseir, and the Ghabbour family, had a similar tax exemption yet they were not able to put any building plans into effect since in 1999 ABC bought them out.

Zayat like other businessmen also cast his web and established business ties with the military. In 1998, Zayat entered into an exclusive nation-wide distribution agreement with the Egyptian army. The army owned *Safi*, a premium bottled mineral-water company. The deal allowed ABC to distribute

Safi through its nationwide network of 29 warehouses and its fleet of over 400 trucks, while the Egyptian Army continued its control over production. The deal between the Army and Zayat was very strategic and important for ABC. ABC was unable to get much access to the lucrative market of Upper Egypt due to prohibitions the police had placed on the sale of alcohol in an area where thousands of police personnel were deployed in fighting militant Islamists in the 1990s. With the Army having the upper hand in all operations in Upper Egypt, the police would not have been able to prevent ABC from distributing its beer.

In 1999 ABC won a bidding battle against the Sawiris and, initially, against Sami Saad, the local agent and producer of Schweppes, for the state monopoly winery, Gianaclis. The 70 percent gross profit margin in the wine industry had made the winery a company worth fighting for. Imported wine was subject to a 3,000 percent customs duty and was thus prohibitively expensive, making Gianaclis all the more attractive as an investment. The Zayats organized a formidable campaign and used their extensive state contacts especially within the public enterprise office, which helped them acquire an edge over the Sawiris. In the end, a higher offer by the Zayats combined with the support of key members of the privatization committee safeguarded their acquisition.

Through these maneuvers, the state had established a monopoly in the alcohol sector that was now in the hands of Zayat. Following the sale of ABC in 1997, the Sawiris family quickly positioned itself to acquire a license to establish a brewery and a winery. Knowing that the state would continue to protect the alcohol sector—also as part of an understanding between the Zayat brothers and the state—they began building a new brewery on their Red Sea resort at El-Gouna, importing grape juice in sealed containers from Italy. Notwithstanding their license, the Sawiris were able to benefit from tax exemptions. Not only did their beer and wine hit the Egyptian market by 2000, but they were able to enter into a price-fixing arrangement with the Zayat brothers. However, this duopoly did not last long. A complete monopoly was once again safeguarded as ABC bought out the El-Gouna brewery and winery, which included a liquor factory that had also been privatized and bought by the Sawiris, Zotos, and Bolonaki. In late 2002, following suit just like Nosseir did in the mid-1990s, the Zayats sold ABC to Heineken for LE 1.3 billion.[15] The ABC acquisition represented the most profitable turnover in Egypt's post-1952 history from its original purchase in 1997 to its 2002 sale to Heineken.

As these anecdotes indicate, the period 1993–2000 did see the rise of network behavior but also some interesting rearranging. Those individuals that belonged in the statist group, that were skeptical about privatization in the late 1980s—Leftists, nationalists (Nasserists), and unionists—continued to be apprehensive about privatization in the mid-1990s onward. In addition, the statist group (not network) was also skeptical about the presence of foreign capital in the 1990s. As the Egyptian capital markets began to boom during the mid-1990s, and foreign portfolio investment became a noticeable trend, questions arose about the real intentions of foreign capital. These concerns were not unfounded and by 1997 the government had, informally, voiced its concern about the speculative nature of foreign holdings. However, Egypt in that way was not different from the observed influx of foreign, often speculative, investment capital in other emerging capital market settings.

The networks that elite businessmen put in place in the mid-1990s were not circumstantial. They were established as a result of the dwindling power of the public sector elite and the regime's intention to see businessmen replace the bosses of the state-owned enterprises (SOEs). The intention of elite businessmen to form networks was to perpetuate their monopoly power in the marketplace. It was not geared toward influencing the political landscape of Egypt whatsoever. These businessmen put in place conglomerates, which for the most part were neither vertically nor horizontally integrated, but were random collections of different business ventures, as a result of rent-seeking patterns rather than competitive attainments. Egyptian elite businessmen are for the most part creations of hit and run operations with quick profits. As such, they had an interest in the 1990s to operate various networks to either forestall or delay the pace of liberalization. Moreover, the same businessmen who acted in a network sometimes formed partnerships with different members of the same elite to either buy out public sector companies or form important monopoly and price fixing arrangements. However, those that did win the spoils of the privatization process in the 1990s were elite businessmen who were in direct proximity to the executive and its entourage. Certainly, the biggest privatization that Egypt experienced in the early stages of the privatization process was the sale of Coca Cola in 1993. It was a deal that involved most prominently, among other members of the political elite, the quintessential elite businessman of the 1990s, Mohamed Nosseir. He benefited from his relations with Atef Sidqi as well as Atef Ebeid to purchase with little competition the Coca Cola factory, which he resold two years later, at a price more than triple his cost. After all, Nosseir and the rest of the crony business elite were only doing what the structure of the economy had allowed them to do: provide politically helpful services to the regime.

The private sector's concentration in the service sector was a reaction to the state's role in the rest of the economy. The commodity producing sectors, such as agriculture, manufacturing, petroleum, and construction, in the 1990s remained dominated by the public sector. The private sector's share of output in the commodity producing sectors in the 1990s did not reach more than one-third, despite the fact that it stood at 32 percent as long ago as 1983.[16]

The complexities of privatization and its role in reshaping interests and networks are further illustrated by examining the sale of the San Stefano Hotel in Alexandria. In 1988 Fouad Sultan, the then minister of tourism and a privatization advocate, proposed the sale of San Stefano. The sale was opposed in parliament and the government was forced to back down from Sultan's proposed sale. A decade later, a consortium of businessmen led by the very powerful contractor of Alexandria, Talaat Moustapha, who also happened to be a member of parliament in 1995–2000, joined forces with another very powerful business family, the Mansours. As if these two businessmen were not enough, Prince Walid Bin Talaal of Saudi Arabia came in as the foreign strategic investor. Also the National Bank of Egypt (NBE) entered as an equity holder alongside the Commercial International Bank, in which NBE has a 20 percent controlling stake. Although initially the government was not willing to allow these businessmen to build a seafront hotel that was more than seven stories high, their ruling was changed after considerable pressure had been brought to bear by exploiting network ties between potential investors, the public sector, and the parliament. The merger of public and private interests that transpired was paradigmatic of the 1990s. Egyptian businessmen had accumulated more capital in the 1990s than in the 1980s, venturing into an array of areas, and they had established powerful networks with the public sector that allowed them to command a powerful presence in many areas of the economy.

During the course of the 1990s, the onset of a more serious privatization effort and an economic upswing felt mainly in the service, import trade, and tourism sectors created incentives for networks to reposition themselves for a share of the spoils. Groups that could have at one point have appeared anti-reformist and anti-privatization oriented readjusted their priorities. These were groups that were well entrenched in the huge public sector. Their motivations were purely self-accumulative; fearing that the bonanza created under the reformist umbrella might not last forever. An attitude of "get it while you can" was prevalent among many public and private sector individuals. Quite similarly, Manzetti and Blake find that, while market reform and privatization take place corruption ensues due to the lack of transparency "as new means to pursue old corrupt ends."[17] And despite the Egyptian government's frequent affirmation of its commitment to the principle of transparency—not least in an effort to reassure the World Bank—the privatization experiment of the

1990s produced relatively little either in the way of transparency or in the way of more accountable processes of economic decision-making.

The government was motivated in maintaining the system for four main reasons. First, the lack of accountability of the reform process coincided with the general lack of political accountability that the government fostered. Second, the government could not have become more accountable about the actual process of privatization in an economic system that supported the opposite. Not only would this have created a structural anomaly, but the regime had few incentives to force different networks to become more transparent. For instance, the state budget is often, in more transparent states, viewed as the government's attempt to justify its expenditure plans to civil society. In the case of the Egyptian state budget, there is neither an attempt to justify the government's spending policy nor is civil society empowered to criticize it. The budget is a document inherently secretive, and full of uncertainties about the precise spending power of each ministry.

Third, the lack of accountability of the system also suited the government's larger agenda of state–business symbiosis. The regime could take decisions to allocate patronage to its narrow base of supporters—of which elite business networks were a central component—without being accountable to anyone. Although criticism could be heard here and there about certain licenses and contracts being awarded to certain actors of the elite business network, there was little that could have been done. As with all other structures that support informality and secrecy of business networks over formality and transparency, for every license and contract that reaches the public eye there are countless others that go unnoticed. Niche markets that were established with the support of the state as a fixer of contracts did not decline during the reform era. On the contrary, the pattern of things has been to create niche markets for businessmen under a completely legal guise. A good example is the way in which the government went about handing out two licenses, one to the Osman family and the other to the Sawiris family, for the involvement of the private sector in the cinema industry in the late 1990s as well as leasing 15 state cinemas on leases of 20 years. No other businessmen were given the opportunity to enter into either the bidding or the actual operations of the cinema industry. Little is known about the monopoly the Osman and Sawiris families have been able to cultivate with the Egyptian military, during the 1990s, on specialized construction contracts. State licenses of private sector ventures have followed the oligopoly route. The Sawiris in the 1990s came to represent the quintessential cronies that rose to new riches as a result of their connections with bureaucrats and politicians.

The only difference between the 1980s and the 1990s is that oligopolies were created in Egypt under a completely legal status. Much less was heard about those businessmen involved in the business of importing sugar, trading in steel, or distributing cement. Fourth, the lack of accountability during the reform process of the 1990s served to hide government uncertainty and often a change of mind about privatization. More specifically, the government would take certain decisions to privatize a company or retract from its promise to sell to a strategic investor without much reason. Lack of transparency served the purpose of containing public scrutiny about privatization sales, including sweetheart deals, undervaluing assets, and so on.

The business elite benefited from the privatization process but some were also the victims of a system that lacked transparency. Bids were cancelled due to "technical" and "legal" matters, documents were not found in time or were outright rejected for not being competitive in price. In financial terms, the established business elite did not benefit from the privatization process of the 1990s as much they did from their proximity to the regime and the ability to diversify their investments. The established business elite made more money through their multiple and diversified operations than by acquiring shares in privatized SOEs. Indeed, elite businessmen flourished under an environment of government contracts as suppliers or subcontractors, and saw greater incentives in keeping the government in business and themselves in close proximity to it than in buying out its SOEs. Interestingly, these businessmen flourished even more during the actual process of privatization not from buying the privatized SOEs but from either establishing parallel oligopoly markets or diversifying into other fields that had a quick-in-quick-out (QIQO) investment scenario. There are instances in which the business elite did buy into privatized firms, but often did so simply to resell assets at a higher price or to use land acquired in the process for real estate development, as in the case of several public sector hotels that were sold off.

Parallel business ventures were established, as mentioned earlier, under the umbrella of the law. This phenomenon did not take place in all sectors, but focused on those that were the most lucrative and where public sector firms were least attractive as investments. Had business elites purchased public sector cement factories, for example, they would have been compelled not only to restructure the management of the newly privatized companies, but agreements with labor unions would have prevented them from cutting labor costs, and would have imposed significant pension and other costs on the new owners. For these reasons, members of the established business elite preferred to use their privileged links to state agencies to launch parallel businesses, rather than encumber themselves with the demands of managing privatized firms. What mattered the most for them, nonetheless, was the maintenance of their proximity to the regime that supported their monopoly arrangements in the economy.

Apart from the Osmans and the Sawiris—two peak business families—a small group of established business elites took advantage of their proximity to the regime. Many started from construction and expanded into other sectors. Ibrahim Kamel specialized in aromatics as well as civilian airplanes but invested in real estate and tourism. Mohamed Farid Khamis developed his business base from his export-oriented carpet factory and began to expand into crony sectors such as real estate development in greater Cairo as well as Sharm El Sheikh. Mohamed Abou El Enein developed one of the most important indigenous ceramics factories in Egypt but benefited from a high import tariff that he pressured the regime to maintain. He also benefited from multiple touristic ventures, profiting from a low purchasing ratio of government land, just like most cronies, during the 1990s, thanks to his ties to the regime. Ahmed Bahghat, who developed as the most important local assembler of consumer electronic products, again being an import substituting industry, benefited from his ties with the military for contracts and patronage.

These and some other elite businessmen had much to lose from a dramatic change of the economic regime in Egypt. Their preoccupation in the 1990s as a network was not only to delay economic liberalization but also to prevent competition outside their ranks from prospective domestic competitors. By making themselves more politically relevant to the regime, their ability to limit competition from aspiring businessmen increased. The elite business network was successful not because of the wealth of its members but due to its informality. There was no given venue—apart from the Presidents Council and other businessmen's associations—that allowed the business network to take form and for its members to share views.

What the Egyptian experience conveys, however, is that economic reforms and programs of privatization did not operate as a zero–sum game pitting one set of business actors against others, based on their fixed positions within the Egyptian political economy. Instead, the reform context permitted multiple groups of business elites to navigate their way through complex networks of economic and political ties to profit from ongoing as well as new opportunities. The core interest of each major constellation of actors, the newer and more established business elites alike, was to protect the generalized environment of cronyism and protect their own access to the distinctive networks of privilege that served them as mechanisms of self-enrichment.

The Privatizing Bureaucrats

Privatization is not a process that merely allows businessmen with important ties to the state to take advantage of opportunities that arise in the economy. Privatization can also permit former bureaucrats and acting bureaucrats and members of the political elite to benefit. In Egypt, the cement sector offers ample evidence of how these collusive forms of state–business networks operated.

Among those who jumped to take advantage of the sale of public cement interests were individuals who had been among the staunchest opponents of privatization in the 1980s. As minister of industry until the early 1990s, Mohamed Abd al-Wahab was one of the most outspoken cabinet defenders of the public sector. With the adoption of structural adjustment policies in the early 1990s, vocal antireformist elements were extricated from the cabinet and Abd al-Wahab was forced out of office. After his departure from the government, Abd al-Wahab became chairman of the Arab Swiss Engineering Company (ASEC). The ownership structure of the company was mixed. Majority control was in the hands of public sector cement companies. Minority stakes were held by Abd al-Wahab as well as by public sector cement managers. Following the privatization of many of the cement companies in 1999 and 2000, majority control shifted into the private hands of previous SOE cement company managers and Abd al-Wahab. ASEC provided specialized management services to the cement industry, and included on its board many former top officials from the Holding Company for Mining and Refractories, under which all of the cement companies are incorporated. ASEC did not simply maintain its market position as a consulting firm but began operating as a sizeable investor in the cement sector, and soon formed a cement cartel. After the introduction of a new prime minister, Kamal al-Ganzouri, in place of an aging Atef Sidqi, the pace of privatization accelerated.[18]

Gradually, ASEC became a powerful player in the cement business. It entered into negotiations with one of the world's best-known cement multinationals, France's Lafarge Coppée, in order to obtain majority control (51 percent) in the state-owned Ameriyah Cement Company. Ameriyah was a highly profitable firm: in 1997 it accounted for nearly 8 percent of Egypt's cement production. ASEC was motivated by two important factors in dealing with Lafarge. It offered an efficient partnership and at the same time it gave the principals in ASEC time to speculate on the share price of Ameriyah. Prior to the actual negotiations, rumors circulated that an agreement was imminent between Lafarge and ASEC. ASEC principals sold shares in Ameriyah during this period, making huge profits. Ameriyah's stock price rose during this period by 35 percent. For Lafarge, ASEC had excellent ties with the PEO office and the very powerful CAA (Central Auditing Agency). The CAA was a very important agency in Egypt's privatization process because it had the power to recommend whether privatization of a company would go through at a given price. It was thought that by having a local partner, as it was often suggested by the PEO office, that the sale would often be smoother and more acceptable to the privatization committee.

However, ASEC's links to the CAA did not necessarily work to Lafarge's advantage. Disagreements surfaced about which of the two would lead the partnership, and Lafarge's claim was rejected following severe pressure from ASEC. Atef Ebeid who then served as the minister of public enterprises announced that the offer was rejected because there was one offer and nothing to compare it with.[19] To support its interest in playing a lead role in the purchase of America, ASEC played on government concerns about foreign control of a strategic industry, arguing that a Lafarge take-out could affect prices at a time of local cement shortage due to the construction boom. This was a sensitive issue for the government because the public sector bought 70–80 percent of the country's cement output. ASEC cement managers also pushed against a majority privatization of Ameriyah, arguing that cement companies were more profitable and better managed than other public sector companies. After the failed talks with Lafarge the government went ahead in December 1997 and sold 17 percent of Ameriyah, fuelling criticism of its abrupt decision. It is believed that ASEC bought a sizeable number of these shares.

However, the cement story was far from over by the late 1990s. As the state increased its expenditure on the major infrastructure projects, notably Toshka and the Peace Canal, its budget deficit also expanded. In 1998–1999 the actual budget deficit, including many off-budget items, was hovering close to 5 percent of GDP, and in 1999–2000 the deficit was clearly above 6 percent. Despite the intent of the government not to sell majority holdings in the cement companies to foreigners it became immediately clear that a large influx of Foreign Direct Investment (FDI) could only come through the sale of the cement companies. Global cement companies were in search of new growth markets in the developing world at a low cost. Egypt fit that acquisition mode quite well. More importantly, profits in the cement sector were substantial. In 1997, according to industry sources, on average, local cement producers made a net profit of around LE 62 per ton.[20]

During the same time the government's privatization program was being criticized for not being fast enough and not touching heavy industry sectors such as cement. It seems at that point that the government was intent on selling some but not all of its cement assets. Under these conditions, the cement cartel was unable to alter the regime's conviction that quick cash had to be infused into the state's coffers one way or another. Hence, within a one-year period starting from 1999 the state sold more shares in the cement sector than in all other years combined. In 1999, Alexandria (74 percent), Assiut (90 percent), and Beni Suef (95 percent) were sold to foreign cement multinationals. A year later, the rest of the shares in Ameriyah cement was sold. Again, the battle for Ameriyah was fierce. This time ASEC did not take the leading role in vying for a controlling share. The lead role was seized by a newly formed company, Al Ahram Cement, established by a group of public sector firms with the involvement of the remaining public sector cement companies. This time, however, the public sector's role in buying out a state-owned cement company was seen as backtracking on privatization, and Al Ahram cement was pressured to disband. Eventually the company was sold to Cimpor of Portugal for $481 million, which stands as the largest cross-border acquisition in Egypt. By the end of 2001, around 35 percent of the cement sector was foreign owned.

Though it was not a party to many of these sales, ASEC did not disappear. The government's interest in selling the Helwan Cement Company was first broached in 2000, when a Saudi company sought to purchase a 48 percent stake. However, the government postponed the sale of Helwan to give ASEC time to make a bid. ASEC, which had an eye on the company since it already had a 3.5 percent stake, bought 99.3 percent of the company in 2001. The last cement battle took place over the majority ownership of Torah Portland Cement. At the forefront of the acquisition mania was Suez Cement, which was majority owned by state entities (even if 44 percent was freely floated), including state banks, state insurance firms, and state cement companies. ASEC had an undisclosed share in Torah as did the National Investment Bank (NIB), another public institution that acted more like an off-budgetary piggy-bank of the state rather than anything else.

Besides Suez Cement, acute interest for Torah was shown from Orascom Construction Industries (OCI) of the Sawiris family. During the 1996–1997 period the Sawiris family was able to land a very lucrative contract to build a cement factory (OCI held 51 percent, Suez Cement held 8 percent) with Holderbank of Switzerland. By 1999, the Sawiris began rolling out the first bags of cement at their ECC (Egyptian Cement Company) site. A year later, they made a bid for the Ameriyah Cement Company. Although some thought that the Sawiris would have the power to carve an important niche for themselves, their bid for Ameriyah was refused by the Capital Markets Authority (CMA),[21] following pressure from within the government that "the Sawiris were going too far too fast."[22] The Sawiris went ahead and formed a consortium with Cimpor of Portugal for the acquisition of Ameriyah. Cimpor had a 75 percent stake while ECC held the remaining 25 percent. The consortium was turned down by the CMA following intense pressure from certain members of the public sector cement lobby as all members of the political elite not to allow the Sawiris access into Ameriyah. The crony system did allow for limitations to the amount of power one crony could amass and the Sawiris were a perfect example of that. Often cronies themselves cannot determine where the limits are. Just like Osman, who in the 1970s expanded at an unprecedented rate, in the 1980s his power in the economy and in politics were curtailed by Mubarak. Having the aftertaste of Ameriyah, the Sawiris continued their quest to bid for 65 percent of Torah. Just as in the case of Ameriyah, open bids were made. Again, the Sawiris bid was refused on "legal grounds" by the Capital Markets Authority. However, it was clear that a segment of the bureaucracy dealing with the cement privatization was unwilling to allow the Sawiris to have a powerful arm in the cement sector. It was enough that the Sawiris were able to develop ECC. A year later the Sawiris announced that they were intending to begin a new plant, the Algerian Cement Company (ACC), in Algeria. Torah was eventually acquired (85 percent) by Suez Cement, and combined the two companies commanded 30 percent of the cement production in Egypt.[23] Finally, Ciments Français acquired 34 percent of Suez with NIB increasing its share to 5 percent after refusing its bid for a 10 percent share that would have allowed it to have a chair on the board.

Conclusion

Privatization as a concept aims at allowing the state to withdraw from sectors of the economy where waste and mismanagement is experienced, adding to fiscal pressures. As the state withdraws the private sector is welcomed, and is expected to bring efficiency and competition that ultimately benefit the consumer. In the case of Egypt after more than a decade of experimentation with privatization the role of the state in the economy, although shaken, did not dissipate. Hence, the state was able to maintain its position as the most important distributor of rent, and as the manager of rent-seeking networks. The state achieved only partial reduction of its fiscal drain due to the sale of loss-making public sector firms. However, some of the more problematic public enterprises, such as textiles, remained untouched. The state in the 1990s opted to sell the better-run public enterprises and postponed tackling those that were burdened with debt, excess labor, and outdated technologies.

Instead of selling them cheaply or liquidating many of them the state decided to follow the much more difficult option of restructuring them. The state in many ways worried more about the fate of its state employees than the double-digit unemployment figures evidenced in the 1990s and the constant issue of underemployment.

For its part, the private sector tried to sustain the monopoly arrangements that characterized the role of the state since the nationalization of Nasser. The private sector succeeded in limiting competition within a group of elite businessmen while at the same time advocating for greater openness of the market. Elite businessmen were able to use their networks for their own advantage during the 1990s both when trying to purchase a state firm or establishing a new one.

Egypt's privatization experiment also has to be tested against the level of structural changes instituted in the economy. The goals that were set from the outset of the process in the early 1990s were not realized more than a decade later. The value of the entire SOE sector cannot be accurately estimated, it is believed to be worth more than LE 600 billion.[24] Out of that total, 314 companies were valued, according to the most generous government estimates, at around LE 88 billion.[25] The much more formidable task—both because of its daunting undertaking and its effects on the state's ability to confer patronage—of privatizing banks, utilities, refining, petrochemicals, rail and air transportation, that is, companies where the state is still the majority owner, is yet to be seen. Despite Atef Ebeid's announcement upon becoming prime minister in October 1999 that the government would complete the sales of all public sector enterprises by the end of 2001, this process is still far from complete.[26] Reforming the rules of the game to make them more market oriented and thus more competitive has not occurred. Moreover, reform attempts in the 1990s failed to break the networks of privilege that kept Egypt's private sector inward-focused.

Networks are an important component of economic life, both in a developed economic setting or a reforming and developing economy. The role of networks in economic life and particularly during the era of belated economic reform in Egypt and other parts of the Middle East is crucial to an understanding of the reformist project and its outcome. Egypt's elite businessmen and bureaucrats benefited from the reform project of the 1990s. Each group established effective networks that provided them privileged access. When privatization came along, these two groups were already well placed to take advantage of the opportunities created. However, competition was not absent nor was intra-elite collusion as well as collusion between elite businessmen and former and acting bureaucrats. Above all, these networks were created to safeguard their monopoly of power in the business landscape of Egypt, and since the early1990s they have successfully done so.

Notes

1. See Walter W. Powell and Laurel Smith-Doerr, "Networks and Economic Life," *Annals of Sociology* (1994): 368–402.
2. Ibid.
3. See Stanley Wasserman and Joseph Galaskiewiez, eds., *Advances in Social Network Analysis* (California: Sage Publications, 1994).
4. Ibid.
5. Mark Granovetter and Richard Swedberg, eds., *The Sociology of Economic Life* (Colorado: Westview Press, 1992).
6. Ibid.
7. See Ronald S. Burt, *Structural Holes: The Social Structure of Competition* (Cambridge: Harvard University Press, 1992).
8. Walter W. Powell, "Neither Market Nor Hierarchy: Network Forms of Organization," in Bernard Staw and Leonard L. Cummings, eds., *Research in Organizational Behavior* 12 (Greenwich, CT: JAI Press, 1990), 295–336.
9. David Stark and Laszlo Bruszt, *Postsocialist Pathways: Transforming Politics and Property in East Central Europe* (Cambridge: Cambridge University Press, 1998); and Luigi Manzetti, *Privatization South American Style* (Oxford: Oxford University Press, 1999).
10. Joel S. Hellman, "Winners Take: The Politics of Partial Reform in Postcommunist Transitions," *World Politics* 50, no. 2 (1998): 232.
11. Stark and Bruszt, *Postsocialist Pathways* 2, 104–105.
12. Ibid., 34.
13. See "Privatization, Capital Flows and FDI Attractiveness," in Economic Trends in the MENA Region, 2000, Economic Research Forum, Cairo, 2001, 4.
14. Data provided by the Public Enterprise Office, Cairo, 1997.
15. The price paid by the Luxor Group was a substantial increase on the Central Auditing Agency estimate of LE 190 million for ABC and the market price of LE 202 million.
16. Research Information Sector, 1998, Ministry of the Economy, Cairo, Egypt, 23.
17. Luigi Manzetti and Charles H. Blake, "Market Reforms and Corruption in Latin America: New Means for Old Ways," *Review of International Political Economy* 3, no. 4 (Winter 1996): 662.
18. These pressures were exogenous in nature and emanated from the IMF's expectations that a total of 25 firms would have to be privatized by the end of 1996.
19. *Al Ahram*, November 27, 1997.
20. Interview with author, Cairo, October 1997.
21. *Al Alam Al Yom*, February 9, 2000.

22. Interview with author, Cairo, July 2000. The privatization of both Torah and Ameriyah was implemented by tender, the first time that tenders have been used in the Egyptian privatization program. Investors interested in acquiring a majority SOE were required under the system to place ads in local newspapers announcing their intentions and requesting shareholders of the holding company and individual and institutional investors in the company being privatized to sell their shares before a set deadline. Meanwhile, competitors had the option of increasing both the offer price and the stake they were seeking to acquire.

23. *Al Alam Al Yom*, February 12, 2000.

24. *Al Ahram*, March 21, 1996.

25. Ibid.

26. *Al Alam Al Yom*, October 23, 1999.

CHAPTER 3

Patterns of Resistance: Economic Actors and Fiscal Policy Reform in Egypt in the 1990s

Ulrich G. Wurzel

Introduction

After a short period of growth in the late 1970s and early 1980s, Egypt's economic and social circumstances deteriorated dramatically. Due to a massive budgetary deficit and external debts of $50 billion at the end of the 1980s, economic stagnation gave rise to an acute crisis. Fiscal policy reform, called for by creditors and international financial institutions during negotiations over the stabilization and structural adjustment program of 1990–1991 aimed at restoring the financial viability of the Egyptian state.[1] Two broad sets of policy and institutional reforms were central to these negotiations. First, general changes needed to be made in budgetary *spending patterns*. This required redefining the role of the state in the national economy to pave the way for the reform of the public sector. Along with other redistributive programs and subsidies, transfers to an inefficient public business sector had contributed to Egypt's fiscal crisis. In the early 1990s, state-owned enterprises (SOEs) still produced roughly 75 percent of Egypt's overall industrial value added.[2] Thus, the IMF and the Word Bank insisted on a structural adjustment program that explicitly included demands for privatization.[3] Second, *patterns of revenue generation* for the budget had to be adjusted, involving a rise in, as well as the introduction of, new kinds of taxes and the intelligent use of privatization proceeds.

However, if decisive fiscal policy reform steps would substantially diminish the huge transfers to loss-making, overstaffed SOEs, the result would be a massive decline in public business sector activities. The consequence would be the lay-off of a noticeable number of workers (up to more than half a million). Remaining state employees would lose their importance in domestic politics.[4] A shrinking of the public sector would also take economic power and political influence away from an important segment of the pre-reform elite comprising public sector administrators and public enterprise management. At the same time, public sector administration, management, and workforce would become less willing to deliver policy support to the government. Finally, those factions of the Egyptian private business sector elite would be affected by privatization, particularly since Sadat's *Infitah* (economic opening) had exploited their close links to the public sector to benefit from the resource flows from the budget to the SOEs.

Mainstream political economy has argued that economic reform "depoliticizes access to resources," and that those who have benefited from their participation in privileged pre-reform coalitions will be the losers in the reform process.[5] However, in his introduction to this volume, Steven Heydemann also points out that empirical research calls this assertion into question. Certainly, in the Egyptian case, many economic actors who were privileged prior to reforms have been able to protect the interests that were threatened by the reform measures as originally designed. Sometimes they were even able to increase their wealth and expand their influence in the reform and post-reform era. On the one hand, such actors or groups of actors still belong to the economic or political elite. On the other hand, a number of changes took place that did, in fact, alter the pre-reform economic and political influence of certain groups of actors. In terms of the impact of reform on privileged actors, the outcomes in Egypt thus appear to diverge from the expectations derived from conventional theories on the political economy of reform.[6] As these findings cannot be explained by such approaches, it appears necessary to find new methods of analysis and additional analytical tools to gain more differentiated insights. This essay explores the possibility of moving research on the political economy of reforms one step further by applying network analysis as developed in economic sociology to the case study of Egypt's privatization as a means of fiscal policy reform.[7]

Networks and Institutions: The Context of Fiscal Policy Reform in Egypt

Economic sociologists use the word "network" to describe "a regular set of contacts of similar social connections among individuals or groups. An action by a member of a network is *embedded*, because it is expressed in interaction with other people."[8] Network analysis focuses on this interaction among actors. In this chapter, I use the term network analysis to designate a theoretical perspective or paradigm and only to a lesser extent to describe the statistical method(s) used as instruments within the general network research framework.[9] However, for inquiries into the political economy of reforms, network analysis seems to be especially useful because economic behavior is understood as social and political, rather than narrowly self-interested. As Granovetter and Swedberg note with respect to undersocialized views of individual utility, economic behavior is socially situated and cannot be explained by abstracting actors from their social contexts.[10] At the same time, network approaches help to avoid oversocialized, deterministic views such as those developed by social scientists such as Parsons, or even classical political economists like Marx in his writings on class or competition in capitalist societies.

Economic and political actors—individuals, families, ethnic groups, and organizations alike—can be part of a number of networks at the same time. Similarly, actors can have different or multiple identities at the same time, that may be expressed in a variety of relations or "kinds of embeddedness." A major advantage of the network approach in economic sociology is precisely this ability to provide more complex conceptions of actors, taking into consideration the multiple nature of identities and interests, and the presence of multiple channels through which both identities and interests can be translated into action during struggles over economic reform.

Moreover, identity, interest, and the actions of individuals are embedded in a historically determined social context, while networks themselves are embedded in larger institutional orders. Therefore, this chapter on the political economy of fiscal policy reform in Egypt takes into consideration the dominant institutional framework of the period in which privatization became a focus of political debate, that is, the socioeconomic and sociopolitical setting of the *rentier system*.[11]

The monopolistic acquisition of rents is a basic function of the rentier state, and is reflected in its organizations and institutions. Yet it is also expressed in the form of networks that arise within it. Among other things, as noted earlier, this connection between institutions and networks tends to complicate understandings of rentier systems that are grounded in coalition-based conception of how economic privilege—access to rents in particular—becomes organized and, subsequently, affects processes of economic reform.[12] While there is little question that economic or political rents are distributed according to political criteria, patterns of distribution are not always captured by conceptualizing an economic order in terms of interest-based coalitions as exclusive economic units or as exclusive modes of collective action. Some recipients of rent will include aggregated and relatively homogenous groups of actors such as the military, public sector management and workers, the religious establishment, or private business sector elites.[13] Yet others, including senior public sector administrators or the private business sector elite operate as prominent, influential individuals embedded in networks with very concrete social, economic, and political links among them. Thus, in contrast to anonymous and homogenous groups organized in the form of coalitions, the privileges granted to high-ranking public or private business figures are distributed to individuals, often acting as patrons, and their clientele.[14] From this perspective, a close link exists between an inquiry into the functioning of the rentier system and the analysis of the behavior of networks of privileged economic actors in the process of economic reform as it unfolded in Egypt in the 1990s.

With regard to this case study of Egypt, the intent of the chapter is to analyze the forms and activities of networks of privileged economic actors to find better explanations for the way in which reforms were drafted, finally agreed upon, implemented, and altered during the course of implementation. Furthermore, I hope to explain how these reform measures have contributed to the disruption or dismantling of privileged pre-reform networks as mechanisms for the appropriation and distribution of rent in various forms. My starting assumption is that the findings generated by network analysis will be particularly interesting whenever economic actors behave in ways that depart from what mainstream, coalition-based theories of economic reform would lead us to expect.

At the same time, by dealing with the behavior of certain types of economic actors in the context of fiscal policy reforms in Egypt, this chapter explores the limits of network approaches in generating insights that other analytic approaches cannot. The key methodological question is to what degree network analysis reveals relationships, dependencies, and causes for the behavior of actors during reforms that other approaches obscure or overlook.

Privatization as a Core Element of Fiscal Policy Reform in Egypt

A major issue in the literature on fiscal policy reform is the privatization of SOEs and public service provision.[15] The overall objective of fiscal policy reform in Egypt was to turn around the financial situation of a heavily indebted state that—by normal accounting standards—had been bankrupt for years before the stabilization program was designed. The main argument for downsizing the public enterprise sector is the inefficiency of SOEs.[16] However, the most important aim of privatization in the framework of this analysis was to relieve Egypt's public finances, which were suffering from the burden of subsidizing SOEs, often heavily. At the same time, however, the privatization process as well as its expected results always have a political dimension through their effect on the vested interests and patterns of interaction among various groups of actors. Theoretically, thoroughgoing privatization could even lead to a new internal power equation. For instance, in a liberalized economic environment, it would not be possible to sustain the old pattern of drawing in major figures from the private sector by offering extraordinary economic privileges, a practice that was established in Egypt during the Infitah period. Economic reform and liberalization could also increase the economic and political importance of entrepreneurs who are not so closely affiliated with the old guard. The way in which Egypt was run by the political elite would thus have to adjust to a new power equilibrium. If, as a result of privatization and other fiscal policy reform measures, the modus operandi of public spending and redistribution were to be altered in any fundamental way, established economic and political networks and alliances would have been disrupted; at a minimum, their influence would have decreased. Privatization decisions, therefore, are equally political decisions.[17]

As outlined in the introduction in this volume, earlier generations of research on the political economy of reforms share this conclusion. However, the models applied by various researchers from these traditions are sometimes based on rather simplistic conceptions of actors, agency, identities, and interests.[18] As a result, empirical findings on the reform processes and outcomes are often not in line with theoretically derived predictions about the roles certain actors play. In particular, economic reform measures often fall short of dismantling the networks of privileged economic actors that exploited pre-reform arrangements. Why, then, did the reforms so often *not* lead to the substitution of pre-market patterns of regulation (such as patronage and clientele networks, family or ethnic links) by market relations that conventional economic theories claim would eliminate major sources of rents and illegal opportunities to appropriate public funds? If it is true that Egypt's privatization has produced results that differ from what conventional wisdom would lead us to expect, and that important actors are behaving far differently from how they should according to existing accounts, then research should focus primarily on the identities and interests of these actors.

Economic Actors and Fiscal Policy Reform

Foreign creditors and donors demanded that Egypt undertake major reforms as a precondition for debt relief, new loans, and other external financial and technical support. It was an external intervention to achieve economic policy aims considered to be of crucial importance by the foreign creditors and donors.[19] To find out whether and how privileged pre-reform networks of economic actors were affected by reform steps and how they reacted to the threat of losing privileges and influence, the identities and related interests of the most relevant privileged economic actors have to be understood.

The Political Elite

Egypt is considered a rentier state with a regime that relies heavily on both economic rents and politically motivated external financial transfers. It turns out that the regime itself is the one actor that benefits most obviously from the existing rentier mechanisms and rent acquisition practices. The circle of the highest political decision-makers can be understood as a network of people (and families) whose fate in terms of status and sources of income immediately depends on maintaining their positions. The regime exploits its far-reaching control of the national economy as well as substantial external resource inflows in order to maintain its political power. In exchange for political support or at least political abstinence, consecutive regimes from Nasser to Sadat and finally Mubarak granted economic privileges to different groups of actors.[20] This implies that the regime has an interest in preserving pre-reform networks and political alliances that are based on existing approaches to the distribution of economic resources. However, fiscal policy reforms are expected to exert a major influence on existing revenue generating and spending patterns.

The principal interest of the regime is to maintain control over the state, society, and economy, but comprehensive privatization would have substantially altered its capacity to secure these ends.[21] Furthermore, the scheduled reform measures—if implemented—would have had negative effects on the future rent income of the government.[22] However, the bankrupt government had no other choice than to accept the donors' reform proposal. It was faced with the dilemma of urgently needing to generate additional external rent income on the one hand, and having to comply with the reform demands of the external donors in exchange for those resource inflows on the other.[23]

Public Sector Technocrats

Besides the top echelons of the political leadership, the state apparatus and the rationale for its actions concerning economic reforms have to be included in the analysis. Dealing with the structures of the state—which is by no means a monolithic bloc—and with the interests of certain governmental actors may help to reveal the obstacles to reform that result from both the functional mechanisms of the rentier system and from the embeddedness of certain actors in privileged networks.[24] Research on the political economy of reforms often suggests that members of state bodies, in particular the economic administration, are among the potential losers in the reform process.[25] According to conventional wisdom, they are therefore likely to do their utmost to prevent fundamental change—both on the institutional level and on the level of the individual actors' activities.

However, the Egyptian case suggests that economic actors may disregard their presumably "natural" roles, which are deduced from their membership in anti-reform coalitions or alliances.[26] One example is a high-ranking administrator in the Egyptian seed sector (a state monopoly) who actively supports newly established private enterprises in taking over core activities from the state—changes that would make his own position redundant as well as the role of the whole governmental seed administration. The question arises as to why this individual acts on the basis of interests that are not captured by his position in the public sector, in contrast to many of his colleagues.

Public Sector Managers

Many public sector managers do not come from wealthy Egyptian families but have worked hard to achieve their positions and status by climbing the ladder of the public sector hierarchy for decades. Newly opened access to higher education for people from their backgrounds and the decreasing influence of the elite of the *ancien regime* in the public business sector after Nasser's policy shift of the early 1960s[27] contributed to their unprecedented socially upward mobility. "These managers fear that even if they are performing well, a wealthy buyer of the public enterprise may replace them with relatives from the wealthy elite."[28]

Therefore, according to prevailing approaches, public sector managers might be expected to form coalitions or alliances, joining as well with the economic administration and other public sector employees to prevent privatization measures. Again, the Egyptian reality is often not in line with such expectations. In some cases, managers of holding or affiliated companies (the main entities concerned with privatizing Egypt's SOEs) did in fact do their best to block privatization. For instance, a network composed of administrators from a number of ministries and high-ranking SOE managers, among others, for years successfully prevented a reorganization of the Metallurgical Industries Holding Company (the former Economic Authority for the Metallurgical Industry) that was necessary to enable the holding company to deal with its primary tasks of portfolio management and privatization.[29]

However, in other instances, SOE chairs embedded in networks that cut across the boundary between public and private sectors[30] took the lead in privatization activities, aggressively taking away positions and privileges from stake-holders outside their networks—for example, former fellow managers engaged in competing "Shillas." In the Holding Company for Public Works, a network of leading managers dominated by the holding chairman even joined forces with the majority of employees (most of them being well-educated, highly specialized engineers) in privatizing most of the affiliates. In other cases, public sector managers used "dirty tricks" to get rid of their presumably "natural" allies or coalition partners in a struggle against privatization. The question arises of how these differences in the behavior of public business managers can be explained.

The Private Sector

In principle, private businessmen are expected to be advocates of economic reforms that put aside politically imposed restrictions to and distortions of the market mechanism as well as heavy-handed state intervention and large-scale public business sector activities. However, as we know from the literature, crony capitalists benefit from these and other distortions and have a vested interest in protecting against the impact of potential reform measures.[31] In Egypt, the delay of the ratification of the new Egyptian customs tariff in 1994, which was part of the IMF agreement, was due to adjustments that had been made as a result of pressure by Egyptian businessmen who feared international competition.[32] As part of Egypt's commitment to the international donors, the Minister of Electricity Maher Abaza announced in October 1994 that electricity prices would be progressively raised to their production costs in 1995. After a request by the Federation of Egyptian Industries (FEI), however, President Mubarak blocked the increase of electricity rates for industrial use.

Throughout the country's modern history, economically powerful businessmen have established close links to the state to enjoy the government's support and protection. In the Egyptian rentier system, the private businessmen linked to the regime would not have been able to accumulate their extraordinary capital and wealth without close ties to the state. Even the entrepreneurs of the new city of 10th of Ramadan, often considered to be the most dynamic in the country,[33] have expressed concerns about the effects of liberalization on Egyptian industry. The minister of industry, Abd Al-Wahab, reassured them in early 1991 that protection would be maintained through tariff barriers and quality control.

In recent years, a number of relatively influential entrepreneurs have emerged as a strong domestic support base for the regime. Parts of the private business community had a vital interest in preventing large-scale privatization as they benefited from the public enterprise sector in many different ways. In this regard, in the terminology of the coalition-based approach, they would be called potential losers of substantial reforms, including certain fiscal policy changes, while others could become winners.[34] Here too, however, empirical findings suggest a more complex reality. The reasons, broadly speaking, are that there are more than just the economically determined identities of the key actors, and that interests are not static over time.[35] One example of the behavior of a leading businessman who built up a highly sophisticated network reflecting a multiplicity of roles and interests—as well as the restrictions to his activities resulting from the rules of the rentier system—is seen in the political career of Muhamad F. Khamis and its sudden end when the regime felt that his network had become too powerful.[36]

Interest-Based Organizations

Certain groups of economic actors that are affected by fiscal policy reform are thought to be represented by interest-based organizations such as business or professional associations, labor unions, and other NGOs. These interest-based organizations should thus be responsive to the interest of their members in the framework of economic reforms. However, in Egypt with its rentier system as the institutional setting, there is a tradition of transforming such organizations into platforms for the realization of certain individuals' and networks' interests instead of protecting the members they formally represent.

Business Associations

Egypt's business associations and chambers of commerce are usually seen in a positive light, and occasionally described as important civil society organizations. Moreover, Doner and Schneider point out that business organizations can play a very positive role for economic development if certain conditions are fulfilled by the organizations.[37] However, a majority of these organizations in Egypt perfectly fit the image of a typical clientele structure shaped by the rules of the rentier system. Some presidents and chairmen run corporatist organizations as their personal domains. In these organizations, modes of interaction are determined by the personality and style of the leader; decision-making processes are centralized, and even the acceptance of new members is often solely at the discretion of the president or chairman as patron and is thus subject to power politics.

After ten years of economic reform, there are numerous indications that influential leaders still use business associations as personal power bases and instrumentalize them to expand their clientele networks. In turn, the regime still uses many of these associations to exert influence and control over businessmen and enterprises among memberships (often, membership in government-controlled associations is obligatory). Most of the business associations do not work in the interest of all their members, but merely for the interest of their leaders.[38] "Lack of autonomy and a tendency to rely on personal contacts inflicts the lobbying system in Egypt. That is partly a consequence of government's co-optation schemes."[39]

Trade Unions

Trade unions are also instrumentalized by high-ranking union bureaucrats to get access to privileges or to establish their personal networks. Their role as a strong and autonomous negotiating partner for trade union bureaucrats in conflicts with the government and private companies ranks second. "In the final analysis, it seems that an effective avenue of lobbying on behalf of labor continues to be absent in contemporary Egypt."[40] The independent trade union movement of the late 1980s and early 1990s was a reaction to the miserable condition of the state-controlled unions.[41] However, it was not strong enough to change Egypt's union landscape, even if important features of real interest-protecting organizations for workers were to be found in these alternative unions.

Nongovernmental Organizations

The same clientelist and exclusive pattern that was outlined for business associations and trade unions applies to the majority of Egyptian nongovernmental organizations (NGOs) as well. The organizations are often dominated by an influential leader (typically the founder of the NGO) who treats the volunteers or employees in an authoritarian way. The beneficiaries are usually seen merely as objects of charity, and are not involved in the planning and implementation of the NGO projects. Many NGOs were founded solely to get access to foreign funding or to support the leader in establishing clientele networks.

The transformation of interest-based representative organizations into platforms for influential actors to pursue their own interests also shapes the actions of these organizations in the struggle over economic reforms. Thus, these organizations do not represent the interests of the majority of their members or target groups, but those of the dominant individual actors or networks who managed to seize them. The networks' misuse of institutions as power bases is camouflaged by a kind of "organizational veil."[42] Observers should not be surprised when union leaders collaborate with the regime in progressively limiting public sector workers' rights in the SOE sector.[43] What drives the actions of union elites is not workers' rights but the union bureaucrats' interest in being rewarded with prestigious positions—for example, seats in parliament or ministerial offices.[44] For the businessmen who dominate associations, it is their personal, political, or economic interest (or the economic interest of their own and their fellows' networks) and not the majority of the members that shape action.

Multiple Identities and Interests

Egypt also provides ample evidence of the instability and multiplicity of actors' interests, underscoring a dynamic quality of politics of economic reform that is often missing in prevailing accounts. For example, when it was discussed in the early 1990s whether the Egyptian soft drink industry, a state monopoly at that time, should be deregulated, certain Egyptian businessmen as potential investors fully supported such liberalization measures. However, after two beverage companies had been privatized with the privatization contract including a market share guarantee (!) for the new owners, the interests of these investors in further deregulation and liberalization of this industry decreased.[45] The same shift occurred with regard to the Egyptian partners of the Luxor Group that took over the Al-Ahram Beverages Company, with its Stella brand enjoying a monopoly in the local-beer market. The new owners of the firm, who had initially pressed for speedy privatization and deregulation, were shocked when the government issued brewery licenses to two other consortia. Reform proponents suddenly turned into opponents of continued liberalization steps in their industry. Due to the unpredictability of the regulatory environment, economic reforms seem to appeal to many businessmen only until they have gotten their piece of the pie. This observation made in the context of the Egyptian reform program is supported by research results on economic liberalization and reform attempts in other Middle Eastern countries as well as in other world regions.

Furthermore, economic actors can have different economic positions or roles at one and the same time. For example, a middle- to high-ranking politician or bureaucrat whose interest should be the maintenance of the system dominated by the state can at the same time be engaged in substantial private sector activities as a middle man, consultant, or trader. During Egypt's renewed aid negotiations with the West under Sadat in the 1970s, Egyptian ministers and top administrators repeatedly attempted to establish private business relations with members of a high-ranking German advisory mission. Sometimes those private ventures could have even damaged the interest of the state they were representing in the negotiations. This confusion of individuals' economic roles and interests in the context of a rentier system, where extraordinary economic privileges are granted to leading politicians or bureaucrats, is not necessarily surprising. However, if the private business ventures of politicians and bureaucrats had later reached a more substantial scale and other family members had developed an identity as business people, these multiple identities and loyalties would inevitably lead to conflicts of interests concerning economic policy reform. In turn, this could have had direct consequences for their behavior in office.

As this suggests, noneconomic identities figure heavily in understanding patterns of agency and the structure of network forms. In the Egyptian setting, as elsewhere, a large variety of intensely socialized identities intersect with official positions and interests in shaping individual responses to processes of regulatory change. Extended family ties play an enormous role, as do sectarian affiliations, school ties, time spent in the armed forces, or shared experiences of labor migration. Regional identities come into play when people settled in Cairo or Alexandria favorably establish economic and social relations with individuals and groups originating from the same village, town, or region. Ideology, for example, Nasserism, Marxism, Islamism, and the like, may be a binding or dividing element in social relations at the workplace of employees, in the neighborhood, or even in economic activities of entrepreneurs. Insider–outsider relations are established in all areas where people define their identities based on certain features related to education, profession, and the like. For example, entering the network of the "Club of Egyptians with German Education," a network that is effective due to the "weak ties" of its members,[46] provides access to invaluable contacts in all sectors of Egyptian society.

However, different economic positions and roles of actors as well as the membership of actors in a number of networks at one and the same time may not only result in the existence of multiple identities but can also lead to competing obligations, loyalties, and possible choices concerning economic or political behavior. In particular, when different network members (or members of different networks) try to influence an actor in parallel (e.g., by mutually exclusive implicit expectations or explicit demands), the characteristics of the respective networks will have an impact on the behavior of this actor in such a situation of conflict. Network theory operationalizes such network features through its attention to attributes such as network density and centralization, the prestige of certain network members or subnetworks, and so on.[47] To make things even more complicated, as David Krackhardt shows in his case study of a failed attempt to establish a union in a high-tech company, behavior can also result from perceived network features or characteristics, rather than from an objective situation.[48]

Different sources of identity and motivation thus merge into a complex mixture of loyalties, social ties, and related incentives for action that vastly complicate usual categories of agency in the literature on the politics of economic reform. For example, M. F. Khamis, the head of the Federation of Egyptian Industries (FEI), always took a very protectionist position during the negotiations on the EU–Egyptian Association Agreement while he himself is a very successful exporter. However, his unquestioned position as the leader of the FEI is an important source of power for his personal network that he couldn't undermine and, seemingly at the same time, is a certain constraint in the sense of Granovetter's notion of "strong ties." Again, different kinds of rationality result from features of multiple identities that transcend simple economic categories. For the case of Turkey, Önis and Webb show that interests in liberalization and protectionism can collide even within one and the same private conglomerate as different corporate divisions follow different strategies.[49]

Privileged Economic Actors and Privatization Attempts in the 1990s

The Regime

To secure its political survival, the network of the top leadership wants to exert influence over all spheres of society, including the economy. Describing Egypt as a rentier state implies that the regime has a vital interest in maintaining certain patterns of government spending and granting economic privileges to other groups of actors in exchange for support on the domestic policy front, even if most of these groups of actors have to be characterized as decision takers and cannot be expected to actively challenge or threaten the authoritarian regime.[50] The regime thus had to try to sustain the flow of political rents without keeping the related reform promises it had made to donors and creditors. The privatization program for the 314 SOEs under law 203 of 1991 is an outstanding example of such an attempt. Criteria set by foreign donors and creditors for the evaluation of Egypt's privatization were based on the amount of public sector business assets sold as well as the number of finalized privatizations.[51] However, the regime seemingly adopted a strategy of "reforms-just-for-show" that limited the scope of the privatization program from the outset. Behind the scenes, regime officials encouraged complex delaying tactics, and used announcements of policy shifts as substitutes for real reform measures to appease external donors.[52]

In instances when the regime was compelled to deliver real reform results as concessions to donors, for example, in policy domains such as trade liberalization or removing state monopolies, it was done in a way that was consistent with the rentier state's need to distribute economic wealth to supporting networks of economic actors. The resulting opportunities for profitable economic activities were granted as a kind of newly designed privilege to its political supporters, mainly from the private business community. On the one hand, instrumentalizing half-hearted reform measures in order to grant privileges to certain actors helped the regime to stay in control despite the short-term consequences of this externally imposed change. On the other hand, such new privileges could compensate pre-reform privileged economic actors and their networks for possible losses resulting from other externally demanded reform measures—for example, in the fiscal policy domain.

Whenever external donors and creditors called for more decisive privatization steps, the regime sacrificed parts of the SOE sector, the sale of which would not result in major losses of the state's control or economic losses for pre-reform networks. Obviously, deciding which SOEs to give up also depended heavily on the strength of the related networks interested in keeping the concerned companies in the public sector. Well-connected networks of public sector managers, administrators in charge, and private businessmen repeatedly managed to get "their" companies on the lists of strategically important SOEs that were excluded from majority sales. Firms associated with the military-industrial complex were excluded from privatization plans right from the beginning. Managers of textile companies often stressed the political risks of closing down whole industrial sectors. Influential private businessmen who depended on inputs from textile SOEs sometimes intervened at the highest levels to get their suppliers off the privatization lists. Others were either less efficiently connected or lost out to competing network interests. Observers, therefore, may also find many examples of networks not being successful in defending or rearranging pre-reform economic privileges.

However, this bargaining of privileged networks or network patrons vis-à-vis the network of the top political leadership had an impact on how reforms were implemented on the micro level. During the struggle over how to distribute costs and benefits of the real reform steps implemented to appease donors, the network of the highest regime members—or its agents in the administration—had to take into consideration the relative importance of different pre-reform privileged networks for its strategy of system maintenance. In other words, the influence of pre-reform networks on the alteration and implementation of reform steps on the micro level depended both on the kind of connectedness of these networks to the regime and on the domestic policy support these networks could offer in turn.

The regime's need for positive signals to the public concerning investment, growth, and job creation, for instance, help account for the tendency to favor networks of relatively younger business people involved in production over networks of the old cronies from the era of Sadat's *Infitah*. Those who had something to offer the regime could shape the way the reforms were drafted and implemented more efficiently than competing, weaker networks. Success or failure of pre-reform networks in preserving their privileges was also dependent on the importance of the particular issue under negotiation. The privatization of a company for land reclamation with a couple of employees meant a less dangerous step (considering the loss of economic control and the potential of becoming a source of internal political unrest) than the sale of Nasr Automotive, a car assembly plant with over 12,000 workers, or of the vertically integrated steel complex HADISOLB with its 23,000 employees.

Nonetheless, given the regime's interest in system maintenance, the general impact of privatization efforts was as limited as the implementation of the measures promised to the donors. When it became clear to the top leadership that fundamental structural change in the public sector would threaten the established relations with influential networks that supported the regime, Egypt's political leaders opted for a postponement, if not denial, of important privatization steps. Although some pre-reform privileged networks of economic actors encountered losses concerning their privileges, the government successfully prevented comprehensive privatization and retained control over major parts of the country's economy.[53] The state is still in a position to appropriate internal and international economic rents and managed to open up new sources of external politically motivated rent income such as debt forgiveness and new financial transfers. After the creditors had written off the last tranche of debt, leverage for exerting external pressure on the Egyptian government concerning economic reform disappeared. Egypt's privatization efforts ended in stagnation. Finally, in February 2002, the Egyptian government officially announced that no further privatization would be implemented.

State Technocrats

By its very nature, privatization is expected to result in a decreased need for public sector administrative capacity. Administrators and technocrats, therefore, will be mostly negatively affected by large-scale SOE sales. However, a case study of privatization attempts in Egypt's seed sector again underlines the fact that identities and interests of economic actors cannot simply be derived from their formal position in the economic and political system.[54]

During the 1980s and early 1990s partial reforms in the state-controlled seed sector permitted the establishment of smaller, private seed producers and traders, though these continued to operate under extensive state control. However, due to their origins in the government seed sector, close networks emerged that included private entrepreneurs who were previously employed in the public sector and administrators still active in governmental agencies. Suffering under considerable restrictions, the private seed producers had been advocating major reforms for years. In the late 1990s, Yusuf Wali, the Minister of Agriculture, Yusuf Abdul Rahman, the head of PBDAC, and Samir El-Naggar, president of the most important private seed producers association (ESAS), suddenly joined forces to push through a fundamental seed sector reform against opposition from within their own agencies on the grounds that senior officials had abandoned their institutional interests and commitment to the defense of their institutions. However, the embeddedness of the main "pro-reform" actors in a network of personal relationships seems to have produced stronger incentives for the top administrators than their formal position in the state apparatus would suggest.

In contrast to the 314 companies affected by the privatization program under law 203 in 1991 (see also later), the intended privatization of the CASP is one of the rare cases of reform steps really being implemented. It shows all the dynamics to be expected whenever the economic privileges of networks of influential actors are redistributed. The formerly unquestioned position of influential actors was endangered by the deregulation or reregulation of this part of the economy. Anticipating the potential changes ahead as well as the related newly emerging opportunities for rent seeking, leading public sector administrators already linked through a network of personal relations with private business people actively designed the privatization scheme in their field of authority. In this sense, pre-reform privileges resulting from public sector activities were transferred to the private sector by network members who were still high-ranking public sector administrators. One of the reform outcomes could be the transition of a public sector quasi monopoly (CASP) into a private one. Insiders assume that one of the new owners would be Yusuf Abdul Rahman, who is not only the head of PBDAC, the owner of a private sector company, and the CEO of a public–private agricultural joint venture, but also the son of a close friend of Yusuf Wali, the Minister of Agriculture, from time jointly spent in the military. The related economic privileges, among others, are results of direct access to IPRs as well as CASP's dominance in particular segments of the seed market. Due to the size and the technological capabilities of the private seed enterprises in the network, the formal liberalization of the seed sector also results in enlarged opportunities for network members to make money. Furthermore, during the reform process the network members jointly influenced the design of related Egyptian laws and regulations to guarantee the long-term protection of their economic privileges.[55]

Public Sector Managers

Conventional wisdom suggests that decision makers in holding companies and individual enterprises would do their best to hinder the implementation of real ownership transfer to the private sector. At first glance, this also holds true for Egypt. In interviews, decision makers on subordinate levels said that in principle, privatization could not progress because of a number of framework conditions for which they were not to blame.[56] Alleged reasons for the delay of case-by-case privatizations of law 203 companies cited by the managers were, for instance, technical problems, legal problems, data and information problems (e.g., concerning balance sheets, the valuation of assets, etc.), unclear decision structures, statements about the strategic importance of certain companies, as well as unresolved debt problems. In order to prevent a real ownership transfer of companies to outsiders, company representatives networked with administrators, business partners, friends, and relatives who started "negotiations" with alleged prospective buyers in order to put off other really interested bidders.

Other networks of managers did run down healthy companies in order to make them unattractive for buyers. Sometimes alleged privatization activities failed due to the prohibitive pricing of the SOEs. "Privatizations-just-for-show" were initiated when other public sector entities whose managers were linked through networks bought SOEs. Another possibility to keep a company in the public sector but to transfer it formally to private ownership was to sell enough shares to public sector banks or their investment funds to prevent private investors who were outside a given network from engineering a majority takeover. Due to the widely dispersed circulation of privatized shares of law-203 companies, the pre-sale management of affiliates was still in place in many cases and often controlled a majority of shares. In some cases, shares that should have been be sold to a larger number of small investors or financial institutions through public offerings on the stock exchange were transferred *en bloc* to other public sector units involved in their networks—for example, public banks, instead of being included in the subscription packages. Insider trading was not considered illegal and was widespread. Public sector managers, well informed about the next steps planned by their companies, could use their knowledge not only to speculate and manipulate but also to transfer shares originally to be sold to private investors to other public sector units. As a result, high-ranking managers of the holding or affiliated companies were often the main beneficiaries of different types of insider privatizations. Indeed, pre-reform networks of privileged actors could even improve their economic positions by implementing rather than obstructing reform measures.

Furthermore, since 1991–1992, when the first privatization announcements were made, public sector managers and administrators started to build up individual alternatives for personal survival in terms of income and status, just in case the government really implemented parts of the privatization program. While some of them were co-opted through the offer of prestigious administrative positions, others started (or continued with increased enthusiasm) their privately run businesses, relying on their ability to drain public sector resources. These practices also fit into the broader picture of privileged economic actors exploiting the environment of partial and inconsistent economic reforms as well as distorting reform implementation on the micro level to protect or rearrange pre-reform privileges. Networks of SOE managers who had already used their access to public sector resources to establish successful private companies were only worried that the streams of cheap inputs and qualified workers from the public sector to their private companies (plus bonuses and additional incomes) would come to a halt. These managers opposed the selling of "their" companies, not privatization and the dismantling of the public sector in general, an observation consistent with Waterbury's judgment on the nonexistence of something like a class of public sector managers.[57]

As a result, hardly any organized resistance in the form of an alliance or coalition of public sector managers (alone or together with the public sector workers) developed in the Egyptian case. The embeddedness of managers in networks generating status and income—whether through political co-optation or through their involvement in other economic activities—was far more important than their economic position in the public sector. Despite this general pattern, high-ranking SOE managers who did not find sustainable alternatives to the status and income previously generated by their public sector positions often lost out by either resisting change or by not being flexible enough to adapt to changing conditions. Many were fired by the Public Sector Minister, Atif Ebeid, and these staffing changes also resulted in the redistribution of economic privileges among particular networks.

For all these activities, networks within an SOE, from other public sector enterprises, from the administration and the responsible surveillance bodies, as well as private sector businessmen had to cooperate closely in order to get the deals done. Social relations established during decades of service in the public sector domain, joint schools, university or army experience, as well as family links or religious ties were of crucial importance in securing personal trust, reliability, and efficiency during the often complex and difficult—not to mention sometimes illegal—operations.[58]

Private Sector Businessmen

In the private as well as public sector, the density of public–private networks led to hybrid and complex reactions to the opportunities and risks presented by privatization. While influential segments of the private sector have long benefited from political patronage and close links to the public sector, a multitude of networks including both representatives of the Egyptian private sector as well as family members of leading politicians and public sector administrators or managers has emerged during the last two to three decades in all conceivable fields of economic activity. These networks are usually based on the cooperation of actors from different backgrounds who jointly exploit the huge bureaucracy, heavy-handed state interventions, and lucrative niches that result from incomplete, contradictory stop-and-go reform steps. The privileges of these networks could potentially be affected by substantial reforms, including fiscal policy changes, and this threat, despite the pro-market rhetoric of entrepreneurs, may result in economic and political action opposing or obstructing privatization.

For example, the boards of holding companies, which should act as the primary organizational structures to facilitate privatization, often included private businessmen from the industry concerned. The entrepreneurs, according to semi-official statements, were expected to add momentum to privatization processes. However, the directors of SOEs often represented exactly the networks that would be deprived of economic privileges as a result of fast and comprehensive privatization measures. This conflict was apparent in the failed attempt of the Textile Industries Holding to restructure, commercialize, and privatize major parts of its affiliated companies. The vice president of the holding, whose entire career had been in the public sector, was an outspoken advocate of fast and large-scale reforms and privatization of the textile industry. His personal motivation, as he claimed in an interview, was to turn around the companies to the extent possible to save tens of thousands of jobs. However, he met fierce resistance from other board members when trying to prepare restructuring and privatization steps. The strongest opponents included one old guard, diehard Nasserist and the two private businessmen on the board. According to the vice president, the Nasserist opposed change mainly for ideological reasons while one of the businessmen provided the dye materials and the other the polyester fibers for nearly all affiliates of the holding. The line of conflict in this case was marked mainly by the confrontation between the vice president of the holding and the workers' representative, both of whom wanted change to make the textile companies more viable, and the private business people who exploited a lucrative niche resulting from the distortions in the Egyptian rentier system. "If they could, they would kill me," summed up the vice president of the situation. This case shows how privatization as a process of reregulation in a concrete micro-level case would have affected the economic privilege of private sector business people (a privilege that only could be obtained by the network links that bound private businessmen with influential public sector administrators). As long as privileged networks of economic actors, including private sector businessmen, do not face severe pressure from the higher echelons of the administration or the political elite, they will block attempts at SOE reform.

Redistribution, Reregulation, and the Reorganization of Economic Privilege

This case study of Egypt's privatization program for 314 law-203 companies generates two major results. On the one hand, it is obvious that due to the hesitant, selective, and inconsistent implementation of privatization measures the expected major structural change did not happen. The basic pattern of economic and political regulation—the rentier system—was effectively maintained. On the other hand, on the micro level, a degree of redistribution and reorganization of economic privilege took place. Even if Egypt, on the reform spectrum, remains close to the end of rather cosmetic or "just-for-show" reforms,[59] the government's stop-and-go measures in individual cases definitely produced the kind of dynamics we associate with the activities of networks of privileged economic actors facing change that possibly threatens their vested interests. Although the overall impact of the announced reform program on the economic and political bases of the rentier system was rather limited, the consequences for individuals were in some instances severe. Therefore, it is reasonable to take Egypt's externally imposed reform attempt as a case study of the role of networks of privileged economic actors during the drafting, alteration, and implementation of economic reforms, as well as for an analysis concerning the disruption or dismantling of such networks as a possible outcome of reforms.

With regard to the first major conclusion just mentioned, obviously the external donors who demanded economic reforms were not able to manage the reform process in a way that would have helped to break the ground for fundamental change. In contrast, the "reforms-just-for-show" strategy of the Egyptian regime was very successful in terms of generating additional external rent transfers that helped the government to stabilize the economic situation of the country while maintaining its political rule in the short term. Regarding the privatization program for the law-203 companies, there was no speedy and comprehensive sale of SOEs. The transformation of many SOEs into *de jure* independent entities did formally cut the direct links between the enterprises and the central budget. However, the regime, through public banks or the holding companies, continues to financially support many deficient enterprises and, thus, can intervene heavily in their affairs. With regard to the major parts of the public sector still under the regime's direct or indirect control, a fundamental reregulation or reorganization of economic privileges hardly took place. The same holds true for the impact of many other reform steps.

As shown elsewhere in greater detail, the overall pattern of the political economy of Egypt's economic reforms in the 1990s can be sufficiently explained by referring to the nonorthodox theory of the rentier system.[60] However, network-based approaches, rather than explaining *why* reform was "just-for-show" in Egypt, can help to understand *how* the "reform-just-for-show" strategy of the Egyptian regime worked and why it finally was so successful. The activities of networks of privileged economic actors resulted, on the one hand, in the obstruction of many case-by-case privatization attempts on the micro level. On the other hand, the regime's announcement policy and delay tactics wouldn't have been so efficient if they were not able to instrumentalize the whole spectrum of often competing networks in order to limit the overall impact while, at the same time, presenting the "reforms-just-for-show" to the international community. Therefore, without resorting to network-based methods, the micro-level dynamics and outcomes of the Egyptian reforms in the 1990s could not be fully understood.[61]

In other words, network analysis as developed in economic sociology can push forward micro-level understandings of how certain reform steps were drafted, agreed upon, and implemented, as well as how the concerned networks of privileged actors were affected by reform measures in concrete, individual situations. Here, network analysis with its strong focus on actors' positions, identities, interests, relations, and roles can deliver valuable insights into the dynamics of processes centered around defending economic privilege, getting access to new opportunities of rent seeking, as well as the competition among different networks and the changing balance of power among them.

However, as the government's preferred strategy to minimize political risk in the wake of the reforms was simply to *abandon* important reform elements, the impact of the reform program on privileged pre-reform networks largely depended on whether a given network was engaged in activities that were exposed to substantial reform steps resulting from donors' pressures. Besides the strategies of the political leadership to prevent large-scale and speedy divestiture of law-203 enterprises, the struggle over privatization also included activities of certain networks trying to benefit from stop-and-go reforms. Privileged actors often managed to exploit incoherent and half-hearted reform measures in the general framework of the privatization program to strengthen their positions and to find new ways of exploiting the government's fiscal policy for their own benefit. The introduction of transparency, the elimination of opportunities for rent seeking, or the illegal appropriation of public funds by networks of privileged economic actors did not occur at all in many areas. Therefore, while some restructuring of networks of pre-reform privileged economic actors was unavoidable, the basic patterns of distribution, regulation, and organization of economic privilege did not change.

Redistributive consequences mainly resulted from those reform steps that the government could not avoid due to donor pressure. However, often, the newly created opportunities for profitable economic activities (e.g., after a partial liberalization of sectors such as telecommunications or within the government's major land reclamation projects in Egypt's deserts) through licensing procedures or other direct and indirect administrative restrictions were exclusively accessible to selected actors with close ties to the regime—usually members of privileged pre-reform networks.[62] Also, individuals and networks that lost privileges in one area of economic activity were compensated by newly created opportunities for making money in other fields. The structure of benefits and opportunities was altered whenever a number of networks of pre-reform privileged actors were competing for access to new opportunities or in trying to defend older privileges in situations where not all could succeed.

Sometimes, along lines similar to those discussed by Béatrice Hibou (chapter 6 in this volume), the regime also exploited the granting or withdrawal of economic privileges to redesign the balance of power among actors who depended on its protection and support and sustain uncertainty among economic actors. Such power brokering enabled some networks to strengthen their positions—e.g., private business sector protagonists of the so-called *Infitah al-Intaj* (the "opening of production," as opposed to Sadat's *Infitah*, which mainly led to the rise of well-connected traders and middlemen). In contrast, other networks suffered severe losses when important network members were removed from key strategic positions in the public sector or the economic administration and lost access to related resources, not only in terms of material resource flows but also regarding access to strategic information, decision makers, and so on.

As other networks of patronage and corruption could continue without being publicly denounced, it seems that some patrons are better connected to circles of influential decision-makers than others. While there exist many examples of failed network activities meant to influence the design or implementation of reforms, some networks achieved their aims simply because they had more to offer to the regime or fit better, however temporarily, into its domestic policy agenda of divide and rule. Furthermore, the success or failure of network activities also depended on the importance of a particular issue for the regime's strategy of system maintenance. As regime stability was the overall aim, the veto of members of the top leadership network, first of all the president himself, could override any bargaining or lobbying attempt by any network of privileged actors.

Despite the arbitrary and fluid dynamics at work, some patterns do emerge from the reorganization of economic privilege during the 1980s and 1990s. In general, there has been a tendency to shift privileges from established networks representing the public–private symbiosis to younger generations of private businessmen who cooperate with public sector entities in various ways. To the extent that this trend is a reality, it coincides with increasing links between the relatives of high political decision-makers and this younger generation of Egyptian businessmen. These intensified links result in the restructuring of the family networks of top politicians as well as the merger of networks dominated by high-ranking politicians and administrators with networks centered around leading businessmen.[63] Additionally, it seems that the regime regards younger, often more outward- and export-oriented entrepreneurs to be more capable of contributing to growth and employment. This too implies, but by no means guarantees, that their networks will be more successful in lobbying for newly designed economic privileges or for the protection of pre-reform access to resources.

However, the opportunities for privileged networks of economic actors to increase their influence and wealth generally grew as a result of changes in regulation that accompanied selective processes of reform. Areas that have been opened for private sector participation include the telecommunication sector, which in turn includes television channels and BOOT (build, own, operate, transfer), highways, airports, ports, power plants, the cement industry, as well as car assembly in cooperation with foreign companies and land reclamation and development, among others. Furthermore, private companies are now allowed to deal in public sector imports—an indication of the rearrangement of the traditionally close relationship between public and private sector activities in Egypt. However, in this regard as well, the interests of certain private sector networks close to top politicians have been furthered by the regime while others were prevented from fully exploiting new opportunities. In the case of the reform of the Egyptian seed sector, after intense lobbying of the influential private seed producers in the network of Yusuf Wali and Yusuf Abdel Rahman, the laws and regulations related to Egypt's membership in the TRIPS-agreement will work to the benefit of these privileged actors. Smaller, less influential private seed producers with less sophisticated technology will have to expect major economic disadvantages.

Networks and Coalitions in the Analysis of Economic Reform

One useful lesson learned from research on Egypt's privatization program is—as discussed in more general terms in the introduction to this volume— that actors and agency quite often do not fit into traditional political economy categories; individuals as well as networks of actors are charac- terized by features cutting across mainstream categorizations. In particular, actors in the Egyptian context cannot be described as being part of homogeneous interest-based groups in the sense that coalition-based approaches use this term. Therefore, in analyzing the dynamics of privatiza- tion in Egypt, aggregating individuals and groups of actors to conceptualize reform in terms of coalitions has more disadvantages than advantages—in most cases.

As the Egyptian case amply demonstrates, economic actors do not engage in reform struggles on behalf of such homogenous and rather anonymous interest groups. Instead, they try to advance their immediate personal or small-group interest vis-à-vis the regime, usually on a personalized basis and often literally in face-to-face interaction. "It should not be surprising that the regime's strategy of co-opting influential individuals into the National Democratic Party (NDP) encourages Egyptian representatives of capital to rely on the personal and hence individualistic methods of lobbying." As Ramy Lakah, one of Egypt's biggest businessmen and employer of approximately 8,000 people, admits, "I am not a member of any [business] association. These channels are not necessary to get through to government. If there is a problem it is better to go directly to government, to one of the Ministers or the Prime Minister. He is accessible so there is no need for organizational [interference]."[64] Most often, it is concrete, personalized, and identifiable *networks* of individuals with a shared—not necessarily economically determined—identity, history of personal contact, sense of group-belonging, and experience of joint action that is the concern of administrators, SOE managers, or private businessmen involved in bargaining with government representatives over certain reform steps.

In fact, a review of coalition-based literature suggests that the empirical evidence presented to support interest group models often contradicts such arguments. Typically, it is a handful of well-connected businessmen rather than legitimate representatives of "the business community," or a few privileged members of the union establishment instead of "the workers" who get their issues on the agenda.[65] And, no less typically, the benefits these actors are seeking or the interests they are trying to protect are their own vested interests and their personal networks. The "peak associations of interest groups" referred to in some coalition-based studies turn out, in fact, to be exploited by some of their leaders (e.g., for getting direct access to the prime minister and the president) instead of protecting the overall interests of the groups they formally represent.[66] Egyptian observers, therefore, do not find it "surprising that businessmen [in parliament] have no positive effect on the legislative process; they enter parliament to do their own deals and have no interest in systemic reform."[67]

Furthermore, privileges granted by the rentier regime will not be allocated in a general way to anonymous coalitions. Particular networks dominated by concrete families, business conglomerates, and the 1956 graduates of the military academy selectively receive access to resources. However, taking on a network perspective can help to explain the related processes and outcomes that interest-based approaches and earlier generations of work on the political economy of reform cannot address in a suitable manner.

Notes

1. It was clear to the external creditors that macroeconomic stabilization would only be successful if Egypt's public finances were fundamentally restructured—hence the call for resolute fiscal policy reform.
2. World Bank, "Technical Assistance Project for Privatization and Enterprise and Banking Sector Reforms," for the Arab Republic of Egypt, 1992.
3. Privatization was intended to contribute to the overall reform objectives: to help reform public finances and provide more momentum to private sector development (including the financial business sector) and to attract foreign direct investment. As the subsidization of loss-making enterprises out of total tax revenues could be prevented through privatization, government spending could be redirected to subsidize social programs or profitable projects. See Peter Heller, Richard Hemming, and Rupa Chakrabarti, "Macroeconomic Constraints and the Modalities of Privatization," in Mario I. Blejer and Teresa Ter-Minassian, eds., *Fiscal Policy and Economic Reform: Essays in Honour of Vito Tanzi* (London: Routledge, 1997), 32–49.
4. It is worth remembering that in the 1980s and early 1990s labor unrest in the public sector had a strong impact on the government's hesitation to undertake substantial reforms.
5. Steven Heydemann, "Rethinking the Politics of Economic Liberalization," unpublished grant proposal submitted to the European University Institute, 1999, 1.
6. This general observation is described as a major point of departure for the research project of which this volume is the result. For a summary of reform results in Egypt during the 1990s, see Dieter Weiss and Ulrich Wurzel, *The Economics and Politics of Transition to an Open Market Economy: Egypt* (Paris: OECD Development Centre, 1998); and U. Wurzel, *Ägyptische Privatisierungspolitik 1990 bis 1998. Geber-Nehmer-Konflikte, ökonomische Strukturreformen, geostrategische Renten und politische Herrschaftssicherung* (Hamburg, Münster: Lit., 2000), 225 ff.
7. For an introduction into the discipline of economic sociology, see the introduction in Mark Granovetter and Richard Swedberg, eds., *The Sociology of Economic Life* (Boulder: Westview Press, 1992). For an overview on network research, see Walter W. Powell and Laurel Smith-Doerr, "Networks and Economic Life," in Neil N. Smelser and Richard Swedberg, eds., *The Handbook of Economic Sociology* (Princeton, NJ: Princeton University Press, 1994), 368–402; and Dorothea Jansen, *Einführung in die Netzwerkanalyse. Grundlagen, Methoden, Anwendungen* (Opladen: Leske und Budrich, 1999).
8. See Granovetter and Swedberg, *The Sociology of Economic Life*, 9.
9. Jansen, *Einführung in die Netzwerkanalyse*, 11 ff.
10. Granovetter and Swedberg, *The Sociology of Economic Life*, 9.
11. To be sure, some commentators have noted a contradiction between network analysis, with its socialized conception of economic behavior, and neoclassical

rent-seeking theory that views behavior solely in terms of means–ends efficiency as conceptualized in rational choice theory or new institutionalism (Thrainn Eggertsson, *Economic Behavior and Institutions* [New York: Cambridge University Press, 1990]). However, it is important to note that research on rent and its consequences for socioeconomic and sociopolitical development has not been the exclusive domain of methodological individualism. See Mushtaq H. Khan, "Rents, Efficiency and Growth," in M. H. Khan and K. S. Jomo, eds., *Rents, Rent-Seeking and Economic Development: Theory and Evidence in Asia* (Cambridge: Cambridge University Press, 2000), 21–69.

12. Rentier states that depend heavily on economic rent income have large organizations of foreign as well as internal trade at their disposal. These organizations are very influential within the domestic economy and hold a monopolistic position in relation to the exterior. Usually there exists an extensive system of state-run economic administration, and quite often an inflated public business sector. Rentier states that depend on external political rents, on the other hand, primarily promote organizations that are responsible for obtaining political rents or supporting the regime's status in regional politics, which is of fundamental importance with respect to rent revenues (foreign ministry, information ministry, ministry of cooperation, as well as the military apparatus). Their actions in domestic as well as in foreign politics are guided mainly by the intention to secure rents.

13. See Stephan Haggard and Robert Kaufman, "Institutions and Economic Adjustment," in S. Haggard and R. Kaufman, eds., *The Politics of Economic Adjustment: International Constraints, Distributive Conflicts, and the State* (Princeton: Princeton University Press, 1992), 3–37; John Waterbury, *Exposed to Innumerable Delusions* (New York: Cambridge University Press, 1993); and S. Haggard and Steven B. Webb, eds., *Voting for Reform: Democracy, Political Liberalization, and Economic Adjustment* (New York, NY: Oxford University Press, 1994).

14. Khan, "Rent-Seeking as a Process," 89 ff.

15. See Mario I. Blejer and Teresa Ter-Minassian, eds., *Fiscal Policy and Economic Reform: Essays in Honour of Vito Tanzi* (London: Routledge, 1997); and Jeffrey Davis et al., *Fiscal and Macroeconomic Impact of Privatization* (Washington, DC: International Monetary Fund, 2000).

16. The privatization of SOEs is also intended to generate positive developments in employment, investment, and growth in the mid-to-long term, as a direct result of enhanced private sector and financial market development, as well as of an increase in foreign direct investment. See S. Kikeri, J. Nellis, and M. Shirley, *Privatization: The Lessons of Experience* (World Bank, 1992), 10. While in larger and more open economies the relative impact of privatization on the proportion of public and private ownership in the economy might be limited, "in a small and relatively closed economy or an economy where public sector assets are substantial as a percentage of total assets, the magnitude of the transfers associated with

privatization could readily lead to significant effects on the portfolios of the private and public sector." See Heller et al., "Macroeconomic Constraints," 37.

17. "Public sector reform and privatization are public policy issues that are always embedded in other issues pertaining to structural adjustment, degrees of state economic intervention, and the regulation of markets. They are organically linked to the quintessentially political issues of public resource allocation, the provision of collective goods, and the distribution of wealth in society. It is an artificial exercise to separate out these issues, especially privatization, from the larger policy context. Public sector reform and privatization never take place in isolation from broader efforts at macro-economic and political adjustment." See Ezra N. Suleiman and John Waterbury, eds., *The Political Economy of Public Sector Reform and Privatization* (Boulder and London: Westview Press, 1990), 1.

18. For examples, see Alberto Alesina, "Political Models of Macroeconomic Policy and Fiscal Reforms," in S. Haggard and S. Webb, *Voting for Reform*, 37–60.

19. External agencies of creditors such as the World Bank, the IMF, and the Paris Club started to impose privatization on the governments of a number of developing countries as an emergency measure, where economic crises became so deep that deficits and debts had spiraled out of control and—at least according to these agencies—continued public business sector activities would have made it impossible to stabilize the respective economies in macroeconomic terms. Egypt is among the developing countries in which direct pressure from donors and creditors had been most obvious. See Suleiman and Waterbury, *The Political Economy*; Weiss and Wurzel, *The Economics and Politics of Transition*.

20. See Robert Springborg, *Mubarak's Egypt: Fragmentation of the Political Order* (Boulder: Westview Press, 1989); John Waterbury, *The Egypt of Nasser and Sadat: The Political Economy of Two Regimes* (Princeton: Princeton University Press, 1983); Waterbury, *Exposed to Innumerable Delusions*; and Weiss and Wurzel, *The Economics and Politics of Transition*.

21. See Suleiman and Waterbury, eds., *The Political Economy*. "In the context of the Government's retreating economic role, the public sector is the prime instrument for social and economic control. . . . Its sale would not only contribute to the further weakening of the State and its ability to direct socio-economic change, but also is a recipe for political suicide"; Dessouki, "The Public Sector in Egypt," 267.

22. Devaluation, which was often called for by the external donors, would lead to the loss of rents that existed due to the economically unrealistic exchange rate. Comprehensive trade liberalization would abolish rents that owe their existence to the state's numerous foreign trade monopolies. Rigorous structural reforms like privatization would abolish internal sources of rent (e.g., public sector monopolies in trading and processing certain products such as cotton and other cash crops).

23. Besides providing new loans, the reform agreements with the IMF, the Word Bank, and the Paris Club guaranteed debt cancellation of the considerable amount of up to $25 billion, on the condition that the government delivered the reform results agreed upon.

24. Khan, "Rents-Seeking as a Process," 70–144.
25. Waterbury, *Exposed to Innumerable Delusions.*
26. This statement holds true also when the phenomenon of the so-called change teams inside the administration is not included.
27. D. Weiss, *Wirtschaftliche Entwicklungsplanung in der VAR (Ägypten)—Analyse und Kritik* (Köln und Opladen, 1964).
28. Paul O'Farell, *Privatization in Egypt: A Review of Program Development and Current Status* (Cairo, 1995), 12.
29. Weiss and Wurzel, *The Economics and Politics of Transition,* 176.
30. S. Heydemann, *Economic Networks and the Political Economy of Fiscal Policy Reform in the Middle East: Conceptual Starting Points and Some Preliminary Hypotheses* (unpublished, 1999), 13 ff.
31. See Z. Önis and S. Webb, "Turkey: Democratization and Adjustment from Above," in S. Haggard and S. Webb, eds., *Voting for Reform: Democracy, Political Liberalization and Economic Adjustment;* Robert Kaufman, Carlos Bazdresch, and Blanca Hereda, "Mexico: Radical Reform in a Dominant Party System," in Haggard and Kaufman, *The Politics of Economic Adjustment.*
32. The maximum tariff was reduced from 87% (except for high-powered cars, cigarettes, and alcohol). Tariffs, previously between 30% and 70%, were decreased by 10%. On the other hand, some customs tariffs were raised (e.g., for tires from 20% to 30%) and additional taxes introduced to "cover the cost of inspection and classification of good." In March the World Bank demanded that these taxes be removed in the shortest possible time as they contravened the objective of the tariff reduction.
33. See Henk Knaupe and U. Wurzel, *Entwicklung der Entlastungsstadt Tenth of Ramadan in Ägypten: Erfolge und Fehlschläge in Industrie, Wohnungswesen und Infrastruktur* (Münster, Hamburg: Lit, 1996).
34. Other businessmen, who established industrial enterprises able to compete successfully on global markets without large-scale protection or hidden support by the government, would gain a lot if economic reforms developed more momentum. A third group constitutes the roughly 95% of entrepreneurs who are just too weak or too absorbed by daily duties to exert any influence on the regime's policy. An improvement of the general business environment—in particular, a fundamental stabilization of the macroeconomic framework conditions—should be in the interest of the vast majority of business people.
35. Haggard and Kaufman, "Institutions and Economic Adjustment," 27–28.
36. Wurzel, *Ägyptische Privatisierungspolitik 1990 bis 1998,* 175 ff.
37. See Richard F. Doner and Ben Ross Schneider, "Business Associations and Economic Development: Why Some Associations Contribute more than Others," *Business and Politics* (December 2000).
38. Ibid., 173–183; S. Gräfe, *Die politische Rolle ägyptischer Privatunternehmer im Prozess wirtschaftlicher Liberalisierung der Saatgutbranche* (Magisterarbeit, Universität Leipzig, Institut für Politikwissenschaft, Leipzig, 2002), 37 ff.

39. Noah El-Mikawy et al., "Institutional Reform of Economic Legislation in Egypt," ZEF—Discussion Papers on Development Policy, no. 30 (Bonn: August 2000), 45.

40. Ibid., 47.

41. Omar el Shafei, *Workers, Trade Unions, and the State of Egypt: 1984–1989* (Cairo: The American University in Cairo Press, 1995).

42. Wurzel, *Ägyptische Privatisierungspolitik 1990 bis 1998*, 347–348.

43. See Omar el Shafei, *Workers, Trade Unions, and the State of Egype: 1984–1989*; Wurzel, *Ägyptische Privatisierungspolitik 1990 bis 1998*, 279–300.

44. "The prevailing co-optation of union leaders into the political system means that it is not unusual to find individuals who, simultaneously, represent workers and the government. An illustrative example of this is the president of the GFELU, Al-Sayed Rashed. He cannot be classified as simply a minister in waiting, but is in fact a veteran member of the President's ruling party, the NDP, a member of the People's Assembly and its deputy speaker." See El-Mikawy et al., "Insitutional Reform of Economic Legislation in Egypt," 37.

45. This shift in interests is captured by Joel Hellman, "Winners Take All: The Politics of Partial Reform in Post-communist Transitions," *World Politics* 50, no. 2 (January 1998): 203–234.

46. Mark Granovetter, "The Strength of Weak Ties. A Network Theory Revisited," in Peter Marsden and Nan Lin, eds., *Social Structure and Network Analysis* (Beverly Hills: Sage, 1982), 105–130.

47. Jansen, Dorothea, *Einführung in die Netzwerkanalyse. Grundlagen, Methoden, Anwendungen*, 121 ff.

48. See David Krackhardt, "The Strength of Strong Ties: The Importance of Philos in Organizations," in Nittin Nohria and Robert G. Eccles, eds., *Networks and Organizations: Structure, Form, and Action* (Boston, MA: McGraw Hill, 1992), 216–239.

49. Önis and Webb, "Turkey: Democratization and Adjustment from Above."

50. Waterbury, *Exposed to Innumerable Delusions*.

51. From the perspective of fiscal policy reform, the former would generate additional budget revenue. The latter would be a yardstick of how many loss-making SOEs would have left the public sector and thus lower the burden imposed on the budget if loss-making SOEs had been sold.

52. Facing donor pressure for increased momentum of the privatization process, government officials blamed decision makers at holding and affiliated company levels for the slow progress of individual privatization projects, but the foiling of privatization on subordinate levels was at least implicitly accepted by the top leadership. See Wurzel, *Ägyptische Privatisierungspolitik 1990 bis 1998*, 244 ff.

53. "However, one should not expect a radical transformation of the Egyptian economic system, as such a transformation would be linked to changes in the nature of the political regime. And such transformation will certainly be a gradual process" (Said Aly, in Olaf Köndgen, "Privatisierungspolitik in Ägypten

zwischen wirtschaftlicher Notwendigkeit und politischen Widerständen," *KAS Auslands informationen* 1 [Sankt Augustin, 1995], 42.

54. The example is based on Sebastian Gräfe's empirical research on agricultural policy reform. See Gräfe, *Die politische Rolle ägyptischer Privatunternehmer im Prozess wirtschaftlicher Liberalisierung der Saatgutbranche.*

55. Ibid., 67 ff., 80 ff.

56. In turn, in negotiations with donors and creditors, the government blamed the managers and said it was not to be held responsible for their faults.

57. Waterbury, *Exposed to Innumerable Delusions*, 10 ff.

58. Author interviews, Cairo, 1996–1999.

59. Wurzel, *Ägyptische Privatisierungspolitik 1990 bis 1998.*

60. See H. Albrecht, P. Pawelka, and O. Schlumberger, "Wirtschaftliche Liberalisierung und Regimewandel in Ägypten," *Welttrends* 16 (Autumn 1997); Weiss and Wurzel, "The Economics and Politics of Transition"; Wurzel, *Ägyptische Privatisierungspolitik 1990 bis 1998*; and Gräfe, *Die politische Rolle ägyptischer Privatunternehmer im Prozess wirtschaftlicher Liberalisierung der Saatgutbranche.*

61. Were the circle of the top leadership around the president not a black box for outside observers, network theory could also be employed to document the agenda-setting, bargaining, and decision-making processes within the regime in great detail. However, for obvious reasons this seems to be impossible. On the implicit use of network analyses regarding the spread of reform ideas and conceptions and the work on change teams, see Haggard and Kaufman, "Institutions and Economic Adjustment," 3–37; and Önis and Webb, "Turkey: Democratization and Adjustment from Above."

62. Manzetti and Blake, in their analysis of corruption in Latin America, relate the reorganization of modalities of corruption in countries pursuing privatization in South America, and resulting failures of reform. "In fact, we believe that market reforms have changed the politics of corruption rather than eliminating this phenomenon," Haggard and Webb, *Voting for Reform*, 668.

63. An early example, of course on the top level, was the marriage of a Sadat daughter with the son of the construction tycoon Osman Ahmad Osman.

64. Author interview.

65. See in particular the country studies on Turkey and Mexico in Haggard and Webb, *Voting for Reform*; and to a lesser extent examples in Waterbury, *Exposed to Innumerable Delusions*. The same holds true for Egypt where "major special interest groups do not function as information managers for the collective benefit of the group they represent," El-Mikawy et al., "Institutional Reform of Economic Legislation in Egypt," 50.

66. Önis and Webb, "Turkey: Democratization and Adjustment from Above."

67. El-Mikawy et al., "Institutional Reform of Economic Legislation in Egypt," 51.

CHAPTER 4

From Negotiation to Rent Seeking, and Back? Patterns of State–Business Interaction and Fiscal Policy Reform in Jordan

Oliver Wils

Introduction and Theoretical Considerations

Fiscal policy reforms are complicated. Empirical evidence suggests that in most countries of the Middle East the tax and tariff systems "remain complex, inefficient, and difficult to administer," although some adjustments have been made in the wake of the financial crises of the late 1980s.[1] But fiscal policy reforms are not only about reorganizing taxes and tariffs. Rather, they deal with more encompassing issues such as reducing the size of the state ("downsizing"), and restructuring various components of the state budget. Therefore, I regard expenditure reduction, privatization, and tax reform as major instruments supporting the goal of fiscal stability.[2] In this broader understanding, fiscal policy reforms are highly subversive as the so-called IMF riots in the Middle East have shown.

The complications of fiscal policy reforms are, however, not limited to the danger of rebellious have-nots. As indicated in Heydemann's introduction, it is also the haves who, as members of powerful economic networks, are manipulating changes in the (re)distribution of public goods and state revenues. Indeed, it is the main hypothesis of this comparative research project that the dynamics and outcomes of fiscal policy reform in the Middle East (and elsewhere) are affected by powerful economic networks and vice versa.

In turn, our main analytic concern is that prevailing accounts of the politics of economic reform are not well equipped to address these network effects.

This chapter contributes to the larger discussion pursued throughout the present volume with a case study of Jordan. In particular, I argue that the specific relationship between Jordanian economic elites of the public and the private sectors is the key to understanding the process of fiscal policy reform in the kingdom.[3] Dating back to the early 1950s, leading businessmen and senior bureaucrats in the kingdom have developed a high degree of collusion and cooperation. I show that until now this relationship has been marked by two distinctive processes: formal negotiation on the one hand and individual, informal rent seeking on the other. While formal negotiation was particularly strong in the 1950s and 1960s and rent seeking became more powerful in the 1970s and 1980s, I argue that during the economic (and political) reform process of the 1990s both patterns played an important role. The patterns of both formal negotiation and informal rent seeking have shaped the worldview and behavior of Jordanian economic elites and are continuously used to protect privileges and manipulate reform policies.

Thus, the essay contributes to the study of the political economy of Jordan, where—as in many other Middle Eastern countries—relations between private and public sectors have not been analyzed sufficiently. It also contributes to the theoretical debate on how to make use of network analysis in the political economy of fiscal policy reform by integrating networks into more encompassing patterns of state–business relations. In this context, economic networks are seen as sets of relations that are being shaped and penetrated by specific patterns of state–business interaction.

A more detailed discussion of networks, state–business interactions, and the politico-economic relevance of rents follows. The second section deals with the historical development of state–business interactions in Jordan, focusing on changes in fiscal policy and the specific patterns that mark the relationship between the economic elites of the public and private sector. The third section covers the economic reform program that started in 1989. In particular, the introduction of a sales tax in 1994 and the privatization of the telecommunication sector serve as examples to show how fiscal policy reform has affected economic elites and how they have tried to manipulate these reforms.

Networks and Patterns of State–Business Interaction

According to standard network theory, a social network is defined as "a specific set of linkages among a defined set of persons, with the additional property that the characteristics of these linkages as a whole may be used to interpret the social behavior of the persons involved."[4] The vagueness of this definition has contributed to the emergence of two different strands of network analysis, namely "networks as analytical tools capable of illuminating social relations and networks as forms of ties that govern relations amongst economic actors in a variety of organizational and cross-organizational settings."[5] Other authors emphasize the regulatory or governance potential of networks. Messner, for example, argues that networks represent a qualitatively new pattern of organization and regulation beyond markets and policy hierarchies.[6] Yet, more or less all network approaches share the basic assumption that networks are more than pure distributional coalitions, underlining that networks affect the behavior and *Weltanschauung* of their participants in one way or another.

In contrast, however, to the theoretical importance of network analysis, its empirical application is difficult. For example, how and according to what criteria can single networks be isolated given that network forms differ and, as Ibarra states, are marked by different degrees of density, connectivity, and hierarchy?[7] Does the often-praised flexibility of networks not force them to change form continuously in order to adapt to rapidly changing environments? What about the network participants, the "defined set of persons"? Do various factions all follow the same strategy without regrouping and reshuffling or do they develop new ad hoc alliances, possibly even outside a given network? And, most important for the purpose of this essay, how and through which specific mechanisms do networks influence, manipulate, or participate in designing economic policy?

Instead of isolating a single network and analyzing the specific characteristics of the linkages between the individuals organized in this network, it is preferable to embed networks in a broader set of patterns that shape, structure, and penetrate these linkages. Embedding networks into the more encompassing patterns of state–business relations allows for a more systematic and historically grounded comparison of network characteristics, their development, and their impact on economic policy formulation. Furthermore, it is a pragmatic approach that takes into consideration that in countries like Jordan data on single economic networks are not easily available and that there are only few studies on the politico-economic system and on state–business relations that might support the application of network analysis.

State–business relations are important for the analysis of a country's political economy. Furthermore, there is little disagreement that specific characteristics of state–business relations have a huge impact on economic development. Variations in the organization of information exchange and participation in economic policy-making as well as different means of conflict regulation enhance or reduce transaction costs considerably. According to neo-corporatist theory, these meso-level governance systems are key to explaining the differences between capitalist economies.[8] In a stimulating study on state–business relations in developing countries, edited by Maxfield and Schneider, the authors inquire about the conditions under which relations between bureaucrats and businessmen contribute either positively to economic growth or negatively to rent seeking. They identify three sets of key variables concerning the effects of state–business relations: first, "soft" characteristics such as the degree of transparency, credibility, and trust; second, "hard" characteristics related to structural-organizational aspects of the state as well as business associations; and third, external factors such as political or economic threats.[9]

A further factor that is important when analyzing state–business interactions is the historical dimension. As scholars of the New Institutionalism in economics and sociology[10] have repeatedly underlined, specific patterns of action must be analyzed against the background of routinized, internalized, or institutionalized arrangements. Lehmbruch, for example, has argued that sectoral governance systems are not only "seen as emerging out of processes of collective social learning in institutional contexts. Rather they become institutionalized themselves. And, as institutions tend to do, they then either constrain or facilitate political action."[11] Initial arrangements between businessmen and bureaucrats may thus be historically contingent. But once they are routinized or institutionalized to a certain degree they become more stable patterns of state–business interactions and, as a result, change only gradually.[12] Therefore, patterns of state–business ties need to be analyzed in a historical perspective. In countries such as Jordan, where no major regime change has taken place since the formation of the contemporary state, modifications of state–business interactions and new patterns are to a certain extent path dependent. Furthermore, as the case of Jordan shows, modes of state–business interaction that had been superceded can reemerge, as is the case with the process of formal negotiation, a dominant pattern of interaction in the 1950s and 1960s that was revitalized during the reform process initiated in 1989.

Rents and Fiscal Policy

The regional circulation of oil rents has been long regarded as a major factor shaping the political economy—and thus state–business relations—of Middle Eastern countries.[13] It has been argued that a huge part of state revenues such as oil income, development grants, and other financial transfers, as well as workers' remittances, were not extracted from the national economy but rather externally generated. As a result of delinking what in classical economics is considered to be the state's main tasks—namely resource extraction and redistribution—from the national productive sectors it is believed that rents lead to a high level of state autonomy vis-à-vis social interests. Rents accruing directly to the state can be used to satisfy strategic groups or, through welfare measures, the populace at large.

Compared to the magnitude of external rents, tax policies seem to play only a minor role for generating necessary state revenues.[14] And in fact, even in the mid-1990s, more than 50 percent of state revenues in the Middle East were other than tax revenues.[15] There is, however, some reason to believe that tax policies affect state–business relations more than conventional theory assumes. This is partly related to the two major weaknesses of rentier state theories. First they are ahistorical in the sense that their analytical focus is on the oil period, while the modes of production and state–business relations in the pre–oil boom era were not covered adequately. Second, they are overly state-centered in the sense that the state is seen as the only actor through which rents are channeled and which is responsible for maintaining this mode of production through means of foreign policy.[16] Cooperation between bureaucrats and businessmen who serve the purpose of rent generation and the manipulation of its allocation are, by definition, a blind spot.[17]

A more nuanced account of state–business relations and how they are affected by sources of state revenue requires an historical approach. Furthermore, instead of focusing only on rents that are generated externally, forms of rent that are generated internally or at least in cooperation with domestic business factions should be taken into consideration. For example, monopoly rents or rents that are created through discriminatory tax policies are generated internally. Another form of rent is created through the taxation of the trade sector, mostly in combination with an overvaluation of the national currency.[18] Although the realization of this rent depends also on an external factor (e.g., inequalities in the world market), the tradables are produced locally. The kind of goods and the channels through which rent is created and appropriated affect the specific patterns of state–business interaction.[19]

In summary, my approach starts from the assumption that rents have long provided a substantial part of state income in the Middle East. Nevertheless, the composition and sources of rent income in a given country have varied over time, affecting its fiscal structure and policy options. In Jordan, for example, the importance of businessmen for the generation of monopoly rents affected the redistribution of public revenues in the 1950s and 1960s.

The influx of oil rents in the 1970s and 1980s changed the fiscal structure of the kingdom and altered the relationship between businessmen and bureaucrats. Thus, changes in the rent and fiscal structure of Jordan serve as the background against which the patterns of state–business interaction are analyzed. However, as I have noted, changes in the patterns of state–business interaction cannot be explained by referring to changes in the rent structure alone, but have to take into account the already existing and routinized patterns of interaction.

Negotiation and Rent Seeking: Jordan's State–Business Interactions in Historical Perspective

Industrialization and Negotiation, 1951–1966

The first significant cooperation between Jordanian businessmen and senior bureaucrats emerged in the 1950s in the industrial sector. Before that, state–business interactions were virtually nonexistent, although it should be noted that during the mandate period (1921–1946) a group of Amman-based traders—mostly of Syrian and Palestinian origin—had developed good relations with Amir Abdallah. They provided financial support for the Amir, who was in dire need of additional funding, because the personal income provided by the British did not suffice to cover his substantial social obligations. The traders, in turn, profited enormously from the shortages created by the Second World War by getting privileged access to import licenses. As Amawi has shown, in a very short span of time a group of some 30 traders accumulated considerable wealth.[20] Therefore, with independence in 1946, Jordan had a very small but unprecedentedly rich group of merchant families. Their later cooperation with the Jordanian bureaucracy was, however, related to the economic and political conditions of the early 1950s.

One of the factors constraining the actions of the Jordanian bureaucracy and the merchants alike was the destitute economic situation of Transjordan. At the end of the British mandate period (1921–1946), Transjordan was a country marked by a low level of economic activity, with agriculture and, to a lesser degree, handicraft and trade serving as the main sources of income. Industrial production was virtually nonexistent. State income was highly limited, since domestic revenue was low, consisting mainly of indirect taxation, especially import duties and licence fees.[21] Foreign assistance provided by the British that made up to 30 percent of Jordan's income was mainly used to finance and equip the army, which, under British command until 1956, was one of the main instruments to enforce Hashemite rule in Transjordan.

This situation of economic underdevelopment deteriorated further when, as a result of the Palestine war of 1948, Jordan had to absorb a huge number of Palestinian refugees and to provide basic services for the West Bank. After the annexation of the West Bank in 1950 and the proclamation of the Kingdom of Jordan, the number of inhabitants tripled from 440,000 to 1.2 million. Furthermore, the Arab–Israeli war cut off the country from coastal Palestine, the traditional market for its agricultural products. There was, however, an acceleration of industrial activity after the war, because the forced isolation had led to some sort of "natural" protection triggering small-scale import substitution, and some Palestinian businessmen had brought considerable financial resources with them.[22] Yet the great majority of the refugees as well as the Jordanian population lived in very poor conditions.[23]

The dire need to develop an industrial base and infrastructure and to broaden the quantity and portfolio of state revenues gave impetus to governmental development measures. In particular, it strengthened a movement of leftist and nationalist bureaucrats who in the 1950s tried to establish their program of state-led modernization. This new generation of Jordanian bureaucrats, educated through public training and scholarship programs initiated during the Mandate, were close knit[24] and strongly influenced by the socialist and nationalist ideologies that spread all over the Arab world in the 1940s and early 1950s. In fact, their relatively strong position in public administration was fostered through the prevailing political situation: after the assassination of Amir Abdallah in 1951, the monarchy was considerably weakened. Both King Talal and King Hussein, crowned at the age of 18, were politically inexperienced and unable to overcome the internal struggles among the palace elite.[25] At the same time, Jordanian civil society was flourishing, stimulated by the political activism of the Palestinian population.[26] New political parties, trade unions, and professional associations were often critical to the monarchy. As a result, King Hussein and the palace elite only regained their political power in 1957 by dissolving the socialist nationalist government and purging the army of antimonarchist officers after a military *coup d'état* had failed.[27] However, the influence of the nationalist movement again increased when Wasfi al-Tall, an outspoken autocrat and nationalist, was appointed prime minister in 1962.

Supported by civil society and the nationalist mood of the 1950s and 1960s, the bureaucrats tried to establish their program of state-led modernization and to gain control over the Jordanian economy. One of the strongholds of the nationalist bureaucrats was the Ministry of National Economy, where Hamad al-Farhan, a leading figure of the nationalists, served as undersecretary until he was ousted in 1957. In an attempt to raise state revenue, the ministry struggled for more state control of development aid from Britain and the United States.[28] Foreign aid had increased in the 1950s, but was only under partial control of the state. A huge part of foreign assistance was used for the security apparatus while other parts were earmarked for the settlement of the refugee population (through UNWRA) and occasional small-scale projects. In the end, the nationalist bureaucrats failed to control the use of foreign aid. Yet they contributed to a qualitative and quantitative extension of state activity.[29] Development planning was streamlined, including closer cooperation with foreign development agencies.[30] Under the tenure of Prime Minister Wasfi al-Tall, bureaucracy became more efficient and anticorruption measures were introduced.[31] In sum, the nationalist bureaucrats contributed considerably to an enhancement of the technical and institutional capacity of the Jordanian state.

The main goal of the nationalist bureaucrats was, however, to initiate major industrial projects and to raise state revenues that could be used for development purposes. Given that development aid was out of reach and that the state budget did not allow for financing the planned investment projects, the bureaucrats had little choice but to cooperate with the small group of wealthy Jordanian merchants and some additional Palestinian businessmen that had fled to the kingdom. In the end, the establishment of all the major Jordanian industries of the 1950s such as the establishment of the Jordan Cement Factories Company in 1951, the reorganization and extension of the Jordan Phosphate Mining Company in 1953, as well as the establishment of the Jordan Petroleum Refinery Company in 1956 and the Jordan Vegetable Oil Industries Company in the same year, were grounded on public–private partnerships. Although many businessmen were in favor of these joint ventures, in some cases the establishment of big industries cut across the interests of leading merchants and top politicians. For example, the local agents for oil companies such as Shell, Caltex, or Mobil were against the establishment of the petroleum refinery. In these cases, the ministry brought its full discretionary power into the process of negotiation, which included a threat to withdraw the import licenses of the businessmen. Consequently, the merchants agreed to take shares in the new companies.[32]

In principle, these first deals of state–business cooperation were based on an open process of negotiation between two more or less coherent interest groups. Although both parties were initially not very appealing to each other, negotiation was facilitated by the fact that none of them had the political power to dominate the other. Nevertheless, the results of these deals were positive for all involved. While the state granted the new companies monopoly concessions, guaranteed their losses, and set market prices and dividend levels, the businessmen responded by investing in the industrial sector. The private shareholders were offered lucrative dividend levels.[33] The state on the other side profited through additional employment opportunities and a diversification of state revenues.[34] Value added in the mining and manufacturing sectors grew by almost 16 percent annually between 1959 and 1966.[35]

This process of negotiation was to become more institutionalized in the following years. The positive synergistic results of state–business cooperation may have contributed to this development no less than the impact that the frequent board meetings of the shareholding companies had on businessmen and bureaucrats alike. In the early 1960s, many companies were established with remarkable government shares.[36] State–business cooperation was even extended to public and private sector institutions. For example, the Central Bank of Jordan (CBJ, established in 1963) and the Industrial Development Bank (established in 1965) co-opted onto their boards influential businessmen from the Shuman, Budayr, Tabaʿa, and Abu Hassan families. Furthermore, representatives of the Amman Chamber of Industry (ACI, established in 1962) were on the boards of many public institutions. Moreover, the Chamber, which up to the present is dominated by the sons and grandsons of the old business elite, also had several state managers on its board.

In sum, state–business cooperation in Jordan began as a process of negotiation born out of both the economic conditions of a late developing country and the political checkmate between a nationalist movement and the palace elite that gave a boost to an etatist bureaucracy. However, the subsequent institutionalization of this process indicates that the different actors secured several advantages with a cooperative approach based on negotiation. Apart from the already mentioned dividends guaranteed by the industrial joint ventures, cooperation with the Jordanian bureaucracy was highly lucrative for the businessmen, because it gave them a high social status—whereas their fathers who were mostly traders and merchants did not receive much respect in the 1920s, 1930s, and 1940s. Furthermore, the cooperation gave them access to rents independent of traditional forms of patrimonial favoritism exercised by the palace elite. For the nationalist bureaucrats, the cooperation with businessmen facilitated their project of state-led modernization and industrialization and, together with their efforts to streamline and rationalize bureaucratic procedure, laid the foundations for a developmental state, if a rudimentary one. Through regular meetings and exchange of information, senior bureaucrats and businessmen got closer to each other and developed a certain degree of cohesion.[37] Finally, the bureaucrats managed to establish themselves as a new segment of the Jordanian elite.

This, however, was only possible because parts of the palace elite had realized that a more modern state administration fit well into the Hashemite policy of nation-building,[38] and that new forms of rent generation and allocation did not endanger, but rather complemented traditional forms.

Oil Boom and Rent Seeking, 1973–1989

The regional oil boom of the 1970s and early 1980s marked the beginning of a new development paradigm in Jordan. With oil prices quadrupling, Jordan was integrated into the regional circulation of petrol rents benefiting from unprecedented high levels of financial transfers. According to official figures, the kingdom received cash payments of approximately $2 billion for the years 1974–1978, and nearly $3.5 billion for the years 1979–1983.[39] As a result, the scarcity of resources that had marked the 1950s and 1960s could now be overcome through these financial transfers leading to a discontinuation of import substitution industrialization. In this context the question arises of how these oil rents have affected the established patterns of cooperation between Jordanian economic elites of the private and public sectors.

The Jordanian economic elite had to adapt to a new political and economic environment that began to emerge during the years 1967–1971. This transitory phase started with the Arab–Israeli war of 1967, the disastrous outcome of which, for the Arab world, led to a serious weakening of the Arab nationalist movement.[40] Moreover, a new wave of some 300,000 Palestinian refugees and the loss of the West Bank gave rise to the *fedayyin* movement in Jordan, whose militancy helped to provoke a civil war in 1970–1971. When economic planning was reinstated in 1972, it was supervised by Crown Prince Hassan and under closer control of the palace.[41] Economic policy-making was further depoliticized by the emergence of a new group of technocrats emanating from the CBJ, which, by an extensive program of scholarships for studies abroad, mostly in the United States, had trained many senior bureaucrats.

These political developments together with the rapid increase of oil rents led, on the one hand, to an extension of the public sector and its involvement in the economy.[42] On the other hand, the institutional and developmental capacity of the Jordanian bureaucracy was considerably weakened. Huge investment projects such as the Jordan Fertiliser Industries Company, the South Cement Industries Company, the Jordan Glass Industries Company, and the Jordan Timber Processing Industries Company were badly planned. Within ten years of their establishment they were either absorbed into other companies or went into receivership. Furthermore, the rapid extension of the public sector increased red tape. The number of ministries and public departments involved in economic policies expanded, yet their responsibilities were not clearly defined and, in fact, often overlapped.[43] Bureaucratic procedure was further complicated through the Economic Security Committee (ESC), established in 1967 to deal with the effects of the Israeli occupation of the West Bank. With martial law remaining in force, the ESC was increasingly used to bypass existing laws and regulations. Especially after 1974, when parliament was dissolved, the ESC developed into one of the major decision-making bodies in Jordan.[44]

Senior bureaucrats in the economic sectors were further concerned with a permanent reshuffling of high administrative posts, similar to the principle of elite rotation in politics.[45] According to Piro, this policy aimed at keeping technocrats within the influence of the state, while simultaneously separating them from their social bases and, thus, making them more dependent on the palace elite.[46] In this context of insecurity and dependency, cooperation with businessmen was important for senior bureaucrats. It provided them with additional power (and on occasion with some pocket money) and, probably most important, served as an exit option from their public sector jobs.

Big business families in Jordan also considered their cooperation with senior bureaucrats important, although for different reasons. The well-established business elite benefited enormously from the private sector boom that accompanied the oil period. Increased government spending gave impetus to high growth rates in the construction, transport, trade, and manufacturing sectors.[47] Another source of wealth derived from the huge amounts of remittances sent back by the approximately 300,000 Jordanians working in the Gulf States. Remittances reached a peak of $1.2 billion in 1984 and went mostly into consumption.[48] Indicating the extent of this boom, private sector investments rose from JD 80 million ($248 million) in the period 1973–1975 to JD 600 million ($1.8 billion) in the period 1976–1980.[49]

Although the Jordanian business elite profited most from this boom, competition had become fierce. With the circulation of oil rents, the financial wealth of the businessmen declined in importance. Moreover, land ownership, real estate speculation, and contracting on behalf of the military and the national airline had led to the emergence of a new stratum of rich people.[50] In addition, some Jordanians, often of Palestinian background,[51] who had acquired resources through employment in the Gulf, started to invest in Jordan in the late 1970s. To defend their privileges against competition from these *nouveaux riches*, the established business elite capitalized on their relations with high-level bureaucrats. These relations provided access not only to information, but also to other material benefits such as obtaining import licenses from the Ministry of Supply or within the framework of bilateral trade agreements.[52] It is important to note that this type of state–business cooperation was not limited to negotiated processes and "good relations," but involved increasingly informal and individual processes of rent seeking.

One of the areas where rent-seeking activities, along with negotiation processes, took place in an excessive manner was the banking and financial sector. This privately owned sector grew rapidly in the 1970s and 1980s and offered high dividends. Assets of Jordanian banks rose twenty-fold from JD 95.5 million in 1973 to JD 1.8 billion in 1983, making Jordan the only Arab country where bank assets exceed GDP since the late 1970s.[53] For the business elite, controlling credit opportunities was also an important means to keep competitors at a distance. Informal lobbying and personal networking was so extensive that the number of banks in Jordan rose from 8 (4 Jordanian and 4 foreign banks) in 1973 to 17 (11 Jordanian and 6 foreign banks) in 1983. In contrast to this development, in 1974 the CBJ had already decided not only to stop the licensing of new banks, but rather to reduce the number of banks through mergers.[54] However, in order to establish new banks private financiers co-opted influential bureaucrats, often from the finance and banking sector itself, to assist them in the procedure of licensing and offered them seats on the banks' boards of directors.[55]

In sum, state–business cooperation continued during the oil period of the 1970s and early 1980s although Jordan's integration into regional rent-circulation channels (through both direct cash transfers and workers remittances) undermined previous efforts of import substitution industrialization. In fact, imports were not discouraged, but, on the contrary, increased due to high consumption demand fuelled by remittances. Also, the import sector was encouraged by a government policy of keeping the exchange rate overvalued, so that custom duties and import levies could be channeled into the treasury.[56] These state efforts to get a share of remittances strengthened existing relations with the business elite from the trading, contracting, and financial sectors. Cooperation between economic elites from the public and private sectors was also strengthened by the need of the business elite to protect its privileges against a stratum of newly rich competitors. Since the business associations had lost importance in the 1970s and 1980s, the business elite made increasing use of its personal relations to the state administration, and even to the palace. To exclude potential competitors from networking with these decision makers, the established business elite used its social status as a gatekeeping mechanism to manage access to channels of informal and individual decision-making. As a result of the fierce competition between the old business elite and new entrepreneurs, and the weakening of administrative procedures that had led to arbitrariness and a lack of transparency, the relevance of informal networking increased. During the 1970s and 1980s, processes of formal negotiation remained important as a means of information exchange and mutual consultation, but they were soon outweighed by informal, mostly individual processes of rent seeking.

In 1985, after international oil prices had dropped dramatically, both Jordan's high dependence on external financial transfers and workers' remittances and the persistence and influence of the rent-seeking networks created after 1973 became obvious. A new government under Prime Minister Zayd al-Rifa'i was mandated with the task of reforming Jordan's economy, but proved incapable and perhaps unwilling to do so. The new government that included prominent businessmen could even be seen as another important network in itself.[57] In order to compensate for the losses in external assistance the government resorted to the international financial markets and signed commercial loans. Soon external debts reached more than $8 billion in 1988. The banking sector suffered huge losses with several banks (among them the Petra Bank, a major Jordanian business bank) falling into bankruptcy and receivership in 1988 and 1989. Moreover, as a result of the financial crisis, the Jordanian Dinar lost 50 percent of its value between 1988 and 1990.

Economic Reform, Tax Disputes, and Privatization

The Reform Program: Jordan After 1989

In 1989, Jordan concluded an economic reform program with the IMF and the World Bank. In its first phase, the program focused on financial stabilization to reduce the national debt to manageable proportions, build foreign currency reserves, and achieve a balanced budget;[58] core measures were increases in the prices of public services and the cutting of subsidies. In the second phase, structural adjustment measures were agreed upon including several subsector reforms in the welfare and tax system, a liberalization of the customs and trade regime, and the privatization of public companies. According to the original indicators set for financial reforms, state expenditure was to be reduced from 40 percent of GDP in 1992 to 35 percent in 1998. Simultaneously, revenues were to be increased from 26 percent of GDP in 1992 to 30 in 1998, leaving a budget deficit of 5 percent of GDP instead of 14 percent. Furthermore, the negative trade balance was to be reduced from 28 percent of GDP in 1992 to 12 percent in 1998.[59]

The simultaneous reduction of import and customs duties to international standards and the aim of achieving a balanced state budget did not harmonize with each other. Yet the introduction of a sales tax contributed to an increase of domestic revenue, which rose from JD 566 million in 1989 to JD 1,451 million in 1995, with customs duties (JD 204 million) and the sales tax (JD 264 million) alone accounting for one-third.[60] The budget deficit shrank to nearly 5 percent of GDP in the first years of the reform program. However, after 1996 it grew again to reach 11 percent of GDP in 1998.[61] At this stage, privatization was considered a core element of financial reform, and an indicator of the state's willingness to withdraw from the economy. Besides its direct contributions to the budget, it was hoped that privatization would trigger foreign investment.

Initially, loan and credit conditionality was relatively strict, leaving Jordanian economic policy-makers with little room for maneuver. Yet external pressure on Jordan's political economy eased when Jordan entered the Madrid peace negotiations and finally concluded a peace treaty with Israel in 1994. In the aftermath, the kingdom received several unconditional grants and loans, often as unspecified budgetary support.[62] Development grants were also channeled through the NGO sector, which is widely controlled by members of the Hashemite family.[63] Obviously, the rationale behind the international assistance was not only developmental, but to a certain degree intended to keep an important regime stable.

Despite this relatively open-handed environment, domestic opposition to the ongoing economic reform process increased. Large parts of the Jordanian population have suffered from high unemployment and poverty rates while excessive red tape and frequent rumors of corruption directed their anger toward the government. The reduction of state spending and, especially, the abolition of subsidies, have posed a political threat as the riots of 1989 and 1996 have shown.[64] Opposition has also been related to the peace treaty and any further reconciliation with Israel. Indeed, the regime's strong determination to continue the peace track and to maintain all the economic benefits associated with it, is the main reason behind the gradual limitation of the political liberalization process initiated in 1989.[65]

As a result, the Jordanian palace elite has had to strike a balance between considerations of regime survival and commitments to international financial agencies. This explains, in part, why sensitive reforms such as the reorganization of public administration and the privatization of public companies have often been postponed. Political considerations also affected the Jordanian economic elite of the public sector. A group of reform experts that had developed good relations with international financial and development agencies has gained in importance because it facilitated the bargaining processes with the IMF, the World Bank, and other donors. However, rent-seeking activities are still widespread and increasingly used to pacify political factions, undermining the reform programs designed by these technocrats.

The first serious crisis in the policy of balancing internal and external factors occurred in 1998. In the previous years, the country had witnessed high growth rates so that international financial organizations had praised Jordan's economic and reform performance as highly successful.[66] However, the fragility of the reform program became obvious when in July 1998 the Jordanian government had to declare that the growth rates for 1996 and 1997, allegedly 5.2 and 5 percent, had been substantially overestimated.[67] Instead, in 1999 official statistics placed these figures at 1.0 and 1.3 percent, respectively.[68]

In the following section, the two major steps of Jordan's fiscal policy reform of the 1990s—the introduction of a sales tax in 1994 and the privatization of the telecommunication sector—are described. Both cases show clearly that the Jordanian economic elite reacted to the challenges of economic reform by resorting to the two familiar patterns of formal negotiation and informal rent seeking in order to secure its privileges and to avoid outright competition.

Tax Reform

One of the centerpieces of Jordan's tax reform was to simplify the tax system and to switch the system from a strong reliance on taxation of trade toward taxing local consumption. In fact, throughout Jordan's history import duties were the single most important source of domestic revenue, accounting for a third of total domestic revenue on average. Small wonder that the IMF and the World Bank demanded a reform of the tax system to keep it in harmony with international and regional standards. Tax losses should be compensated by increasing the consumption tax (qualitatively and quantitatively) that was introduced in 1988. In 1994, the consumption tax was replaced by a sales tax that finally was converted into a VAT system in 2001.

The business elite and parts of the economic elite of the public sector were not particularly happy about exiting the long-standing source of rent generation offered by the taxation of trade. Big merchants and traders were to lose their privileges related to obtaining import licenses and exemptions from import duties, but forced to pay sales taxes. Industrialists were to lose the high-tariff protection for their mostly uncompetitive products. All were concerned that the tax reform would affect their profits that were already reduced by the regional economic stagnation of the early 1990s.

A first confrontation between the government pushing for tax reform and the business elite occurred in November 1991 in the run-up to a new stand-by agreement with the IMF. At that time, import duties on more than

200 items were reduced while 43 (imported and locally produced) new items were charged with a consumption tax between 5 and 15 percent (for some luxury goods 25 percent). In response, the private sector and particularly the ACI organized conferences and seminars to lobby against these regulations. Furthermore, it used the recently liberalized media (especially the newspapers) to describe the negative impacts on the industrial sector. In the end, the government did not withdraw these regulations. The private sector, however, had sent a very clear signal that a reform of the tax system is only possible with its participation.

When the conversion of the consumption tax into a sales tax was discussed in 1992, the ACI and the ACC participated in the preparations. In November and December of 1992, intensive negotiations took place among the Ministry of Finance, the Ministry of Economy, the Customs Department, the CBJ, and the ACI and ACC.[69] Nevertheless, their different positions could not be bridged and no agreement was reached, leading to a delay of the introduction of the sales tax from January to April 1993. Finally, the whole process had to be postponed to the period after the elections of November 1993.

The ACI demanded that the sales tax be reduced from 10 to 5 percent, and that far-reaching tax exemptions be created for industrial raw materials and for certain industries such as textiles that were not competitive. Furthermore, it preferred that the basis for tax assessment of imported goods should include the customs duties. The ACC demanded, as well, a low rate of import taxation, but suggested that taxes be calculated before customs are included. Nevertheless, both the ACI and ACC were in agreement that the details of the sales tax should be regulated by parliament and not by the cabinet.

After the elections of November 1993, a new committee was established to discuss the matter further. Although four different draft tax bills were discussed, the basic differences could not be resolved.[70] Finally, in February 1994, Prime Minister 'Abd al-Salam al-Majali pressured the parliament into deciding on the draft law. Since the version under discussion was not the one favored by the private sector, the ACI and the ACC started another lobby campaign. The ACI distributed studies and sent memoranda to parliamentarians and members of the cabinet. Furthermore, it met with a delegation from the Islamic Action Front faction after having already talked to former prime minister and renowned opposition figure Taher al-Masri, then the speaker of parliament. Also, seminars were held and the ACI's position was publicized in full-page newspaper ads.[71] It is remarkable that between the two chambers, the ACI was far more professional and effective than the

ACC, which was internally factionalized and ineffective.[72] Instead of using the public and the possibility of negotiation, members of the ACC opted for individual rent-seeking and tried to get their goods on a list of tax-exempt items.[73]

In the end, the sales tax law was passed in parliament. Yet tax rates were fixed at 7 percent and not 10 percent as originally intended, and it was decided that its conversion into VAT should not take place before 1999 and then only with the approval of parliament. As an appendix to the law, a list of tax-exempt items was added. Since this list could be modified by the cabinet (and not parliament), members of the private sector elite were favored because they had better means to influence such decisions.

In September 1995, the sales tax rate was increased to 10 percent. At that time, demands from the private sector were partly addressed by an extension of the list of tax-exempt items while the industrial sector benefited from a reduction or even elimination of customs duties for a range of primary and intermediary goods.[74] Simultaneously, the private sector economic elite received further substitutes for their lost privileges. Income taxes, for example, were considerably reduced in 1995 from a previous peak rate of 45 percent to a peak of 30 percent. Corporate taxes were also reduced from previous rates of 38–55 percent (according to the classification of enterprises) to 15–35 percent. Furthermore, in 1995 a new investment law was launched that offered a range of tax and customs reductions for investment projects in the agriculture, industry, tourism, and transport sectors. Small wonder that the business elite, with its easy access to commercial loans due to large ownership of parts of the banking and finance sector, participated in most of the new investment projects.

Privatization

Another component of Jordan's fiscal policy reform was related to privatization. In this context, private enterprises were gradually allowed to enter sectors hitherto monopolized by the state. One of the first areas was education where, since 1989, private universities have offered their services,[75] followed by other sectors such as telecommunications and electricity. In addition, privatization included the direct sale of public companies or public shares to the private sector. As early as 1986, some transport companies, the Telecommunications Corporation (TCC), and Royal Jordanian (the national airline), were considered eligible candidates for privatization. In reality, however, political factors led to postponing the sale of state companies and only a few shares in minor industries and some public companies in the tourism sector (e.g., the Intercontinental Hotel and the Ma'in Spa) were sold. When the IMF and

World Bank started to increase their pressure in 1996, the Jordanian government responded. In 1998 it sold public shares in the Jordan Cement Factories Company and, one year later, sold 40 percent of the Jordan Telecommunications Company (JTC).

The telecom sector provides a good case for analyzing privatization in Jordan because the privatization process included both the opening of the sector for private companies and the direct sale of state assets. Furthermore, the telecom sector offers highly lucrative business opportunities involving local as well as international companies. In the following, I describe two short examples related to the privatization of the telecom sector; the first dealing with the licensing of cellular phone services, the second with the struggles surrounding the sale of 40 percent of JTC.

The licensing of a private mobile services provider was part of the national telecommunications strategy that the Jordanian government elaborated in cooperation with the World Bank in 1993. In August 1994, the license was given to Jordan Mobile Telephone Services Company (*al-sharikat al-urdunniyya li-khidmat al-hawatif al-muntaqila*)—in short, Fastlink. The main investors behind Fastlink were the former chief of staff and chief of police 'Abd al-Hadi al-Majali and his son Sahil, the London-based Iraqi investor Nathmi Awji, and the Abu Jaber business family; the foreign partner of the consortium was the American Motorola company.[76]

The license was granted for a period of 15 years. Fastlink enjoyed a monopoly position for the first four years until November 1998, when a second provider for cellular phone services was to be established. In return, Fastlink had to pay $10 million for the license and 20 percent of its income to the government.[77] Yet the mobile market expanded at a much faster pace than expected, with the number of Fastlink's customers growing from 24,000 in 1996 to 86,000 two years later. It is worth noting, however, that the licensing of Fastlink did not remain unchallenged. A competitor for the cellular license took the case to court, revealing interesting details of the licensing process.

The competitor[78] argued that serious mistakes had been made in the review of bids. For example, its lawyers complained that the licensing committee, which was set up by the cabinet in 1993, was not independent. On the contrary, the membership of this committee was identical to the board of directors of the TCC, except for the chairman of the board, who was the minister for post and communications. Another argument was that in August 1994, when the license was granted to Fastlink, Motorola—the foreign partner of Fastlink—was not allowed to operate in Jordan because it was named on the boycott list of the Arab League. In May 1996, the

Jordanian Higher Court for Justice dismissed the suit arguing that the appointment of members of the board of TCC to the licensing committee did not violate the law. Regarding the boycott of Motorola, the judges pointed out that the Arab League allows for exempting telecommunications companies from boycott regulations, especially if these companies were market leaders in the sector. Therefore, the cabinet decision to grant Motorola the license should be seen as equal to an explicit exemption ruling for the company.[79]

To an outside observer, the arguments of the Higher Court seem flimsy. If the cabinet could retrospectively justify a technical flaw in the licensing process, administrative procedure is considerably weakened by political intervention. Similarly, an overlap between the members of the licensing committee and the board of the state-owned TCC (appointed by the cabinet) eliminates administrative control over the political process. Companies interested in the telecom business will therefore direct their resources to influence the politicians involved. In this regard, Fastlink may have profited from better *wasta* (personal mediation) than its competitors.[80]

The second case—the partial transfer of ownership of the JTC—reveals a similarly high degree of political interference in the process of selling JTC shares. During this process, matters of procedure overlapped with conflicting interests of rent-seeking networks.

The privatization of JTC started in 1995. Telecommunications law #15 of 1995 provided for the establishment of a Telecommunications Regulatory Commission (TRC) and the commercialization of the TCC as a first step toward privatization. In 1997, the TCC was converted into a commercial company (JTC) with a capital base of JD 250 million (around $400 million). In October 1997 the cabinet—after TCC/JTC had been evaluated by the investment companies Price Waterhouse and Merrill Lynch—decided to sell 40 percent of the shares instead of 26 percent as originally intended, and to grant JTC the second license for cellular phone services.[81] The British firm Cable and Wireless as well as the American Southern Bell Company—two global players in the telecom market—indicated their interest and finally submitted their offers.

Behind the scenes, however, discussion was still ongoing concerning whether the sale of shares to a strategic partner or an alternative public offering on local and/or international capital markets would better suit the country's needs. The group of government ministers that brought forward the strategic partner option argued that only an international telecom company could provide for up-to-date technology and sophisticated management techniques. In some cases, these reformers had close personal links to international telecom companies. For example, Nasir Lawzi, who was minister of information from 1995 to 1996, worked previously as a consultant for Siemens.[82] Jamal Sarayrah, who was minister of post and telecommunications from 1991 to 1993 and from 1995 to 1997, was a chief consultant for FLAG (Fiberoptic Link Around the Globe) Ltd., a company that runs a huge communication net to which Jordan was connected in 1999. More importantly, Sarayrah was a member of the board of the Export and Finance Bank whose investors include the son and son-in-law of Sharif Zayd Bin Shaker, prime minister in 1995 when the bank was established, and a cousin of King Hussein.[83] Other shareholders of the bank were former governors of the Central Bank and the family of Ziyad Faris, who was appointed new CBJ governor in 1996. Major investments also came from the Darwazah, Abu Jaber, Qa'war, and Nuqul business families. The Export and Finance Bank was the local partner of Merrill Lynch, the investment company that in January 1997 was selected as technical advisor for selling telecom shares. The involvement of the Export and Finance Bank suggests that, similar to the process of licensing a cellular service provider, the administrative/technical and political aspects of JTC's privatization are not properly separated.

However, the strategic partners option did not go unchallenged. Opposition parties and parts of Jordan's civil society argued that instead of transferring national assets to foreign companies, the revenues of a public offering could be used to modernize the JTC by purchasing the newest technology available on the market. In March 1998, the government's privatization policy came under heavy pressure from parliamentarians criticizing the social risks associated with privatization and the sell-out of public companies.[84] Army and security circles were also worried since the army provided parts of JTC's communication net—that is, international connections and the links to the Syrian and Iraqi nets. The most influential critic was, however, 'Ali Shukri, who as the director of royal communication and of the king's personal office was one of Jordan's most powerful men.

Shukri was in charge of a satellite–earth station and two satellite communication systems, named Hashim 1 and Hashim 2, that provided for the international communications of the royal palace (e.g., it connected the Mayo clinic, where King Hussein stayed repeatedly for cancer treatment, and Al-Hussein Medical Centre in Amman). In spring 1998, it seemed that Shukri intended to convert the satellite–earth station into a second carrier for international telecommunication services. Internet providers started to lease international connections via Hashim 1 and 2 with rates that were much cheaper than JTC's.[85] Furthermore, a private company (Trans Jordan for

International Communications) was established in June 1998 with a capital stock of JD 10 million. The main investors were the Mu'asher family, a renowned business family involved in textile and chemical industries and owners of the Jordan National Bank. According to Yusif Abu Jamus, the chairman of the Telecommunications Regulatory Commission (TRC), the company applied for a license for national and international connections and planned to serve as an umbrella for military, security, as well as royal communication needs.[86]

Yet the establishment of a second telecom company would have thwarted the whole privatization process initiated so far. In the course of the showdown between Shukri and the government, Shukri seemed to have lost the first round. The Mu'asher company was never licensed and Shukri left the palace. For his opponents there was, however, little reason to rejoice, since Shukri was appointed the new chairman of the JTC.

From his first day in office, Shukri announced his opposition to the strategic partner option.[87] The situation escalated further leading to the intervention of King Hussein to solve the dispute. Yet the meeting that took place in the United States with King Hussein, 'Ali Shukri, Jawad al-'Anani, the chief of the Royal Court, and Prime Minister Fayez Tarawneh came too late: Southern Bell withdrew its offer. Having little choice with only one contender left, the government announced the temporary halt of the privatization process on October 27, 1998.

The winner of the day was 'Ali Shukri, but when King Hussein died on February 7, 1999, Shukri lost his political mentor. The government that was formed under the new king, Abdallah, included Jamal Sarayrah, Nasir Lawzi, and Rima Khalaf, who were all known for preferring the strategic partner option. Finally, Shukri resigned on March 6, 1999. A few days later, the chairman of the TRC followed, complaining that the TRC was not an independent body as stated by law and that members of the new government were constantly interfering with his work.[88] Soon, the new government resumed privatization proceedings and issued a new tender. In November 1999 the lot was knocked down to a consortium headed by France Telecom and the Arab Bank, which had offered $508 million for the shares.

Conclusion

These examples of privatization and the case of tax reform both underline the basic argument of this research project; that the outcomes of fiscal reform processes are to a large degree shaped by powerful economic networks. I have analyzed these networks, their characteristics, and the specific ways they affect policy making within the framework of more general patterns of state–business interaction. These patterns were shaped by a fiscal structure that has been marked by the sources and channels of rent generation and allocation. Therefore, changes in this fiscal structure have led to a modification of these patterns. However, state–business interactions are not easily altered because routinized patterns shape the perception of opportunities of the actors involved and are continuously reproduced. Jordan provides for a good case where established patterns were maintained or, as was the case with processes of formal negotiation, were even revitalized under changing politico-economic conditions. Processes of formal negotiation and informal rent seeking are not limited, of course, to the two examples described here of tax reform and privatization, but take place in many other areas too; for example in the agricultural sector, in the context of investment promotion policies, and of Jordanian–Israeli joint ventures.[89] Both patterns are familiar to the Jordanian economic elite and both are effective in protecting privileges as well as manipulating policies that were often formulated by external actors such as the IMF and the World Bank.

While fiscal policy reform in Jordan has not changed the larger pattern of allocation and reallocation of privileges thus far, its experience resembles that of Egypt as discussed in chapters 2 and 3 by Wurzel and Sfakianakis in this volume: reforms have in fact fostered changes in the organization of rent generation and distribution that threatened the privileges of economic elites in both the private and the public sectors. As a result, some senior bureaucrats tried to avoid, postpone, or cushion serious policy measures. The business elite for its part joined the rest of the private sector in complaining. As the example of tax reform has shown, the interests of the economic elite in matters of reform are, to a certain extent, ambiguous. In contrast to pure distributional coalitions the privilege system of the Jordanian economic elite is linked to a highly cooperative approach. Membership in these elite networks is exclusive and goes hand in hand with high social status or, at least, the prospect of enhancing one's social status. Thus, maintaining these linkages and their exclusivity is more important than gaining partial material benefits that risk the severing of these ties. A further reason for ambiguity among the business elite is related to the presence of many Jordanian business families in different economic sectors, so that defending narrow sectoral interests is not always common. While certain policies might affect parts of the family business negatively, other parts might profit.[90] Therefore, Jordanian businessmen neither rebelled nor tried to establish pro-business parties as was the case in Morocco and Tunisia. Rather, their actions remained within the frame of a cooperative approach using familiar patterns of interaction.

However, while the persistence of rent seeking under conditions of economic and fiscal reform may not be surprising, the return of negotiation is quite an interesting phenomenon. What might play a role in this regard is that some of the political and economic constellations of the 1990s resemble the situation of the 1950s and 1960s. First, political liberalization increased the importance (and widened the room for maneuver) of civil society, parliament, and the media. Second, the topic of development has a high political priority. And third, private investments are a necessary or at least required element of development planning. Furthermore, both in the 1950s–1960s and the 1990s negotiations focused largely on medium- or long-term arrangements between the state and the business community. The establishment of joint industries in the 1950s, the co-optation of business families into economic decision-making bodies such as the Central Bank in the 1960s and the involvement of business in the design of tax policies in the 1990s was meant to establish a continuing privilege system. The business elite demands monopoly status or favorable exemptions from tax or import regulations and, in exchange, accepts or even participates in the generation of rent through monopoly enterprises and the taxation of trade (and later consumption) that is fostered by an overvalued exchange rate. Negotiation has taken place at the board meetings of major public institutions, through the representatives of the Chambers of Industry and Commerce, and at the meetings of the highly influential Jordanian Businessmen's Association, an organization that comprises most of Jordan's economic elite from the private and public sectors. Negotiation is thus a collective and formal procedure that frequently involves even the public through political parties, parliamentary discussion, and the media.

In contrast to negotiated arrangements, rent-seeking processes are normally related to single government decisions such as the granting of import licenses as well as the establishment of banks in the 1970s and 1980s and the acceptance of a bid in the process of privatization in the 1990s. Here, privileges are directly granted to certain business families and, sometimes, top politicians. Under the conditions of regime survival and omni-balancing that marked the 1990s, the palace elite resorted to this means of privilege allocation to satisfy political allies and other influential groups. Since direct financial transfers are not easy to justify, rent-seeking opportunities related to privatization and politically risky undertakings such as doing business with Israel serve as substitutes.[91] These high-level rent-seeking processes are, unsurprisingly, very informal and individual; normally they involve members of the palace elite and the top business families.

In sum, the networks that have emerged within these patterns of state–business interactions in Jordan were based on mutual cooperation and collusion. Although the membership, scope, and characteristics of these networks varied over time, they remained highly important for members of the economic elite as a means of rent generation and allocation, but also of conflict regulation and information exchange. With their exclusivity they provide also an important channel to the major political decision-makers of the palace elite. In this regard, even the networks that were based on negotiation cannot really be regarded as developmental,[92] although they certainly contributed to economic growth. State business synergies are outweighed by the negative side effects of a private sector oligarchy that works with all means at hand to prevent competition.

Fiscal policy reform as the core measure of a larger economic reform program has to take the existence and impact of these economic networks into consideration. Since bypassing them seems impossible, any serious reform attempt has to integrate the interests of these networks into the policy design. In this context, it may be advisable for policy makers to identify the patterns of state–business interaction in which these networks are embedded and to strengthen the patterns that contribute most to economic development and the aims of fiscal policy reform. In a further step, these patterns should be modified to reach the larger goal of economic reform. In Jordan, historical experience suggests that growth-oriented processes of negotiation can be strengthened by administrative reform including capacity building and the introduction of transparency regulation. Also, a strong civil society seems to be supportive.

However, a viable reorganization of fiscal policy in Jordan will require dissolving private sector oligarchies by offering alternative business opportunities and fostering a competitive system. Being a small and sparsely populated country, Jordan will have little choice but to boost its export sectors and strengthen its integration into the global economy. A considerable devaluation of the Jordanian Dinar is unavoidable. Theoretically, economic hardships associated with devaluation could be compensated by international loans and grants channeled into funds to satisfy basic needs. There is, however, little reason to believe that the European Union or the United States will assist such a politically risky undertaking. They are basically interested in keeping Jordan's monarchy stable.

Against this background, it is quite understandable that the tax system in Jordan is complex, inefficient, and difficult to administer, as I indicated in the introduction, and that privatization means little more than the transfer of public rents into the hands of a private sector oligarchy. It is a part of the fiscal policy arena that allows for formal negotiation as well as informal rent-seeking arrangements between and within economic networks. As long as the economic elite can secure its privileges through these and similar mechanisms, they will not protest. Will small manufacturers or petty traders? Probably. But is the palace or the international donor community listening?

Notes

1. George T. Abed, "Trade Liberalization and Tax Reform in the Southern Mediterranean Region" (IMF Working Paper 98/49, Washington, 1998), 11.
2. According to Bangura, privatization "contributes to fiscal stability in two main ways. First, gains can be made on the expenditure side by withdrawing subsidies to loss-making companies and imposing hard budget constraints on the economic decisions of managers.... Second, the revenue derived from selling state enterprises to the public can help governments close their fiscal gaps"; Yusuf Bangura, "Public Sector Restructuring: The Institutional and Social Effects of Fiscal, Managerial and Capacity-Building Reforms" (UNRISD Occasional Paper No. 3, Geneva, 2000), 15.
3. I define economic elites rather pragmatically as the main or leading decision-makers in the field of economic activity and regulation. For a further discussion, including of important social and economic attributes of economic elites in Jordan, see Pamela Dougherty and Oliver Wils, "Between Public and Private: Economic Elite in Jordan," in Ricardo Bocco, ed., *The Hashemite Kingdom of Jordan, 1946–1996. Social Identities, Development Policies and State-Building* (Paris: Karthala, forthcoming); Oliver Wils, "Private Sector Monopolies and Economic Reform in (Post) Rentier States. The Case of Jordan," *Asien Afrika Lateinamerika* 28, no. 4 (2000): 365–397; and Oliver Wils, *Wirtschaftseliten und Reform in Jordanien: Zur Relevanz von Unternehmer-Bürokraten-Netzwerken in Entwicklungsprozessen* (Hamburg: Deutsches Orient-Institut, 2003).
4. This definition given by Mitchell in 1969 is cited in Thomas Schweitzer, *Muster sozialer Ordnung. Netzwerkanalyse als Fundament der Sozialethnologie* (Berlin: Dietrich Reimer Verlag, 1996), 16; see also Linton C. Freemann, "Social Network Analysis: Definition and History," in A. E. Kazdan, ed., *Encyclopedia of Psychology*, vol. 6 (New York: Oxford University Press, 2000), 350–351.
5. Ira Katznelson, "Embeddedness Beyond Networks: Reflections on Sociology's New Institutionalism" (unpublished draft, 1999), 25.
6. See Dirk Messner, *Die Netzwerkgesellschaft. Wirtschaftliche Entwicklung und internationale Wettbewerbsfähigkeit als Probleme gesellschaftlicher Steuerung* (Köln: Weltforum Verlag, 1995); see also Helmut Willke, *Systemtheorie III: Steuerungstheorie* (Stuttgart/Jena: Gustav Fischer Verlag, 1995).
7. Hermina Ibarra, "Structural Alignments, Individual Strategies, and Managerial Action: Elements Toward a Network Theory of Getting Things Done," in Nitin Nohria and Robert G. Eccles, eds., *Networks and Organizations: Structure, Form, and Action* (Cambridge: Harvard Business School, 1992), 165–188.

8. For example, see J. Roger Hollingsworth, Philippe C. Schmitter, and Wolfgang Streeck, eds., *Governing Capitalist Economies: Performance and Control of Economic Sectors* (Oxford: Oxford University Press, 1994); Colin Crouch and Wolfgang Streeck, eds., *Political Economy of Modern Capitalism: Mapping Convergence and Diversity* (London: Sage Publications, 1997).

9. Sylvia Maxfield and Ben Ross Schneider, eds., *Business and the State in Developing Countries* (Ithaca: Cornell University Press, 1997). According to Maxfield and Schneider, state–business collaboration that is marked by information, transparency, credibility, reciprocity, and trust is likely to contribute positively to economic growth. Regarding the second point, they argue that state–business collaboration is affected by state characteristics as well as the nature of business associations. An insulated and Weberian bureaucracy on the one hand and business associations that are either encompassing or able to monitor and sanction the behavior of their members on the other tend to inhibit temptations for rent seeking. And finally they state with reference to their third point that the reasons for time consuming and costly state–business collaboration are related to (perceived) economic or political threats or strong incentives for the production of goods requiring close cooperation. On business associations, also see Richard F. Doner and Ben Ross Schneider, "Business Associations and Economic Development: Why Some Associations Contribute more than Others," in *Business and Politics* 2, no. 3 (2000): 261–288.

10. For an overview on the different strands of New Institutionalism, see John Harriss, Janet Hunter, and Colin M. Lewis, eds., *The New Institutional Economics and Third World Development* (London: Routledge, 1995); Paul DiMaggio, "The New Institutionalism: Avenues of Collaboration," *Journal of Institutional and Theoretical Economics* 154, no. 4 (1998): 696–705; and Geoffrey M. Hodgson, "Institutional Economics: Surveying the 'Old' and the 'New,'" *Metroeconomica* 44, no. 1 (1993): 1–28.

11. Gerhard Lehmbruch, "The Organization of Society, Administrative Strategies, and Policy Networks: Elements of a Developmental Theory of Interest Systems," in Roland M. Czada and Adrienne Windhoff-Héritier, eds., *Political Choice: Institutions, Rules, and the Limits of Rationality* (Frankfurt/Main: Campus, 1991), 127.

12. The resistance of institutionalized governance systems to change is described by Lehmbruch referring to the German health system, which, despite huge financial pressures, is only gradually and slowly adapting.

13. See Hazem Beblawi and Giacomo Luciani, eds., *The Rentier State* (London: Croom Helm, 1987); Claudia Schmid, *Das Konzept des Rentier-Staates: Ein sozialwissenschaftliches Paradigma zur Analyse von Entwicklungsgesellschaften und seine Bedeutung für den Vorderen Orient* (Münster: Lit-Verlag, 1991); and, Peter Pawelka, "Staat, Bürgertum und Rente im Vorderen Orient," *Aus Politik und Zeitgeschichte* 33 (1997): 3–11. For a more critical view, see K. A. Chaudhry, *The Price of Wealth: Economies and Institutions in the Middle East* (Ithaca: Cornell University Press, 1997).

14. See Giacomo Luciani, "The Oil Rent, the Fiscal Crisis of the State and Democratization," in Ghassan Salamé, ed., *Democracy without Democrats? The Renewal of Politics in the Muslim World* (London: I. B. Tauris, 1994), 130–155.
15. Abed, *Trade Liberalization and Tax Reform*, 22. It should be noted that, because direct taxation is very low, indirect taxation accounted for the highest share of regional tax incomes.
16. See Schmid, *Das Konzept des Rentier-Staates*.
17. Even rentier economy approaches do not take state–business interactions into consideration seriously. Laurie Brand, e.g., noticed that the state participated in the circulation of remittances through the taxation of imports. However, the resulting networks between state officials and business families were not integrated into analysis; see Laurie A. Brand, *Jordan's Inter-Arab Relations: The Political Economy of Alliance Making* (New York: Columbia University, 1994).
18. See Hartmut Elsenhans, *Abhängiger Kapitalismus oder bürokratische Entwicklungsgesellschaft: Versuch über den Staat in der Dritten Welt* (Frankfurt/Main: Campus, 1981; English version: *State, Class and Development*, New Delhi/London/Columbia, MO: Radiant, Sangam, South Asia Books, 1996).
19. See Hartmut Elsenhans, "Integrating Political Economy in the Comparative Study of Administration," in H. K. Asmeron and R. B. Jain, eds., *Politics, Administration and Public Policy in Developing Countries: Examples from America, Asia and Latin America* (Amsterdam: VU University Press, 1993), 16–36.
20. Abla M. Amawi, "The Consolidation of the Merchant Class in Transjordan during the Second World War," in Eugen L. Rogan and Tariq Tell, eds., *Village, Steppe and State: The Social Origins of Modern Jordan* (London: British Academic Press, 1994), 162–186.
21. While import duties accounted for 40% of domestic revenue in the early 1940s, they reached a peak of 73% of tax revenues in 1956.
22. Others, such as 'Abd al-Hamid Shuman, founder and chairman of the Arab Bank, managed to transfer their business to Jordan. According to the World Bank, it is estimated that JD 10 million of bank deposits were transferred and that refugees brought around the same amount of money with them, which altogether accounted for more than half of Jordan's GNP; see International Bank for Reconstruction and Development (IBRD), *The Economic Development of Jordan: Report of a Mission*, organized by the International Bank for Reconstruction and Development at the request of the government of Jordan (Baltimore: John Hopkins Press, 1957), 45.
23. By 1954 more than half of the refugee workforce was still unemployed and a considerable part of the other half, as well as the local population, had only seasonal or casual employment; see IBRD, "The Economic Development of Jordan," 5.
24. Prominent figures among these young nationalists such as Hamad al-Farhan, Wasfi al-Tall and Khalil al-Salim had been classmates at the secondary school in Salt and, in the 1940s, studied together at the American University in Beirut.

25. See Robert B. Satloff, *From Abdullah to Hussein: Jordan in Transition* (Oxford: Oxford University Press, 1994). Initially, the palace elite consisted mainly of the Hashemite family, some loyal Palestinians (such as Tawfiq Abu al-Huda and Samir al-Rifaʻi), and some co-opted tribal and minority group leaders (e.g., Christians and Circassians). The Jordanian/Bedouin element of the palace elite, although often referred to as the backbone of Hashemite rule, emerged only gradually; see Shmuel Bar, "The Jordanian Elite—Change and Continuity," in Asher Susser and Aryeh Shmuelewitz, eds., *The Hashemites in the Modern Arab World* (London: Frank Cass, 1995), 221–228; and Tariq Tell, "Les origines sociales de la glasnost jordanienne," in R. Bocco and M. R. Djalili, eds., *Moyen-Orient: Migrations, démocratisation et médiations* (Paris/Geneva: PFUF/IUEHEI, 1994).

26. Betty Anderson, "Jordanian Political Parties of the 1950s: Social Transformation and the Dynamic Role of Nationalist Ideology," in R. Bocco, ed., *The Hashemite Kingdom of Jordan, 1946–1996: Social Identities, Development Policies and State-Building* (Paris: Karthala, forthcoming).

27. Satloff, *From Abdullah to Hussein*.

28. Paul Kingston, "Breaking the Patterns of Mandate. Economic Nationalism and State Formation in Jordan, 1951–57," in Rogan and Tell, *Village, Steppe and State*, 187–216.

29. At the same time the amount of state expenditure earmarked for development rose from JD 2.76 million (or 16% of the total) in 1955 to JD 11.27 million (24% of total) in 1965.

30. Cooperation with foreign development agencies was important since they had built up a parallel administrative infrastructure (Great Britain with the Jordan Development Board, the United States with the cooperative departments); see Paul Kingston, "Failing to Tip the Balance: Foreign Aid and Economic Reform in Jordan, 1958–1967" (unpublished manuscript, 1999).

31. In 1962, al-Tall purged some 200 bureaucrats and transferred more than 400 others who were charged for corruption; see Paul Kingston, "Failing to Tip the Balance," in Asher Susser, *On Both Banks of the Jordan: A Political Biography of Wasfi Al Tall* (London: Frank Cass, 1994).

32. Muraywid al-Tall (former economist at the Ministry of National Economy) interviewed in Amman, May 19, 1998 and Hamad al-Farhan (former undersecretary at the Ministry of National Economy) interviewed in Amman, May 27, 1998.

33. The concessions were very favorable for business. Concerning the Jordanian Cement Factories Company, a World Bank mission voiced its criticism in 1957: "While agreeing that special legislation is preferable, the mission seriously questions whether industrial concessions of this kind are really in the interest of Jordan's economy.... The degree of security given to its shareholders ... is so excessive as to give rise to a distorted notion of what should be considered reasonable risk bearing in industrial ventures," IBRD, *The Economic Development of Jordan*, 244.

34. According to official figures, the cement factory contributed JD 1.5 million to the state in 1966–1967, and the refinery more than JD 3.3 million in 1968; see al-Qita' al-Sina'i (Amman: Ministry of Culture and Information, 1969), 19, 27. In 1968, total domestic revenue stood at JD 26.3 million.

35. E. Kanovsky, *The Economy of Jordan: The Implications of Peace in the Middle East* (Tel Aviv: University Publishing Projects, 1976), 7.

36. Examples are the Jordanian Cloth Manufacturing Company (1962), the Arab Pharmaceutical Manufacturing Company (1964), and the Jordan Paper and Cardboard Factories Company (1965).

37. Dougherty and Wils, "Between Public and Private."

38. See Schirin H. Fathi, *Jordan—An Invented Nation? Tribe-State Dynamics and the Formation of National Identity* (Hamburg: Deutsches Orient-Institut, 1994).

39. Central Bank of Jordan, *Special Issue on the Occasion of the Fifteenth Anniversary of the HKJ Independence: Yearly Statistical Series, 1964–1995* (Amman: CBJ, 1996).

40. Furthermore, the nationalist movement in Jordan lost one of its key figures in 1971, when the Prime Minister Wasfi al-Tall was assassinated.

41. According to the former governor of the CBJ, Muhammad Sa'id al-Nabulsi, it was the initiative of Crown Prince Hassan to select some economists in 1972 to formulate the three-year development plan from 1973 to 1975; Interview with al-Nabulsi, Amman, June 8, 1998.

42. Initially, expansion of the public sector came in response to the adverse effects of soaring oil prices. Inflation skyrocketed because of higher import prices and an increased money supply. This was accompanied by exploding land prices caused by speculation and, after 1975, the arrival of tens of thousands of Lebanese refugees fleeing the civil war. In some sections of Amman, land prices rose by as much as 1,000% in the span of one year. See Jawad Anani, "Adjustment and Development: The Case of Jordan," in *Adjustment Policies and Development Strategies in the Arab World*, Said El-Naggar, ed., 131 (Washington DC: International Monetary Fund, 1987). In order to counterbalance the effects of inflation on the purchasing power of wages, the Ministry of Supply was established in 1974 and was given a monopoly over the import of basic foodstuffs and responsibility for setting the prices of other items. In 1975 the Civil Consumer Corporation was established to provide civil servants with goods at cost price. At the same time, the state began to expand its role through the provision of basic infrastructure and services, housing, and employment.

43. Timothy J. Piro, *The Political Economy of Market Reform in Jordan* (Lanham: Rowman and Littlefield, 1998), 66–67.

44. As Brand has held, "if the prime minister wanted something done quickly or something done that was officially illegal, he could refer it to the committee. The committee also made decisions about liquidating companies, borrowing to the ceiling of the Central Bank and then legalizing more borrowing, allowing the Central Bank to deposit with other banks to support the currency, issuing more currency than had been permitted, evicting people from commercial establishments,

and allowing someone who would otherwise have been forbidden, to sit on the board of directors of a company," Brand, *Jordan's Inter-Arab Relations*, 67–68.

45. Marius Haas, *Husseins Königreich: Jordaniens Stellung im Nahen Osten* (München: Tuduv, 1975).

46. Piro, *The Political Economy of Market Reform in Jordan*, 52–53.

47. State expenditure rose nearly six-fold within ten years from JD 120 million in 1973 to JD 705 million in 1983.

48. Frank Czichowski, *Jordanien: Internationale Migration, wirtschaftliche Entwicklung und soziale Stabilität* (Hamburg: Deutsches Orient-Institut, 1990).

49. Michel Chatelus, "Rentier or Producer Economy in the Middle East? The Jordanian Response," in Adnan Badran and Bichara Khader, eds., *The Economic Development of Jordan* (London: Croom Helm, 1987), 214.

50. See Wils, *Wirtschaftseliten und Reform in Jordanien*.

51. In this essay, no particular attention is being paid to the Jordanian-Palestinian question. Yet it is often assumed that there is high tension between a bureaucracy staffed by (Trans-) Jordanians and a private sector dominated by Palestinians. These tensions do certainly exist. Within the Jordanian economic elites, however, this question does not seem to play a major role. Most big businessmen would consider family background, social status, and rootedness in Amman's power networks as more important factors than regional background. Regarding the economic elites of the public sector, Palestinians and (Trans-) Jordanians are both to be found in high administrative offices dealing with the economy.

52. Dougherty and Wils, "Between Public and Private."

53. Rodney Wilson, "The Role of Commercial Banking in the Jordanian Economy," in Adnan Badran and Bichara Khader, eds., *The Economic Development of Jordan* (London: Croom Helm, 1987), 48.

54. 'Abdallah al-Maliki, *Al-mawsu'a fi tarikh al-jihaz al-masrafi al-urdunni*, vol. 1, *Al-bank al-markazi al-urdunni wa al-siyasa al-naqdiyya* (Amman: Al-urdunniyya li-l-tasmim wa al-taba'a, 1996), 138.

55. Wils, *Wirtschaftseliten und Reform in Jordanien*.

56. State revenues through custom duties rose by a factor of 10 from JD 12 million in 1973 to JD 121 million in 1983, whereas total state revenues rose by a factor of 6.5 from JD 103 million in 1973 to JD 674 million ten years later; see CBJ, *Special Issue on the Occasion of the Fifteenth Anniversary of the HKJ Independence*, 22.

57. Dougherty and Wils, "Between Public and Private."

58. Edouard Maciejewski and Ahsan Mansur, eds., "Jordan: Strategy for Adjustment and Growth," IMF Occasional Paper 136 (Washington DC: International Monetary Fund, 1996); Pamela Dougherty, "The Pain of Adjustment—Kerak's Bread Riots as a Response to Jordan's Continuing Economic Restructuring Programme: A General Overview," *Jordanies* 2 (1996): 95–99.

59. Fahid al-Fanik, Barnamaj al-tashih al-iqtisadi, *1992–1998: ahdaf wa mubararat barnamaj al-in'ash wa al-tashih li-l-iqtisad al-urdunni al-muttafiq 'alayha sunduq al-naqd al-duwali* (Amman: Mu'assasa Fahid al-Fanik, 1992), 46–48.

60. Revenues increased considerably from 1989 to 1995 as a result of the introduction of a consumption tax and, in 1994, a sales tax (from JD 78 million to JD 264 million), the raising of fees, and the doubling of imports with still high custom duties. In addition, the rates for government services have been raised, e.g., in the telecommunication sector (from approximately JD 60 million to JD 150 million); figures are presented by the CBJ Annual Reports (various issues).

61. Wils, *Wirtschaftseliten und Reform in Jordanien*, 145–146.

62. Oliver Wils, "Foreign Aid Since 1989 and Its Impact on Jordan's Political Economy: Some Research Questions," in *Jordanies* 5/6 (June–December, 1998): 100–120.

63. Katja Hermann, *Aufbruch von Unten. Möglichkeiten und Grenzen von NGOs in Jordanien* (Hamburg: Lit, 2000).

64. The social unrest took place in the southern parts of the country where poverty is above average.

65. Renate Dieterich, *Transformation oder Stagnation? Die jordanische Demokratisierungspolitik seit 1989* (Hamburg: Deutsches Orient-Institut, 1999); Laurie A. Brand, "The Effects of the Peace Process on Political Liberalization in Jordan," *Journal of Palestine Studies* 28, no. 2 (1999): 52–57.

66. Jordan's growth rates had been related to the fact that in the wake of some 300,000 returnees from the Gulf in 1991 the Jordanian economy witnessed a boom in construction and investments. After concluding a peace treaty with Israel in 1994, Jordan received new development aid accompanied by further debt rescheduling and substantial debt forgiveness.

67. See *Middle East Economic Digest*, June 26, 1998.

68. CBJ, Monthly Statistics, March 1999.

69. Amman Chamber of Industry (ACI), *Taqrir majlis al-idara li-'am 1992* (Amman: ACI, 1993).

70. Pete W. Moore, "Business Associations, Politics, and Economics in Jordan," paper presented at the annual MESA conference, Chicago (1998).

71. For more details see Wils, *Wirtschaftseliten und Reform in Jordanien*.

72. The ACC was established in 1923 and is the largest private sector organization with membership exceeding 30,000 in 1995. Although the ACC was throughout its history dominated by members of the business elite, in 1994 Haydar Murad, who was not a member of the established elite, was elected president. Moore explains this leadership change with reference to the basic law of the ACC, which gives every member the same voting rights, whether it is a big business bank or a small vegetable trader. In contrast, voting in the ACI depends on a certain company size. As a result, however, the ACC has lost in importance and is weakened by internal struggle; see Pete W. Moore, "Business Associations, Politics, and Economics in Jordan," paper presented at the annual MESA conference, Chicago, 1998.

73. Ibid., 23.

74. See Amman Chamber of Industry (ACI), *Taqrir majlis al-idara li-'am 1995* (Amman: ACI, 1996). It took quite some time until this agreement was put into practice. The ACI has demanded repeatedly to realize the tax exemptions with

little success. Then in May 1998, it used the opportunity to lobby directly to King Hussein when he honored 99 founders and pioneers of the Jordanian industry (*Rawad wa bunat al-sina' al-urdunniyya*). Some weeks later, tax exemptions were realized, and new goods were added to the list of items that fell under the sales tax.

75. See Jean-Christophe Augé, "Das jordanische Hochschulwesen zwischen staatlichem Aufbau und Privatisierung," *INAMO* 14 (1998): 14–17.
76. Wils, *Wirtschaftseliten und Reform in Jordanien*, 192.
77. In 1999, Fastlink contributed $12 million to the treasury.
78. National Telecommunications Co. (*al-sharika al-ahliyya li-l-ittisalat*) cooperating with the U.S.-company Millicom.
79. See Wils, *Wirtschaftseliten und Reform in Jordanien*.
80. It is worth noting that the official representative of Fastlink, 'Umar al-Nabulsi, and the chairman of the licensing committee, 'Ali al-Nusur, were close acquaintances, knowing each other from the Arab Potash Company and the cabinets of 'Abd al-Hamid Sharaf and Qasim al-Rimawi (1979–1980). Probably more important was the fact that the prime minister at the time of licensing was 'Abd al-Salam al-Majali, the brother of 'Abd al-Hadi al-Majali, one of Fastlink's main shareholders.
81. *Jordan Times*, October 19 and 21, 1997.
82. Personal communication with Siemens officials, Amman, March 1999.
83. The son-in-law of Sharif Zayd Bin Shaker is 'Ali al-Husri, the nephew of the renowned Arab nationalist Sati' al-Husri.
84. *Jordan Times*, March 29, 1998.
85. *Jordan Times*, August 8, 1998.
86. *Arab Daily*, March 13, 1999; personal communication, Amman, March 6, 1999.
87. See Wils, *Wirtschaftseliten und Reform in Jordanien*, 198–200.
88. *Arab Daily*, March 13, 1999.
89. For more details see Wils, *Wirtschaftseliten und Reform in Jordanien*.
90. The Tabba' family offers a good example for a highly diversified and intersectoral family business. The Tabba' Group of companies (annual turnover in 1995: $250 million) consists of the Al-Tewfik Automobile and Equipment Co. that was established in 1941 and is managed by Hamdi S. Tabba'; Jordan Flour Mills, established in 1945 and managed by Bander S. Tabba'; Arab Traders Inc., established in 1976 and managed by 'Abd al-Ilah Tabba'; Abdallah Tabbaa Maintenance and Contracting Establishment, established in 1986 and managed by Abdallah Tabba'; Tabbaa and Associates Marketing Consultants, established in 1992 and managed by Mustafa Tabba'; and Modern Information Systems Design, established in 1994; see Wils, *Wirtschaftseliten und Reform in Jordanien*, 164.
91. The most outstanding example of a Jordanian company that is involved in joint ventures with Israeli and international companies is the Century Investment Group, founded in 1995. After three years, Century employed more than 2,000 people and was active in the textile, food processing, electronic, and software

sectors. Century was also the major force behind the preferential trade agreement with the United States. Goods produced in Irbid's "qualifying industrial zone" (i.e., Century's area) with Israeli components will get unrestricted and tax free entry into the U.S. market. Major shareholders of Century include the Salah family, public institutions, and members of the palace elite. According to Century's chairman, the inclusion of the Majali and Rifa'i families should guarantee that they are not against the project; interview with Omar Salah, chairman of Century Investment Group, Amman, March 8, 1998.

92. The term "developmental" is used in the sense of Maxfield and Schneider, *Business and State in Developing Countries.*

PART 2

Fiscality, Economic Reform, and the Role of Networks

CHAPTER 5

Nobody Having too Much to Answer for: Laissez-Faire, Networks, and Postwar Reconstruction in Lebanon

Reinoud Leenders

When typhus and cholera breaks out, they tell us that Nobody is to blame. That terrible Nobody! How much he has to answer for! More mischief is done by Nobody than by all the world besides. [...] Nobody has a theory, too—a dreadful theory. It is embodied in two words: Laissez-faire—Let alone. Samuel Smiles, *Thrift* (Chicago: 1889), 358–359, cited in H. Scott Gordon (1971).

L ebanon has long been considered a rare exception to the state *dirigisme* and plan economies prevailing in its neighboring countries and, indeed, the developing world at large. While other countries resorted to inefficient state enterprise, fixed multiple exchange rates, marketing boards, and consumer subsidy schemes, Lebanon appeared to enjoy the fruits of an open and liberal economy characterized by consistent surpluses on its balance of payments, no public debt to speak of, and steady economic growth. Indeed, between 1950 and 1974 national income against constant prices is estimated to have risen by 617 percent, or an average of more than 8 percent per year—unusually high for a Middle Eastern country lacking oil resources.[1] Especially between 1970 and 1974 growth of GDP skyrocketed. With an average growth rate of 16 percent per year in this period, Lebanon seemed to have consolidated its role as financial entrepot for the region, absorbing large inflows of foreign currencies from the Gulf countries. In the process, relatively high living standards were achieved, as illustrated by high literacy rates, high life expectancy, and high levels of consumption and education.[2] Even during the Lebanese wars (1975–1990), the country's economy continued to outperform most of its non–oil producing Arab neighbors, leaving one Lebanese economist to describe the country's "credo of laissez-faire" as so deeply engrained that no warlord—no matter how "socialist" in outlook—would think of touching it.[3]

Unsurprisingly, this inclination to laissez-faire (al-siyasa al-yad al-marfu'a) also had its discontents. These critics maintained that Lebanon's minimalist state caused wide socioeconomic disparities and a neglect of the country's productive sectors. Generally, however, even such skeptics subscribed to the view that Lebanon's political economy could be best captured by the notion of laissez-faire. The debate, in other words, was predominantly phrased in terms of the perceived benefits and ills of laissez-faire versus those of state intervention, without questioning the validity or exact ramifications of such notions in Lebanon let alone in the study of political economy at large.

In the early 1990s, after Lebanon finally turned its back on more than 15 years of war and destruction, there was little effort to revaluate common understandings of the country's economic history. In fact, Lebanon's long tradition of laissez-faire has been persistently regarded as a favorable condition for postwar economic recovery. Whereas most neighboring countries still needed to go through painful reforms away from statism, policy makers and international financial organizations saw Lebanon as being one important step ahead by virtue of its thriving private sector and liberal state policies. For example, the World Bank concluded with satisfaction in a survey in 1995: "Lebanon has always been an economy dominated by the private sector. Unlike most of its neighbors, Lebanon never flirted with statism and the country was renowned for its laissez-faire policies, its minimalist state, and its entrepreneurial tradition."[4]

This strategy served Lebanon well. Most Lebanese policy-makers and political actors shared this view, even to the extent that the country's commitment to laissez-faire received explicit mention in the 1989 Ta'if Peace Accord and the preamble of the postwar amended Constitution.[5] Subsequently, postwar reconstruction plans and government policy statements celebrated laissez-faire as the economy's only hope for private-led recovery and a return of Lebanese assets placed abroad during the war years. Especially when one major exponent of Lebanon's legendary entrepreneurship, business tycoon Rafiq al-Hariri, formed his first government in November 1992, Lebanese and international commentators alike were confident that the country would be neatly in line with the Washington consensus and soon reap the fruits of private-led growth.

Roughly ten years into Lebanon's reconstruction program, actual outcomes could not have been more at odds with expectations. From 1996 onward, growth has stagnated, leading to a fall in per capita real GDP. According to the IMF, the Lebanese economy is currently characterized by "very large and persistent macroeconomic imbalances, the loss of competitiveness, and structural and administrative impediments."[6] Interestingly, the IMF now lists a range of economic ills that previously only befell the planned economies of neighboring countries. Thus Lebanon suffers from soaring public debt ratios and budget deficits, slackening (foreign) private investment, high costs of doing business, and government reluctance to implement swift reforms and structural adjustment. Privatization and the introduction of VAT are way behind schedule and, in fact, achievements in these fields pale in comparison to other countries in the region such as Egypt, Morocco, and Tunisia. Curiously, however, the current and prolonged economic malaise has failed to persuade Lebanon's advocates and critics of laissez-faire to reconsider their original characterizations of the Lebanese economy. If Lebanon was initially considered a prime example of free market enterprise in the developing world, why then did it end up being crippled by the very structural and macroeconomic imbalances from which the economy was supposed to be immune?

In this essay, I suggest an explanation that hinges heavily on the notion of networks as a qualitative alternative to pure markets and state intervention in organizing and determining economic activity. In doing so, I first identify entrepreneurs' perceptions of Lebanon's market accessibility and state–business relations based on opinion surveys and unstructured interviews with Lebanese business elites. I subsequently discuss the relevance and meaning of networks in the Lebanese context and identify the ways such networks emerged and became embedded in Lebanon's postwar political settlement. While acknowledging that most if not all hierarchical organizations should be seen as evolving around networks, this chapter argues that the exact nature of how networks operate and relate to state actors determines whether they contribute to or impede economic performance. Via this approach, I hope to introduce the notion of networks into the Lebanese debate on laissez-faire and statism for the purpose of explaining the seemingly anomalous outcomes of this country's postwar reconstruction program. Finally, I discuss the chapter's findings in the light of prevailing understandings of how and under what circumstances networks can be functional or dysfunctional in terms of economic performance.

Laissez-Faire Without Markets

Though rejected by some as the pipedream of sterile theoreticians, criticized by others for neglecting political or social underpinnings and institutional ramifications, or outright dismissed as a narrowly construed and Eurocentric conception of capitalism, the "market" continues to be the dominant starting point for understandings of economic behavior and conventional explanations of economic outcomes. Of course, no brief discussion can do justice to the overwhelming amount of study that has been devoted to the notion of the market as the guiding principle of neoclassical economic thought. But stripped to its very essence, the notion conceives of economic action as a meeting place of isolated buyers and sellers wherein prices form the only criterion for a transaction and purely economic competition generates efficient outcomes. Accordingly, neoclassical theory conceives of markets as "a spontaneous coordination mechanism that imparts rationality and consistency to the self-interested actions of individuals and firms."[7] As such, access is guaranteed to all utilitarian players who wish to enter the market irrespective of their social affiliations, and neither restrained or advantaged by third parties including the state. Hence, the market presupposes "an atomized, *under*socialized conception of human action"[8] while assuming a minimal role for the state to give free course to the forces of supply and demand. Within this context and phrased in its ideal-typical version, neoclassical theory advocates a "doctrine of laissez-faire" as being "the perfection of the competitive system; the harmony of interests that reigns within a society so organized; the illegitimacy and perverse consequences of governmental interference."[9] Let us assume at this stage—however unrealistically—that this conceptualization of the market indeed captures the essence of how capitalist societies operate. How, then, does this case study of laissez-faire in Lebanon fit in? By applying equally broad standards while taking into account that the real world always deviates from the ideal, do economic realities in Lebanon show even a remote resemblance to the market?

As already hinted at here, the Lebanese debate on laissez-faire never formulated the question as such. All it postulated is that Lebanon never witnessed the kind and the magnitude of state interventions experienced by most neighboring countries. Conventional arguments in this respect stress that Lebanon has sustained relatively free exchange and interest rates, witnessed few government-imposed restrictions on domestic and foreign trade, and created very few state monopolies, whereas the state generally respected private property rights and refrained from subsidizing or otherwise manipulating credit and consumer prices.[10] Some celebrated these characteristics as Lebanon's comparative advantage in the region, often by drawing on the ideas of Michel Chiha (1891–1954), a Catholic banker and prominent constitutional lawyer who regarded laissez-faire as both an economic imperative for the country's open and trade-based economy and as a major ingredient of Lebanon's national identity.[11] In contrast, others saw in laissez-faire a major source of society's inequalities, a cause of its lopsided development solely based on "financial-mercantile capital," a source of its regional and sectarian tensions, and even as having contributed to the civil strife culminating in the wars of the 1970s and 1980s.[12] But despite their disagreements regarding the desirability of laissez-faire, both its advocates and its critics argued that, to a large extent, the country's tradition in minimal state intervention has continued to characterize major policy domains in the 1990s.

First, regarding fiscal policies, income and corporate taxes continued to be extremely low by international standards. In fact, a major tax reform in 1993 was directed at attracting capital held by Lebanese expatriates via a reduction in nominal tax rates on corporate profits from 26 percent to a very low 10 percent. Traders based in the country's two free zones enjoyed a 10-year tax holiday. On top of this, a law was adopted in 2000 that exempts companies from paying any taxes if they base themselves in south Lebanon. Also the top marginal rates of individual income taxes were set at 10 percent; down from 32 percent. Partly as a result, in the 1990s direct tax revenues averaged only 2 percent of GDP.[13] Characteristic of Lebanon's outward orientation, nominal tariff rates rank among the lowest in the region. Average tariffs are merely 10 percent and very few trade items are subjected to formal restrictions. Lebanon's industrial Effective Rates of Protection (ERPs)—which measure price effects of trade restrictions regarding locally produced goods— are on average only 22 percent significantly lower than Jordan's 50 percent and Egypt's 70 percent.[14]

Second, Lebanon's monetary policies suggest a generally liberal regime. Since 1992, the Lebanese pound has been nominally anchored to the U.S. dollar and is allowed to float freely within a bandwidth defended by the Central Bank.[15] Market interventions are rare and limited to correcting fluctuations caused by political crises rather than economic or financial developments. The Central Bank made it clear that its support is not without limits as illustrated by its refusal in March 1992 to continue delving into its foreign reserves in order to boost the pound. Lebanon does not apply multiple exchange rates, as for example in Syria, and its currency can be freely traded both domestically and internationally. No official restrictions apply to movements of capital in or out of the country.[16]

Moreover, and in sharp contrast to its neighbors, Lebanon has never witnessed much state enterprise except for some public utilities (water, electricity, transport, and communications) and a few companies belonging to the Intra Investment Company, which was taken over by the state following its bankruptcy in 1967. In fact, the war years caused the de facto privatization of many state-run facilities due to the collapse of public institutions or serious damage to their assets. Thus, private generators began to supply electricity both for households and firms, a state-held monopoly on postal services was broken by the mushrooming of private couriers, and telephone connections to the outside world were similarly provided by private companies. In the oil and energy sector, private distributors began arranging their own imports with little or no interference by the Ministry of Industry, which formally enjoyed the exclusive rights to such operations.[17] Private clinics and hospitals replaced the faltering public health care system, which suffered from excess demand, bombings, and looting.[18] Services formerly provided by the state including garbage collection, street cleaning, and repairs on municipal roads and other public infrastructure were, beginning in 1977, mostly taken over by private companies associated with specially created authorities set up by political groupings and their militias.[19]

This trend toward further state disengagement has continued after the war. In its postwar reconstruction program, the state increasingly resorted to schemes wherein certain state assets or functions were leased, contracted out, or otherwise delegated to the private sector. The most frequent strategy in this respect has been to grant private companies Build-Operate-and-Transfer (BOT) or Operate-and-Transfer (OT) contracts in areas including postal services, oil imports, GSM networks, airport and port facilities, and waste collection.[20] Also the building of public infrastructure has in some cases been left to the private sector via complex contracting schemes, most notably in the Beirut Central District where a private shareholding company, Solidère, carried out and financed infrastructure works on behalf of the state in return for the right to own and exploit landfills in the area.

In line with these developments, postwar governments envisaged a dominant role for the private sector in the country's reconstruction program. Horizon 2000, the government's 1993 targeting plan, foresaw total private investments to reach levels twice as high as public investments, or nearly $42 billion for the period 1993–2002, based on historical data suggesting that the private sector traditionally accounted for 85 percent of GDP.[21] Since 1992, the state's share in total capital expenditures has risen sharply but the private sector still accounts for 80 percent of GDP, 95 percent of domestic investment, and 92 percent of consumption.[22]

To a large degree, therefore, the term laissez-faire seems to capture the Lebanese state's role reasonably well whereas in some areas the state has even further disengaged itself from playing an active role in the economy. But what about Lebanon's markets? Does the minimal state in Lebanon imply that the free forces of demand and supply determine economic outcomes as the perfection of the competitive system, as neoclassical theory suggests?

It was in fact this question that was put to Lebanese and foreign businessmen in several surveys conducted in Lebanon's postwar era. When asked about which factors they held responsible for their failures and/or successes in business, entrepreneurs very rarely pointed at market dynamics in the pure sense. Thus, a 1995 World Bank survey among entrepreneurs operating in various sectors revealed that market participants were much less troubled by market factors such as "domestic competition," "foreign competition," or "lack of demand."[23] Instead, this survey indicated a high cost business environment due to erratic government policies, corruption, complex procedures, and delays on customs as well as a stifling state bureaucracy at both central and municipal levels. Similarly, a 1999 cross-sector survey of businessmen's views cited factors like "corruption," "government procedures," and "informal competition" to be the biggest obstacles to doing business in Lebanon.[24] Again, market factors like "weak demand," "scarcity of technical workers," and "costs of labor" were much less frequently mentioned as major bottlenecks to business.

Neither did Lebanon's reputation of laissez-faire convince foreign investors of the country's hospitable and accessible markets. Indeed, despite its reputation as the region's champion of economic openness and laissez-faire, in the 1990s Lebanon attracted very small flows of foreign direct investment (FDI). Measured as a percentage of GDP, FDI in Lebanon was among the lowest in the region; much lower than Egypt or even Syria.[25] A survey of foreign businessmen operating in Lebanon by the UN's Economic and Social Council for West Asia (ESCWA) found that corruption, lack of transparency, slow customs procedures, and inconsistent economic policies are among the main factors discouraging investors from doing business in Lebanon.[26] In a similar survey conducted by the U.S. Foreign Policy Council, Arab traders indicated that Lebanese customs were as costly to their business as the notoriously antiquated and elaborate customs regime in Syria.[27] Again, contrary to what enthusiasts of Lebanon's laissez-faire postulate, entrepreneurs all over the region found Lebanon a difficult country to export to due to costly and complicated procedures in customs and the state administration generally.

Such negative perceptions partly account for Lebanon's disappointingly low ranking by Arab entrepreneurs of the region's leading site for FDI; Lebanon stands at number four, after Saudi-Arabia, the United Arab Emirates, and Egypt. But the 1995 World Bank survey is even clearer when it explored the reasons for the great reluctance among Lebanese expatriates to set up their business in Lebanon:

> [T]here is a perception in the expatriate community that corruption has become institutionalized in networks of protection, beyond the law, for self-dealing, bribes, and the bartering of favors and influence. These potential investors argue that so long as this [continues], the rules of factional and familial fealty will dictate economic entry and determine success. Consequently, many in the expatriate community state they will take investment risk only to the extent they can know and control events and actors, without reliance on legal recourse and national institutions.[28]

Several Lebanese businessmen who had nevertheless returned to Lebanon expressed similar frustrations to the author while showing awareness of the apparent contradiction between their experiences and Lebanon's overall reputation. One Lebanese representative of a major foreign company active in Lebanon said: "Some may say that Lebanon has a wonderful tradition in laissez-faire and respecting liberal values, but most of my days are wasted on dealing with inefficient state bureaucrats and port officials, negotiating with ministers or their delegates, and on the never-ending struggle to obtain the right licenses and approvals." Hence, Lebanon may be classified as a laissez-faire economy with reference to the minimal role played by the state, but this by no means implied that the free forces of demand and supply were given free reign. In order to understand the ways in which access to markets has been restricted and regulated, we will have to focus on the role of networks in enabling and confining economic activity.

Networks and Lebanon's Postwar Political Settlement

Renewed interest in the role of networks of social relations has largely resulted from a growing unease about neoclassical conceptualizations of economic life as autonomous from social structures and relations. Economic activity, it is argued, should be seen as constrained and enabled by social relations among economic agents engaged in reciprocal, preferential, and mutually supportive actions. In a sense, therefore, network approaches go beyond the neoclassical realm of universalistic rules of economic exchange and enter the much murkier domain of social ties between agents.[29] Naturally, this appreciation of particularism makes it much harder to generalize about patterns of economic exchange.[30] Such is already apparent from the literature's vagueness or elusiveness regarding the exact meaning of networks. .

One often cited definition, for example, describes networks as "a specific set of linkages among a defined set of persons, with the additional property that the characteristics of these linkages as a whole may be used to interpret the social behavior of the persons involved."[31] Formulated as such, the notion of network risks becoming a residual category wherein some sort of false coherence is attributed to all factors left unexplained or ignored by neoclassical theory. To make matters even more confusing, wide disagreement exists on the question of how social networks relate to types of "formal" organization. For example, Nohria and her contributors postulate that *all* types of formal organization should be understood as social networks and be studied accordingly.[32] Powell, on the other hand, conceives of networks as distinctively different from and presenting an alternative to markets and hierarchies.[33] I do not attempt to resolve these daunting methodological issues here. Instead, I provisionally regard networks as "intricate, multifaceted, durable relationships in which horizontal forms of exchange are paramount."[34] Furthermore, I argue that the ways in which networks relate to formal organizations in general and state institutions in particular are not *a priori* given or a matter of definitional interest, but that these linkages depend on the reasons and nature of their existence. In fact, we believe that such linkages may provide some important clues as to whether networks can be conducive for or act as an impediment to economic performance.

The notion of networks as informal relations between businessmen and politicians and their lubricating effect on economic transactions is a recurring theme in Lebanon's popular discourse on postwar reconstruction. We have already seen from the surveys of expatriate Lebanese entrepreneurs that networks are generally perceived as a predominant fact of economic life. In a similar fashion, Lebanese from different economic backgrounds refer to the importance of informal contacts when asked about their conception of Lebanese politics and business. They stress the role of *wasta* (personal connections) in achieving both political and entrepreneurial goals and allude to the general tendency of wheeling and dealing *à la Libanaise* to facilitate sweetheart deals among befriended or connected businessmen and politicians.[35] And, indeed, even a casual look at the sectors that have been particularly active under conditions of postwar reconstruction suggests that economic life is predominantly based on particularistic relations rather than universalistic rules such as those of bureaucratic organization and market competition.

Thus, a list of contractors in state-financed road construction reads like an inventory of the country's political elites and their associates or relatives, thereby strongly suggesting that personal connections rather than pure merit or competitive advantage determine the chance to obtain contracts. In fact, the state's financial watchdog, the Court of Accounts, revealed that most public procurements were based on informal arrangements between ministers, bureaucrats, and affiliated entrepreneurs, in violation of legal tendering procedures.[36]

The government's BOT contracts followed a similar pattern. For instance, the terms of two GSM contracts granted to private operators in 1994 are widely believed to have been molded to serve the interests of Prime Minister Rafiq al-Hariri, Defence Minister Muhsin Dallul, and Syrian Vice President Abd al-Halim Khaddam after each of them obtained a controlling share in these companies.[37] Likewise, one joint venture received a highly lucrative contract to build and operate Beirut Airport's duty free shopping zone amidst allegations that one of the company's principal owners had obtained far-reaching concessions due to his business links with Hariri whereas other companies were allegedly not offered an opportunity to present their bids.[38]

Yet another example relates to the country's oil imports. Here also strong links exist between importing business actors and politicians—both in terms of ownership patterns and via strong alliances between entrepreneurs and politicians, or both. In fact, the importance of *wasta* was blatantly illustrated here when, in 1997, two importers who failed to secure such ties were effectively pushed out of business.[39]

The lucrative quarrying business has also been characterized by complex networks linking politicians with entrepreneurs and law enforcement officials.[40] Such ties were crucial in allowing some individual quarries, mainly in Mount Lebanon, to continue operating despite calls for their closure on environmental or public health grounds. In the process, vast profits were made as quarried materials were used in the building hub of Beirut and its immediate surroundings. Others who did not enjoy such ties saw themselves either excluded from the business or suffered from declining terms of trade as a result of the strong political backing enjoyed by their business rivals.

No list of examples can be exhaustive, especially because network-based business practices seem to have been prevalent in all domains of economic activity. In fact, the pervasiveness of networks is so compelling that actors *expect* networks to govern relations within institutions regardless of whether organizational blueprints project forms of bureaucratic organization or not.[41]

Of course, one could argue that even in advanced capitalist societies social networks play a crucial role in what only superficially appears as pure market relations based on universalistic and impersonal criteria of supply and demand. As Granovetter cautions, there is a risk of just noting the importance of networks in "other countries" (i.e., non-Western societies) and highlighting supposedly different cultural peculiarities as overriding explanations.[42]

In Lebanon, this risk is imminent because culturalist dispositions on how society and the economy are organized are particularly dominant, especially among politicians and business actors who are asked to express their views to a Western researcher. Thus, most politicians and businessmen interviewed by this author emphasized cultural factors in their explanations of "Lebanese wheeling and dealing," the admiration of "cunning" (*shatara*) in business and politics, and the importance of networking in contrast with Western values of business and governance.[43]

However, the phenomenon appears much less enigmatic when we place the emergence and operation of social networks firmly in their political and institutional context. By doing so, we will be able both to offer an explanation of why actors rely on network forms of organization and obtain a clearer picture of the nature of these networks in relation to the distribution of power and institution building.

A key to understanding the role of networks in postwar Lebanon is the nature of the political settlement that emerged after the signing of the Ta'if Peace Accord in 1989.[44] While defining the political settlement as the fundamental rules of public decision-making (in the text of the Accord and the Constitution, their application and actual practice), we can observe some striking patterns whereby the political settlement obstructed or prevented the formation of hierarchical and bureaucratically organized state institutions and encouraged actors to seek for alternative forms of organization.[45] Although we do not have the space here to do justice to all its complexities, the political settlement can be said to have contained four main elements that had a profound and debilitating effect on bureaucratic institution building.

First, as the Ta'if Accord placed heavy emphasis on incorporating virtually all contestants in the decision-making process while granting the leaders of the three main confessional groupings (the Maronites, the Shi'ites, and the Sunnites) almost identical powers, routine decision-making soon broke down. Consequently, the formation of public policy and institution building came to be dominated by informal bargaining between the "troika," or the three presidents—the president of the Republic, the president of the Council of Ministers (the prime minister), and the president of the National Assembly (the Speaker).[46] Watched over and refereed by the Syrian leadership, the most common outcome of this bargaining was the apportionment (*muhasassa*) of the spoils of public office, privileges, and state resources.

Second, the executive has been paralyzed by a quasi-permanent cabinet crisis due to an extreme dispersal of power and multiple veto points held by the cabinet's constituent members. In particular, the principle of "collegial government" (*sirat al-hukm al-jama'iya*), as well as the inability of the prime minister to enforce a minimum of cohesion in his cabinet, complicated and frustrated public decision-making.

Third, parliament became increasingly marginalized and failed to carry out its role as an independent counterweight to the executive whereas the speaker used his wide powers to turn parliament into a tool to bolster his bargaining power in the troika.[47]

Fourth, even when the Ta'if Accord proscribed an inclusive coalition in government, electoral practice was manipulated to cater for the rise of a selective and highly unrepresentative political elite, primarily to serve Syrian interests in securing a leadership in Beirut loyal to its foreign policy aims in Lebanon.[48] In turn, these imperatives made political incumbents extremely sensitive to local or regional interests as they tried to compensate for their lack of real support among their local constituencies.

These four elements of the political settlement both obstructed forms of bureaucratic organization while providing incentives for political actors to look for alternative institutional arrangements. The result was that, even by the region's poor standards, Lebanon had a much weaker bureaucratic environment than its Arab neighbors.[49] A few examples may suffice for demonstrative purposes.

Ever since a private concession for the Port of Beirut expired on December 31, 1990, continuous political stalemate between the troikists and various members of the cabinet prevented the emergence of bureaucratic structures to institutionalize the port's management. Capitalizing heavily on their effective veto power in the political settlement, the various contestants failed to come to an agreement on whether the port should become part of the state's administration, be transferred to an autonomous office attached to the public sector, or be privatized with or without minority government participation. Following more than two years of inertia, a provisional governmental "Commission" was appointed to replace temporarily the port's private operators. As if to underline that all options were still considered open, all contenders were allocated a seat on the Commission. However, none of these members could be considered public servants. Nor was the Commission given a clear mandate or status vis-à-vis either the public administration at large or the private sector. This ambivalence was apparent, for example, from the salary scales and bureaucratic hierarchy. Administrative structures that prevailed under the private concession were kept intact, even when they were now financed by the state. Furthermore, the port's revenues, a major source of income for the Treasury, were not deposited with the Central Bank as is customary for public institutions, but kept in a private bank account.[50] For the state's Court of Accounts, the port was not considered part of the public administration and thus no effort was made to audit the Commission's books. This situation continues until today. "It is unknown today what the final administrative status of the Port will be," the port's chairman said at the end of 1997.[51] "But [in the meantime] we regard the Port as a public utility that for all its flexibility resembles a commercial enterprise." Thus, lacking bureaucratic structures, the port became a state entity entirely managed by social networks wherein politicians relied on their personal links to the members of the Commission to govern its operations.

The oil sector presents another example of the ways in which the political settlement prevented the rise of bureaucratic forms of organization. When armed hostilities were brought to a halt in 1990–1991, oil-importing companies were in no hurry to help design a general framework wherein the tasks and obligations of the Ministry of Industry and Oil (IO) would be defined. The main obstacle in this respect was that some core individuals of the postwar elite had themselves acquired large stakes in the business. In fact, two of them, President Elias al-Hrawi and Speaker Nabih Birri, were particularly intent on keeping decisions about the role of the Ministry of IO in a gridlock due to their position in the troika. Hrawi contributed to this situation via his alliance with the minister of IO, Shahe Barsumian, who made no attempt to design an institutional framework that would clarify the ministry's role as either importer of oil derivatives or as regulator of a market run by private companies. Prime Minister Rafiq al-Hariri, on the other hand, had no stake in the oil business and therefore suggested several schemes to regulate importing by drawing up clear criteria for new entrants. But due to their solid position in the political settlement, Hariri's opponents were able to prevent such an institutional framework from emerging and the Ministry of IO continued to enjoy vast discretionary powers in granting licenses to importers linked to Hrawi, Birri, and the Druze leader Walid Junblatt.[52] Again, the nature of the political settlement caused networks rather than bureaucratically organized institutions to govern distributional issues.

When the distribution of material or political resources gained local or regional dimensions, political elites were particularly keen to use the powers codified in postwar settlements to obstruct the rise of bureaucratic institutions. Thus, attempts to rehabilitate the country's municipalities via local elections were consistently voted down, at least until the spring of 1998. One of the main reasons for this seemed to be that some political elites feared that local elections would expose their lack of popular support among their own constituencies as gerrymandering would be much more difficult to apply than in parliamentary elections. Moreover, the reinstatement of municipal government would reduce these political elites' importance, as public services would then no longer be provided by the central government but by elected municipal councils. As a result, centrally collected taxes and fees earmarked for the municipalities were kept in an Independent Municipal Fund and provisionally managed by Hariri's allies in the cabinet.[53] Without any defined organizational status let alone bureaucratic structures, the fund was made to finance all sorts of public procurement by state institutions controlled by Hariri's associates, including the Council of Development and Reconstruction (CDR) and the Governorate of Mount Lebanon.[54] Companies that secured contracts included Geneco, a construction company managed by Hariri's brother Shafiq, and the waste management company Sukleen/Sukkar, whose managing director acknowledged that his business would not have flourished were it not for his close connections to Hariri.[55]

But whereas the political settlement often thwarted the formation of bureaucratic institutions, individual strategies to circumvent the cumbersome decision-making process were similarly obstructive to bureaucratic development and further highlighted the importance of social networks as an alternative organizational form for the provision of governance. It was mainly Hariri who pursued such strategies in order to compensate for his relatively weak power as prime minister and in order to get around the continuous bargaining in the troika.

Thus, from 1992 on, the Council for Development and Reconstruction (CDR) grew into the government's main instrument for planning, financing, and implementing the country's reconstruction program.[56] Directly attached to the prime minister's office, the CDR fell under Hariri's responsibility and, this way, the latter could insulate his policies from the continuous challenges to his power in the cabinet and from the calls for *muhasassa* of his rival troikists. But to keep shielding the CDR from these political pressures, principles of bureaucratic organization were readily sacrificed. For instance, the CDR's mandate was extremely ambiguous. It was granted "planning duties," "advisory functions," "executive duties," "supervisory duties," and the authority to solicit domestic and foreign loans to finance the projects it decided to carry out.[57]

External audits and checks were equally absent.[58] Moreover, its 270 staff members were not regarded as ordinary public servants and this way the CDR escaped the qualification standards and selection procedures set by the

Civil Service Board. In fact, Hariri stuffed the CDR with his own associates and private employees. Many of these officials continued to work for the prime minister's private companies, or were part of his ever-expanding string of private advisors and business partners; a loose group that became popularly referred to as *le Bureau*.[59] When Hariri was once asked about allegations that many of his former private employees in the CDR were still paid salaries out of the prime minister's own pocket, he merely replied by threatening to withdraw them from the public service.[60] Similar practices characterized the operations of the Investment Development Authority of Lebanon (IDAL). Originally set up in 1995 to encourage foreign investment, IDAL became an agency distributing lucrative BOT contracts as a substitute for full-fledged privatization, which would have required parliamentary approval.[61] Unhindered by bureaucratic standards of management and headed by an associate of Hariri, IDAL clearly favored business allies of the prime minister, including Muhamad Amin al-Hijazi who was granted the right to build and exploit a large commercial and leisure complex at the state-owned Sports Stadium in Beirut.[62]

Hariri's efforts to insulate the country's reconstruction efforts from the debilitating effects of the political settlement reached near perfection in the highly complex scheme designed for the rebuilding of the Beirut Central District (BCD). In 1991, a private real estate company, later named Solidère, was charged with rebuilding and developing the heart of Beirut, including its public infrastructure.[63] In return, all assets held by more than 120,000 original claimants to property rights in the area were transferred to Solidère after judicial valuation and became tradable in the form of company shares.

Furthermore, the company was granted the right to own and exploit half of reclaimed land gained from a landfill in the BCD and an additional surface of publicly owned land in the area. As a result, the private company began exercising many state powers including city planning and supervising its own public infrastructure works.[64] To secure the entire scheme from any challenges by his rivals, Hariri controlled the project via a network of business allies and former employees. Thus, the prime minister's allies dominated Solidère's board of directors (as large shareholders), its private contractors, and all state institutions whose authorities touched upon the works in the BCD, including the CDR, the Higher Council for Urban Planning (*Majlis al-'Ula li-at-Tanzim al-Madani*), the City Council of Beirut, the Land Registry (*Cadastre*), and the Ministry of Finance.[65] To further seal the scheme from outside political interference, the judges who were to evaluate the original owners' properties needed to be protected from the political pressures that permeated the judiciary. Mainly for this reason, the judges were literally taken out of their institutions (the judiciary), placed in "judicial committees," and *paid salaries by Solidère*.[66] Moreover, the original property owners were denied their constitutional right to appeal against these committees' decisions in court, so that their evaluation of the properties concerned were considered to be final. In effect, the judicial power of the state was used to endorse the transfer of property but was at the same time divorced from the institutions designed to exercise this power because the latter might have been vulnerable to interference by Hariri's rivals.[67] In sum, in an elaborate maneuver to circumvent the debilitating effects of the political settlement, Hariri had "privatized" important state prerogatives including city planning, supervision of the building of public infrastructure financed by state resources, and judicial legitimation of what was tantamount to a massive and involuntary transfer of property to Solidère. In the final analysis, the entire scheme was anchored in Hariri's tightly knit network of contacts and allies, who acrobatically crossed the boundaries between public and private whenever required. As Saree Makdisi concludes, Solidère became "the ultimate expression of the dissolution of any real distinction between public and private interests or, more accurately, the decisive colonization of the former by the latter."[68]

As stated by Powell, "[m]arkets, hierarchies, and networks are pieces of a larger puzzle that is the economy."[69] However, very little is known about the reasons or bases for the seemingly endless variance such puzzles show between and within different societies.[70] Perhaps mainly for this reason, network theorists have been reluctant to make universalist claims concerning the causes of certain forms of embeddedness and networks.[71] This limited case study cannot, of course, contribute a great deal to an understanding of networks in general. But what it does suggest is that the rise and pervasiveness of social networks should be firmly placed in their political contexts in general and in processes of institution building in particular. Just as institutions are "political to the core,"[72] so are social networks, both in their formation and in their effects on the overall distribution of resources. In Lebanon, the proliferation of networks as a predominant form of organization correlates strongly with the nature of this country's postwar political settlement, or the rules of public decision-making and their application since the Ta'if Accord. Whereas the political settlement made it virtually impossible to take authoritative decisions regarding the formation of bureaucratic organizations, political actors gained strong incentives to look for alternative forms of organization. Under these conditions, social networks began to *substitute* for bureaucratic governance, and clearly operated at the latter's expense. By doing so, social networks both shaped opportunity structures while they acted as sources of constraint in an economy that otherwise appears as an oasis of free or unregulated transactions and laissez-faire.

Networks and Economic Performance

A growing research literature has emphasized the functionality of network forms of organization. Sociologists and other students of networks argue that networks can promote economic performance because they generate larger degrees of flexibility, adaptability, and trust than markets or hierarchical organizations can provide on their own, if at all.[73] This stress on positive effects is understandable given the fact that network theory has been largely formulated in response to neoclassical approaches that treat social relations among actors as "a frictional drag that impedes competitive markets."[74] Studies of the astounding growth of the East Asian economies similarly called for a deeper understanding of the "successful network structure of Asian capitalism," and also praised the functionality of networks in contradiction to more conventional approaches.[75]

Interestingly, some of these themes have been echoed in Lebanon, where Prime Minister Hariri and his associates have time after time stressed that "getting things done," "having the right contacts," and adopting flexible approaches to governance are equally if not more important than bureaucratic development. In fact, the latter has often been referred to in a pejorative sense as in posing unnecessary obstacles to adaptive and flexible governance. For example, Hariri and his associates consistently portrayed the state's financial watchdog, the Court of Accounts, as a cumbersome, legalistic agency frustrating the government's reconstruction efforts.[76] Fu'ad Siniora, the Minister of State for Finance and a staunch ally of Hariri, even argued at one point that a more prominent role for the Court of Accounts would be undesirable as its employees are "obsessed with form and have no eye for substance."[77] A similar reasoning recurred in Hariri's defense of his first six years in power. Hariri released a pamphlet after he was deposed as prime minister in November 1998 for, among other things, failing to implement administrative reform and institutional development.[78] In this document, Hariri spends many pages highlighting his close contacts and friendships with businessmen in the Lebanese diaspora, Western heads of state, and high-ranking officials in international financial organizations as having been instrumental in kick-starting the country's reconstruction program. Answering critiques that under his management bureaucratic institutions failed to emerge, Hariri states rather apologetically:

> Public institutions cannot play their fundamental role in development when they are suppressed, unable to benefit from highly qualified staff and made dependent on the interventions of politicians. While appreciating the importance of integrity and civil duty of the official [i.e., bureaucratic rules of governance], one has to acknowledge that his competence, his productivity, his ability to implement, his decisiveness and his responsibility are equally essential factors. To deny this can only impede economic recovery and harm the position Lebanon deserves in the regional and international economy.[79]

Hariri's turbulent career in Lebanon's postwar politics has made such views into a major issue of the political debate on reconstruction with positions ranging between those in favor of "the party of reconstruction without cleanliness" (i.e., Hariri's forceful but nontransparent and crony-like approach), and those adhering to "the party of cleanliness without reconstruction" (i.e., opposition leader and former prime minister Salim al-Huss and his emphasis on bureaucratic procedures and the rule of law in government and business).[80]

It is not my intent to quarrel with the literature's emphasis on the functionality of networks or to side with the neoclassical bias against social networks. Instead, I want to suggest that in order to assess whether networks contribute or impede economic performance one has to look closely at two interrelated factors: the specific forms of networks and their relation to the state's institutions.

What is striking about Lebanon's networks is that foreign and domestic investors alike perceive the country's business environment as erratic, unpredictable, and unfathomable. World Bank surveys of the views held by expatriate entrepreneurs offer ample evidence for this. In addition, Atallah found that a large majority of his respondents regarded "the level of uncertainty created by the Lebanese state institutions" as the most important obstacle to doing business.[81] My own unstructured interviews with Lebanese businessmen confirm these complaints. For example, one contractor had returned to Lebanon from Saudi Arabia. He told the author on condition of anonymity that after four years of unsuccessfully trying to disentangle and deal with the relevant networks to obtain contracts in state-financed reconstruction projects, he was about to give up: "In Saudi-Arabia, it was clear who places orders and at what price. The system there is predictable so that I simply added the costs of the commissions I had to pay to my offering price. But here no one knows who is in charge of what, and if you think to have found the right guy, somebody else appears to demand his share [*hissa*]."[82] Such observations suggest that networks in postwar Lebanon are extremely volatile whereas enduring competition between them has failed to put in place coherent, durable, and hence predictable forms of social interaction on which entrepreneurs can rely to formulate their business strategies. In other words, the specific forms of networks in Lebanon defy their supposed purpose of providing a lubricant for economic transactions or generating trust in competitive environments.

Under these conditions, social networks exacerbate investment insecurities, add to the costs of business, and discourage productive investment. Publicized cases wherein entrepreneurs found themselves to be overwhelmed by demands of competing networks confirm this pattern. For example, the British joint venture SAR Marine General and Mowlem International Ltd (Sar-Mowlem) lost its contract to clear the Port of Beirut of sunken vessels and debris after it refused to give in to unexpected requests to subcontract the work to a rival Lebanese company.[83] The Lebanese agent of Sar-Mowlem told the author that he was astonished by the move, because he thought he had built excellent personal contacts with the relevant public officials who were supposedly in charge of the port's operations.[84] In a similar fashion, the Saudi business tycoon Prince al-Waleed Bin Talal pulled out of a $120-million hotel development project in the Beirut Central District in spite of his close relations with Hariri.[85] Al-Waleed complained that he had been besieged by numerous well-connected middlemen who insisted on playing a role in the project by removing (and creating) all sorts of administrative obstacles. That same month, Habtoor—a large investor from the United Arab Emirates—withdrew a $200-million real estate project because of similar obstacles amounting to a "discouraging investment climate."[86]

Whereas social networks may in certain forms be value enhancing, extreme volatility and unpredictability seem to correlate with the kinds of relations networks establish between private entrepreneurs and state actors. In this context it is relevant that in cases where social networks seem to have played an important if not vital role in promoting productive investment and economic growth, such networks were *complementary* to strong or "autonomous" bureaucratic institutions, as for example observed in East Asia until the late 1980s.[87] Thus, even when acknowledging the centrality of social networks in explaining economic behavior, bureaucratic institutions provided one of the conditions under which relations between state officials and entrepreneurs contributed to economic growth.[88]

The difference with postwar Lebanon could hardly be more extreme. The formation of social networks occurred here because the political settlement failed to produce bureaucratic institutions. Thus, networks *substituted* for bureaucratic institutions, which may also explain why their specific manifestation has been extremely fragmented and failed to put in place the secure business environment and predictability of rules required for productive investment and economic growth. In fact, it is in this context of weak bureaucratic institutions that social networks degenerated into a tool of rampant corruption, to the extent that in Lebanon networks and corruption came to be perceived as being virtually identical.[89] Given the failure of bureaucratic institutionalization and the absence of even a minimal degree of state autonomy, competing social networks consistently fell short of generating the qualities of trust and durability they might have produced in different political contexts.

Like state interventions in the economy, social networks provide, restrict, and regulate access to business opportunities. As such, networks are not intrinsically value enhancing, nor are they by definition detrimental to economic growth or necessarily indicators of corruption. In postwar Lebanon, however, social networks seem to have acted against productive investment and growth. This can be explained by their volatile and fragmented nature and, related to this, by weak bureaucratic institutions and their general failure to grant networks some degree of coherence, durability, and predictability. In the final analysis, these traits can be brought back to the nature of the postwar political settlement, which failed to put in place a workable arrangement for generating and sustaining strong bureaucratic institutions.

Historically, this analysis appears to make sense too. However, some caution against drawing historical comparisons is warranted as no research has been done on the nature of social networks before the war. Despite all its weaknesses and internal contradictions, the political settlement of prewar Lebanon showed a much larger degree of coherence characterized by, among other things, a hegemonic presidency, Maronite predominance in parliament, and greater exclusivity in allowing elites access to public decision-making.[90] This political settlement has been associated with the domination of a relatively unified coalition that includes a "commercial-financial bourgeoisie" and the (mainly Maronite) notable families or *zu'ama*.[91] This may explain the much greater centrality of state institutions and, presumably, the more complementary role of social networks in facilitating more secure and thriving business environments. In the course of the 1970s and during the war years, the influence of this dominant coalition waned (but did not disappear),[92] primarily because of the political ascendancy of rival elites, including militia leaders,[93] politicians parachuted into Lebanon and backed by the Syrian leadership,[94] and expatriate business tycoons.[95] The post-Ta'if political settlement reflected this dispersal of political power and attempted, under the guise of restoring confessional parity, to appease and incorporate all these heterogeneous elites into the public decision-making process. Most commentators on the Ta'if Accord initially praised these adjustments to the political settlement as a welcome development toward more genuine democracy. As one of the Accord's architects put it, the political reforms formulated in the Ta'if Accord were aimed at a transition "away from governance by subjugation [*qahr*] and hegemony [*haymana*]."[96] But because it generated such an extreme dispersal of political power in the public decision-making process, the political settlement fragmented and undermined the very state institutions that were supposed to carry Lebanon into an era of "reconciliation [*taswiya*] and participation."

Conclusion

The notion of social networks offers an interesting window into the seemingly enigmatic nature of Lebanon's political economy. Even when a strong case can be made for the prevalence of laissez-faire (whether by default or design), a focus on the role of networks and their effects on the organization of economic activities underscores the extent to which Lebanon's economy remains highly regulated and restricted. The notion of the market, at least in a strict neoclassical sense (and recognizing that economists today are more inclined to integrate the social into their work), fails to capture these dynamics, thereby making postwar Lebanon a case in point of "Nobody" (the notion of laissez-faire) having too much to answer for. An inquiry into the origins and economic repercussions of social networks in Lebanon highlights some specific traits of the forms such networks take and the ways in which they link up business and state actors. I have argued that an analysis of these characteristics should start from an appreciation of the nature of the postwar political settlement (the fundamental rules of public decision-making both in the texts of the Ta'if Accord and the Constitution and in their application and actual practice). With this as the starting point, it became clear that the extreme dispersal of political power inherent in this political settlement undermined the formation of bureaucratic institutions, whereas incentives were high for political actors to circumvent bureaucratic organizations when they did exist. Under these conditions, social networks substituted for, rather than complemented, forms of bureaucratic organization. I have argued that under these political circumstances social networks became extremely fragmented, erratic, and unpredictable, and failed to put in place the secure business environment that (*ceteris paribus*) is required for productive investment and economic growth. As the Lebanese case shows, it is the specific nature of the political and structural contexts in which networks originate and operate that determine their developmental consequences.

It is tempting to view the dynamics and shortcomings of laissez-faire in postwar Lebanon as an omen of what awaits the economic and political outcomes of structural adjustment programs and fiscal policy reforms currently being implemented in neighboring Arab countries. One could argue, for example, that "rolling back the state" and adopting reforms that resemble Lebanon's general outlook of laissez-faire will equally fail to put in place market-based economies as social networks take on restrictive and regulatory functions, especially when insufficient attention is paid to bureaucratic development. However, as is often the case with analogies, such interpretations are superficial. In the final analysis, the exact forms and role of social networks in Lebanon originate in this country's unique political settlement, which in itself reflects exceptional political and structural developments associated with elite fragmentation between and within confessional communities.[97] Furthermore, the political battles accompanying the dismantling of state-led economies, often under external pressures, are likely to affect the nature of the outcomes of reform, which, consequently, may show little resemblance to Lebanon's experience of sustaining an economic order characterized by laissez-faire and fragmented networks. But what Lebanon's experience does remind us is that the dichotomy between markets and states only tells part of the story, if it tells us anything at all. Social networks should be taken seriously in understanding economic and political outcomes, especially when societies fail to live up to the expectations of reformers and their backers based in Washington.

Notes

1. See Y. Sayigh, *The Economies of the Arab World: Development since 1945* (London: Palgrave Macmillan, 1978), 283.
2. See Lebanon's Physical Quality of Life Index for the 1970s calculated by the U.S. Overseas Development Council, cited in I. Harik, "The Economic and Social Factors in the Lebanese Crisis," in *Journal of Arab Affairs*, April 1982.
3. See A. Chaib, *L'Aventure de la liberté: essai sur le libéralisme économique au Liban* (Beirut: Pub. and Marketing House, 1983).
4. World Bank, *Lebanon Private Sector Assessment* (Washington, DC: World Bank, November 1995), 1.

5. The text of the Ta'if Accord and the 1990 Constitution can be found in: B. Menassa, ed., *Constitution Libanaise, textes et Commentaires et Accord de Taef* (Beirut: 1995). For an analysis of the references in both texts to laissez-faire, see A. Chaiban, "Les aspects économiques de Taef: une doctrine économique?" *Travaux et Jours*, no. 59 (Spring 1997).

6. International Monetary Fund, *Article IV Consultation with Lebanon 2001* (Washington, DC: JMF, October 29, 2001).

7. W. W. Powell, "Neither Market nor Hierarchy: Network Forms of Organization," in *Research in Organizational Behavior* 12 (1990): 302.

8. M. Granovetter, "Economic Action and Social Structure: The Problem of Embeddedness," in M. Granovetter and R. Swedberg, eds., *The Sociology of Economic Life* (Boulder: Westview, 1992), 55.

9. H. Scott Gordon, "The Ideology of Laissez-Faire," in A. W. Coats, ed., *The Classical Economists and Economic Policy* (London: Methuen and Co., 1971), 196.

10. For example, see C. Issawi, "Economic Development and Liberalism in Lebanon," *Middle East Journal* 18, no. 3 (1964); S. Makdisi, *Financial Policy and Economic Growth: The Lebanese Experience* (New York: Columbia University Press, 1979); R. Owen, "The Economic History of Lebanon 1943–74," in H. Barakat, ed., *Toward a Viable Lebanon* (Washington, DC: Center for Contemporary Arab Studies, Georgetown University, 1988); B. Labaki, "L'économie politique du Liban indépendant, 1943–1975," in D. Haffar and N. Shehadi, eds., *Lebanon: A History of Conflict and Consensus* (London: Center for Lebanese Studies, 1988); C. L. Gates, *The Merchant Republic of Lebanon: Rise of an Open Economy* (London: Center for Lebanese Studies, 1998); and A. Dagher, *L'Etat et l'économie au Liban, action gouvernementale et finances publiques de l'Indépendance à 1975* (Beirut: Cahiers du CERMOC, 1995).

11. See M. Chiha, *Propos d'économie libanaise* (Beirut: Fondation Michel Chihi, 1965); F. Trabulsi, *Sallat bi-la Wasl, Michel Chiha wa al-Idiyulujiya al-Lubnani* (Beirut: Riyad al-Rayyis lil-kutub wa-al-Nashr, 1999); and N. Shehadi, *The Idea of Lebanon, Economy and State in the Cenacle Libanais 1946–54* (Oxford: Centre for Lebanese Studies, 1987).

12. Among others, see T. Gaspard, *The Limits of Laissez-faire: A Political Economy of Lebanon 1948–87* (unpublished Ph.D. thesis, Sussex University, 1992); T. Kaspar, "Qara'at ukhra fi Iqtisad Lubnan wa mustaqbalihi," in N. Beyhum et al., eds., *Beyrouth: Construire, l'avenir, reconstruire le passe?* (Beirut: Dossiers de l'urban Research Institute, 1993); C. Dubar and S. Nasr, *Les Classes Sociales au Liban* (Paris: Presses de la fondation nationale des sciences politiques, 1976); K. Hamdan and M. 'Aql, "At-Tughma al-Maliya fi Lubnan," in *At-Tariq* 4 (1979); E. Yachoui, *Restructuration et Croissance de l'Economie Libanaise* (Beirut: Librarie du Libon, 1983); H. F. Aly and N. Abdun-Nur, "An Appraisal of the Sixth Year Plan of Lebanon (1972–1977)," in *Middle East Journal* 29, no. 2 (1975); M. Johnson, *Class & Client in Beirut, The Sunni Muslim Community and the Lebanese State 1840–1985* (London: Atlantic Highlands, 1986); H. Charif,

"Regional Development and Integration," in D. Collings, ed., *Peace for Lebanon? From War to Reconstruction* (Boulder: Lynne Rienner Publishers, 1994); A. Fahas, *Az-Zuruf al-Iqtisadiya li-al Harb al-Lubnaniya* (Beirut: Matabi Lubnan al-Jadid, 1979); S. Nasr, "Backdrop to Civil War: The Crisis of Lebanese Capitalism," in *Middle East Report*, no. 73 (December 1978); and N. E. Chammas, *L'Avenir Socio-économique du Liban en Questions, Eléments de Réponse* (Beirut: Harvard Business School Club of Lebanon, 1995).

13. See T. Helbling, "Postwar Reconstruction, Public Finances, and Fiscal Sustainability," in S. Eken and T. Helbling, eds., *Back to the Future: Postwar Reconstruction and Stabilization in Lebanon* (Washington, DC: JMF, 1999), 14, table 3.1.

14. See A. Fedelino, "Association Agreement between Lebanon and the European Union," in Eken and Helbling, *Back to the Future*, 72.

15. In 2000, however, the Central Bank announced its new policy of allowing the exchange rate to float within a narrower band than before. For more details, see S. Eken et al., *Economic Dislocation and Recovery in Lebanon* (Washington, DC: IMF, 1995), 32 ff. For a regional comparative perspective, see P. D. Karam, *Exchange Rate Policies in Arab Countries: Assessment and Recommendations* (Abu Dhabi: Arab Monetary Fund, December 2001).

16. In comparison with other Arab countries, Lebanon scores extremely low on various indices used to measure and compare exchange rate and capital controls. See Karam, *Exchange Rate Policies in Arab Countries*, 30, table 3.2.

17. Prior to the outbreak of hostilities in 1975, the state acted as the country's sole importer of oil and derivatives. This role was confirmed by Legislative Decree 79 (June 27, 1977). For details, see A. Mudawwar, *Dalil Qita' An-Naft fi Lubnan* (Beirut: al-markaz, 1996), 29 ff.

18. For more details on the collapse of Lebanon's public health service and its "privatization by attrition," see S. Azar, *La Politique de Santé au Liban depuis 1945* (Beirut: Rabieh, 1996).

19. See J. Harik, *The Public and Social Services of the Lebanese Militias* (Oxford: Centre for Lebanese Studies, September 1994).

20. For a list of such schemes, see J. Wetter, "Public Investment Planning and Progress," in Eken and Helbling, *Back to the Future*, 10, table 2.4.

21. Ibid., 6.

22. Ibid., 2.

23. See World Bank, *Lebanon Private Sector Assessment*.

24. S. Atallah, *Roadblocks to Recovery: Institutional Obstacles Facing the Private Sector in Lebanon* (unpublished, Lebanese Centre for Policy Studies, Beirut 1999), 35, figure 44.

25. In 1998, FDI measured as part of GDP amounted to 3.45%; extremely low compared to 7.96% (Syria), 13.06% (Morocco), 16.53% (Jordan), 20.2% (Egypt), and 26.6% (Tunisia). See A. T. Sadik and A. A. Bolbol, *Mobilizing International Capital for Arab Economic Development with Special Reference to the Role of FDI* (Abu Dhabi: Arab Monetary Fund, November 2000), 67, table 13.

26. See *Daily Star*, June 14, 2001.

27. See Bernard Hoekman and Patrick Messerlin, *Harnessing Trade for Development and Growth in the Middle East* (Council on Foreign Relations, Study Group on Middle East Trade Options, 2002), tables 3 and 5.

28. See World Bank, *Lebanon Private Sector Assessment*, 20.

29. Especially Granovetter's notion of "embeddedness" captures this approach well. See Granovetter, "Economic Action and Social Structure."

30. On this point, see C. A. Heimer, "Doing Your Job *and* Helping Your Friends: Universalistic Norms about Obligations to Particular Others in Networks," in N. Nohria, and R. G. Eccles, eds., *Networks and Organizations: Structure, Form, and Action* (Boston, MA: Harvard Business School Press, 1992).

31. J. C. Mitchell, "The Concept and Use of Social Networks," in J. C. Mitchell, ed., *Social Networks in Urban Situations* (Manchester University Press, 1969).

32. N. Nohria, "Is a Network Perspective a Useful Way of Studying Organizations?" in Nohria and Eccles, *Networks and Organizations*.

33. See Powell, "Neither Market nor Hierarchy," 299.

34. Ibid., 306.

35. For an inquiry into the *wasta* phenomenon, see C. D. 'Adwan, *'Al-Wasta', Bayna as-Shabab wa al-Mujtam'a* (unpublished paper delivered at Conference of Arab researchers in Amman, 2000).

36. In a special report the Court of Accounts detailed its finding that 74% of all transactions made by the state failed to meet tendering requirements. See *An-Nahar*, December 1, 1994.

37. Most strikingly, there were no immediate price tags attached to these contracts. Instead, both operators committed themselves to pay the state a progressive share of their future revenues and apply a surcharge to customers to the benefit of the state. See *Contract for Build, Operate and Transfer Undertaking for Implementing Cellular GSM Services in Lebanon* [...], *By and Between the Republic of Lebanon—Ministry of Post and Telecommunications* [...] *and Telecom Finland International* (Beirut, June 30, 1994). Note that Dallul's son Nizar—who directly participated in the deal—is married to Hariri's daughter. He is alleged to have relied on credits from Hariri's bank *Banque de Méditerranée* for his start-up capital in one of the private networks, Liban Cell.

38. See N. Wakim, *Al-Ayadi as-Sawd* (Beirut: Sharikat, 1998), 210–213; *An-Nahar*, November 20, 1997.

39. In August 1997, import licenses were withdrawn from the U.S. company Falcon International and Lebanese UniTerminal, on the pretext that "the state strives to ensure revenues for the treasury by restricting private imports according to the law [...]." See *As-Safir*, September 29, 1997.

40. On such ownership patterns, see Dar al-Handasah, *A Nation-Wide Study of Quarries*, vols. 1 and 2 (Beirut: Ministry of Public Works and General Directorate for Urban Planning, January 1996).

41. For example, a long-serving official at the Port of Beirut critical of political intervention in his administration was approached by a new minister close to Hariri

and repeatedly asked which network he "belonged" to. After the official insisted that his role was purely professional and unrelated to any network of influence, the minister eventually categorized him into a rival network and he was treated accordingly. Interview with a high-ranking official at the *Commission de gestion et d'exploitation du Port de Beyrouth* who requested his name to be withheld.

42. See Granovetter, "Economic Action and Social Structure," 67.

43. Interestingly, such perceptions were shared by virtually all our interviewees irrespective of their confessional affiliation. For overly culturalist accounts touching on the issue of networking in politics and business, see *An-Nahar*, December 13, 1994; *An-Nahar*, May 5, 1995; P. Skaff, *Ali Baba and the Forty Thieves: The Myth and the Reality (Tracing the Roots of Corruption in the Arab Personality)*, paper presented at the International Anti-Corruption Conference in Prague (Transparency International, 2001). Also note a similar reference to "traditional" Arab culture in the title of Shams ad-Din's book on state procurement policies and corruption in postwar Lebanon: "The cave [of 'Ali Baba and the forty thieves] of reconstruction." See M. I. Shams ad-Din, *Mugharat al-'Imar, bi al-Haqā'iq wa al-Arqam* (Beirut: 1999).

44. For useful analyses of the Ta'if Accord and its implementation, see B. Menassa, ed., *Constitution Libanaise, textes et Commentaires et Accord de Taef* (Beirut: Les Editions l'Orient, 1995); J. Maila, *The Document of National Understanding: A Commentary* (Oxford: CLS, 1992); A. Mansur, *al-Inqilab 'ala at-Ta'if* (Beirut: 1993); and A. Mansur, *Mawt Jumhuriya* (Beirut: Dar al-Jadid, 1994).

45. Weber famously defined a "bureaucratic agency" as a hierarchical organization that meets six main criteria. Following Page, we grouped these criteria into three main components: (a) clear goal formulation and rules governing the agency's operations, (b) the existence of external control and audit mechanisms, and (c) strict separation between public office and private interests. See respectively M. Weber, *Economy and Society: An Outline of Interpretive Sociology* (Berkeley: University of California Press, 1978), 956–958; E. Page, *Political Authority and Bureaucratic Power, A Comparative Analysis* (Knoxville, TN: University of Tennessee Press, 1985), 9.

46. On the "troika" phenomenon, see V. Perthes, "Problems with Peace: Post-War Politics and Parliamentary Elections in Lebanon," *Orient* 33, no. 3 (September 1992); D. as-Sayyigh, *An-Nizam al-Lubnani fi Thawabitihi wa Tahawwulatihi* (Beirut: Dar al-Nahar, 2000); and Joseph Maila in *L'Orient-Le Jour*, December 7, 1994.

47. For further details on the demise of parliament in public decision-making, see J. Bahout, "Lebanese Parliamentarism: Shadow Plays and the Death of Politics," in *The Lebanon Report* (Spring 1996); M. D. Young, "Misreading the Signs: Parliament and the Second Republic," in *The Lebanon Report* (Spring 1996); F Sassine, "Is Parliament's Credibility in the Red?" in *The Lebanon Report* (Spring 1996).

48. For an analysis of gerrymandering, especially in the 1992 parliamentary elections, see F. el-Khazen, *Lebanon's First Postwar Parliamentary Election 1992: An Imposed Choice* (Oxford: Centre for Lebanese Studies, 1998); T. 'Atalla, *Taqniyat at-Tazwir al-Intikhabi wa Sibul Mukafahatiha* (Beirut: Lebanese Center for Policy Studies, 1996), 15–21; J. Maila, "Elections sous influence," in *Les Cahiers de l'Orient*, no. 28 (4th trimester 1992); F. Abi Sa'ab et al., *al-Intikhabat an-Niyabiyya al-Lubnaniyya 1996, 'Azmat ad-Dimuqratiyya fi Lubnan* (Beirut: 1997); V. Perthes, "Libanons Parlamentswahlen von 1996: die Akzeptanz des Faktischen," in *Orient* 38, no. 2 (1997b); N. Nassif and R. Bu Munsif, *al-Masrah wa al-Kawalis, Intikhabat 96 fi fusuliha* (Beirut: Dar an-Nahar, 1996). For a more detailed analysis of Syria's foreign policy interests in Lebanon as well as Syria's increasing influence in Lebanon's intra-elite politics, see V. Perthes, *Der Libanon Nach dem Buergerkrieg, Vom Ta'if zum Gesellschaftlichen Konsens?* (Ebenhausen: Stiftung fuer Wissenschaft und Politik Forschungsinstitut Internationale Politik und Sicherheit, 1993), 105–116; H. C. Malik, "Lebanon in the 1990s: Stability without Freedom?" *Global Affairs* 7, no. 1 (Winter 1992); A. R. Norton, "Lebanon: With Friends like These," *Current History* (January 1997).

49. In one comparative study of the perceived effectiveness of bureaucracies in the MENA region, Lebanon scored lowest on a set of relevant variables compiled in a "Bureaucratic Quality Index." See Economic Research Forum, *Economic Trends in the MENA Region* (Cairo: 1998); *Daily Star*, September 8, 1998.

50. See *An-Nahar*, December 13, 1997.

51. Cited in *Ad-Diyar*, December 16, 1997.

52. President Elias al-Hrawi represented the Swiss firm GAT-Oil after having resigned as the managing director of Total-Liban in 1990. He is believed to have stakes in various Lebanese oil-importing companies including Naftomar and EuroGulf, via his son Roy, the Lebanese entrepreneur Naji 'Azzar, and the Syrian business tycoon Sa'ib Nahhas. Speaker Nabih Birri allegedly has close links to another major importer and wholesaler of petroleum products, Al-Taqa. Walid Junblatt holds a majority share in various oil-importing companies including *Cogico*.

53. By law, the Independent Municipal Fund is only an account with the Central Bank and not an institutional entity by itself. The Fund's resources consist of revenues derived from taxes and fees collected directly by the municipalities (such as licenses for cinemas, restaurants, and property taxes), and taxes and fees collected by the central government (such as a 10% share of custom duties, and fees collected on utility—electricity, water, and telephone—bills). See "Legislative Decree 118" ("the Law on the *Baladiyat*"), in *Al-Jarida Ar-Rasmiya*, June 30, 1977.

54. The CDR was headed by Fadil Shalaq, a former director of Hariri's Oger-Lebanon and board member of the prime minister's private charity. He was succeeded in 1995 by Nabil al-Jisr, the former president of Oger in Paris. The appointed governor of Mount Lebanon, Yamut as-Suhayl, is the brother of the

representative of Hariri's charity organization in Brazil. 'Abd al-Qadir Itani, also a former employee of Hariri's Oger Company, played a key role in granting contracts on behalf of the governorate to numerous companies including Geneco.

55. See interview with Maysara Sukkar, managing director of Sukleen/Sukkar, in *Daily Star*, April 13, 1999. In 1999, the Court of Accounts found that virtually none of the projects financed via the Independent Municipal Fund had fulfilled tendering requirements, and therefore declared these contracts nil and void. For excerpts of the Court's report, see *An-Nahar*, April 1, 1999; and *Magazine*, April 9, 1999.

56. Between 1992 and 1999, the CDR spent nearly $5.4 billion or 80% of total public capital expenditure in this period. See Republic of Lebanon, Council for Development and Reconstruction, *Progress Report* (Beirut: March 1999), 75.

57. See law 117, in *Al-Jarida ar-Rasmiya*, December 12, 1991.

58. This point was one of the main findings of a 1991 survey of the CDR's administrative structures prepared by the private consultants Coopers & Lybrandt-Deloitte. See also C. Raye, "CDR: L'Etat et son Double," *L'Orient-Express*, October 1997.

59. On Hariri and his reliance on private consultants and business associates in formulating public policies, see Joseph Samaha in *Al-Hayat*, July 20, 1993.

60. See *Al-Hayat*, August 10, 1998. It has mainly been Beirut MP Najah Wakim who repeatedly lambasted the prime minister for these practices. For example, see *An-Nahar*, December 14, 1995.

61. This stipulation is laid down in the Constitution, Article 89. See Sh. Juha, ed., *ad-Dustur al-Lubnani, Tarikhuhu, Ta'adilatuhu, Nassuhu al-Hali 1926–1991* (Beirut: Dar al-Ilm lil-malayin, 1998).

62. Efforts to circumvent parliament's approval of any privatization scheme were stretched in this case by setting the maturity of the BOT contract at 45 years. See Investment Development Authority of Lebanon, *Beirut Sports City Commercial Center* (Beirut: n.d.); Wakim, *Al-Ayadi as-Sawd*, 202–203.

63. See law 117, in *Al-Jarida ar-Rasmiya*, December 12, 1991.

64. See C. Rayes, "Voyage au bout de Solidère," *L'Orient-Express*, November 1996; H. Sarkis, "Territorial Claims: Architecture and Post-War Attitudes Toward the Built Environment," in S. Khalaf, and P. S. Khoury, eds., *Recovering Beirut: Urban Design and Post-War Reconstruction* (Leiden: Brill, 1993), 114.

65. The main players in this network included Fadil Shalaq and Nabil Jisr (successive heads of the CDR and former employees of Hariri's Oger), Muhamad Ghaziri (appointed president of the Municipal Council of Beirut and another of Hariri's former employees), Nicolas Saba (successor to Ghaziri and a former employee of Hariri's Oger in Saudi Arabia), Yusif Khalil (head of the *Cadastre* and widely seen as one of Hariri's associates), Fu'ad Siniora (Minister of State for Finance and formerly head of one of Hariri's commercial banks), several high officials at the Higher Council for Urban Planning (whose relatives were known to be or have been employees with Hariri's companies), Nasir as-Sham'a

(chairman and general manager of Solidère and formerly head of Operations and Maintenance at Hariri's Oger company in Saudi Arabia), Sami' Nahas (member of Solidère's Board of Directors and formerly legal advisor to Hariri), Basil Yarid (member of Solidère's Board of Directors and a manager with *Groupe Méditerranée* in which Hariri has a majority sharehold), three Saudi members of Solidère's Board of Directors (who all established business relations with Hariri during his stay in Saudi Arabia), and, of course, Hariri himself in his capacities of major shareholder (he declared to possess $125 million in shares, or about 7% of Solidère's total capital) and prime minister. Finally, other major shareowners are alleged to have included Siniora and several of his relatives, Hariri's sister Bahiyat Hariri, Fu'ad Sa'd (advisor to Hariri), Suhayl Yamut (*muhafiz* of Mount Lebanon and former employee with Oger), the wife of Bahij Tabbara (Hariri's private lawyer and Minister of Justice), Nadim al-Munla (former director of Hariri's Future Television), Ziyad 'Itani (employee of Oger), and Ghassan Hamud (Hariri's candidate for the parliamentary elections in the south in 1992). See N. Wakim, *Al-Ayadi as-Sawd*, 129–130, 147.

66. In response to a query submitted by Beirut attorney Muhamad al-Mughrabi, the Higher Council of Judges (*Majlis al-Qada' al-'Ali*) ruled on February 21, 1994 that the "judicial committees" should not be seen as an integral part of the judiciary, for the simple reasons that the Council had played no part in forming them and that it did not exercise any authority over these committees. This, of course, left the question open as to how these judges, then, could have legally taken up employment—and fees—outside the judiciary. See *Li aj-Janib Majlis al-Qada' al-'Ali*, Letter by Muhamad al-Mughrabi to the Higher Council for Judges, Beirut, October 9, 1995. For Solidère's payment of the judges' salaries, see *Al-Bayan*, July 1999.

67. The Lebanese judiciary has been heavily politicized and was often used as a tool by all players in the political settlement to further their own interests. This has been widely admitted by politicians and members of the legal profession alike. In February 1998, the Higher Judicial Council and the Bar of Beirut and Tripoli issued a joint statement deploring mounting political intervention in the judiciary and calling upon political leaders to stay out of the legal process. See *Le Commerce du Levant*, March 12, 1998. On the lack of independence of the judiciary in postwar Lebanon, see Sulayman Taqi ad-Din et al, *Al-Qada' al-Lubnani, Bina' wa Tatwir al-Mu'assasat* (Beirut: LCPS, 1999).

68. Saree Makdisi, "Laying Claim to Beirut: Urban Narrative and Spatial Identity in the Age of Solidère," *Critical Inquiry* 23 (Spring 1997): 672.

69. Powell, "Neither Market nor Hierarchy," 301.

70. See the critique by J. M. Podolny and K. L. Page, "Network Forms of Organization," *Annual Review of Sociology* 24 (1998): 66–70.

71. See Granovetter, "Economic Action and Social Structure," 75–76.

72. K. A. Shepsle, *The Political Economy of State Reform: Political to the Core*, Lecture originally presented at the Seminar for State Reform, Bogota, Colombia, 1998.

73. For an overview of "Growth-Oriented Networks," see S. Haggard, S. Maxfield, and B. R. Schneider, "Theories of Business and Business-State Relations," in Maxfield and Schneider, *Business and the State in Developing Countries* (New York: 1997), 55–57.

74. Granovetter, "Economic Action and Social Structure," 56.

75. N. W. Biggart and G. G. Hamilton, "On the Limits of a Firm-Based Theory to Explain Business Networks: The Western Bias of Neoclassical Economics," in Nohria and Eccles, *Networks and Organizations*, 472. Also see C. A. Johnson, *MITI and the Japanese Miracle* (Stanford: 1982).

76. Interview with Samir Shankir, advisor to OMSAR, in Beirut, May 6, 1999. Also see C. Ingels, "L'Administration libanaise an sortir du conflit civil: permanence de l'enjeu politique partisan et impératifs fonctionnels de la reconstruction à portée nationale," Ph.D. dissertation, Université Aix-marseille III (marseille), 227.

77. Cited in *An-Nahar*, January 18, 1995.

78. After his third mandate expired, Hariri failed to form a new government due to a clash of personalities with the newly elected president Emile Lahud. The latter had made it clear in his inaugural speech in November 1998 that reconstruction policies should not go at the expense of the "rule of law" and a "state of institutions" (*dawlat al-mu'assasat*). For the full text of Lahud's speech, see *An-Nahar*, November 25, 1998.

79. R. Hariri, *Pouvoir et Responsabilité, Coût de la paix, perspectives d'avenir* (Beirut: 1999), 79.

80. See the commentary by Muhamad Husayn Shams ad-Din in *Mulhaq an-Nahar*, January 16, 1999. In as far as electoral results in Lebanon can be regarded as reflecting public sentiments, the Lebanese overwhelmingly answered in favor of the "party of reconstruction without cleanliness" in the autumn of 2000. One reason for this is likely to have been a widespread perception that Huss's "legalistic" style of government had exacerbated the economic crisis.

81. These "institutional uncertainties" featured "corruption," "informal competition," and "unpredictability of economic policies." Note that the survey also found that this level of uncertainty was significantly higher than in the MENA region at large. See Atallah, *Roadblocks to Recovery*, 10, figure 9.

82. In Atallah's survey, 60% of respondents expressed their fear that, once they had resorted to bribing, they would be asked by officials for more money. See ibid., 19.

83. For more details on this case, see R. Leenders and C. Adwan, "In Search of the State: the Politics of Corruption in Post-War Lebanon," *Mediterranean Politics* (2004, forthcoming).

84. Interview with Wissam Shaqur, Lebanese representative of Sar-Mowlem, in Beirut, October 10, 2000.

85. See *Daily Star*, March 3, 1998.

86. See *Daily Star*, March 11, 1998.

87. Evans's notion of "embedded autonomy"—where state actors have close ties to business but are still able to formulate preferences and act autonomously—captures well this apparently contradictory combination. See P. Evans, *Embedded*

Autonomy: States and Industrial Transformation (Princeton: Princeton University Press, 1995).

88. This observation is consistent with the findings of Schneider and Maxfield who suggest that "[t]he key conditions for sustaining benign collaboration [between state and business elites] include embedded Weberian bureaucracy." See B. R. Schneider and S. Maxfield, "Business, the State, and Economic Performance," in S. Maxfield, and B. R. Schneider, eds., *Business and the State in Developing Countries* (Ithica: Cornell University Press, 1997), 30.

89. This observation is consistent with Evans's view that with a "[l]ess cohesive and coherent state, connectedness risks becoming captured, and growth-oriented networks threaten to deteriorate into rent-seeking networks." See P. Evans, "State Structures, Government-Business Relations, and Economic Transformation," in Maxfield and Schneider, *Business and the State in Developing Countries*, 82. On rampant corruption in postwar Lebanon, see Leenders, "In Search of the State."

90. See T. Hanf, *Coexistence in Wartime Lebanon: Decline of a State and Rise of a Nation* (London: Center for Lebanese Studies, 1993), 86–96; F. El Khazen, *The Breakdown of the State in Lebanon 1967–1976* (Cambridge, MA: Harvard University Press, 2000), 241–249.

91. See M. Johnson, *Class & Client in Beirut: The Sunni Muslim Community and the Lebanese State 1840–1985*.

92. For details on the waning power of the *zu'ama*, see J. Bahout, "Les élites parlementaires Libanaises de 1996, Etude de composition," in J. Bahout and Chawqi Douayhi, eds., *La Vie Publique au Liban: Expressions et recompositions du politique* (Beirut: CERMOC, 1997); F. El-Khazen, *Lebanon's First Postwar Parliamentary Election, 1992: An Imposed Choice* (Oxford: Center for Lebanese Studies, 1998); V. Perthes, "Libanons Parlamentswahlen von 1996: die Akzeptanz des Faktischen," *Orient* 38, no. 2 (1997); and F. Kiwan, "Forces politiques nouvelles, système politique ancient," in F. Kiwan, ed., *Le Liban aujourd'hui* (Beirut/Paris: CERMOC/CNRS éditions, 1994).

93. On the rise of militia leaders in postwar politics, see K. A. Beyoghlow, "Lebanon's New Leaders: Militias in Politics," *Journal of South Asian and Middle Eastern Studies* 12, no. 3 (Spring 1989); F. Trabulsi, "At-Takawun at-Tabaqi li as-Sulta as-Siyasiya ba'd al-Harb," in *Ab'ad*, no. 6 (May 1997); and E. Picard, *The Demobilization of the Lebanese Militias* (Oxford: Centre for Lebanese Studies, October 1999).

94. For details on the increasingly prominent role of Syria's allies in Lebanon, see F. El-Khazen, "The Making and Unmaking of Lebanon's Political Elites from Independence to Taif," *The Beirut Review*, no. 6 (Fall 1993); J. Maila, *The Document of National Understanding: A Commentary* (Oxford: Centre for Lebanese Studies, 1992), 81–97; J. Maila, "Le Traite de fraternité: une analyse," in *Les Cahiers de l'Orient*, no. 24 (4th trimester 1991); and V. Perthes, *Der Libanon nach dem Buergerkrieg, Vom Ta'if zum gesellschaftlichen Konsens?* (Ebenhausen: Stiftung fuer Wissenschaft und Politik Forschungsinstitut Internationale Politik und Sicherheit, 1993), 33–37.

95. On the rise of the businessman-turned-politician, see E. Bonne, *Vie publique, patronage et clientèle: Rafic Hariri a Saida* (Paris/Beirut: IRENAM/CERMOC, 1995); R. Naba, *Rafic Hariri, Un homme d'affaires premier ministre* (Paris: L'Harmattan, 1999); Trabulsi, *Sallat bi-la Wasl, Michel Chiha wa al-Idiyulujiya al-Lubnani*; and Hamdan, "At-Tughma al-Maliya fi Lubnan," 169 ff. A profile of new business/political elites and an interesting discussion of the phenomenon can be found in an essay by May Abi 'Aql in *An-Nahar*, April 18, 1998.

96. Mansur, *Mawt Jumhuriya*, 249. Mansur was one of the members of parliament who drafted and signed the Ta'if Accord.

97. It seems to be exactly these anomalous developments that made most authors decide to leave out Lebanon from their cross-comparative analyses of the region's political economy. For example, see N. N. Ayubi, *Over-Stating the Arab State, Politics and Society in the Middle East* (London: I.B. Tauris, 1995); S. Bromley, *Rethinking Middle East Politics, State Formation and Development* (Cambridge: Polity Press, 1994); and R. Owen, *State, Power and Politics in the Making of the Modern Middle East* (London: Routledge, 1992).

CHAPTER 6

Fiscal Trajectories in Morocco and Tunisia

Béatrice Hibou

U nderstanding fiscal relations demands an exhaustive knowledge of politics. Without a doubt, the tax system is one of the clearest reflections of power relations within a given society. Yet to go beyond such general remarks and to understand concretely the current situation in Morocco and Tunisia we must take a detailed look at recent changes in fiscal relations and the events associated with them. This means integrating them into a historical perspective. For example, the way in which tax (or legitimate extraction) has been modeled historically depends on the particularities of a specific context and on specific sociopolitical configurations. Tax cannot be taken merely as an economic concept; it is simultaneously a historically constructed political concept. In order to understand contemporary transformations in fiscal relations in the North African contexts of Morocco and Tunisia, we must first clarify the historical processes through which some forms of extraction became legitimate while others did not and some forms of taxation became accepted while others did not.[1]

The events I have chosen to observe in both countries took place between the years 1994 and 2000. In Morocco, I focus on the latest fiscal amnesty, which in reality represents the resolution of the famous "purification campaign" ("*campagne d'assainissement*") of 1995–1996, bringing to an end the confrontation between the "central power" and the "economic community." In the case of Tunisia, I have chosen as my central point of observation the establishment of a genuinely *private* system of taxation, which reveals the ambiguous nature of taxes and their role in power relations. An account of these two episodes that places them in perspective will clearly demonstrate the complexity of fiscal relations and their historical significance and, at the same time, the impossibility of understanding fiscal reforms without taking into account not only the role and operation of networks and the play of lobbies and coalitions, but also the weight of sociopolitical constraints and especially, the specificity of modes of government.

Morocco and the Fiscal Amnesty of 1996

The official aim of the "purification campaign," which took place between the end of 1995 and the beginning of 1996, was to attack smuggling, drug trafficking, tax evasion, and corruption. During this period, and especially in January and February 1996, a huge publicity campaign was directed against these "new evils," which were accused of weakening the Moroccan economy and jeopardizing its integration into the international community.[2] A number of merchants and industrialists were arrested or simply convicted.

The Facts

The campaign is interesting for our analysis on several counts. It brought to light for the first time, officially and with great publicity, the scale and importance of activities situated on the margins of the law. Official statistics should naturally be viewed with caution, given the underground nature of the activities they are presumed to record and the politicized character of government data in general. However, with these caveats in mind, customs data for 1994–1995—figures that provided the rationale for launching the campaign—show the turnover of smuggling activities that year was as high as $3 billion (DH 27 billion). This sum is equivalent to Morocco's entire industrial production and represents one-third of the country's GNP. Smuggling was estimated to provide a livelihood for approximately 600,000 individuals out of a total working population of 8 million. The loss to customs from illicit trade was estimated at DH 6 billion, or about 50 percent of total customs income. This figure was confirmed by the tax administration, which indicated that tax evasion represented a loss of around 50 percent of tax revenues. It goes without saying that such activities were widely acknowledged prior to the purification campaign, yet it was at this precise moment that they were brought into the public eye and that quantitative figures were supplied.[3]

In addition, the campaign showed that these activities were by no means marginal. On the contrary, they involved virtually every sector of Moroccan society, including (or rather, beginning with) well-known big businessmen.

Above all, the campaign, and the data that were used to justify it, suggested that illegal activity—customs and tax fraud, as well as corruption and drug trafficking—did not constitute a dysfunction, but were instead part and parcel of Morocco's economic and political system.[4] The identification of activities as illegal and immoral was not stable and predictable, grounded in a consistent norm of legality, but politically determined. What the Moroccan case shows, in other words, is the impossibility of distinguishing the legal from the illegal, the licit from the illicit, and the public from the private; the law is not a unique and universal referent that demarcates a clear boundary between such domains.

Given their privileged position within a system of political power, fiscal relations are not univocal, singular, or the same for all, but fluctuating. As a result, the purification campaign was widely understood not as an attack directed against those guilty of fraud or the contravention of various clear-cut rules—and thus an effort to revitalize Morocco's economy. Rather, it was seen as a determined and powerful display of *arbitrary rule* on the part of the centralized power, and as a moment of extreme uncertainty for all. Centralized power moved unilaterally to alter long-standing patterns of economic activity, destabilizing norms that gave confidence to economic actors. The significant slowdown of the economy and the near paralysis of the country's principal ports during the first half of 1996 testify to this interpretation of the campaign among Moroccans.

A "gentlemen's agreement" brought the campaign to an end a short time after it was initiated. Although it was a brief moment in Morocco's political life, the campaign was nonetheless very important symbolically. Prompted by the economic consequences of the campaign, attempts on the part of the business community to defend itself against the arbitrary exercise of state power, as well as instances of violence between authorities and suspected smugglers, discussions were opened in the middle of 1996, principally between business interests and the minister of the interior. Apparently, the discussions focused on techniques to raise ethical-legal standards in the conduct of economic activity. These included the reform of accounting practices, the modification of economic legislation, discussion of (and criticism from business leaders about) the modalities of privatization and the outsourcing of public services (such as the concession of the Casablanca RAD data communications network to Lyonnaise des Eaux), the clarification of customs operations (in particular the system of temporary imports), the elaboration of rules in specific sectors of the economy (e.g., in the pharmaceutical sector), and the establishment of a committee of ethics.

However, the technico-economic packaging of the talks failed to hide from participants the political dimension of the discussions. In reality, what was at stake was the need to put an end to a violent confrontation between the central power and economic actors who were considered at that moment, rightly or wrongly, to be potential dissidents. In other words, negotiations over how to end the purification campaign were a matter of redefining norms and recovering an equilibrium between divergent interests and forces, and not at all a question of assuring legality or the uniformity of fiscal relations.

Following nearly a year of negotiations, a fiscal amnesty brought this episode to a close. The intent of the monarchy to secure the reconciliation negotiated by the Ministry of the Interior was realized, technically, by the Ministry of Finance, which was all the more engaged in the process due to its pressing need for new income. Concretely, the negotiation between the General Confederation of Moroccan Entrepreneurs (CGEM) and the Ministry of Finance resulted in what was called the "*mise à niveau amnistiante*" or "updating amnesty," a double process that combined the updating of company accounts and bookkeeping with a fiscal amnesty for firms. In exchange for the government's withdrawal of all pending litigation and its agreement not to audit corporate accounts for a four-year period (1994–1997), enterprises agreed to pay between 0.16 and 0.65 percent of their annual turnover in taxes.

Two characteristics of this compromise clearly reveal its political character. First, the compromise was reached on issues of fiscal policy, the most political and symbolic of economic domains. Second, all the sectors of the economy, even those that were not *a priori* affected by massive fraud (e.g., large banks or groups such as Omnium Nord Africain or Société Nationale d'Investissement) were covered by this law. Apart from that, in order to make clear the contractual nature of the amnesty as a bargain between business and the government, Moroccan business leaders promised to create employment for 1,200 young postgraduates and to apply the "civic enterprise charter" in accordance with directives from the ethical committee of the CGEM.

The Campaign's Meaning: A Political Recentering of the Authoritarian System

A technical and ahistorical reading of the tax evasion and purification campaign presents the campaign as an operation "against corruption and tax evasion." In this reading, the campaign is associated with ongoing efforts by the central authorities to master and control fiscal subjects, and the resistance to such efforts, both individual and collective, by Moroccan political and economic actors. However, a more critical anthropological and historical reading calls into question this somewhat naive vision of the facts. In my view, the campaign and its aftermath established a new equilibrium between the central power and Moroccan political and economic actors in the context of historically constructed fiscal relations. We must see it through the traditional filter of the twists and turns of political relations and interpret it as an adjustment in the authoritarian Moroccan regime's methods of regulation.[5] This adjustment is less a matter of contestation regarding questions of supreme authority than a redefinition of modes of action that are considered acceptable and legitimate. It is in this sense that the purification campaign and the fiscal amnesty reveal both the Moroccan mode of government and the Moroccan imaginary, in particular its fiscal dimension.

The purification campaign cannot in any way be considered as a clean-up operation, properly speaking, or as an operation to apply moral norms to economic practices. Rather, it must be seen as the affirmation of the primacy of central power; as the exercise of the arbitrary authority of this power. As the impossibility of passing judgment on the numerous affairs brought to light demonstrates, the sole ambition of the central power was to show itself as the only master—the only party capable of changing the rules of the game—to make it clear that at any moment it could break other powerful actors and that at the heart of its method of exercising power was the preservation of confusion.[6] The feelings of fear, uncertainty, and perplexity, which were experienced by entire economic community can be explained precisely by this redefinition of fiscal norms without the participation of economic actors in the negotiation, as well as by their awareness that the system had been momentarily destabilized by and for the central power. The only principle to have functioned effectively in the production of the new norm was that of loyalty.

One symbol of the will to affirm and concentrate power, which escaped nobody's attention, was the transfer of customs administration to Rabat, leaving empty and abandoned a brand new building constructed for this purpose in Casablanca. At the same time, the judicial system did not fulfill its function of applying the law, but rather took on the function of a forum for announcements: judicial actions expressed the concern of the central power that at a given moment economic actors had "gone too far" in their interpretation of the negotiated norm, and that it was time to readjust the system. The central power felt itself to be under threat (or pretended to be), believing that the potential for dissidence had become too powerful. The adjustment of the system thus consisted of reintegrating activities and individuals that had escaped its control, and in affirming that the central power had a monopoly on the definition of the rules of the game.[7] Another sign of this strongly affirmed supremacy is suggested by the vocabulary employed in the campaign. Even though the political character of the campaign was well understood, nobody dared to refer to it in public by anything other than the official term: a purification campaign.[8] In the same vein, it is interesting to note the skepticism that developed *post facto* concerning the statistics put forward during the campaign: the figures for tax evasion or drug revenues were highly political, and the central authorities never really confirmed these numbers. Here again, the production of references mobilized during the confrontation and debate was monopolized by the central power. To put it another way, there was no serious questioning of the system. On one hand, the principle of legality was flouted. There was no difference in treatment among actors according to their real fiscal situation, no unification of new modes of taxation, and no reference made to the law in evaluating past fiscal behavior. On the other hand, the central power monopolized the production of new norms and discourse surrounding economic practices. There was no possibility of a dissenting discourse concerning the Moroccan tax system or the reorganization of the tax structure. Neither was there a redefinition of the function of tax administration and the role of the economic networks at its heart.

The campaign did have an effect on economic issues that were the subject of interest in the press. It helped to legitimate official discourse on the importance of healthy and formalized relations with Europe, the absolute need to restructure the tax system in keeping with European and global requirements, and the need to encourage competitiveness. Yet it did not have any effect on its purported object: it entirely failed as an assault on illegality and systematic fraud. To the contrary, rather than being eradicated, these activities even increased. Those convicted during the purification campaign have all been pardoned today, and nobody has been able to verify if they actually paid the fines that were imposed upon them.

In this context, the gentlemen's agreement must be understood as a redefinition of those groups of intermediaries that gravitate around the central power: on one hand, the Ministry of the Interior and on the other, certain businessmen. The agreement expresses the compromise forged among the actors of the "purification campaign" and, in one sense, the normalization of a form of uncertainty created by the central power to better affirm its supremacy. We should not give too much credibility to the thesis which claims that the campaign was stopped thanks to the organization of business leaders and their ability to impose their position, even if this group was able to make itself heard, in particular, concerning the negative effects of the campaign on the country's economic activity and image. Rather, the independence of the economic sphere from the political is as limited and fragile as ever, insofar as the Makhzen is an economic force that continues to rely on confusion and opacity and where the imaginary of the economic actors remains marked by this vision of submission to the central power.

A more subtle interpretation would argue that the presidency of the CGEM was co-opted into the ranks of the political establishment, participating not as a political actor, but as an authorized mediator, among other personalities of the economic sphere. The negotiation did indeed take place, but not at the initiative of the business leaders; rather, it was an act of the prince, via the intermediary of the Ministry of the Interior. On this point, it is revealing to note the absence of the government at the negotiating table and the omnipresence of the central power. Here once again we find illustrated the dominant principle of the Moroccan political system: the circumvention of legality and the primacy of loyalty constituting a servile relationship.

The negotiations between the Ministry of the Interior and certain businessmen, as well as the application of the *"mise à niveau amnistiante"* by the Ministry of Finance, must therefore be interpreted in terms of ruse tactics and the respect of form. In so far as it was materially and politically impossible to put everybody in prison, the only solution was to pardon everyone; hence the general amnesty and its application through the law.[9] The legislation was necessary in order to provide large enterprises with foreign investors an argument for their non-Moroccan shareholders concerning an operation that was an aberration from a strictly legal, economic, and financial point of view.

The *"mise à niveau amnistiante"* thus constituted above all a new form of the principle of disassociation between the infraction and its legal proof since there was no distinction made in the treatment of the concerned businesses on the grounds of whether they engaged in corrupt practices or not, whether they had broken the law or not, and whether their activities were illicit or not. The amnesty was a royal initiative, and different governments had little choice but to accept these liberties taken with the law. It was up to the new opposition government to apply this measure, which it did with few scruples as it was in need of income. The amount raised from the amnesty was by no means negligible, estimated today at DH 3.7 billion.[10] This amount was obtained thanks to the application of an accord to the entire economic community, revealing thus its political significance: loyalty and submission to the central power as opposed to a selective measure reflecting the actual state of infractions of the law. The CGEM negotiated the end of the confrontation for all of the economic actors, without any distinction between large and small businesses, or those whose activities were more or less respectful of the law. This episode implicitly underlines the disparate, particular, fluctuating, ambivalent, and by nature diverse character of tax relations. That certain individuals, due to their privileged relations of allegiance, pay no taxes with total impunity was not questioned. If the campaign occurred, it was by no means to address the nature and methods of taxation, but rather to show that the central power was still present, active, and the unique arbiter of fiscal norms.

Additionally, the "*mise à niveau amnistiante*" comprised an absolution, an erasure of the past, and a forgetting of disputes—in sum, a form of amnesia. In allowing a fresh start for all, the regularization of accounts linked to the amnesty constituted the normalization of fraud (and of the corruption that allowed it). It goes without saying that it by no means resolved tax problems and the lack of respect for the law. Today, as in the past, fraud is pervasive; the possibility of avoiding taxes or paying the minimum continues to depend on the nature of one's political relations, especially with the central power, and the system of exemptions is still stimulated by specific inequality-generating interests. The amnesty was never conceived as a guarantee of the rationalization and modification of economic practices. In particular, it was not accompanied by any measures encouraging openness and honesty. Today, as in the past, Morocco's economic fabric has a split character: big business rarely stoops to vulgar fraud, yet like any large enterprise in any other country, it plays on the amount and nature of reserves, expenditures, and the repatriation of funds. Small and medium-sized businesses have still not regularized their accounts. As for those businesses partially or totally in the informal sector, they have scarcely been touched by the amnesty, since its application depended upon declared turnover. The inefficacy of the "*mise à niveau amnistiante*" was all the more patent since it was far from being the first operation of its kind. It was thus immediately interpreted as a sort of seasonal operation, or a new procedure for the adjustment of the system.

Finally, the amnesty can be viewed as the recognition of illegality and fraud as essential cogs in the administration of Morocco's economy (via corruption). Yet recognition does not mean condemnation, and even less, suppression. The amnesty was understood as the purchase from the administration of its right to interpret the norm, and yet it was a temporary purchase, as the amnesty concerned only four years. In addition, nothing was done about the organization and role of the administration whose disorganization and institutional dispersion remain the instruments of confusion and power.

In short, the purification campaign, the gentlemen's agreement, and the "*mise à niveau amnistiante*" in the fashion of the *harka* of the olden days, form part of the state's engineering, as do the conflicts and confrontations with important local personalities.[11] The "controlled dissidence" created by the central power as an instrument allowing it to manage the political space more easily was inscribed, once again, in the economic sphere. It symbolized the exercise of power from the center and allowed the center to guide the negotiations on its own terms. It thus provided the central power with unchecked freedom, since there exist no countervailing powers capable of resisting integration into the central power's game. The purification campaign and its consequences were the central power's instruments in its project to reorganize political and economic space through ruse and negotiation. Yet the renegotiated norm is fundamentally the same as the one it replaced. It continues to depend on manipulating the ambiguity of status and position with respect to the law (in particular, public/private, legal/illegal, licit/illicit); on the definition of the norm in affirming the primacy of loyalty; on the multiplication of exceptional arrangements; and more generally, on the diversity of different legal statuses and tax relations. Moreover, it remains the unique referent for all large-scale operations.[12] The muddling of bearings is a mode of government: the confusion between legal and illegal, as well as the play on two incompatible but coexisting criteria of government (legality and loyalty) are widely used instruments of power.[13]

A History of Exceptions, Privileges, and Allegiance

We need to return to history in order to grasp the specificity of tax relations and the understanding that political and economic actors have of them. The language that speaks of power relations conveys the authoritarian and criminal attributes of the traditional system, but at the same time accounts for the deep links between the past and the present. Historical continuity is not simply inscribed in the lexicon of everyday life, but refers above all to those constructed discourses that enable the description and comprehension of the current political and, more recently, economic situation of contemporary Morocco. That certain journalists, even businessmen, invoked the concept of *harka* (the military campaign undertaken by the sultan to pacify rebellious tribes and collect taxes in the nineteenth century) to explain the arbitrary methods of the purification campaign shows clearly that the historical and anthropological depth of actions and the representations that animate them is neither an anachronism nor a simple intellectual invention; this depth is claimed by the actors themselves.

In Morocco, contemporary practices (political management in the field of illegal, even criminal activities; the fragmentation of the administration, especially the fiscal administration; and the discontinuous and arbitrary interventions from the Makhzen, particularly in the tax domain) constitute a modernized form of the discontinuous nature of the Makhzen's exercise of power. In a context where he was incapable of permanently controlling the whole of the country, the sultan encouraged, even contributed to, the fabrication of dissident spaces. Controlled dissidence resulted in the *harka* as well as permanent conflicts and confrontations with important local personalities. This organization of space more through ruse tactics and negotiation than through violence and command extended to the tax system and the control of economic activities, allowing but also controlling the private enrichment of these privileged individuals.[14] In the Makhzen spaces, even if there were numerous exemptions (in particular, in favor of religious brotherhoods), taxes were levied regularly (Koranic and exceptional taxes in the case of financial difficulties) or were negotiated against the provision of soldiers (*guich* tributes). Yet this tax base was largely insufficient, and the sultan was obliged to organize regular campaigns. Indeed, the rebelliousness of the dissident areas was more often expressed by a refusal to pay taxes than through explicitly political modes of protest. Thus the obvious response on the part of the central power, whose authority was nonetheless intermittent and partial, was to collect taxes by force. When negotiations failed (taxation being an act of allegiance and the recognition of sovereignty), taxes were collected by the *harka* (or *razzia*) during which the central power physically displayed its authority in taking its due through violence. The authority of central power imposed itself in dissident areas by the frequent organization of the *harka*, even under the reign of the most powerful and centralizing sultans. These expeditions became *de facto* the rule: it was a matter of displaying the sovereignty of the sultan in contexts where it had been fiscally contested. As such, the campaigns, then as now, constituted a "form of itinerant power."

The absence of homogeneity and uniformity in fiscal relations is illustrated by the difference in treatment between the tribes/Makhzen space and the tribes/Siba space, but also by the mobility of these groups and thus the treatment that was accorded them. Historians and anthropologists have shown the nuances of the Makhzen/Siba distinction. On the one hand, the borders between these two categories of space were unstable and fluid, the object of a continual remodeling. In the imaginary and the political reality of Morocco, no fixed or rigid distinction existed between them. As a result, the differences in fiscal relations, related at the outset to differences in status and in the nature and type of relations entertained with the central power, were themselves constructed and constantly reconfigured as a function of relations and negotiations with the central power. On the other hand, the dissident spaces were strongly encouraged, even created by the central power faced with the impossibility of controlling everything directly in a permanent and centralized fashion. In these conditions, tax relations could not be explained in terms of an alternative between submission and dissidence (the payment of taxes by agreement or under force). The dissidence was for the most part fictive, negotiated, and under control. Here again it was, above all, a matter of a power struggle between the central power and its fiscal subjects that, in the end, rarely resulted in acts of violence.

However, this absence of uniformity found another and even more striking expression through the existence of a special tax system for "protégés." This system of protection is relatively recent, developing from 1830 to 1840.[15] In the beginning, it was designed to reassure foreign agents and protect their commercial partners from the arbitrary nature of the *alouite* tax system, laws, and justice. The sultan accorded fiscal favors to foreigners on political or religious grounds, or to Jewish and sometimes Muslim traders for commercial reasons. Under European pressure, the system became so widespread that it began to weaken the Makhzen. The principle of protection was gradually extended to foreign powers and the number of protégés grew very rapidly due to illicit procedures (fictitious associations, trafficking in the consulates). More importantly, many of the Sultan's protégés came under the protection of foreigners. These developments led the Makhzen into a vicious circle from which it could not extricate itself: the growth of protection had begun to erode its economic and financial capacities to an extent that became even more disquieting as the wealthiest traders came under foreign control. The important drop in the Makhzen's resources led it to increase fiscal pressure on its less wealthy subjects and on the tribes, thereby undermining its legitimacy. In the aim of reestablishing the latter, the Makhzen granted new exemptions, reducing its fiscal base even further. It should be noted, and this holds equally for the current situation, that the protégés were by no means delinquents or marginals; rather they were particularly powerful members of the highest sectors of Moroccan society, exercising real influence.

What this historical detour reinforces is that in the Moroccan imaginary there exist no fiscal relations that are uniform, universal, and equally valid for all. Taxation expresses less a specific economic relation than a political one, which is thus by nature differentiated, fluctuating, and perpetually open to renegotiation. This specific relationship is not so much between a fiscal subject and an abstract bureaucratic state as between a fiscal subject and the state personalized by the sultan and the Makhzen.

Tunisia and the Private Tax System

In the case of Tunisia, despite the odd campaign in recent years against tax fraud (in particular against customs fraud and fraud in relation to social security contributions) the country has not, properly speaking, experienced an episode or important event in this domain. On the other hand, the creation at the end of 1993 of what I call a private tax system, through contributions to the National Solidarity Fund or NSF (Fonds de solidarité nationale, FSN), and the National Employment Fund or NEF (Fonds national de l'emploi,

FNE), enables us to grasp Tunisian fiscal relations in all their ambiguity, and in their capacity to elucidate power relations in the same vein as the purification campaign in Morocco. In order to understand clearly this dimension, we must examine this highly particular tax system in the framework of the broader Tunisian fiscal system.

General Characteristics of the Tax System

As in Morocco and other developing countries, the Tunisian tax system comprises two complementary characteristics with respect to tax legislation and fiscal relations. On one hand, the systemic failure to declare income, the underdeclaration of income, and the low rate of tax collection are estimated by the Tunisian Internal Revenue Service to represent 50 percent of tax income. In keeping with our Moroccan example, these figures should also be taken with great caution, and for the same reason. Statistics are no less a matter of politics in Tunisia as in Morocco, and we can see clearly in the Tunisian context the latitude such estimates allow. In concrete terms, figures such as these serve to justify controls and levies of all sorts, and enable the discrediting of "businessmen" who have fallen out of favor.

On the other hand, tax controls have been intensified in recent years to make up for the losses resulting from the free-trade agreement with Europe (estimated at some 70 percent of customs income, or 18 percent of total tax income), as well as the decrease in income from oil. Today, entrepreneurs complain about the arbitrary nature of these controls and the weight of back payments. It must be noted that for three decades, tax evasion was openly tolerated by the central power in order to increase its legitimacy, but also and above all to encourage the development of a national bourgeoisie. The current context, with the decline, or even the disappearance of income from oil and phosphates and the application of liberal norms, in particular budgetary rigor, no longer permits this. But this by no means undermines the role of taxation as an instrument of negotiation.

Although obviously never explicitly stated, tax fraud, a common practice among the large majority of entrepreneurs, continues to be tolerated and even encouraged. On one hand, a great deal of tax legislation is ambiguous; for example, laws pertaining to the VAT. On the other hand, there is often a large gap, in time as well as content, between presidential statements, the adoption of a law, and its actual application. It is not uncommon to seek without success legal texts pertaining to certain decisions that have nonetheless been applied. Tax fraud enables the justification by political power of its arbitrary intervention in economic matters, and allows civil servants in the tax administration to benefit from bonuses in proportion to the back taxes recovered. At times the back taxes are so consequential that they result in a negotiation between the government and the taxpayer; for the most serious cases, such negotiation takes place directly between the director of the enterprise and the president of the Republic. One of the biggest conglomerates in the country, which owed back taxes of three or four times its annual profit, managed to have them reduced by half in exchange for a contribution to the NSF (or the "26.26" as it is known from its bank account number) and placing one of its companies on the stock market.

Exchange is indeed at the heart of fiscal practices, as suggested by the contrary example of perfectly legal enterprises that do not contribute to the 26.26 or the NEF (known as the "21.21" account). It is thus by no means certain that the business community is the financial loser in this game, as they claim. Hence in Tunisia (as in Morocco), tax evasion should not be interpreted as a sign of lack of controls: it is widely acknowledged and tolerated. In the case of excessive opportunism or overstretched ambitions, an audit and back payment can always be imposed. On this point it is interesting to note that the name for the General Bureau of Taxes in Tunisia is the Bureau of Tax Controls!

The 26.26 and the 21.21: Current Instruments of Negotiation

Today, these negotiations take place increasingly through tax levies. In exchange for tolerating tax evasion and illegal activity or to obtain political or economic favors, sums were paid to the NSF (theoretically until the beginning of 2000) and later to the NEF, to the ruling party, to diverse organizations, or to associations close to the power in place. Thus there occurred a sort of substitution of "private" taxation for public, or "private" taxation for "public" benefits.

The NSF, better known under the name of 26.26, is a fund created, according to official rhetoric, to "wipe out the shadow zones," eradicate poverty, and provide for the basic needs of the excluded sectors of Tunisian society by the year 2000. Thus, according to the official justification provided by the presidency, the NSF expresses a different mode of social policy, one that relies on the solidarity of the entire citizenry. However valid these arguments may be, we cannot take them at face value since, on the one hand, numerous programs were already in operation in 1994 (such as the programs for integrated rural development or the program of help for needy families), and on the other, the methods of financing the 26.26 are highly peculiar.[16] The same holds true today for the NEF (or 21.21), intended to reduce unemployment, especially among the young (this time a deadline for results was wisely omitted).

214 • Béatrice Hibou

From the point of view of 26.26 revenue, it is widely known today that "voluntary" donations are largely made under constraint: every company and business must contribute two Tunisian Dirhams per employee per month to the NSF. In the same vein, they must give significant amounts at one time or another during the year, often during the anniversary of President Ben Ali's rise to power on November 7, Solidarity Day on December 8, election periods, or in order to solicit favors from the administration. This constraint may well be implicit, but it is nonetheless real: a businessman who fails to honor this duty of solidarity in a visible way risks serious difficulties, including tax audits, diminished access to capital markets, and administrative hassles. Each civil servant must pay one day of salary per year, and farmers 1 percent of their sales. Tunisian subjects, whether they live in Tunisia or abroad, are constantly pressured to contribute when they have to renew their personal documents or have other dealings with the administration. Finally, the state itself provides a substantial contribution to the fund. Moreover, it is very difficult to know how much the 26.26 collects; officially, its revenue averages DT 15 million, not including budgetary allocations. However, many observers dispute these figures. The economist Mahmoud Ben Romdhane estimates that income from businesses alone is as high as DT 24 million per year, or twice as much as the official revenues registered in 1997 of DT 11.7 million.[17] In economic circles, revenues from businesses are estimated at DT 40 million, of which DT 38 million are contributed solely by big businessmen.[18]

From the point of view of expenditure, it is practically impossible to obtain detailed figures other than those presented in official publications, as attested to by the difficulties faced by donors in their attempts to quantify social aid.[19] There exists no real budget, no list of recipients, no organization chart of the management system, no scale for the distribution of resources, and no evaluation of actions undertaken. For example, due to political interference, an evaluation undertaken by a research center, the CERES, provoked a split between researchers involved, and the complete report was not published. This does not mean that funds are not distributed; they are, even if in a discretionary and clientelistic fashion with little accountability.[20]

Even if the contributions do weigh on some businesses accounts, the amounts paid to the 26.26 are not that significant, especially as social policy has multiplied its arsenal of interventions over the past three decades. Yet their visibility is indicative of the underlying motivations behind the creation of the 26.26. It is, simultaneously, a political discourse directed toward the middle classes,[21] a means of political control, a mechanism for weakening the appeal of Islamic fundamentalism using methods borrowed by the latter from the single party (as the vocabulary used to justify the NSF suggests[22]), as well as an additional instrument of exchange between the business community and Carthage. There is a strong relationship between official tolerance for violations of certain rules or agreements and contributions to the 26.26.[23] Contributions to the 26.26 reveal a process of the "privatization of the state" in so far as the obligatory nature of contributions and the lack of any control on the part of public institutions enable the 26.26 to be interpreted as a form of private taxation.[24] Finally, it is a symbol of the personality cult surrounding President Ben Ali. Since the NSF was created on his initiative, he remains its sole master. The fund is not subject to parliamentary controls or the Court of Public Accounts (*Cour des Comptes*). The activities supported by the fund are undertaken in the president's name rather than the name of the state or the oft-denigrated administration.[25]

But the most interesting aspect for our discussion is that the 26.26 or the 21.21 can be understood as a private tax system—a system of taxation because of the obligatory nature of contributions; "private" due to the absence of any public controls and in terms of the methods of gathering and distributing funds in the name of a single personality (even if he plays on his dual public/private image). The quotation marks around "private" refer to the ambivalence and relativity of the notion. Even if the account is not included in the national budget nor subject to parliamentary control, and even though the fund belongs personally to the president of the Republic (in private, Tunisians call it a racket, and refer to the existence of a shadow account, the 26.27, used to finance the private residences of the head of state or for security expenses), nonetheless, we cannot say that the 26.26 or the 21.21 constitutes simply a process of extraction. We cannot reduce this mechanism to the simple capture of wealth, albeit used for social welfare purposes. Rather, these funds constitute a form of "exchange" in which real services are traded for control and other political benefits. The "shadow zones" are demarcated by the RCD, who designates them as such to the president. Contributors are listed and receive a receipt for their contribution, even those living abroad. Entrepreneurs and other influential businessmen who fail to make their voluntary contributions find themselves excluded from public markets and other economic opportunities, and run the risk of an audit or other administrative scrutiny.

A History of Delegation to the "Private" and the Tension Between Universality and Particularity

Even if, in contrast to the Moroccan case, historical references are less present in the everyday lexicon and less explicit in current political and economic discourse, they are no less active in the Tunisian imaginary. They are expressed through representations of the tax system, through understandings of fiscal relations, and through the changing limits, over time, of what constituted legitimate fiscal practices. Thus in the past in Tunisia, central authority was limited to levying taxes, the protection of the cities and peasants, the defense of Islam, and the administration of justice.[26] The centralization of the state was inseparably linked to the autonomy of the tribes, and methods of "indirect enforcement" ("*faire-valoir indirect*") were diffused throughout the society. "The nation is entirely under the submission of the Bey of Tunis, but governs itself," noted an eighteenth-century observer.[27] But commercial exchanges with the West, following the examples of the *Course, djihad*, piracy, and the use of militias[28] constituted both a principle and resource of government fundamental for the construction of Tunisia.[29] Modes of generating state revenue under the Ottomans, including taxation, were leased out.[30] In a parallel development, social and cultural activities were privatized by the *ulamas*, in particular via the *waqf*, but also through the educational and justice systems. Yet the ties between religious leaders and central power were close;[31] the former constituting the intermediaries or the liaisons between society and the state. Tunisia was "a society of private law whose activities rested upon contractual agreements among partners, while state intervention remained marginal."[32] The history of the Ottoman Ancien Regime suggests that in a general sense throughout the Empire, "privatization" was less synonymous with resistance and contestation of central authority than a process of permanent negotiation over rights and the organization of provincial administration in changing political, social, and economic situations.[33]

We find in this account an element of the current problematic of "private" taxation, insofar as the notions of public and private, state and non-state were and remain hazy, changing, and in any case, much less clearly defined than political theory would have it. Today, the references used by actors to interpret and understand the tax game arise from this history of delegation, privatization, decentralization, and attempts to centralize power. Reformism in Tunisia and Egypt at the end of the nineteenth century targeted this method of indirect fiscal management and attempted to concentrate power in the apparatus of the state. The contemporary privatization of the tax system, and above all, of social and cultural activities, may be interpreted as an attack on this recentering of power and a reinvention of institutions whose principles have been borrowed from the *waqf* and other private institutions of the Ottoman *beylicat*. The return to the privatization of certain social and economic functions is not in this case synonymous with a loss of control. To the contrary, it helps to fill the gap between perceptions of the "practical necessity" of state control over these functions and the limited material capacities available to the central power to carry them out.[34]

A second historical experience important to an understanding of contemporary tax relations in Tunisia is the constant tension, from the middle of the nineteenth century, between the reformist myth of universality and the various social forces encouraging differentiation and fragmentation. It is interesting to note that today, as in the past, there persists a contradiction between an ideal (which we would qualify today as the modern legal state) and the Tunisian mode of government, which runs up against it. Whether we consider the current institutional reforms and conditionalities inspired by the legal state model, or the reformism and desire in the past to establish fixed laws and centralize political action, the idea is the same—to define fixed rules that are known in advance and identical for all, and to reduce pockets of particularistic regulation and politico-administrative discretionary power. The stability and predictability of rules and economic laws should reassure economic actors, accelerate growth, and promote investment. And the depoliticization of economic decisions should result from the strict definition of public and private spheres and the clear relation between them.

We can clearly see which implicit definition of the law as well as the public and political action this idea of reform promotes. The implicit model is that of bureaucratic and repetitive state intervention; the incarnation of political principles such as legality, universality, and direct control; and a clear distinction between political and economic ends, between state and market, and between legal and illegal. The tension between this model and reality lies in the fact that the Tunisian mode of government is characterized by a multiplicity of referents; by the fluidity between public and private; by the confusion among legal, authorized, tolerated, and illegal; and by the instability of legal texts. Historical studies clearly show that power in Tunisia has always taken its force from the ambiguity of its manifestations and its nature, and that arbitrariness is a central element of the exercise of power.[35] This historical specificity of power may be translated in terms of fiscal behavior. During the period of the Bey, the tribes never paid at the first demand[36] since what was at stake was negotiation with the central power, and taxation was the ideal site for such negotiation. During these occasions, both taxes and status were negotiated.

Conclusion: Fiscal Reforms and Historical Trajectories

This long detour via historically constituted fiscal imaginaries and recent changes in the political lives of Morocco and Tunisia should enable us to reconsider current experiences of fiscal reform. Placing events in Tunisia and Morocco in historical perspective enables us to explain easily why results have failed to meet the aspirations of financial and aid sponsors, the reformers, and certain sectors of the population. Such a historical view allows us to go beyond explanations in terms of failure, the sociopolitical constraints linked to rent-seeking behavior, and the composition and actions of networks by showing (1) the importance of political, thus fiscal, representations and imaginaries; (2) the complexity of social relations and the impossibility of distinguishing between poles such as central power/economic networks; (3) the impossibility of thinking of fiscal reform in terms of demand and sup-ply when economic policy is formed by an ensemble of actors and is not con-trolled by civil servants and political leaders, and when the actors involved in reform processes have such fluctuating and ambivalent positions.

In the preceding analysis, I attempted to show how tax, fiscal reform, and fiscal relations are not essentially economic concepts, that they should not be understood uniquely in an economic sense. The examples of fiscal evasion in Morocco and Tunisia should not be understood principally as the economic expression of political contestation, or in terms of the contestation over cen-tral power. Likewise, the "privatization" of fiscal relations should not be interpreted as a profound questioning of the centrality of state power in the economy. To the contrary, I hope to show that the political imaginary is cen-tral to present-day practices of fiscal evasion and the privatization of taxation. The contemporary contours of the fiscal relations are drawn through histor-ical experiences. This is why, to return to the comments made by Steven Heydemann in the introduction to this book, fiscal reform is not under-stood, in the disputes under study, as an essentially liberal project. Rather, it is apprehended as a continual process of sociopolitical regulation and the reorganization of the inequalities that are inherent to relations of power.

Likewise, then, it is less important to identify the different actors, their identities, and the networks in which they act (this having been done in pre-vious research) than to identify the historical processes that define the limits of understandings of fiscal relations, as well as the limits of what is legitimate and what is not. This change in perspective leads, most notably, to the rejec-tion of a strict division between "public" and "private," leading us, instead, to underscore the fluid nature of these categories and the participation of actors and interests in one and the same political economy—whether they be pub-lic or private, whether they be in conflict or in consonance, and whether or not they share the same values or understand fiscal relations in the same terms. These latter processes are the subject of the preceding pages. This subject mat-ter leads me to reject an analysis in terms of group interests and political stakes and to refuse the logic of the winners and losers of reforms. To the contrary, it brings to the fore the importance of the question of economic subjectivity: suggesting how actors (here Moroccan and Tunisian fiscal subjects) understand fiscal reforms according to an analysis of historical processes of the institutionalization of fiscal relations in these two countries.

Notes

1. See Janet Roitman, *Fiscal Disobedience: Economic Regulation in Central Africa* (Princeton: Princeton University Press, 2004).
2. Béatrice Hibou, "Les enjeux de l'ouverture au Maroc: dissidence économique et contrôle politique," *Les Etudes du CERI* no. 15 (April 1996).
3. In the national press (*La Vie économique, Libération, Maroc Economie, Al Bayane, L'Opinion, La Nouvelle Tribune, L'Economiste*), employers' bulletins (*CEDIES Informations*) as well as through the debate on the evaluations provided by the Observatoire géopolitique des drogues (*Géopolitique des drogues* [Paris: La Découverte, 1995]; *Etat des drogues, drogue des Etats* [Paris: La Découverte, 1994]; *Rapport d'enquête sur les enjeux politiques, économiques et sociaux de la production et du trafic des drogues au Maroc*, photocopy, February 1994), the American agencies (Bureau for International Narcotics and Law Enforcement Affairs, *International Narcotics Control Strategy Report* [Washington, DC: United States Department of State, March 1995]), and the responses given in 1996 by the Minister of the Interior (*Livre Blanc* responding to the estimations of specialized organizations).
4. For a convergent analysis, even if it is not based on the same anthropological references, see John Waterbury, "Endemic and Planned Corruption in a Monarchical Regime," *World Politics* 25 (July 1973): 534–555.
5. For a detailed analysis from a political anthropological perspective, see Béatrice Hibou and Mohamed Tozy, "Anthropologie politique de la corruption au Maroc: fondement historique d'une prise de liberté avec le droit," *Revue Tiers Monde*, no. 161 (January–March 2002): 23–47.
6. This is not unique to the Moroccan political regime: in sub-Saharan Africa, e.g., all operations against fraud must also be read as central events in political life (especially in the resolution of political conflicts) and anticorruption commissions must be seen as quintessential places for the affirmation of presidential power. On this subject, see Louis Gouffern, "Les limites d'un modèle? A propos d'*Etats et bourgeoisie en Côte d'Ivoire*," *Politique africaine* no. 6 (May 1982); Jean-François Bayart, *L'Etat en Afrique: La politique du ventre* (Paris: Fayard, 1989); Béatrice Hibou, *L'Afrique est-elle protectionniste? Les chemins buissonniers de la libéralisation extérieure* (Paris: Karthala, 1996); and Jean-François Bayart, Stephen Ellis, and Béatrice Hibou, *La criminalisation de l'Etat en Afrique* (Brussels: Complexes, 1997).
7. Hibou, "Les enjeux de l'ouverture au Maroc."

8. Even if in private, a number of expressions such as "the Makzhen is showing its muscles" and "the power is tense" suggests that nobody was fooled.

9. According to financial law for the budget year 1998–1999 (*Bulletin Officiel* no. 4627 October 5, 1998).

10. This amount should be put in perspective; although it represents an unusually large sum for the budget year, this is simply because it comprises income normally due over a four-year period. The fiscal amnesty must be compared to the result of four years of fiscal controls. Such a result, according to the tax services, shows an income from control of DH 1.2 billion per year, or DH 4.8 billion over four years. We can see here an important aspect of the amnesty: an urgent measure among others (levies on national companies) in order to maintain the budget deficit at 3% (as opposed to the 5% foreseen).

11. On the political and symbolic importance of the *harkas*, see Tozy, "Anthropolgie politique de la corruption au Maroc" and for their contemporary economic importance, see Hibou, "Les enjeux de l'ouverture au Maroc."

12. This has not fundamentally changed since the death of Hassan II and the arrival of Mohamed VI, as illustrated by the episode of the allocation of the funds from the sale of the GSM license. The decision was taken to place the funds, in contravention of all legal principles, in a foundation (la Fondation Hassan II) out of the reach of all budgetary and parliamentary controls.

13. Béatrice Hibou, "De la privatisation de l'économie à la privatisation de l'Etat," in B. Hibou, ed., *La privatisation des Etats* (Paris: Karthala, 1999).

14. Pierre Guillen, *Les Emprunts marocains, 1902–1904* (Paris: Editions Richelieu, 1971); Ganiage, "North Africa," in Olivier and Sanderson, eds., *The Cambridge History of Africa* 6 (Cambridge: Cambridge University Press, 1985); and El Mansour, *Morocco in the Reign of Mowlay Sulayman* (New York: Middle East and North African Studies Press, 1990).

15. Leland Bowie, *The Impact of the Protégé System in Morocco, 1880–1912* (Ohio University, Papers in International Studies, Africa Series no. 11, 1970); Mohammed Kenbib, "Protection et subversion au Maroc (1885–1912)," in Jean-Claude Santucci and Mohammed Kenbib, eds., *Le système des protections au Maroc* (1996); Mohammed Kenbib, "Protection et subversion au maroc (1885–1912)," in Jean-Claude Santucci, ed., *Le Maroc actuel* (Paris: Editions du CNRS, 1992).

16. On the 26.26, see Salvatore Lombardo, *Un printemps tunisien: Destins croisés d'un peuple et de son président* (Marseille: Editions Autres Temps, 1998), and the Tunisian newspapers for official discourses and justifications as well as the amounts officially received. For a critical analysis, see the French and Belgian (*Le Monde, Libération, Croissance, La Croix, Le Soir, La Libre Belgique*). The best article is no doubt that of Chédly Ayad, "Le 26.26, c'est le président Ben Ali!" *Le Soir*, August 2, 1999. There are very few scientific accounts: see Khalil Zamiti, "Le fonds de solidarité nationale: pour une approche sociologique du politique," in *Annuaire de l'Afrique du Nord* 35 (Paris: CNRS, 1996), 705–712, and Béatrice Hibou, "Tunisie, le coût d'un miracle," *Critique Internationale* 4 (June 1999): 48–56.

17. Mohamed Ben Romdhane: interviews and citations in Ch. Ayad, "Le 26.26, c'est le président Ben Ali!" *Le Soir*, August 2, 1999.
18. Interviews and citations in Catherine Simon, "Les appétits d'un clan," *Le Monde*, October 22, 1999.
19. Document produced by a research bureau for a development agency.
20. Zamiti, "Le fonds de solidarité nationale," 705–712.
21. S. Benedict, "Le mirage de l'Etat fort," *Esprit* (March–April 1997): 230–231, and J. P. Bras, "Tunisie: Ben Ali et sa classe moyenne," *Pôles* 1 (April–June 1996): 174–195.
22. A reading of the Tunisian press is instructive on this point: the fund is to "wipe out the shadow zones" [*"d'éradiquer les zones d'ombres"*] (NSF booklet); to go from "darkness" to "light" (*Le Renouveau*, December 8, 1996, which takes up religious terms); to "pick up those left by the wayside" previously attracted by Islamic groups (*Le Renouveau*, December 11, 1994); and to "channel the gifts and donations" (*Le Temps*, March 22, 1993). "Faced with the inherent dangers of a situation which threatens to shake the foundations of the nation and destroy its homogeneity" through the 26.26, proceed to "reintegrate whole swathes of the national territory" (*La Presse*, December 9, 1996); "the aim is not so much to reduce social inequality as to build the foundations of a society committed to its indivisibility and whose principal force is its seamless unity" (*La Presse*, December 9, 1994).
23. Hibou, "Tunisie: le coût d'un miracle," 48–56.
24. Béatrice Hibou, "De la privatisation de l'économie à la privatisation de l'Etat," in Béatrice Hibou, ed., *La privatisation des Etats* (Paris: Karthala, Collection "Recherches internationales," 1999).
25. Michel Camau, "Politique dans le passé, politique aujourd'hui au Maghreb," in Jean-François Bayart, ed., *La greffe de l'Etat* (Paris: Karthala, 1996), 63–93; "D'une République à l'autre: refondation politique et aléas de la transition libérale," *Monde arabe, Maghred-Machrek* (July–September 1997), 157:3–16.
26. LucetteValensi, *Fellahs tunisiens. L'économie rurale et la vie des campagnes aux 18 et 19 emes siècles* (Paris: Mouton, 1977).
27. French informant cited by Camau, "Politique dans le passé," as well as by Valensi, *Fellahs Tunisiens*.
28. Fernand Braudel, *La Méditerranée et le monde méditerranéen à l'époque de Philippe II*, vol. 2, 1990 edition (Paris: Armand Colin, 1949).
29. Camau, "Politique dans le passé." With the upheavals it created in terms of taxation, the effects of exchange with Europe were felt in every corner of the country. See Valensi, *Fellahs Tunisiens*, and M. H. Cherif, "Document relatif à des tribus tunisiennes des débuts du XVII ème siècle," *Revue de l'Occident Musulman et de la Méditerranée* no. 33 (1983): 67–87.
30. Abdelamid Hénia, *Le Grîd, ses rapports avec le beylick de Tunis (1676–1840)*, doctoral thesis (Tunis: Université de Tunis, 1980); Anne-Marie Planel, "Etat réformateur et industrialisation au XIX siècle," *Monde arabe, Maghreb-Machrek*

(July–September 1997), 157:101–114; M. Hédi Chérif, "Fermage (lizma) et fermiers d'impôts (lazzam) dans la Tunisie des XVII-XVIII siècles," *Etats et pouvoirs en Méditerranée, Les Cahiers de la Méditerranée* (Université de Nice, 1898), 1:19–29.

31. On this point see Khayr ed-Din, *Essai sur les réformes nécessaires aux Etats musulmans, Paris, 1868* (Aix-en-Provence: Edisud, 1987). Throughout time, these bonds were strengthened to the point that the reformism constituted an initial handing-over of *waqf* assets to the state, which indeed finished by being completely brought under the control of the state at the moment of independence. See L. Carl Brown, *The Tunisia of Ahmed Bey, 1835–55* (Princeton University Press, 1974), and A. Hourani, *La pensée arabe et l'Occident* (Paris: Naufal Europe, 1991) (1983 for the second English edition).

32. Magali Morsy, "Présentation" (1987) in Khayred-Din, "*Essai sur les réformes nécessaires*," 61.

33. Ariel Salzmann, "An Ancient Régime Revisited: 'Privatization' and Political Economy in the Eighteenth Century Ottoman Empire," *Politics & Society* 21, no. 4 (December 1993): 393–423.

34. See Camau, "Politique dans le passé," 63–93.

35. Jocelyne Dakhlia, *Le divan des rois* (Paris: Aubier, 1998); M. Hédi Chérif, *Pouvoir et société dans la Tunisie de H'usayn Bin'Ali (1705–1740)* (Tunis: Publications de l'Université de Tunis I, 1984 and 1986); Taoufik Bachrouch, *Le Saint et le Prince en Tunisie* (Tunis: Faculté des Sciences Humaines et Sociales de Tunis, 1989).

36. Brown, "*The Tunisia of Ahmed Bey 1835–1855.*"

CHAPTER 7

Participatory Development and Liberal Reforms in Tunisia: The Gradual Incorporation of *Some* Economic Networks

Jean-Pierre Cassarino

Since the early 1990s, political economists have devoted a great deal of attention to the potential impact of liberal and fiscal reforms on the economic structures and social and political systems of Mediterranean Non-Member Countries (MNCs), while focusing, among other things, on the gradual exposure of domestic firms to international competition, the dismantling of trade barriers, and the consequential loss of fiscal revenue. The need for enhanced credibility and financial support from foreign donors are often mentioned to explain the adherence of some MNCs to the drastic measures advocated by the World Trade Organization (WTO) and the European Union (EU). However, scant attention has been given to the multifarious ways in which liberal and fiscal reforms have been *understood*—if not reinterpreted—by some Middle Eastern governments. This chapter deals with the ways in which the Tunisian government has been successful in reinterpreting the scope of its liberal economic reforms, and with the dynamics that have gradually shaped the relationships between the government and some leading entrepreneurs of the Tunisian manufacturing industry since the early 1990s, while redefining the patterns of participatory development in Tunisia.

As a prerequisite to showing that the government has been keen on incorporating economic actors into its realm to secure its own centrality in the reform process rather than bargaining with such actors, this chapter analyzes the various factors that have led gradually to the political inclusion of some leading Tunisian entrepreneurs. These factors pertain not only to the definition of new account-abilities to which business actors must respond, but also to the resilience of neo-patrimonial patterns of resource allocation that demonstrate the state's ability to preserve its central position in the political economy during the course of purportedly market-oriented economic reforms.

The first part of this chapter examines how economic reforms have been deepened and reinforced since the late 1980s, without diminishing the persistent interference of the ruling party in Tunisia's economy and society, and with little movement toward state divestiture of public assets. The analysis refers to the specific characteristics of an institutional environment that, despite its liberal orientation, has retained most of the traits of neo-patrimonialism, evident in the government's efforts to construct the impression of a social consensus around matters of economic and social policy, the production of an ethic of governance, the selective allocation of resources, and the definition of new accountabilities that made economic actors more responsible for mismanagement and entrepreneurial failure or bankruptcy. In other words, instruments of control have been designed to secure, as former minister of industry, Slaheddine Bouguerra, put it, the "balance between economic growth and social stability" in today's Tunisia.[1]

The second part of this chapter focuses on the gradual incorporation of specific entrepreneurial groups into the political arena. These groups are only one part of the overall configuration of the private sector in Tunisia and consequently cannot be viewed as representative of the Tunisian private sector as a whole. They are elements of a business elite that existed well before the reinforcement of open-door economic policies in the late 1980s. Hence, the point is not to give a global picture of state–entrepreneur relations, but to analyze the material and symbolic factors that favored a rapprochement between the state and leading entrepreneurs. While drawing on the theoretical insights of network analysts and exchange theorists, the purpose of this second part is to shed light on the patterns of exchange and the complementary interests that have shaped, if not institutionalized, the relationships between the leading entrepreneurs of the manufacturing industries and the Tunisian government in the framework of a network organization that is subject to examination.

The Partial Inclusion of Economic Networks

There is no question that the patterns of participatory development in Tunisia have changed dramatically since 1988. New economic actors have entered the private sector while taking advantage of the pro-business reforms that followed the signing of the 1995 Euro-Tunisian partnership agreement. Moreover, even though liberal reforms were reinforced, the centrality of the state and its ability to adjust to the demands of conditionality imposed by its main donors (the IMF, the World Bank, and the EU) remains a given and is central to understanding the Tunisian pattern of participatory development, including the expansion of the private sector and the revival of entrepreneurs as valued social actors.

Since the adoption of the 1988 National Pact and the government's efforts to expand its social base, entrepreneurs have been referred to by the government as full-fledged actors in the development process of Tunisia. The Pact was intended, in part, to gain the confidence of the private sector and thus strengthen the social bases of President Zin El-Abidin Ben Ali's new regime, the so-called New Era. It was also seen as one element in the government's egalitarian vision of global reconciliation among social and economic actors in Tunisia. Most importantly, the National Pact constituted a way of dealing with a society that was increasingly diverse demographically, in terms of expectations for the future, ideology, and economic power.

Given the irreversibility of liberal reforms, entrepreneurs were asked, under the umbrella Union Tunisienne de l'Industrie du Commerce et de l'Artisanat (UTICA), to adhere to a new framework of relationships between the state and society, and also within society itself. Moreover, defining the National Pact as a normative consensus, albeit one imposed from above, was a prerequisite to the state's incorporation of diverse and not always compatible social and economic forces, while fostering new patterns of control. This point is essential as it shows that the gradual incorporation of economic networks started by creating the appearance of an all-pervasive social consensus, which, at the same time, helped to consolidate the centrality of the state in all spheres of private initiative.[2] In fact, since 1988 the relationships among the state and associations, as well as the state and entrepreneurs in Tunisia have been deeply intertwined. Moreover, though often taken for granted today, this tightly linked relationship ran counter to prior trends: until 1988, no specific privileges were granted to entrepreneurs as such. Yet by the late 1980s, the state was keen on making entrepreneurs more compliant with its rhetoric of social consensus. This concern became explicit during the early 1990s when the government undertook what it called the "decompartmentalization"[3] of firms, through associative action. This recent coinage refers metaphorically to the need to pull down the walls that separate the various components of Tunisian society from one another (e.g., citizens, entrepreneurs, and political militants), with a view toward mobilizing their collective participation. The "decompartmentalization" of firms constitutes the second step—the 1988 National Pact being the first—that led to the gradual incorporation of entrepreneurial groups by the state.

This new orientation may have stemmed from the government's awareness that entrepreneurs in Tunisia could represent, in a context of reinforced liberalization and privatization, a potential threat to the government's top–down management of the economy and to its efforts to legitimate reform policies as the expression of a national consensus on issues of economic development. Five years after the endorsement of the National Pact, on April 23, 1993, the state introduced the annual celebration of the "Journée Nationale des Associations." This can be seen as an official attempt to reaggregate social forces, whether influential or not, in order to complement the actions of the government.[4] This concern has been explicit since 1993, even though, as explained later, its scope appears different in today's Tunisia. The most illustrative example of the government's awareness of the existence of potentially competitive initiatives led by private entrepreneurs concerned the associative activities of the Institut Arabe des Chefs d'Entreprises (IACE). In the context of this essay, the IACE can be understood as a financially autonomous network of economic actors whose main objective was to promote market information about economic development in Tunisia. Created in 1985, the IACE developed substantially thanks to the initiatives of its chairman, Mansour Moalla. However, in June 1993, Moalla resigned following a defamatory public campaign denouncing the existence of a "Masonic lodge" whose main objective was to turn itself into an "unavoidable lobby" in order to "control the structures of the national economy."[5] There is no question that the 1993 BIAT (Banque Internationale Arabe de Tunisie)-IACE episode revealed the threshold beyond which autonomous private initiatives could not prosper. At the same time, the retaliation against Moalla marked a milestone in the relationship between the government and entrepreneurs. It constituted a clear signal regarding the government's willingness to support private initiatives, provided they did not infringe on the government's centrality.

However, while determined to preserve its authority, the government nonetheless needed to adapt to shifts in the economic environment, and to the demands of reorganizing its social base though the incorporation of business networks. This was especially apparent in the developments that followed the implementation of the New Investment Incentives Code (NIIC) in December 1993. The NIIC standardized incentives for foreign and Tunisian investors, who were expected to increase exports, promote the transfer of technology, and generate additional employment. Foreign investors were granted fiscal advantages, which varied according to the legal status of the firms and their sectoral distribution. For instance, foreign business companies in Tunisia, which are wholly export-oriented (i.e., offshore companies), benefited from a ten-year tax exemption on all income and profits. Moreover, they could also import freely all the products and materials they needed for their production line, and could sell up to 20 percent of their output on the local market. Regarding the textile and clothing industries, the NIIC offered large benefits, since foreign firms are not subjected to a 17–43 percent customs duty on the import of textile manufacturing equipment and materials, as well as to VAT. As for business concerns that are partly export oriented, the NIIC stipulates that they benefit from incentives similar to those granted to offshore companies, but only on the exported portion of their output. In other words, such business concerns benefit from a ten-year tax exemption on all income and profits stemming from their export activities. Moreover, the products, goods, and services required for exports are not subjected to VAT.[6]

While additional tax advantages have been granted to all entrepreneurs, those who run export-oriented businesses are the most favored by the measures contained in the NIIC. For instance, tax exemption is applied to a share (35 percent) of their reinvested profits and income. Imported goods and equipment that are not available on the domestic market are subject to a 10 percent customs duty. Most of the measures contained in the NIIC have been introduced to stimulate exports and attract foreign direct investments (FDIs) to Tunisia. Others have been implemented in the wake of the principles of participatory development, which present the state as the main guarantor of social mobility and the advocate of private entrepreneurship.

The tax and fiscal advantages that have been granted to Tunisian and foreign investors, together with the creation of an array of financial funds aimed at supporting private entrepreneurship, give only a partial impression of the context of participatory development in which the gradual incorporation of economic networks took place. Formal institutions have been mobilized by the Tunisian government to supervise the expansion of the private sector in the framework of the NIIC. This concerns more particularly the Bourse de la Sous-Traitance et du Partenariat (BSTP),[7] the purpose of which is to select business companies eligible for industrial subcontracting in Tunisia. The improvement of quality production and the evaluation of transaction costs are also part of the BSTP program. The scope and cost of reforms initiated by the government is also reflected in the creation of the Fonds de Promotion et de Décentralisation Industrielle (FOPRODI),[8] the Fonds de Promotion et de Maîtrise de la Technologie (FOPROMAT),[9] the Fonds de Dépollution (FODEP),[10] the Fonds de Développement de la Compétitivité Industrielle (FODEC),[11] and in the tax exemption granted to promote vocational training in industrial firms through the Centre National de Formation Continue et de Promotion Professionnelle (CNFCPP).[12]

It is difficult to evaluate the extent to which such financial funds have been incidental to the development of the private sector in Tunisia. Few official reports exist on the concrete outcome of their activities that are, arguably, directed to only one component of the national economy, namely the private sector. If anything, the existence of such funds is congruent with the export-led economic policies that have been reinforced since the late 1980s, following the 1986 structural adjustment program.

Significantly, the creation in June 1992 of a Ministry for International Cooperation and Foreign Investment, and the subsequent opening in several European industrial cities of branch offices of the Agence de Promotion de l'Investissement Extérieur (APIE),[13] support the argument that investments and exports constitute a priority in the growth strategy of the Tunisian government. Such sectors as agriculture, textiles, mechanics, and food processing have increased their contribution to growth. However, as shown in figure 7.1, the yearly number of operative firms in manufacturing industries has decreased steadily since 1990, as have employment levels in this sector.[14] The decreasing number of active firms created in the Tunisian manufacturing sector does not mean that the contribution of the manufacturing sector to growth in GDP has diminished accordingly. On the contrary, the manufacturing sector accounted for 16.5 percent of GDP in 1992 and for 18.8 percent in 1995.[15] Rather, this phenomenon shows that the reforms contained in the 1993 NIIC have not been beneficial to the expansion of the private sector itself.

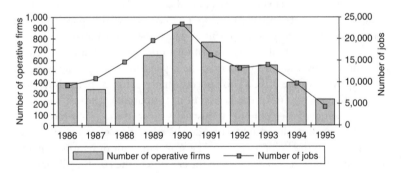

Figure 7.1 Growth and decline in the number of operative firms and job creation in the .... of .... industries (1986-1995).

Source: Data elaborated on by the author on the basis of *Le Courrier de l'Industrie* no. 73 (March 1996).

Three interrelated factors may account for this causal relationship. First, the impediments to the expansion of the private sector lie in the high cost of the contributions to national insurance, namely, the Caisse Nationale de la Sécurité Sociale (CNSS), which amounts to 40 percent of labor costs, on average. This policy, based on the principle of the welfare state, turns out to have a double-edged effect: on the one hand, it reinforces "the alliance between economic growth and social stability" in Tunisia, while contributing to the redistributive effects of growth;[16] on the other hand, however, the high social cost of labor induces employers (and employees) not to declare the actual amount of wages in order to limit the financial burden of the CNSS on their profits and salaries.[17] This constraint results in the development of a black market and tax fraud, which was officially evaluated at 36.9 percent in 1989.[18] At the same time, tax fraud of this sort should not be viewed exclusively as an illegal strategy for survival by overregulated economic actors. Such practices, whether real or hypothetical, may also allow dissent, in its various forms, to be monitored through tax aggressiveness. Tax aggressiveness constitutes not only a means of strengthening the control of the government over zealous entrepreneurs, but also publicizes the ethical and moralistic principles on which the government has built its self-image.

The second factor constituting an impediment to the development of entrepreneurship is related to structural characteristics. Despite the adoption of various policies aimed at guaranteeing the process of state divestiture and privatization, state-owned enterprises (SOEs) remain the central actors of the national economy, not only in terms of market outlets but also in terms of employment.[19] Figures related to the number of privatized firms remain unclear and contradictory. In 1989, the government introduced another legal definition of SOEs, which was also defined under Bourguiba in 1985. Law 89-9 stipulated that an SOE is a firm in which 50 percent of its capital is owned by the state or public bodies (article 8). Following this new definition, the number of SOEs dropped from 307 to 200.[20] However, it has to be said that this mathematical approach to the process of privatization is not automatically conducive to state disengagement.

In fact, in accordance with law 94-102, even after their privatization former SOEs remain subject to the control of the state or the public administration, for public administrators can veto both the merger of a newly privatized firm with another entity and its possible liquidation.[21] Moreover, the shares of a privatized firm can be neither subject to the prior approval of the minister in charge of privatization nor transferable for a certain period of time.[22] In other words, regardless of the different definitions and the official number of SOEs in Tunisia, their privatization does not necessarily imply a loss of state control over their management. Government interference in the management of a privatized firm stems from its desire to minimize the social consequences of privatization, in terms of dismissals, and to maximize its centrality in the field of economic control by impeding the potential formation of mergers. Moreover, such interference contributes to the blurring of boundaries between the Tunisian private and public sectors; so much so that IMF officials consider that the amount of investments dedicated to the private sector tends to be statistically overstated, "as investment by public enterprises is generally included in the data for private sector investment."[23] In the same vein, Riadh Zghal, a Tunisian economist, confirms that "there are no statistics related to the [specific] contribution of the private sector to Gross Domestic Product (GDP)."[24] Further, the commitment of the state to the management of privatized firms secures its position of social provider, but does not conceal the impediments that the expansion of Tunisian private entrepreneurship faces. The technical and legal foundations of the privatization process are important to understand the extent to which these have shaped the configuration of the private sector in Tunisia, and how these have allowed the commitment of the GoT in the economy to be readjusted since the late 1980s.

The third impediment to the expansion of private entrepreneurship is related to the second and refers to cumbersome bureaucratic procedures. Owing to the existence of import quotas on raw materials and equipment, and to the introduction of import licenses, entrepreneurs find it difficult to deal with a public administration that remains "protectionist."[25] Moreover, while in the late 1980s Eva Bellin observed that "a project [required] signatures from over one hundred offices before it [could work] its way through the bureaucratic approval process," hindrances persist today despite the "freedom to invest" that was reasserted in the 1993 NIIC.[26] For example, customs clearance procedures constitute a serious hurdle to the survival of private firms. Although Abdelkader Ammar, the director of Tunisian Customs, has promised to simplify customs clearance by reducing to about ten the number of required documents, some sixty administrative documents are still required to clear imported materials.[27]

Undoubtedly, the "freedom to invest" constitutes one of the basic building blocks of the liberal policies that have been reinforced since the late 1980s. Official statistics confirm the growing number of private firms licensed by the Agence de Promotion de l'Industrie (API) from 1986 to 1993. However, these figures do not reflect the actual number of entrepreneurial projects that led to the effective creation of manufacturing firms. In other words, for an entrepreneurial project to obtain an API license does not automatically lead to its actual realization. Table 7.1 demonstrates that the ratio between *licensed* and *operative* firms in the manufacturing industry has decreased steadily

Table 7.1 A comparison between the number of licensed and operative firms in Tunisian manufacturing industries (1986–1993)

	Licensed firms (number)	Operative firms (number)	Operative firms/licensed firms ratio (in percent)
1986	929	393	42.3
1987	923	333	36.0
1988	1,942	434	22.3
1989	3,416	647	18.9
1990	4,321	931	. 21.5
1991	4,406	768	17.4
1992	3,629	550	15.1
1993	2,918	555	19.0
Total	22,484	4,611	20.0

Source: API internal documents, 1996.

during this period. This ratio illustrates that despite the growing popularity of private entrepreneurship (i.e., the large number of *licensed firms*), a large number of projects did not materialize.

Possible explanations for this downward trend in the access to entrepreneurship (i.e., the decreasing ratio of operative to licensed firms) include not only a "problem of communication" between the public administration and Tunisian firms, but also difficulties encountered by firms in accessing financial capital.[28] The interest rates applied to bank credits remain relatively high, varying between 12 and 17 percent, depending on the sector of activity.[29] Finally, as a World Bank official claimed, "the state is too present: it swallows too large a share of available savings, which is earmarked for public investment."[30] The legal context of privatization, the high level of interest on bank loans, as well as stifling bureaucracy, have had a certain bearing on the configuration of the Tunisian private sector, as well as on business–government relations. These became more intertwined following the signing of the Euro-Tunisian Partnership Agreement in 1995, which entailed not only the gradual dismantling of tariff barriers that exposed the domestic economy to international competition, but also the loss of import revenue and the bankruptcy of a great number of private business concerns. In the context of this chapter, the point is not to analyze the various costs and benefits for Tunisia in connection with the Agreement, but to pinpoint two factors thanks to which the Tunisian government has gradually mobilized some prominent figures of Tunisian entrepreneurship while reinforcing its centrality.

The "*programme de mise à niveau*" (upgrading of the private sector, PMN), which has been implemented in the wake of the Euro-Tunisian Partnership Agreement, has substantially contributed to reshaping not only the economic environment in Tunisia, but also the relationship between the state and leading entrepreneurs. The PMN is aimed at buttressing the ability of Tunisian firms to face international competition, thanks to an array of formal institutions and financial funds promoted by the government and the EU, while modernizing and optimizing their production line, developing vocational training, and promoting export. At its inception, this program was based on voluntary applications on the part of entrepreneurs.[31] However, faced with their lack of enthusiasm, the government adopted more pro-active measures in May 1997 to "induce [entrepreneurs] to adhere to the PMN."[32] Beyond the technical and legal issues related to the ways in which the government has gradually reoriented the implementation of the PMN,[33] it is important to stress that the PMN appears in today's Tunisia as a prism through which the "challenges of globalization" and the "distribution of roles in society"[34] can be understood. Moreover, there is no question that it has established a hierarchical system that has gradually set up the government and its leadership as paternalistic "educators" who make citizens more sensitive to their accountabilities and are intent on securing the "alliance between economic growth and social stability."

In this revamped hierarchical system of interaction, the Tunisian business association (UTICA), professional associations, and some leading entrepreneurs have been mobilized since the mid-1990s while acquiring various privileges. While becoming prominent figures among Tunisian entrepreneurs, these businessmen have been endowed with the privilege of debating such matters as the need for "enhanced privatization and state divestiture," the "persistence of bureaucratic hindrances," and the "challenge of globalization." It is important to recall that these leading entrepreneurs have been, as it were, *ennobled*; some of them were decorated by President Ben Ali himself during the "Journée Nationale de l'Entreprise," which has been celebrated annually since 1996.[35] In keeping with the "Journée Nationale des Associations," the celebration of the "Journée Nationale de l'Entreprise" may be viewed as an attempt to reinvigorate, through the umbrella of UTICA, a spirit of corporatism among Tunisian entrepreneurs at large.

Today, the institutional context of the PMN has strengthened the *rapprochement* between a limited group of actors and the government. As argued before, it is possible that leading Tunisian entrepreneurs will reinvigorate the self-image of the state, but at the same time, the government is clearly working to reorient some segments of the economy toward the gradual development of conglomerates. Although no regulation related to conglomerates exists in Tunisian law, the government has been keen to make leading entrepreneurs more sensitive to the possibility of concentrating their business activities.[36] As a Tunisian official suggested, "it is necessary to help Tunisian corporate groups develop their dimension, also through the processes of mergers and takeovers."[37] This statement appears to be in sharp contrast to the official rhetoric of the late 1980s, in that it explicitly shows the existence of complementary interests between Tunisian conglomerates and the government, in the wake of the "presidential option" for the PMN. Also, it demonstrates that the terms "corporate group" and "conglomerate" have now joined Tunisia's business lexicon. In a nutshell, the gradual decompartmentalization of the firm, plus the implementation of the PMN and the explicit reference to mergers and conglomerates on the part of Tunisian officials have resulted in a new pattern of top–down participatory development in Tunisia, as well as in the emergence of an institutionalized network organization that I now examine.

Configuration of a Network Organization

The top–down pattern of participatory development is part and parcel of a governance pattern that has been reinforced since the mid-1990s in Tunisia. Governance, as defined by Goren Hyden, pertains to "the conscious management of regime structures with a view to enhancing the legitimacy of the public realm."[38] The specificity of the Tunisian pattern of governance seems to lie in the government's ability to incorporate social and economic forces even while transforming itself. The gradual incorporation or inclusion of leading entrepreneurs into the political arena constitutes not only a response to the need for tactical adjustments and legitimacy on the part of the regime, but also a strategy aimed at securing its own political survival and centrality in a context marked by increased economic openness and (controlled) liberalization. Undoubtedly, the government has been successful in legitimizing its own pattern of development management, for there has been a sort of interdependence of actors' roles—whether these belong to the public administration, the state, the ruling party, voluntary associations, or the private sector—which has been imposed by the presidential leadership and the regime since the mid-1990s without any kind of public contest or dissent.[39] Official rhetoric and ceremonies not only allowed the accountabilities of citizens to be defined, but also permitted new roles and privileges for leading entrepreneurs to be enhanced.

Moreover, the environmental conditions that were analyzed in the preceding section assist in understanding the motivations of leading entrepreneurs in participating actively in the Tunisian pattern of development management. It may be argued that this participation has taken place in the framework of a network organization, as Wayne Baker would suggest. For Baker, a network organization pertains to patterns of roles and relationships that induce in-group ties and intergroup affiliation, so much so that formal categories or groups are not significant barriers to interaction. On the one hand, a network organization is characterized by a certain degree of "differentiation," which "refers to the formal division of an organization into ranks, functions, departments and work teams [...]."[40] On the other hand, the reference to network organization also pertains to the degree of "integration" among groups or categories of actors. The last characteristic of a network organization lies in the fact that it is intentionally created by means of integrating mechanisms.

Network organization appears to be a useful analytical tool to describe the inclusion of some leading Tunisian entrepreneurs in the government realm and to understand how the relationships between the state and leading entrepreneurs have been, as it were, mutually empowering. In the context of this study, three integrating mechanisms can be identified.

The first element pertains to institutional reforms and environmental conditions. As explained before, measures have been taken that favor the emergence of mergers and corporate synergies in the Tunisian economic landscape. For large Tunisian firms, such new measures yield three main material advantages for their business activities. First and foremost, they reduce transaction costs owing to large economies of scale. Second, the acquisition of state-of-the-art technologies of production and the improvement of human resources reinforce their ability to face international competition, in anticipation of the complete dismantling of tariffs. Finally, the last material advantage lies in their ability to be granted preferential access to large-scale government projects.

As for the government, the encouragement and promotion of mergers and corporate synergies allows a certain degree of control over economic openness and social order to be secured. Moreover, the rapprochement between the government and some leading entrepreneurs of Tunisian manufacturing industries has allowed the state to develop a liberal image, appearing as an exemplar of market-oriented values and economic reforms. This demonstrates that the mobilization of leading entrepreneurs has not taken place in a vacuum. In fact, as explained in the preceding section, before the consolidation of a network organization, a series of institutional reforms and legal provisions has been necessary to make complementary and mutually empowering the interests of the government and those of leading entrepreneurs.

The 1994 parliamentary elections,[41] which marked the political inclusion of some members of business circles, constituted just one step among all those that led to the gradual formation of the network organization under study.

The second aggregating element of the network organization stems from the exchange of what Karen Cook and J. M. Whitmeyer call "valued items."[42] According to the two exchange theorists, valued items may include material, informational, and symbolic elements. In other words, they pertain to resources that are mutually relevant, whether these are tangible or not. The relevance of such exchanges is two-fold. For the leadership and the government, the distribution of titles of nobility to leading entrepreneurs allows a modicum of alliance between economic growth and social stability to be guaranteed, while securing their interference in the economic sphere and control over the expansion of the private sector in a context marked by state disengagement, the reinforcement of privatization, and reform of the public administration. Contemporaneously, through the implementation of the *programme de mise à niveau*, the government has maintained its monopoly on the selective allocation of the financial resources and subsidies needed to improve the ability of business firms to face international competition. This monopoly has certainly been incidental on the formation of an alliance with some prominent figures of the Tunisian manufacturing industries, while reinforcing the coercive power of the state and the leadership.

However, such an alliance, based on the dynamic of a network organization, may also stem from previously existing ties between the firms of some leading entrepreneurs and the state apparatus. Actually, one has to consider that some prominent figures of Tunisian entrepreneurship are, by family descent, the sons (or daughters) of the industrialists who, during the 1970s, took advantage of the open-door economic policies (or *infitah*) implemented by the state in order to set up their own firms in such nonstrategic sectors as the mechanical, electric, and food-processing industries.[43] Today, these family-run business concerns have grown substantially, while controlling large segments of industrial sectors. The point is not so much to recall that the 1970s industrialists benefited from the *largesse* of the state to provide for the survival of their firms, as to highlight the fact that their descendants have inherited, if not reproduced, the client relationships that their fathers had maintained with the Tunisian administration. This inherited relational capital not only increases access to financial and informational resources, but also makes the aforementioned patterns of exchanges more valuable. Moreover, the legacy of clientelist relationships with the Tunisian administration has probably led to the reproduction and resilience of oligarchic, if not, monopolistic structures in the Tunisian economy.

Importantly, in terms of generations, one essential difference between the industrialists of the 1970s and their heirs has to be stressed. While the industrialists were viewed as "dispensable to the regime,"[44] their heirs are now playing a central role in refurbishing the image of the state and increasing its capacity to control economic and social forces in today's Tunisia. Undeniably, the government and the presidential leadership have been aware of how the inclusion of some prominent figures of Tunisian entrepreneurship into the political realm could contribute to securing the political survival of the regime as well as to resilient state control of the economy *and* society. Leading entrepreneurs are now part and parcel of a pyramidal network organization, which can be schematically represented as follows:

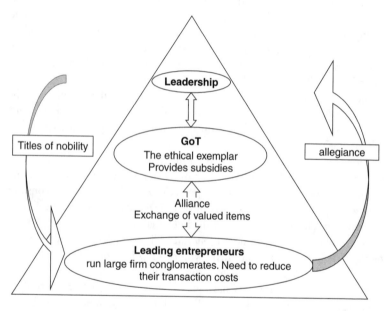

The last aggregating element is related to the second one and pertains to the emergence of roles and prerogatives that define themselves mutually in the framework of this network organization. Actually, while the presidential leadership presents itself as the craftsman of the "New Era" and as sympathetic to those who are wary of the effects of the Euro-Tunisian Association Agreement on the national economy, the government has turned itself into the ethical exemplar of economic reforms. This redefinition of roles would have been impossible without the inclusion and active participation of some leading entrepreneurs of the Tunisian manufacturing industries. Whether the latter are referred to as the paragons of progress and economic accountability, the ambassadors of the "New Era" abroad, or the captains, their mobilization in the context of the forementioned network organization has been crucial in legitimizing the resilient control of the state over the economy.

Further investigations are needed to evaluate the extent to which the exchange of valued items has been incidental to patterns of identification with the network organization. In other words, it seems necessary to go beyond the functionalist approach to network organization to avoid viewing the exchanges of valued items as being exclusively instrumental. Rather, such exchanges may also lead to patterns of identification that have been mutually rationalized or taken as a given.[45]

Conclusions

Following Joel Migdal, this study has demonstrated that "the [Tunisian] state is not a fixed ideological entity. Rather, it embodies an ongoing dynamic, a changing set of goals, as it engages other social [and economic] groups."[46] The desire of the Tunisian government to secure the "alliance between economic growth and social stability" is illustrative of how it has become wary about the promotion of the private sector without controlling its expansion. The resilient structural impediments to the expansion of the private sector have shaped the current configuration of the private sector in Tunisia, while reinforcing the centrality of the state (see the first section). At the same time, the government needed to legitimize this resilient centrality, which led to the incorporation of economic forces while allowing it to establish new patterns of participatory development.

The incorporation of some prominent figures of the Tunisian private sector into the public realm materialized in the framework of what was referred to as a pyramidal network organization (see the second section). Although further investigation is needed to explore the relational content of the exchanges that lubricate this network, the participation of leading entrepreneurs has turned the latter into above-the-average citizens, in stark contrast to the egalitarian principles contained in the 1988 National Pact.[47] Actually, the roles and prerogatives with which leading entrepreneurs have been overtly endowed since the implementation of the PMN have been incidental to the economic orientation of the regime from the mid-1990s to date, and to the selective allocation of financial and informational resources. Clearly, the state-led PMN and the subsequent inclusion of leading Tunisian entrepreneurs appear to be respectively the cause and the effect of the aforementioned pyramidal network organization. On the one hand, the reference to network analysis could not be made without focusing on the contextual factors that favored the emergence and consolidation of this network organization. On the other hand, the reference to network analysis was also a way of demonstrating that the PMN was successful in legitimizing the resilience of the state and in reinforcing a top–down framework of participatory development. In contrast to the 1993 NIIC, the PMN turned out to be more encompassing, as it constituted not only an economic adjustment program for the Tunisian economy but was also erected as a social consensus for society.

Finally, the government's policies aimed at favoring the emergence of conglomerates and the groupings of firms, through mergers and takeovers, will certainly make the transition more manageable, while giving leading entrepreneurs a stronger interest in building alliances with the regime. As mentioned earlier, development is no longer solely the business of the state, but this statement remains contingent upon how leading entrepreneurs intend to take advantage of their participation in such a network organization.

Notes

I am grateful to Steven Heydemann as well as the whole research team involved in the project, for their fruitful comments on an earlier draft. I also thank Richard Perruchoud, my former colleague at the International Organization for Migration (IOM, Geneva), for his criticisms.

1. See *Jeune Afrique* no. 1853 (July 1996): 95.
2. This is consistent with the view expressed by Hibou, Chapter 6 in this volume, reflecting similar strategies of governance in the domains of fiscality and taxation as in economic reform.
3. See, "L'entreprise et l'association: ensemble pour l'avenir," *La Presse*, May 13, 1991, which refers to the need for close collaboration between private firms and associations in Tunisia in order to "decompartmentalize the firm and to reinforce associative action."
4. This aspect was explicitly highlighted during the third celebration of the "Journée nationale des associations," on April 23, 1995. President Ben Ali declared that "an association is a social school. Moreover, it constitutes another area where good deeds materialize, so much so that it complements the action of the government and makes the role of civil society tangible enough to reach its objectives." See the daily newspaper *Le Renouveau*, April 23, 1995.
5. *La Presse de Tunisie*, June 5, 1993.
6. All the incentives granted in the framework of the NIIC, which contains 67 articles, cannot be detailed. I refer to some legal aspects that, arguably, are of interest to this chapter related to the relationships between the government and entrepreneurs. For a more technical approach to the NIIC, see the report of the U.S. Embassy in Tunis

entitled "Foreign Investment in Tunisia: Incentives Under the New Code," *Middle East Executive Reports* 17, no. 9 (1994): 19–21. See also République Tunisienne, *Nouveau Code d'incitations à l'investissement* (API, 1994).

7. The BSTP was created by the API in September 1986, in the wake of the Structural Adjustment Program, and thanks to financial aid granted by the UNDP. Today, the BSTP organizes the Salon Méditerranéen de la Sous-traitance et de l'Approvisionnement (SAMEST) every two years, in the ambit of a fair sponsored by the EU and the API, namely the Carrefour des Affaires et de la Technologie.

8. The FOPRODI was created on October 20, 1977, following Tunisia's open-door economic policies. This fund encouraging industrial decentralization as well as the promotion of small and medium-sized businesses in depressed area in Tunisia. The New Promoters program is partly supported by the FOPRODI.

9. The FOPROMAT was created on December 31, 1990, in accordance with finance law 90-111. It collaborates with the API and is in charge of financing the industrial and technological projects of small firms and of enhancing their competitiveness. Financial aid is provided up to 50% of the global amount of the technological and quality audit, for a maximum of TD 10,000. Following the 1993 NIIC, and in accordance with decree no. 94-878, dated April 18, 1994, the functioning and organization of the FOPROMAT were changed to improve the acquisition of technological equipment. Financial aid is granted up to 50% of the acquisition of technological equipment, for a maximum of TD 100,000. Technical assistance is subsidized up to 50% of the global cost, for a maximum of TD 50,000. Financial requests must be submitted to the API-based Commission technique du FOPROMAT and financial aid is granted following the decision of the Ministry of Economy. Cf. *Journal Officiel de la République Tunisienne* (April 26, 1994): 663–664; see *La Presse*, May 30, 1995.

10. In accordance with law 92-122, the FODEP was created on December 29, 1992. Its purpose is to finance investments made with a view to tackling the problem of industrial pollution, by promoting the construction of sewage plants, or firms recycling waste.

11. On December 26, 1994, and in accordance with article 37 of finance law 94-127, the FODEC was created within the Ministry of Industry. It is in charge of "stimulating the intervention of technical centres with a view to guaranteeing the development of the industrial sector and to facilitating the promotion of quality."

12. Since April 5, 1993, in accordance with decree 93-696, all private firms that adopt vocational training programs are entitled to benefit from a partial or total tax exemption on their profits.

13. In accordance with law 95-13, dated February 6, 1995, the Agence de Promotion de l'Investissement Extérieur (APIE or FIPA) was created in order to promote cooperation between foreign and Tunisian investors. It was created under the aegis of the Ministry for International Co-operation and Foreign Investment. See *Le Courrier de l'Industrie* no. 69 (April 1995): 46; *Le Courrier de l'Industrie* no. 76 (December 1996): 25.

14. A distinction has to be made between firms that are operative and those that obtained the "licence" from the API, but did not start their activities. This distinction allows the gap between the expected number of entrepreneurial projects and the actual number of operative firms to be analyzed.
15. Source: Banque Centrale de Tunisie, *Statistiques Financières* no. 118 (March 1997).
16. See *Jeune Afrique* no. 1853 (July 1996): 95.
17. This argument is analyzed by Riadh Zghal, "Le Développement participatoire. Participation et monde du travail en Tunisie," in Driss Guerraoui and Xavier Richet, eds., *Stratégies de privatisation: comparaison Maghreb-Europe* (L'Harmattan/Casablanca/Paris: Les Editions Toubkal, 1995), 210.
18. Zghal, "Le développement participatoire," 210. In order to tackle the problem of tax fraud, in 1995 the government put forward a "tax amnesty program" for employers, which linked the levy of the CNSS tax to charges paid on outstanding debts. See *Le Renouveau*, November 30, 1995, 6; and *La Presse*, December 1, 1995. Later, in accordance with law 97-4, dated February 3, 1997, employers' contribution to the CNSS decreased from 17.5% to 15.5%, and employees' contribution went from 6.5% to 5%. This decrease in the tax burden was officially presented as a policy aimed at favoring the development of private entrepreneurship. It has to be said that it also demonstrates the will of the government to curtail the black market. See *L'Economiste Maghrébin* no. 178 (April 1997): 13; and *Réalités* no. 575 (November 1996): 11.
19. In 1995, 75% of global employment was dependent on the public sector. See *L'Economiste Maghrébin* no. 172 (December 1996): 63.
20. See law 89-9, dated February 1, 1989. Article 24 also stipulated the creation of the Commission d'Assainissement et de Restructuration des Entreprises à Participation Publique (CAREPP), which is, since then, the public body in charge of organizing the restructuring program of SOEs. The CAREPP can give its opinion in an advisory capacity.
21. Fayçal Lakhoua, "Le Processus de privatisation de l'appareil productif public en Tunisie," *Revue tunisienne d'économie* no. 7 (1996): 144.
22. Article 32-2 of law 94-102 also stipulates that one or two administrators are members of the board of directors and that the minutes referring to mergers, divestment of assets, and/or liquidation must be endorsed by an administrator. *Journal Officiel de la République Tunisienne*, law 94-102, dated August 1, 1994, no. 62 (August 9, 1994): 1290–1291.
23. Saleh M. Nsouli and Jörg Decressin, "Peace, Investment and Growth in the Middle East," *Finances et développement au Maghreb* no. 18 (March 1996): 20.
24. Zghal, "Le développement participatoire," 207.
25. Ibid., 211.
26. Eva R. Bellin, *Civil Society Emergent? State and Social Classes in Tunisia* (Ann Arbor: UMI), 164. The author refers to the documentary and oral data she collected in Tunisia in 1988 and 1989.

27. Nonetheless, it has to be said that not all business concerns are subject to such hindrances. In accordance with the New Investment Incentives Code, export-oriented firms benefit from a privileged treatment from the customs, as long as they are legally labeled "non-residents," namely, when at least 66% of their capital is owned by nonresident investors and financed by means of the import of foreign currencies.

28. *L'Economiste Maghrébin* no. 145 (December 1995): 57. The "problem of communication" is one of the euphemistic phrases that leading entrepreneurs referred to during the numerous professional meetings organized by the business association, UTICA.

29. See "2001: l'Odyssée de la concurrence," *Jeune Afrique Plus* no. 1867–1868 (October 1996): 119 (dossier).

30. Cited in Michel Camau, "D'une République à l'autre: Refondation politique et aléas de la transition libérale," *Monde Arabe Maghreb-Machrek* no. 157 (1997): 15.

31. In effect, when the PMN started on December 25, 1995, in accordance with finance law 95-109, it was based on the principle of voluntary action. "Voluntary action is the fundamental principle of the mise à niveau. Nobody will urge you to apply for the mise à niveau. Without your will and your ambition to do better, the mise à niveau of your firm can hardly be achieved." UTICA, *La mise à niveau de l'entreprise* (Tunis, 1995), 23.

32. *L'Economiste Maghrébin* no. 183 (May 1997): 18.

33. For a more comprehensive analysis of the PMN, see Jean-Pierre Cassarino, "The EU-Tunisian Association Agreement and Tunisia's Structural Reform Program," *The Middle East Journal* 53, no. 1 (1999): 59–74.

34. See "Esprit d'initiative, effort et don de soi pour renforcer la société civile," *La Presse*, April 24, 1997, 4.

35. In 1996 and 1997, the "Journée nationale de l'entreprise" was celebrated on October 5; see *L'Economiste Maghrébin* no. 168 (October 1996): 10. However, perhaps with a view to reinforcing the corporatist dimension of this celebration, in early 1998 President Ben Ali changed the date of the "Journée nationale de l'entreprise." Since then, its yearly celebration takes place on January 17, which coincides with the anniversary of the creation of the Tunisian business association (UTICA) in 1947; see *L'Economiste Maghrébin* no. 201 (February 1998): 10.

36. In effect, the definition of a conglomerate in Tunisian law does not exist. Since early 1998, and on the initiative of Moncef Ben Abdallah (the newly appointed minister of industry), a *code des sociétés* should allow this juridical gap to be bridged. The *code des sociétés*, which is being considered by the Ministry of Justice, should "be aimed at developing, through an array of incentives, the sizes of firms. Also, it should include provisions designed to promote the groupings of firms," *L'Economiste Maghrébin* no. 203 (March 1998): 18.

37. Excerpt from Fadhel Zrelli's speech, General Director of Industry, during a conference organized by UTICA, and entitled "Conglomerates and Economic Openness," in April 1997. See *L'Economiste Maghrébin* no. 182 (May 1997): 33.

38. Goren Hyden, "Governance and the Study of Politics," in Goran Hyden and Michael Bratton, eds., *Governance and Politics in Africa* (Boulder, CO: Lynne Rienner Publishers, 1992): 7.

39. Sadiq Rasheed and David Fashole Luke, "Toward a New Development Management Paradigm," in Rasheed and Fashole Luke, eds., *Development Management in Africa: Toward Dynamism, Empowerment, and Entrepreneurship* (Boulder, CO: Westview Press, 1995), 4. "Development management" pertains to the fact that "development is no longer solely the state or public sector responsibility."

40. Wayne E. Baker, "The Network Organization in Theory and Practice," in Robert G. Eccles and Nitin Nohira, eds., *Networks and Organizations: Structure, Form, and Action* (Boston: Harvard Business School Press, 1992): 400.

41. Tunisian entrepreneurs' political inclusion culminated in March 1994, when Hédi Jilani was elected in Parliament as a representative of the first constituency *(dâyrat)* of Tunis. Together with Jilani, five other entrepreneurs were also elected. See Majlis an-nuab, *Â'dâ' majlis an-nuab (1994–1999)* (Tunis, 1994).

42. Karen S. Cook and J. M. Whitmeyer, "Two Approaches to Social Structure: Exchange Theory and Network Analysis," *Annual Review of Sociology* 18 (1992): 110. In an earlier article, and with reference to "valued items," Cook argues that "ties between actors are established, maintained, or broken primarily in terms of the 'value' provided by exchange relations [...]." See Karen S. Cook, "Network Structures From an Exchange Perspective," in Peter V. Marsden and Nan Lin, eds., *Social Structure and Network Analysis* (London: Sage Publications Ltd. 1982): 195.

43. The industrialists of the 1970s had been employed previously as civil servants who "were permitted a two-year leave of absence to try their hand in the private sector, during which time their positions and seniority in the public sector would be guaranteed." Eva R. Bellin, "Tunisian Industrialists and the State," in I. William Zartman, ed., *Tunisia: The Political Economy of Reform* (Boulder, CO: Lynne Rienner, 1991): 51.

44. Eva R. Bellin, "The Politics of Profit in Tunisia: Utility of the Rentier Paradigm?" *World Development* 22, no. 3 (1994): 431.

45. See Russell Hardin, *One for All: The Logics of Group Conflict* (Princeton: Princeton University Press, 1995).

46. Joel S. Migdal, "The State in Society: An Approach to Struggles for Domination," in Joel S. Migdal, Atul Kohli, and Vivienne Shue, eds., *State Power and Social Forces: Domination and Transformation in the Third World* (New York: Cambridge University Press, 1994): 12.

47. As this was explicitly declared during a meeting presided over by former Prime Minister Hamed Karoui and organized by UTICA, on January 13, 1997: "Tunisian businessmen cannot be viewed as mere citizens." The need for a special status was recognized with reference to the problem of visas. *L'Economiste Maghrébin* no. 183 (May 1997): 13.

PART 3

The Limits of Network-Based Approaches

CHAPTER 8

Challenges to Networks of Privilege in Morocco: Implications for Network Analysis

Melani Cammett

An implicit assumption in the literature on Morocco and in many studies of state–society relations in developing countries is that "real" politics, lobbying, and policy making take place in the realm of the informal. Because the institutions governing the market and state–society relations are arguably less articulated outside of advanced, industrialized countries, analysts presume that dense personalized networks fill the void where formal organizations would otherwise operate. Although this image sets up a false separation between networks and organizations, which more often than not coexist both in developing and developed countries, I accept that until recently interest transmission and policy making indeed largely functioned through personal channels in Morocco. Yet the shifting structure of local economic interests and consequent changes in long-standing patterns of business–government relations demonstrate that traditional modes of interaction between public and private elites are unraveling. In the last decade, factions of the industrial bourgeoisie increasingly expressed their demands publicly, relying heavily on the emergent economic press. Using preexisting organizational structures as a locus for constructing effective producer lobbies, new exporters from relatively modest backgrounds sought more formalized relations with technocrats to advance their claims. These developments mark a significant transformation in Moroccan business–government relations and signal changes in the nature and role of traditional elite networks. This chapter focuses on social struggles played out among producers in the domestically oriented textile and export-oriented ready-to-wear apparel assembly sectors[1] to illuminate the relationship between personal networks and formal organizations in Morocco.

What is driving these shifts in Moroccan state–society relations that appear to threaten the famed influence of well-connected elites? To answer this question, I focus on the shifting structure of the local industrial bourgeoisie and specific factional battles over proposed and implemented trade liberalization policies in the 1980s and 1990s. The combination of a new export-oriented trade regime and rising international manufacturing opportunities initiated important changes in the composition of the private sector. Taking advantage of favorable economic conditions, hundreds of would-be Moroccan "entrepreneurs" from nonelite families launched export-oriented factories from the mid-1980s to the early 1990s, particularly in sectors with low technical and financial barriers to entry such as ready-to-wear garment assembly. Thus, a substantial group of small-scale producers from modest backgrounds emerged alongside traditional protectionist elites, who dominate the textile sector. Paradoxically, the very existence of a cohesive and well-connected protectionist elite mobilized the more disparate clothing manufacturers, enabling them to overcome presumed obstacles to collective action plaguing small interests.[2] In turn, the efforts of new exporters fueled a trend toward formalization of business–government relations reflected in the increased codification of regulatory and fiscal frameworks as well as a new style of open and direct consultation between government officials and producers working through professional associations. In a sense, therefore, the cohesive networks linking big protectionist manufacturers to each other and to the administration contained the seeds of their own destruction—or at least erosion.[3]

The chapter begins with a brief review of network analysis in social science research to show how it can and cannot illuminate the Moroccan case. In particular, network analysis has primarily focused on how cross-sectional snapshots of social networks influence outcomes. This approach can yield a rich account of how established business–government linkages shape politics in times of relative stability. Yet a static approach fails to capture the dynamics of producer politics in Morocco after trade liberalization, when new manufacturers organized collectively and induced change in entrenched business–government linkages. To provide the background, the following section traces the rise of post-independence industrialists in the textile sector, describing the tight linkages that developed both within an elite group of large-scale business interests and between these businessmen and the administration. In the next two sections, I discuss important trade and legal reforms implemented in the

1980s and 1990s that altered the structure of the industrial class and, hence, patterns of producer politics manifested in personal networks and formal producer associations. The chapter culminates by examining the implications of evolving Moroccan business–government linkages for network analysis.

Capturing Change in Network Structures

Network analysis suggests that role or position in a relational web constrains or shapes individual behavior and thus outcomes, but comparatively less attention in this literature has explored how networks themselves emerge or evolve.[4] In Morocco, where family relationships are a key building block of social and business ties, attention to informal networks and their intersection with formal organizations is indispensable. In the 1990s, shifting patterns of Moroccan business–government relations and the apparent inability of big capital holders to mobilize effectively against new challengers began to erode powerful, entrenched elite networks. Morocco is, then, a "critical" case for exploring a key area of ambiguity in the literature on networks.

Until recently, many analysts have used network models as techniques or methodological tools to quantify or describe interactive relationships between individuals or organizations rather than as causal theories. The "apparent primacy of method over substance"[5] in network analysis is in part due to an emphasis on mapping the ties binding separate actors rather than on probing their substance. Network analysis has been used to generate empirically rich and complex cross-sectional pictures of social structure, but less research has explored the implications of insertion in personal networks for social behavior. Proponents argue that network analysis can and should be a causal theory. To move beyond formal modeling of network structures, analysts increasingly recognize the need for a theory of individual-level motivation founded on information about actor attitudes and characteristics.[6] DiMaggio argues,

[N]etwork analysis cannot, for two related reasons, be *purely* structural, if, by that, one refers to explanations based solely on formal modeling of social relations without reference to cultural and subjective aspects of action. First, it cannot do without a theory of action, a set of guiding assumptions about situated actors' orientations toward one another and the world. Second, because it must take account of the substance of cognition..., it cannot dispense with data on actor attributes and attitudes.

Problematizing the microfoundations of human behavior not only makes the approach more theoretically compelling but also provides insights into the sources of change in relational networks and the mechanisms through which they constrain behavior.[7]

In its emphasis on "comparative statics,"[8] network analysis has suffered from many of the problems plaguing historical institutionalist research, which has only recently begun to grapple with theorizing processes of institutional change. For analysts working in this tradition, stable national institutions such as patterns of labor, business, and state organization shape responses to external shocks and therefore social outcomes, reflecting an inbuilt bias toward institutional stability. Conceptualizations of "national models" of capitalism based on contextually specific patterns of business–labor–government relations exemplify the institutional rigidity endemic to historical institutionalist analysis.[9]

An emerging literature on institutional change acknowledges the drawbacks of presuming institutional stasis, particularly in the face of global economic changes. Taking institutional flux as its baseline assumption, this work explicitly problematizes mechanisms of change, with a particular emphasis on path-dependent models of evolutionary transformation.[10] Similarly, the literature on networks has increasingly recognized that networks themselves change, raising questions about the microprocesses underlying network transformation and the nature of their influence on actors if they do not structure behavior in a constant fashion.[11] For example, if socioeconomic conditions sustaining postindependence business–government linkages in Morocco have changed, and new private capital holders have emerged, is it no longer feasible to presume that elite networks structure politics in the same way. Further, the emergence of new networks of manufacturers with their own linkages to state officials can alter the substance and operation of prior networks.

Models of institutional change cannot be applied to network analysis without modification for the obvious reason that institutions and networks are not interchangeable.[12] Nonetheless, Thelen's model of "functional conversion," a model of institutional change that suggests an alternative to a gradual, path dependent trajectory, offers insights that may illuminate sources of change in informal networks.[13] "Functional conversion" identifies a process of potentially rapid change, set in motion when a new set of actors emerges and actively takes over existing organizational forms. Thelen's conceptualization captures many of the dynamics exhibited in the Moroccan case, where new export-oriented producers commandeered a dormant professional association representing industries traditionally controlled by elite families with privileged linkages to palace officials. The successful collective-action strategies of these relative upstarts undercut the policy making influence of networks of large-scale interests in the industrial sector, spurring change in both the institutions governing business–government relations and the nature of elite networks. The empirical material presented in this chapter describes this process and in so doing suggests ways that the substance of elite networks evolved in Morocco in the reform period.

Powell and Smith-Doerr advocate "process-oriented" field research as a means of getting at the microfoundations of networks. This kind of research, they argue, would "generate insight into how ties are created, why they are maintained, what resources flow across these linkages, with what consequences."[14] Furthermore, a micro-level focus could illuminate the mechanisms of change in networks: identifying the ties that sustain specific networks would clarify potential sources of change or breakdown. Economic reform and integration in global production processes have profoundly influenced the local contexts within which Middle Eastern and North African networks of privilege developed and flourished, as micro- and meso-level case studies such as this research demonstrate.[15] These developments buttress recent directions in network analysis, which emphasize the dynamics of change alongside depictions of networks as forms of structure and governance in periods of relative isolation.

Serious obstacles prevent a methodologically rigorous analysis of personal networks in Morocco and other settings in and beyond the Middle East and North Africa. Although a substantial secondary source literature exists documenting the rise and content of family ties among Moroccan public and private elites prior to the 1980s, it is impossible to gather systematic data on the nature of these linkages in the contemporary period.[16] Documentation on current business holdings is virtually nonexistent or, at a minimum, unreliable. Because tax evasion is widespread, industrialists—particularly those with large holdings—are generally unwilling to discuss their business affairs in detail. As a result of these largely political obstacles, it is impossible to thoroughly investigate the substantive ties that compose Moroccan business networks in accordance with Powell and Doerr-Smith's useful methodological prescriptions. My goals are therefore more modest: by tracing the ascendance of new, small exporters and their efforts to block lobbying by heretofore powerful protectionist elites, I aim to highlight how these new social relationships altered the structure and efficacy of historically constituted business–government networks.

The Genesis of a "Network": The Rise of Postindependence Private Elites in Morocco

In the postindependence period, network analysis can be applied fruitfully to show how elite politics, grounded in selective access to economic opportunities, functioned in Morocco. Protectionist trade policies constituted a key tactic used to shore-up elite support for the monarchy in this period. Customs duties and other trade-related fiscal measures not only provide an important source of income for many developing countries but also institutionalize networks of privilege in a national political economy. Protective trade regimes often overlay historically constituted relationships of power, influence, and even collusion between private economic interests and the state.

The Moroccan bourgeoisie has a long history of close linkages to the state, reflecting Morocco's long-standing position as a regional commercial hub. Dating back even centuries before independence, a number of families developed extensive commercial links with West African traders. Many of the most prominent families from the *Fassi*[17] bourgeoisie were merchants operating in regional circuits. To safeguard their economic interests, they developed tight links with the *makhzen*,[18] the seat of Moroccan ruling power. In exchange for paying taxes to the governing power, merchant families enjoyed protection from invading tribesmen. Thus, at independence in 1956, these Moroccan families, who enjoyed independent financial bases, constituted the embryo of an indigenous bourgeoisie. The royal family immediately recognized the importance of obtaining the support of these families and, as numerous sources attest, the palace actively wooed local capital—particularly agrarian capital—by transferring land from departing French settlers to local holders and implementing other favorable measures.[19] The Moroccan monarchy has been known for its liberal policies and pro–private sector position since independence and the particular brand of Moroccan family-based capitalism arose in part as a result of government policies.[20]

Extensive overlapping relationships between public authority and private interests emerged such that establishing a boundary between "public" and "private" in describing the Moroccan political economy is potentially misleading.[21] Families with extensive economic interests placed members in key administrative positions, while major industrialists and bankers have frequently held high-ranking government posts themselves.[22] In this way, dense networks of public officials and private interests arose, blurring the lines between business and government and establishing an entrenched set of state and societal interests benefiting from protective trade policies.

Networks not only traversed the public and private sectors but also developed among private interests. Since independence, a tight-knit matrix of private interests formed, based around a handful of privileged families who cemented their ties through marriage and business contracts.[23] The Moroccan private sector is highly concentrated, with a small number of holders controlling a diverse array of activities throughout the economy.[24] Big capital holders tended to have interests spanning the industrial, agricultural, and financial sectors. These multisectoral *groupes*,[25] structured as holding companies, are founded on strategies of horizontal expansion in multiple activities. The royal family controls the largest group, the Omnium Nord Africain (ONA), which contains at least 40 companies in sectors such as mining, agro-industry, automobile assembly, transportation, real estate, and manufacturing. French and Dutch banks originally founded the ONA in 1919 to consolidate their holdings in Morocco. In the early 1980s, Cogespar, a holding company owned by the Prince Moulay Ali, acquired the ONA as well as a Danish holding company, Siham, and merged the three companies while retaining the ONA name. Henceforth, the conglomerate adopted an aggressive strategy of acquiring interests in diverse sectors, with a high degree of intra-group trade and a complex management structure. The ONA even acquired stakes in the textile industry by purchasing shares in several important textile factories established by foreign investors, notably SCIM and Masurel.[26]

Many of the families at the head of the major holding companies originated in the textile sector or at least acquired holdings in the industry as they expanded their operations. The Kettani group, with interests in manufacturing, electronics assembly, commercial distribution, real estate, maritime transport, construction, and banking, traces its origins to the textile trade. Prior to independence, Moulay Ali Kettani was a cloth merchant, and the family's first industrial ventures centered on the textile industry. In 1957, just after independence, Kettani acquired his first textile factory, Manatex, which he purchased from an Italian company. Subsequently, the head of another leading family, Hadj Mohamed Lazrak, whose son married Kettani's daughter, acquired shares in Manatex, which grew over the years to become one of the world's largest producers of velour cloth. The Kettanis later established a number of other textile and clothing firms, notably Tisbrod and Pantco, while branching out into other sectors, such as banking and finance, through a centralized holding company, the Société de Participations or Sopar. Wafabank, a major Moroccan bank owned by the Kettani family, heavily invested in the group's industrial and commercial holdings. Joint participation in a diverse array of companies as well as intermarriage among prominent families was common practice, engendering the rise of a tight-knit group of large-scale private interests since independence if not earlier.[27]

The Lamrani group, founded in the 1960s by Mohamed Karim Lamrani, has interests in commercial activities, industry, finance, sea transport, and tourism. The group also had stakes in the textile sector through Mafaco, a cloth firm established under the Protectorate that the family acquired from French industrialists in 1973, and Filroc, the first thread factory in Morocco established in the late 1960s. Through its ownership position in three major holding companies—Safari, Sofipar, and Cofimar—the Lamrani group gradually acquired over 30 companies in diverse activities. The Kettanis and Lamranis are but two examples of wealthy, elite families that developed important interests in the textile industry in the early years following Moroccan independence.[28]

As part of its efforts to shore-up elite bases of support by promoting local private capital, the monarchy instituted a protectionist trade regime soon after the French departed. The initial rise of the local textile industry in the postindependence era was intimately related to the adoption of import substitution industrialization (ISI) policies in the first five-year plan implemented from 1960 to 1964. Considered the industry with the greatest prospects for success in such a development strategy, the textile industry held a privileged place under the plan.[29] Investment codes also played an important role in promoting the industry in the context of broader economic development plans. The 1958 and 1960 codes encouraged the creation of local firms through reduced local taxes and fiscal incentives to facilitate intermediate good imports, and provided capital transfer guarantees to foreign investors. Despite such liberal foreign investment terms, the codes did not give rise to significant foreign capital inflows, yet local industrialists benefited from the advantageous terms to establish factories.[30]

Changes in the trade regime bolstered investment incentives to local capital holders. In 1957 the government undercut the terms of the Act of Algéciras, a treaty signed with France under the Protectorate that established a liberal trade regime in Morocco, by instituting protective national trade barriers. While primary goods and equipment for industrial and agricultural activities were taxed minimally, semi-finished products faced duties of 5 to 20 percent and finished products were taxed at a rate of 15 to 35 percent. In 1961, duties were increased and, in 1962, under pressure from the textile producers' association, tariffs on textile products were further augmented.[31] Henceforth, tariffs increased progressively until trade liberalization policies, first implemented in the 1980s as part of a World Bank–led structural adjustment program, began to dismantle the protective trade regime. High taxes on imports served the interests of both the state, for which the duties constituted an important revenue source, and the local private sector, which profited immensely from the barriers to outside competition.

Policies adopted in the 1970s consolidated the position of the local industrial bourgeoisie. In the early 1970s, the government passed a series of laws, known as the "Moroccanization" laws, designed to at least nominally transfer majority ownership of previously French-owned companies to Moroccan hands.[32] Despite the government's declared intention of shoring-up the nascent middle class, the laws primarily enabled the preexisting economic elite to cement its holdings while important, new large-scale groups formed. A number of major textile families trace their origins to this period, when they acquired firms from departing European investors or went into partnership with the previous owners. Examples include the Alami family,[33] which owns a number of textile and clothing firms in and around Meknes; the Sakkat family, which concentrated its investments heavily in textiles with three major firms in the Casablanca area; and the Bel Abbes Bennani family, which first acquired its wealth under the Protectorate in the cloth trade and subsequently expanded its investments to include other areas while participating in joint ventures with the Lamrani and other families.[34]

Linkages to the palace through family members and personal contacts constituted the main channel for elite interest transmission to the administration. At the same time, elite families nominally institutionalized their influence through formal producer organizations, which were little more than elite social clubs. The textile manufacturers' association, or the Association Marocaine de l'Industrie du Textile (AMIT), was created in 1960. From its founding until 1991, official AMIT headquarters were located in a small office in the heart of the Casablanca commercial district of Derb Omar, where almost all major textile producers had established their factories and sales outlets. Although AMIT officially represented both the textile and clothing sectors, representatives of prominent cloth and thread producing families continuously held the presidency, reflecting the dominance of textile interests in the organization. While the presidential term was technically limited to two years, in practice AMIT presidents held office for lengthy periods. Mohamed Lahlou, the former director of the Kettani textile firm Manatex, was president for over 20 years.[35] Although he officially spoke for both the textile and clothing industries, Lahlou clearly represented the interests of cloth and thread producers, and sources within the association attested that he frequently engaged in heated disputes with clothing producers in association meetings.[36] Indeed, it was not surprising that textile producers enjoyed vast influence on policy making given that textile manufacturing requires large capital investment.[37] Only large-scale private industrialists, who generally had more political influence and often held simultaneous high-ranking government posts, were able to enter the thread and cloth industries. Furthermore, because ready-to-wear garment assembly was not a significant activity in Morocco until the early 1990s, clothing manufacturers did not play a decisive role in the association for much of its history.

Until the last five years, textile industrialists—specifically thread and cloth producers—controlled the policy-making agenda for the textile and clothing sectors. Textile producers established close links with administration officials and, as a result, cultivated a network of "friends in high places,"[38] enabling them to successfully push for favorable trade and tariff levels. Formal organizational channels such as AMIT were of less consequence than personal contacts. In policy terms, this meant that the thread, cloth, and finishing industries remained highly protected by trade barriers. For many years, this well-organized group of textile producers pursued strategies and successfully lobbied for measures that favored their interests without consulting export-oriented clothing producers, who held divergent positions on key policy issues.[39] Many industrialists, particularly owners of small and medium textile firms as well as clothing producers, viewed the organization as an elite club serving the interests of large textile producers, particularly the interests of major families dominating the national economy who relied on privileged relationships with key policy makers and controlled the organization's administration. The same group of textile interests that dominated AMIT also held high-level positions in other national associations, notably the Confédération Nationale des Entreprises du Maroc (CGEM), the peak-level Moroccan businessmen's association.[40] Nonetheless, until the reform period, producer associations were not important vehicles for interest transmission and lobbying. Elite families nominally participated in these organizations but relied on direct contacts to well-placed palace officials to advance important claims. Before trade liberalization threatened to upset elite social relationships, then, a relatively static version of network analysis could depict the anatomy of Moroccan business–government relations.

Unraveling the Textile Lobby: New Sectoral Dynamics in the Reform Period

Economic Change and Shifting Industrial Capital Structure

In the 1980s and 1990s, the broader national and international economic contexts of the Moroccan industrial sector changed markedly, threatening the foundations of elite influence. Shifts in the structure of industrial capital and the rise of new, export-based networks of manufacturers highlight the limitations of a cross-sectional view of economic networks.

Beginning in the early 1980s, the Moroccan government adopted a number of policy measures that altered the business context, facilitating the rise of a group of export-oriented interests. The adoption of a structural adjustment program (SAP) in 1983 with World Bank support was one step in this

Table 8.1 Selected tariff levels on textile and clothing imports, 1985 and 1996

Product	Customs duty (%)		Import tax (%)		Total	
	1985	1996	1985	1996	1985	1996
Cotton thread	40	25	25	15	65	40
Synthetic fiber thread	60	10	40	15	100	25
Wool thread	40	25	25	15	65	40
Wool cloth	90	35	60	15	150	50
Artificial cloth	120	35	55	15	175	50
Clothing	100	35	60	15	160	50

Sources: Kingdom of Morocco, *Tarif des Droits de Douane et Nomenclature Générale des Produits* (Rabat, Morocco: Customs Administration, Ministry of Finance, 1985); Kingdom of Morocco, "Loi de Finance Transitoire pour la Période du 1er Janvier au 30 Juin 1996," in *Bulletin Officiel* no. 4339 (December 31, 1995): 867–969.

process. The program entailed reductions in protective trade tariffs from rates as high as 300 percent to levels ranging from 0 to 35 percent and loosened foreign trade restrictions by abolishing the requirement for import licenses by 1992.[41] Table 8.1 shows changes in selected textile and apparel tariff levels, demonstrating the scope of tariff dismantling during the 1980s and 1990s.

The tariff cuts engendered much resistance from industrialists as well as from certain government ministries. Well-connected producers—largely oriented to the domestic market—were the most vociferous opponents, voicing their sentiments directly to administration officials. Although the Ministry of Commerce and Industry supported the reforms, it was forced to concede to a number of demands by industrialists, notably the institution of reference prices on imports. Reference prices vastly increased the effective rate of protection for certain activities, including cloth and thread production, by stipulating a minimum or floor price against which import duties would be calculated.[42] Like most industrialists, the Ministry of Finance only supported the SAP's proposal to simplify trade procedures and the structure of import duties but, like the Central Bank, opposed the program overall on the grounds that it would exacerbate the current account and budget deficits.[43] Conveying their concerns through personal channels, industrialists found allies in certain government agencies, which shared producer hesitations about structural adjustment.[44]

At the same time, trade reforms implemented as part of the SAP and modifications in European production strategies compelled important shifts in the structure of local Moroccan private capital by fostering the rise of a new export sector. Emerging exporters adopted novel interest transmission tactics, introducing important changes in producer mobilization strategies that bolstered formal channels such as producer associations. In particular, a 1983 investment code abolished many of the stipulations of the 1973 "Moroccanization" laws, enabling foreign companies to invest in Morocco without limitations and to repatriate profits.[45] The code stipulated a unified system of investment incentives such as preferential tax treatments and exemptions for new projects, attracting modest amounts of foreign direct investment. Most importantly, the new code boosted linkages between local industrialists and foreign clients. The 1995 Investment Charter, which provided additional fiscal incentives for new non-agricultural business activities, further consolidated the position of emerging export firms in the local economy.[46]

A less tangible but equally important change affecting the structure and interests of the Moroccan industrial sector was the expansion of subcontracting relationships and joint production opportunities with European companies. During the 1980s, European firms increasingly transferred the production of manufactured goods, such as garments, to developing countries with lower wage costs. Indeed, the rise of a group of Moroccan subcontractors and export-oriented producers probably owes more to increased possibilities for working with European firms than to specific trade liberalization policies implemented through the SAP.[47] European companies first began to produce overseas in the late 1970s but increased their foreign subcontracting relationships significantly in the mid-1980s, compelling hundreds of Moroccan "entrepreneurs" to launch garment assembly factories.[48]

Aspiring entrepreneurs from nonelite backgrounds invested heavily in apparel production, which has relatively low barriers. Unlike cloth and thread production, sewing and even knitwear factories require minimal start-up capital and technical expertise. Threatened by the expansion of pro-liberalization manufacturers, bitter textile producers claimed, "Anyone can found a garment assembly company." Exploring the social origins of many factory owners almost confirms this allegation. The vast majority of investors had little or no experience in textile and clothing manufacturing. At the height of the boom, professionals such as doctors, pharmacists, lawyers, and bank employees— anyone who had a small amount of capital and could obtain credit—established garment factories. Labor, usually young women between the ages of 18 and 25, was plentiful and the equipment required was minimal and relatively inexpensive. Changes in the composition of the private sector promised to unsettle entrenched business–government networks of privilege. The majority of new export entrepreneurs did not hail from the tiny privileged elite that had dominated economic and political life since independence, opening the way for new social elements to gain access to wealth.[49]

Between 1985 and 1991, the number of clothing assembly factories grew exponentially, with enormous capital investment and job creation in ready-to-wear garment manufacturing. Although exact figures on the informal market are not available, many new factories were not registered, allowing them to evade taxes and neglect minimum wage standards.

Producer Politicization and the Institutionalization of AMITH

By the early 1990s, a critical mass of internationally competitive clothing exporters boasting extensive direct relations with overseas clients had developed. Under the leadership of a few key individuals, these manufacturers gradually organized themselves through a preexisting trade association, in the process creating a loose network that could challenge the policy influence of protectionist elites.

Because high-quality cloth and thread could be obtained inexpensively on global markets, particularly from Asian suppliers, exporters were not interested in purchasing locally made inputs. Since the investment code reform of 1983, clothing producers benefited from the *Admissions Temporaires* (AT) system, which enabled exporters to import inputs duty-free provided that they reexport the goods in finished products within six months. Yet customs processing delays and other administrative hassles as well as long delivery times for inputs gradually induced them to favor total liberalization of the local textile industry. Lucrative subcontracting relationships with European clients accelerated competition on world clothing markets, and declining global demand for garments in the mid-1980s made such questions of vital importance for exporters.

A bust in international apparel markets initially politicized ready-to-wear garment producers. By 1991, when the Gulf crisis closed off key export channels and compelled European clients to cancel their orders, the clothing industry faced a crisis. Many of the factories were poorly managed from the outset and only those that had mastered the production process could remain competitive in a tighter market. Furthermore, because salaries—the main component of production costs—rose during the 1980s, profit margins shrunk and many industrialists shut down their factories. Nonetheless, a core group of clothing producers remained, vastly outnumbering cloth and thread manufacturers. Members of this group of exporters, who subsequently held leadership positions in the textile and garment producers' association, became outspoken advocates for the interests of ready-to-wear clothing manufacturers.

The urgency of the situation compelled a group of clothing producers to organize within AMIT, the only existing body formally representing the interests of textile and clothing producers. Numerous ready-to-wear garment exporters followed suit, becoming active members of the association. While only three or four core individuals attended AMITH meetings for much of the association's history, the meeting rooms have been packed to capacity since the early to mid-1990s.[50] The association's swelling ranks raised its importance as a representative body, fueling a trend toward greater institutionalization of the organization that continued throughout the 1990s.

In 1991, AMIT moved to a new location, leaving behind its small office in the heart of the old Derb Omar commercial district to occupy a large villa in the chic Casablanca neighborhood of Anfa. The association also increased its permanent staff, over the course of the decade growing to include about 15 fulltime employees who oversee the daily administration of the organization, manage external and member relations, and produce and catalog association publications and documentation.

In 1993, the association officially changed its name to the Association Marocaine des Industries du Textile et de l'Habillement (AMITH), explicitly adding the word "clothing" to the name that for over three decades had only referred to the textile industry. AMITH officials downplay the significance of the amendment, noting that the organization has always been the only representative of both branches of the sector and that the word "textile" implicitly encompasses both textiles and clothing. But, they argued, European clients had been misled by the name, believing that it only represented cloth, thread, and textile finishing companies.[51] Yet the association's name change represented more than an attempt to clarify its role to foreign clients. The explicit inclusion of the clothing branch in the association's title reflected the growing preponderance of garment manufacturers in the organization.

Major reforms in AMITH's administrative structure also demonstrated the rising influence of clothing exporters and the concomitant declining weight of older textile manufacturers in leadership positions in the association. In 1993, Abdelali Berrada, an industrialist with extensive holdings in the garment export branch, was appointed director of VETMA, an agency that organizes trade shows for clothing exporters. The Centre Marocain de Promotion des Exportations (CMPE), a governmental export promotion agency headed by Lahlou, initially launched the annual clothing trade show in 1991 with nominal assistance from AMIT as well as the sponsorship of three major Moroccan banks and the Office du Développement Industriel (ODI), an official industrial promotion agency.[52] With Berrada's appointment, VETMA began operating out of AMITH headquarters and the association, which took over control of the annual trade show, devoted increasing attention to the event. Since then, the VETMA program has expanded substantially, hosting a trade fair within Morocco as well as several shows in various European cities annually.

Much to the chagrin of elite textile families, Berrada's duties expanded beyond organizing VETMA. In the mid-1990s, Berrada became general director of AMITH, co-administrating the association with Lahlou. Although Lahlou ostensibly had the highest position in the organization, Berrada took increasing control over AMITH affairs and, with Lahlou's impending retirement, he and a pro-liberalization faction of garment exporters increasingly had the upper hand in decision making.[53] Although Berrada claimed to have abandoned his holdings in clothing export factories in order to devote himself fully to the association's administration, many doubted his sincerity. A manager of a large cloth factory noted, "Most people think he is there to '*faire son beurre*' [promote his own interests], even though he behaves like Mother Theresa," by pretending to sacrifice his own business interests for the good of the sector as a whole.[54] Other representatives of textile firms concurred. From their perspective, AMITH had deviated from its mission because it was controlled by clothing exporters and neglected the concerns of textile producers, who constituted a vital component of the sector in terms of investment and capital stock.[55]

The rising influence of exporters and subcontractors within AMITH dovetailed with efforts initiated by foreign agencies to strengthen the role of professional associations throughout Moroccan society. In the early 1990s, the World Bank and other international donors launched programs to reinforce the private sector throughout their creditor countries. A 1994 World Bank program as well as various U.S. Agency for International Development (USAID) and European Union (EU) initiatives provided technical and material support for certain Moroccan business associations, including AMITH. Simultaneously, the increased weight of membership dues in its budget reflected the association's growing institutionalization and organization. Annual dues—3,000 Moroccan Dirhams or approximately US$300—were used largely to subsidize the costs of participation in VETMA and other trade shows. In 1995, AMITH began to receive state funding, benefiting from its share of an ad valorem import tax of 0.25 percent used to support professional associations and export promotion agencies.[56] As a result of the *de facto* takeover of the AMITH by export interests, the association became one of the most structured and outspoken producer organizations in Morocco.

Despite the growing influence of clothing exporters in AMITH, tensions had not yet reached the boiling point in the mid-1990s. Issues of common concern for all branches of the industry galvanized the association politically, reflecting the organization's continued internal coherence at this point. A major issue uniting the association as well as the private sector writ large through the Confédération Générale des Entreprises du Maroc (CGEM), the peak-level employers' association, was the *Campagne d'Assainissement*, or "purification campaign," a state-led crusade launched in 1996 to collect unpaid taxes and punish evaders.[57] Organized by the former minister of the interior, Driss Basri,[58] the event marked a major shift in Moroccan politics. Traditionally, big business was virtually immune from prosecution for illegal practices such as tax evasion. Yet during the campaign, even businessmen from prominent families were imprisoned, sometimes for as much as two years. The textile and clothing industries were particularly affected, with numerous exporters fined and even jailed for failing to justify their accounts under the AT system.[59] Through the CGEM, AMITH leaders lobbied vigorously for the release and pardon of association members, regardless of their branch affiliation within the organization.[60]

After the CGEM and the administration resolved the crisis by signing a "Gentlemen's Agreement,"[61] the garment producers' committee of AMITH and the customs authority launched cooperative negotiations aiming to establish a more reliable customs processing system for cloth imports intended for reexport under the AT program. AMITH and the customs authority also initiated discussions on an important question raised during the *Campagne d'Assainissement*—the measure used to establish the amount of cloth imported by a firm for use in garments for export. Most European textile firms used *length* as the unit of measurement for their shipments. The Moroccan customs authority, however, measured cloth imported for garment assembly according to *weight*, using a standard formula based on the length listed by the supplier to calculate import duties. Discrepancies between the weight declared by the customs authority and the actual weight led to countless problems during the *Campagne*. Many clothing exporters were falsely accused of tax evasion by failing to reexport the same weight of cloth declared upon arrival.[62] While this issue directly concerned only clothing exporters, textile producers were implicated insofar as streamlining AT procedures threatened their interests. Ongoing efforts to reform the AT system touched upon questions that were potentially divisive for the sector and, indeed, gave rise to dissension in the late 1990s within AMITH.

Rising Stakes: The EU Free Trade Accord and Fractures Within AMITH

The reform of the AT system provided the spark that ignited mounting tensions within AMITH between networks of textile and clothing producers over trade liberalization. Struggles of this central component of the domestic trade regime brought these distinct sets of manufacturers into direct conflict and highlights how interactions between networks can induce changes in their substance and operation.

As long as the market remained relatively sheltered from foreign competition, potential controversies between opposing camps of producers remained dormant. But trade liberalization posed a direct threat to established industrialists who had developed and flourished under a protected national market. The signing of a free trade accord with the EU in 1996 vastly accelerated the process of reducing protective tariffs and taxes, raising the stakes of trade reform and eliciting fierce responses from local manufacturers. Never before had economic reforms touched so directly on industrialist interests. The rise of a vocal group of exporters in the 1980s and early 1990s, described earlier, exacerbated tensions within the private sector and heightened the difficulties facing large-scale producers from privileged families.

The European Union Association Agreement (EUAA) called for the progressive dismantling of trade barriers over a 12-year period, culminating in the total elimination of protective measures by 2012. Reductions in customs duties and other trade taxes with similar effects, such as reference prices, on goods imported from the EU would be implemented according to a preestablished schedule (see table 8.2).

Table 8.2 EU association agreement, import tariff dismantling schedule (in percent)

Year	Equipment	Primary materials	Spare Parts	Goods not produced in Morocco	Goods produced in Morocco
0 (1998)	100	25	25	25	10
1 (1999)		25	25	25	10
2 (2000)		25	25	25	10
3 (2001)		25	25	25	10
4 (2002)					10
5 (2003)					10
6 (2004)					10
7 (2005)					10
8 (2006)					10
9 (2007)					10
10 (2008)					10
11 (2009)					10
12 (2010)					10

Source: Kingdom of Morocco, *Guide de la mise à niveau de l'entreprise* (Rabat, Morocco: Ministry of Industry, Commerce and Artisinal Activities, February 1999), 4.

Despite initial efforts to block the agreement, local industrialists soon realized their attempts were futile and instead oriented themselves toward agitating for delays and loopholes.[63] Simultaneously, an increasingly influential group of exporters sought to accelerate its tariff dismantling timetable. Nowhere was such private sector divisiveness more apparent than in AMITH, which teetered on the edge of dissolution as a result of disputes between textile and clothing producers over issues related to the EU agreement.

Tensions within AMITH came to a head in July 1997, when the government voted on tariff level amendments for inclusion in 1998 budget. The Asian financial crisis made competition in international apparel markets even more fierce, compelling apparel exporters to launch an offensive to reduce protective trade barriers on key textile inputs. Their demands focused on the elimination of reference prices on thread and cloth imports and the dissolution of the AT system, which forced delivery delays due to its cumbersome bureaucratic procedures.[64] Lahlou and other AMITH officials publicly downplayed the intensity of the disputes, but the outspoken local economic press reported that the disagreements were fierce.

Although the AMITH charter stipulated that disputes should be resolved within the association, members of each faction went directly to the Ministries of Industry and Finance to plead their cases. In exchange for fulfillment of their demands, clothing exporters proposed to compensate the treasury for revenues lost from eliminated reference price taxes by paying a 1 percent tax on all materials imported through the AT system. To assuage the concerns of thread and cloth producers, they proposed the establishment of a fund financed by garment exporters to support textile factory upgrading and reductions in energy costs, which constitute a major production cost for textile firms.[65] To eliminate the AT system altogether would effectively wipe out the local textile industry by allowing duty-free imports of cloth and thread. The question of AT reform, then, was no longer a matter concerning only the customs authority and clothing exporters. Now textile manufacturers were directly engaged in the debate.

The conflict acquired new dimensions when textile producers began to question the motives of garment exporters in calling for total liberalization of the sector. The AT system effectively enabled clothing exporters to divorce themselves entirely from the local market by importing inputs tax-free and reexporting the assembled garments. Dismantling the in-bond system would entail full liberalization of the local economy, granting apparel exporters the right to sell domestically as well as to foreign clients. From the perspective of textile manufacturers, therefore, eliminating the system could only mean that clothing producers wanted to step on their turf—that is, the local market.[66]

Although Morocco's adherence to the GATT Accords in 1995 and the EUAA in 1996 would liberalize the sector within a decade, causing foreign clothing imports to flood the local market, textile producers viewed the ambitions of Moroccan clothing manufacturers to sell domestically with a mixture of disgust and a sense of betrayal. As long as the export and national markets remained separate, a kind of moral equilibrium prevailed, albeit fraught with tension. The beneficiaries of decades of protective trade policies, Moroccan *textiliens* at least rhetorically envisioned a cooperative, national response to the challenges posed by global market pressures. In their view, the new group of clothing exporters, most of whom were relative newcomers to the Moroccan business world and thus were not insiders in the dense personal networks of older industrialists, were opportunistic and greedy. Of course this should not imply that textile producers had more noble intentions. Their brand of economic patriotism clearly emanated from a self-serving vision of the national market.

In both the 1998 and 1999 budgets, the demands of clothing exporters to accelerate the EUAA tariff and reference price dismantling timetable did not prevail.[67] Two main reasons account for their failure: the enduring influence of the textile producers' lobby and government concerns over tax revenue losses. Despite being outnumbered in AMITH by the growing clothing exporters' faction, the "Route de Mediouna," a label for the protectionist textile lobby, retained its policy-making influence in key government circles.[68] Furthermore, the arguments of textile manufacturers resonated with the administrative and fiscal concerns of Ministry of Finance officials, who were apprehensive about a sudden decline in tax revenue with accelerated implementation of the free trade accord.[69] Thus, common economic concerns coupled with enduring personal linkages between postindependence business and government elites blocked the most extreme demands of the increasingly powerful exporters' lobby. Many clothing exporters remained bitter about the continued protection of the textile industry and resented the persistent policy influence of textile manufacturers, who benefited for decades from favorable tariff and tax policies.[70]

Personal Networks, Producer Mobilization and Shifting Business–Government Relations in Morocco

The efforts of new exporters to undercut the perceived policy influence of entrenched, protectionist networks ultimately brought about substantial shifts in the broader context of Moroccan business–government relations in the industrial sector, as well as in AMITH itself. Many AMITH members and outside observers of the association's internal conflicts were certain that the organization would dissolve as a result of the fierce disagreements between textile and apparel manufacturers over trade liberalization. Much to their surprise, however, AMITH executive board members devised a middle-ground approach to address the major concerns of all the warring parties. With the help of an outside consultant, board members from all industries represented in the association produced a document—the *Contrat-Programme*—outlining the major policy goals and demands of the two sectors.[71] In August 1999, AMITH presented the document to the government in a meeting with key administration officials from the Ministries of Industry, Finance and Labor as well as representatives from the prime minister's office.[72]

The *Contrat-Programme* seemed to reflect the interests of textile manufacturers. The participation of ready-to-wear producers in drafting the document therefore seemed inexplicable. But an important underlying point of consensus compelled textile and clothing manufacturers to seek a compromise, notably recognition of the mutual benefits of sectoral integration, or the development of linkages between firms in the upstream (i.e., thread, cloth) and downstream (i.e., garments) activities of the textile and clothing industries within Morocco. According to the logic of sectoral integration, textile producers would gain by selling more of their production to local clothing exporters while the latter would benefit by cutting down on input delivery time and bureaucratic hassles with the customs authority by buying at home.

Before garment subcontractors could purchase locally produced thread and cloth, the quality of these inputs needed to be improved substantially. Furthermore, clothing exporters were most interested in the possibility of buying from European textile firms that planned to move their operations to Moroccan and other nearby lower cost manufacturing sites.[73] Upgrading local textile production was therefore another key focus of the *Contrat-Programme*.

To be sure, joint economic concerns played a role in compelling textile and clothing manufacturers to seek government support for sectoral integration. Because both sectors faced serious economic crises in the mid- to late 1990s, exacerbated by the 1997 Asian financial crisis, all AMITH members had an incentive to lobby for government aid. Furthermore, sectoral integration would ideally benefit textile and clothing producers alike. But garment exporters were still profiting immensely from lucrative contracts with European clients, enabling them to avoid contact with local textile producers altogether, and increasingly relaxed government trade regulations ensured that their high earnings would continue at least in the short to medium term. The participation of clothing manufacturers in drafting and defending the *Contrat-Programme* was anomalous given the relative profitability of their activities and the apparent inexorable trend toward trade liberalization spelled out in treaty commitments with the EU and World Trade Organization. Economic interest alone does not explain AMITH's apparent decision to suppress the divisions within its ranks through a collaborative solution.

The enduring political influence of large industrialists with textile holdings was an important reason for AMITH's decision to pursue sectoral integration. Despite their numerical minority status within AMITH and the growing politicization of newer, nonelite export interests, *textiliens* retained sufficient power to ensure that their concerns remained on the forefront of the association's agenda. Dense personal and professional ties among big capital and the state enabled textile interests to lobby effectively through informal channels for policies protecting their holdings. Despite the increasing export orientation of the Moroccan economy, this history of collective action serving mutual goals remained useful as *textiliens* fought to forestall "inevitable" cuts in protective trade taxes and promote sectoral integration.

Powerful industrialists had extensive interests throughout the Moroccan economy, enabling them to shift their holdings into areas that remained profitable such as finance or real estate speculation, but the stakes remained high. Textile production is a relatively capital intensive industry, so factory closures mean that the financial impact is palpable. The Kettani family, for example, took huge losses when they sold the Cofitex thread factory to a French textile firm, Caulliez Frères, in 1996. The factory, which had been entirely upgraded and modernized in the late 1980s at considerable expense, experienced major labor unrest and repeated strikes throughout the 1990s, effectively shutting down the plant for almost five years. In the end, the Kettanis sold the factory to the French firm for a nominal price.[74] Furthermore, because the varied investments of prominent industrialist families were often overlapping, the crisis in the textile sector had broader consequences for their portfolios. Again, the experience of the Kettanis is illustrative. Among its vast holdings, the Kettani family owns one of the largest banks in Morocco, Wafabank. It is widely known that Wafabank suffered heavily as a result of underwriting extensive loss-making loans to a Kettani textile firm, Manatex.[75] For these reasons, large industrialists had good reason to try to minimize their losses in the cloth and thread industries.[76]

The continued influence of big protectionist capital over policy making in the textile and clothing sectors galvanized garment subcontractors to lobby forcefully for unfettered access to global production opportunities. The existence of a formidable, cohesive block of local industrialists opposing the rapid or even timely implementation of trade liberalization encouraged clothing exporters to fight as vociferously for their interests. Thus, the presence of the well-entrenched textile lobby acted as a catalyst for the politicization of emerging producers from relatively modest backgrounds.

Key representatives of garment interests, notably the director of VETMA and the head of the garment exporters AMITH subcommittee, increasingly took over the reins of control of the association, driving changes in the *de facto* rules governing business–government relations. Modes of interaction between producers and administration officials shifted substantially. While traditional elites relied on informal, interest transmission channels institutionalized through personal networks, new exporters initiated a more open style of business–government communication, at times verging on confrontational. The mobilization of exporters through AMITH had concrete ramifications for the business regulatory framework, particularly in the reform of the AT program and customs processing procedures.[77] AMITH established an ongoing dialogue with the Ministries of Finance and Industry, which were increasingly responsive to producer demands, and association subcommittees working on a range of other issues, such as quality control and labor code reform, began to meet regularly with relevant officials to discuss their concerns through institutionalized channels.[78]

Conclusion

Examining the struggles between textile and clothing manufacturers over trade-related fiscal issues provides a lens into the relations between two distinct groups of industrialists, their shifting linkages to the state and the erosion of traditional networks of influence in the Moroccan industrial sector. By virtue of their overwhelming importance in the national economy, textile and clothing production are representative of the Moroccan industrial sector as a whole. Likewise, textile and clothing manufacturers are a proxy for larger divisions within the private sector, notably between an older generation of large-scale industrialists that has dominated the Moroccan economic and political landscape for decades and newer export-oriented industrialists who developed distinct patterns of communication with the administration in the last decade. The interactive dynamics between well-entrenched large-scale elites and increasingly organized exporters set in motion broader changes in relations between the local private sector and the administration.

If purely economic considerations led to the predominance of one faction of the industrial class over another, then garment exporters would have pushed through their pro-liberalization agenda easily. After all, apparel exports far surpassed textile production throughout the 1980s and 1990s. Yet the influence of exporters was not uncontested, as reflected in outcomes of struggles between textile and apparel manufacturers. The *Contrat-Programme* reflected the enduring influence of textile producers, who ensured that their concerns remained important in AMITH's agenda. In the decades since independence, textile producers became influential in policy-making circles by cultivating direct links to administration officials and benefiting from monarchical patronage by placing family members in high-ranking government positions. Big capital had developed close internal ties through marriage and business deals spanning multiple sectors of the economy. This intricate web of interpersonal ties enabled protectionist industrialists to constitute an influential *de facto* pressure group, safeguarding their interests by attaining favorable tariff and trade policies. Until newer export interests forced a new set of concerns onto the national policy-making agenda in the 1990s by mobilizing through formal organizational structures, local *textiliens* had largely relied on personal channels to pursue their goals.

Unquestionably, the power of protectionist manufacturers is waning within the Moroccan textile and clothing sectors—and even in the broader industrial sector—as a result of economic conditions in global markets and national trade liberalization policies that disfavor their economic activities. Big business interests have retreated into other areas with high barriers to entry such as finance, where their predominance is as yet virtually uncontested. The collective-action successes of newer export-oriented manufacturers with distinct policy preferences have further eroded the predominance of the domestic textile lobby and undercut traditional elite business–government ties.

Just as purely economic analyses are inadequate, however, static networks models also cannot explain the outcomes of struggles between textile and apparel manufacturers. The rise and constitution of a "counter-network" of exporters opposing the perceived influence of protectionist *textiliens* shows that we cannot deduce policy outcomes from the existence of entrenched business–government linkages.

Nonetheless, the resilience of protectionist policy networks conditioned the ways that producers in the textile and clothing sectors interacted in response to economic opening. Without the countervailing presence of the historically constituted textile lobby, whose influence was grounded in personal relationships crosscutting the public and private spheres, key clothing manufacturers would not have been equally motivated to construct a powerful pressure group. Changes in the structure and organizational strategies of producer groups in the 1990s brought about more formal modes of interest transmission based on publicly articulated demands through professional associations and the economic press.

The Moroccan case raises interesting questions for network analysis. The enduring influence of protectionist public–private linkages suggests that networks not only constrain the behavior of their constituents but also shape the actions of "outsiders." In constructing their lobbying strategies, exporters from modest backgrounds were forced to contend with the formidable opposition of well-connected traditional elites. Thus, networks influence the political behavior of marginalized individuals and can even promote collaboration among otherwise disparate, excluded parties. In accordance with Thelen's model of "functional conversion," the successful mobilization of new producers suggests that formerly excluded individuals or groups may act as a catalyst for change. While Thelen's conceptualization explicitly addresses *institutional* change, it has implications for shifts in the coherence and efficacy of personal networks as well. If networks operate within, reinforce, and perhaps even generate a given set of "rules" or institutions, then changes within these institutions will not only affect how networks constrain actor behavior but may also reflect shifts in the coherence of networks themselves. The actions of marginalized, out-group individuals can erode preexisting networks or create new social groupings that alter the broader field within which entrenched networks operate.

Political mobilization among Moroccan ready-to-wear garment exporters highlights an interesting question about the genesis of networks. Did the successful collective-action efforts of small-scale, nonelite producers sow the seeds for the rise of new networks with influence over policy making? It is too early to tell whether the experience of joint political organization and the creation of institutionalized linkages with state officials will give rise to lasting relational webs between a new generation of public and private actors. But short-term organizing in favor of specific shared policy interests is unlikely to forge the same kind of enduring marriage and business-based linkages that evolved over decades among elite families. Furthermore, intense competitive dynamics within the ready-to-wear garment sector do not lend themselves to the construction of solid producer networks as envisioned in the "industrial districts" model.[79] The shape of emerging informal business–government linkages is still undetermined, but it is clear that the existence of historically constituted elite networks profoundly conditioned social struggles among factions of Moroccan producers in the 1990s over the terms of the national market.

Notes

I thank Chris Ansell, Steven Heydemann, David Meyer, the participants of the Workshop on Economic Networks at the European University Institute, and

Networks of Privilege in Morocco • 269

two anonymous reviewers for their useful comments. However, I take sole responsibility for any errors of commission or omission.

1. I refer to textiles and apparel as separate sectors because they involve distinct production processes, although a single producers' association represents the two activities in Morocco. Textiles encompass thread spinning, cloth weaving, and cloth finishing (i.e., dyeing and printing) while apparel refers to manufacturing of finished products such as knitwear and tailored clothing.

2. Mancur Olson, *The Logic of Collective Action* (Cambridge, MA: Harvard University Press, 1965); Michael Shafer, *Winners and Losers: How Sectors Shape the Developmental Prospects of States* (Ithaca, NY: Cornell University Press, 1994), ch. 2.

3. I am not claiming that an inexorable market logic resulting from integration in the global economy has driven these institutional and social changes, as proponents of neoliberal economic prescriptions would contend. Rather, my argument is sociological, focusing on conflicts between contextually specific social groups. Furthermore, I do not idealize emerging export interests. The behavior of new Moroccan exporters does not entirely conform to favorable images of the new "entrepreneur" prevailing in policy prescriptions that envision increased transparency with economic reform and implicit in the literature linking economic and political liberalization. (For example, see Milton and Rose Friedman, *Free to Choose: A Personal Statement* [New York: Harvest, 1990].) Some apparel exporters routinely ignore official labor regulations and violate the in-bond trade regime by selling on the local market. While most newer industrialists have developed distinct patterns of interaction with the administration, largely through AMITH, some have resorted to practices that subvert greater openness in business–government relations, in this way paralleling the behavior of traditional elite networks.

4. Emirbayer and Goodwin argue, "[Network analysis] either neglects or inadequately conceptualizes the crucial dimension of subjective meaning and motivation . . . and thereby fails to show exactly how it is that intentional, creative human action serves in part to constitute those very social networks that so powerfully constrain actors in turn." Mustapha Emirbayer and Jeff Goodwin, "Network Analysis, Culture, and the Problem of Agency," *American Journal of Sociology* 99 (May 1994): 1413.

5. Walter W. Powell and Laurel Smith-Doerr, "Networks and Economic Life," in Neil J. Smelser and Richard Swedberg, eds., *Handbook of Economic Sociology* (Princeton, NJ: Princeton University Press, 1994), 368–402. For an application that maps out actual networks but neglects their origins and sources of change, see Naomi Rosenthal et al., "Social Movements and Network Analysis: A Case Study of Nineteenth-Century Women's Reform in New York State," *American Journal of Sociology* 90 (1985): 1022–1054.

6. Paul DiMaggio, "Nadel's Paradox Revisisted: Relational and Cultural Aspects of Organizational Structure," in Nitin Nohria and Robert G. Eccles, eds., *Networks and Organization: Structure, Form and Action* (Boston, MA: Harvard Business

School Press, 1992), 118–42. Emirbayer and Goodwin ("Network Analysis," 1414–1415) question whether the approach as it stands can support causal arguments: "Network analysis is not a formal or unitary 'theory' that specifies distinctive laws, propositions, or correlations, but rather a broad strategy for investigating social structure." But they maintain that it contains basic theoretical foundations in that it rejects categorizations according to attributes such as class membership and instead focuses on patterns of relations among individuals or other social actors.

7. Some analysts either explicitly or implicitly link individual-level motivations to network theory. For example, Scharpf's "actor-centered institutionalism," a modified rational choice framework, focuses on how institutions and social contexts, including networks, shape individual perception (Fritz Scharpf, *Games Real Actors Play: Actor-Centered Institutionalism in Policy Research* [Boulder, CO: Westview, 1997], 6–7, 137). Burt explores the individual strategic maneuvering within networks through attempts to maximize "structural holes," which are relationships between contacts that are additive rather than redundant (Ronald S. Burt, "The Network Entrepreneur," in Richard Swedburg, ed., *Entrepreneurs: The Social Science View* [New York: Oxford University Press, 2000], 291); See also Ronald S. Burt, *Structural Holes: The Social Structure of Competition* (Cambridge, MA: Harvard University Press, 1992); Krackhardt shows how friendship or philos ties, a form of Granovetter's "strong" ties, provide the comfort needed for individuals to accept change in organizations (David Krackhardt, "The Strength of Strong Ties: The Importance of Philos in Organizations," in Nohria and Eccles, *Network and Organization*, 218; Mark Grannoveter, "The Strength of Weak Ties," *American Journal of Sociology* 78 [1973]: 1360–1380). Kilduff and Krackhardt link the individual and network levels of analysis by arguing that individual perceptions of network ties, rather than actual ties, complement and strengthen network structures (M. Kilduff and David Krackhardt, "Bringing the Individual Back In: A Structural-Analysis of the Internal Market for Reputation in Organization," *Academy of Management Journal* 37 [February 1994]: 87–108). For a conceptualization of how individual agency, rooted in established habits but oriented to visions of the future, reforms structure, see Mustapha Emirbayer and Anne Mische, "What is agency?" *American Journal Of Sociology* 103 (January 1998): 962–1023. White connects "identities," which are distinct from people, to a higher level of analysis by arguing that they produce social structure through attempts to control contingencies in the environment (Harrison White, *Identity and Control: A Structural Theory of Social Action* [Princeton, NJ: Princeton University Press, 1992]); Ansell also uses a culturally grounded linkage of micro- and macro-foundations, arguing that cross-cutting networks promote solidarity, particularly when they tap into diverse cultural meanings (Christopher K. Ansell, *Schism and Solidarity in Social Movements: The Politics of Labor in the French Third Republic* [New York: Cambridge University Press, 2001]).

8. DiMaggio, "Nadel's Paradox," 121. Wasserman and Galaskiewicz's description of the "network perspective" stresses that networks are "enduring patterns of

relations among actors" (Stanley Wasserman and Joseph Galaskiewicz, "Introduction: Advances in the Social and Behavioral Sciences from Social Network Analysis," in Wasserman and Galaskiewicz, eds., *Advances in Social Network Analysis: Research in the Social and Behavioral Sciences* [London: Sage, 1994], 13).

9. See in particular, John Zysman, *Governments, Markets and Growth* (Ithaca: Cornell University Press, 1983); John Zysman, "Dynamic Diversity: Institutions and Economic Development in Advanced Countries," in Robert Delorme and Kurt Dopfer, eds., *The Political Economy of Diversity: Evolutionary Perspectives of Economic Order and Disorder* (Hants, UK: Edward Elgar, 1994), 126–146. For reviews of historical institutionalism and the various other brands of the "new institutionalism," see Peter A. Hall and Rosemary C. R. Taylor, "Political Science and the Three New Institutionalisms," *Political Studies* 44 (1992): 936–957; and Kathleen Thelen and Sven Steinmo, "Historical Institutionalism in Comparative Politics," in Sven Steinmo, Kathleen Thelen, and Frank Longstreth, eds., *Structuring Politics: Historical Institutionalism in Comparative Analysis* (New York: Cambridge University Press, 1995), 1–32.

10. For conceptual discussions of path dependence in political science and sociology, see James Mahoney, "Path Dependence in Historical Sociology," *Theory and Society* 29 (August 2000): 507–548; Paul Pierson, "Increasing Returns, Path Dependence, and the Study of Politics," *American Political Science Review* 29 (June 2000): 251–268; Paul Pierson, "Not Just What, but When: Timing and Sequence in Political Processes," *Studies in American Political Development* 14 (Spring 2000): 72–92. Path dependence has been used loosely to suggest that prior events condition outcomes but, as Mahoney and Pierson argue, this definition is vague and neglects causal mechanisms. Mahoney stresses the importance of contingency in the initial event setting off historical sequences with "deterministic properties." Path-dependent models first appeared in the social sciences in the economic literature on evolutionary change and technological lock-in. See in particular Paul David, "Clio and the Economics of QWERTY," *American Economic Review* 75 (May 1985): 332–337; as well as W. Brian Arthur, "Competing Technologies, Increasing Returns, and Lock-In by Historical Events," *Economic Journal* 99 (March 1989): 116–131; W. Brian Arthur, *Increasing Returns and Path Dependence in the Economy* (Ann Arbor, MI: University of Michigan Press, 1994); Richard Nelson and Sidney Winter, *An Evolutionary Theory of Economic Change* (Cambridge, MA: Harvard University Press, 1982); and Richard Nelson, "Recent Evolutionary Theorizing about Economic Change," *Journal of Economic Literature* 33 (March 1995): 48–90. Liebowitz and Margolis critique these applications in economics (S. J. Liebowitz and Stephen E. Margolis, "Path Dependence, Lock-In, and History," *Journal of Law, Economics and Organization* 11 (1995): 205–226).

11. Some approaches provide insights into network genesis and change. Without explicitly problematizing the emergence of business networks, Granovetter elaborates different dimensions along which the structure of business groups may

vary (Mark Granovetter, "Business Groups," in Neil J. Smelser and Richard Swedburg, eds., *The Handbook of Economic Sociology* [Princeton, NJ: Princeton University Press, 1994], 453–475). See also, Walter W. Powell, "Neither Market Nor Hierarchy: Network Forms of Organization," in L. L. Cummings and B. Staw, eds., *Research in Organizational Behavior* (Greenwich, CT: JAI Press, 1990), 295–336. Saxenian shows how immigrants forge crossnational business networks (Annalee Saxenian, "The Role of Immigrant Entrepreneurs in New Venture Creation," in Claudia Bird Schoonhoven and Elaine Romanelli, eds., *The Entrepreneurship Dynamic: Origins of Entrepreneurship and the Evolution of Industries* [Stanford, CA: Stanford University Press, 2001], 68–108). Powell and Brantley show how research and knowledge exchange give rise to networks and create new patterns of inter-firm linkages (Walter W. Powell and Peter Brantley, "Competitive Cooperation in Biotechnology: Learning Through Networks?" in Nohria and Eccles, Network and Organization, 366–394). From a different perspective, Boisot argues that information exchange and diffusion create institutions, which in turn shape the spread of information (Max H. Boisot, *Information Space: A Framework for Learning in Organizations, Institutions and Culture* [London: Routledge, 1995]).

12. Following North, I view institutions as "the rules of the game in a society or...the humanly devised constraints that shape human interaction" (Douglass North, *Institutions, Institutional Change and Economic Performance* [New York: Cambridge University Press, 1991], 3). But North's definition is incomplete: a workable definition must also incorporate the sociological aspects of institutions, or the social and economic interests contained therein. Networks, like organizations, are structures within which institutions operate.

13. Kathleen Thelen, "Timing and Temporality in the Analysis of Institutional Evolution and Change," *Studies in American Political Development* 14 (Spring 2000): 101–108. In addition, Thelen usefully argues that models of institutional change need not emphasize distinct trajectories—whether evolutionary or rapid—but rather should focus on shared underlying processes of change, regardless of the how they unfold. See also Kathleen Thelen, "Historical Institutionalism in Comparative Politics," *Annual Review of Political Science* 2 (1999): 369–404.

14. Powell and Smith-Doerr, *Networks and Economic Life*, 372.

15. Most academic research on Morocco focuses on the macro-political level, emphasizing the role of the monarchy in shaping the fortunes of local social groups. As a result, many observers highlight the remarkable degree of institutional stability in Moroccan politics in the face of massive economic restructuring. See, e.g., Azzedine Layachi, "Economic Reform and Elusive Political Change in Morocco," in Yahia H. Zoubir, ed., *North Africa in Transition: State, Society, and Economic Transformation in the 1990s* (Miami, FL: University Press of Florida, 1999), 43–60; and I. William Zartman, "King Hassan's New Morocco," in I. William Zartman, ed., *The Political Economy of Morocco* (New York: Praeger, 1987), 1–33.

I argue, however, that this approach obscures important elements of change that can only be captured by situating the analysis on a micro or mid-range level. Focusing on specific sectors, e.g., this research demonstrates that shifts in the institutions governing business–government relations in certain parts of the economy unfolded in the reform period.

16. See in particular Mohamed Saïd Saâdi, *Les Groupes Financiers au Maroc* (Casablanca, Morocco: Okad, 1989).

17. Fassis refers to inhabitants of the old imperial city of Fes in north central Morocco. Many of Morocco's most renowned and wealthy families trace their origins to the city, thus members of the private elite are often termed "Fassis" regardless of their exact origins and current places of residence.

18. The *makhzen* is the term developed in French colonial historiography for the precolonial Moroccan central authority. The *bled al makhzen*, or the "land of government," is often juxtaposed to the *bled al siba*, or the "land of dissidence," populated by tribes and other local power bases, which largely refused to pay taxes to the Moroccan sultan. Despite critiques of this dichotomous depiction of precolonial Moroccan society, some analysts continue to rely on the framework. See Pennell for a discussion of the origins and evolution of the *makhzen* and *siba* concepts (Richard Pennell, "Libya and Morocco: Consensus on the Past," in George Joffé, ed., *North Africa: Nation, State and Region* [New York: Routledge, 1993], 203–220).

19. Rémy Leveau, *Le Fellah Marocain: Défenseur du Trône* (Paris: Presses de la Fondation Nationale des Sciences Politiques, 1985); John Waterbury, *The Commander of the Faithful: The Moroccan Political Elite, a Study of Segmented Politics* (London: Weidenfeld and Nicholson, 1970); and Zartman, "King Hassan's New Morocco." Although he focuses on the "cultural foundations" of Moroccan monarchial rule rather than the postindependence development of key social groups and their relations with the state, Hammoudi provides a good overview of the literature on state–society relations in Morocco (Abdellah Hammoudi, *Master and Disciple: The Cultural Foundations of Moroccan Authoritarianism* [Chicago: University of Chicago Press, 1997], 25–43).

20. Abdelkader Berrada, "Etat et Capital Privé au Maroc (1956–1980)" (Ph.D. diss., University of Mohamed V, Rabat, Morocco, November 1991).

21. Some Moroccan scholars reject this division as an artificially imposed analytical tool that is inappropriate for the Moroccan case (Personal communication with Abdelkader Berrada, Professor of Economics, University of Mohamed V, Rabat, Morocco, November 1999).

22. In a table listing major government and banking posts and their occupants shortly after independence, Waterbury demonstrates the extensive representation of the urban bourgeoisie in these spheres (John Waterbury, *The Commander of the Faithful: The Moroccan Political Elite, a Study of Segmented Politics* [London: Weidenfeld and Nicolson, 1970], 107). Just one of numerous more contemporary examples, Mohamed Lahlou, the owner of Polyfil, a major thread factory

founded in 1990, was minister of finance in the 1980s and is the current director of the national phosphate company, the Office Chérifienne de Phosphates. In fall 1999, the current administration, led by the former opposition leader Abderrahmane Youssoufi, proposed a law that would explicitly forbid government officials from owning and managing private companies while they are in office. In practice, however, the law would be hard to enforce and easily evaded by temporarily placing family members in top management positions of companies (textile firm administrator and owner, interview by author, Casablanca, Morocco, November 16, 1999; thread firm commercial director, interview by author, Berrechid, Morocco, January 13, 2000).

23. For a sociological discussion of marriage and business linkages between elite private sector elements, see Ali Benhaddou, *Maroc: Les Elites du Royaume, Essai sur l'Organisation du Pouvoir au Maroc* (Paris: L'Harmattan, 1997). Interestingly, an industrialist from a prominent Moroccan capitalist family recommended Benhaddou's book, citing its accuracy in depicting inter-family relations in the private sector. Nonetheless, he objected to the book's underlying pejorative tone (Textile firm director, interview by author, Ain Sebaa, Casablanca, January 27, 2000).

24. The discussion refers to large-scale private interests that control the bulk of economic activity. Small shopkeepers, who are primarily from the Swasa ethnic group in southern Morocco, constitute a numerically important group yet do not act as a cohesive political unit (John Waterbury, "Tribalism, Trade and Politics: The Transformation of the Swasa of Morocco," in Ernest Gellner and Charles Micaud, eds., *Arabs and Berbers* [London: Duckworth, 1972], 231–257).

25. Here I am referring to the French understanding of the business group (groupe), which is similar to the notion of a holding company.

26. In the mid-1990s, the ONA sold a substantial portion of its shares in these factories to Canadian investors (apparel firm director, interview by author, El-Jedida, Morocco, February 2, 2000).

27. Saâdi, *Les Groupes Financiers au Maroc.*

28. Ibid.

29. Jaidi argues, however, that innate inconsistencies in ISI policies ultimately sent mixed signals to industrialists, inhibiting the development of a solid local textile industry. Furthermore, subsequent national economic plans, notably the Three-Year Plan of 1965–1967 and the Five-Year Plan of 1968–1972, placed greater emphasis on tourism and agriculture, relegating the industrial sector to the backburner in development priorities (Larabi Jaidi, *Industrie Textile et Processus d'Industrialisation au Maroc* [Rabat, Morocco: Editions de la Faculté des Sciences Juridiques, Economiques et Sociales de Rabat, Université Mohamed V, 1979], 36–37).

30. J. P. Houssel, "L'Evolution Récente de l'Activité Industrielle à Fes," *Révue du Géographie du Maroc* 9 (1966): 78; Jaidi, *Industrie Textile,* 39–40.

31. *La Vie Economique*, May 24, 1991, 18; Jaidi, *Industrie Textile*, 40–41.

32. Although Moroccanization was ostensibly designed to enable Moroccans to take over businesses from foreigners, many locals benefiting from the reforms established partnerships with foreign interests, allowing foreign capital to retain a significant stake and even expand its holdings in the Moroccan economy (Abdelkader Berrada, "La Marocanisation de 1973: Eclairage Rétrospectif," *Economie et Socialisme* 8 (1988): 29–68; Saâdi, Les Groupes Financiers av Maroc).

33. Indeed, Tazi Alami, the current minister of industry and the head of the Alami family, married the daughter of the French owner of the factory that he acquired (thread factory director, interview by author, Casablanca, Morocco, November 25, 1999).

34. Saâdi, Les Groupes Financiers av Maroc.

35. Clothing company administrator, interview by author, Salé, Morocco, January 25, 2000; AMITH official, interview by author, Casablanca, Morocco, March 2, 2000. A new director, Salah-Eddine Mezouar, took over in 2002. The election of Mezouar, who is considered a moderate, reflected changes in the organization described later.

36. Former AMITH employee and clothing firm administrator, interview by author, Casablanca, Morocco, September 20, 1999; clothing firm director, interview by author, Marrakesh, Morocco, December 3, 1999.

37. As a textile engineer described, cloth production is particularly difficult to launch. Not only is the necessary equipment extremely expensive and complex, but factories require effective ventilation systems and machine operators must have a certain level of technical expertise (thread firm director, interview by author, Casablanca, Morocco, November 25, 1999).

38. Former AMITH employee and clothing firm administrator, interview by author, Casablanca, Morocco, September 20, 1999.

39. Clothing firm administrator, interview by author, Salé, Morocco, January 25, 2000.

40. Ibid.; cloth firm director, interview by author, Settat, Morocco, November 29, 1999; thread firm commercial director, interview by author, Berrechid, Morocco, January 13, 2000.

41. Mouna Cherkaoui, *Inventaire des Mésures de Politiques Economiques Prises au Maroc de Janvier 1982 à Juillet 1992* (Rabat, Morocco: Groupement de Recherche en Economie Internationale, University of Mohamed V, October 1992), 34; AMITH official, interview by author, Casablanca, Morocco, October 11, 1999; World Bank, *Growing Faster, Finding Jobs: Choices for Morocco* (Washington, DC: World Bank, 1996). Eliminating import licenses had a direct impact on the influence of both administration officials and industrialists who had benefited from this policy. Government officials lost a significant source of discretionary power—and income from bribes—while licensees found it increasingly difficult to maintain monopolies over economic activities (Ministry of Industry official, interview with author, Rabat, Morocco, March 7, 2000).

42. Brendan Horton, *Morocco: Analysis and Reform of Economic Policy* (Washington, DC: World Bank, 1990), 66.

43. Theoretically, the VAT would compensate the loss of trade tax revenues, yet in practice the prospect of societal opposition to the new tax, extensive exemptions, the deficiencies of the Moroccan fiscal administration, and widespread tax evasion made this unlikely.

44. Horton, *Morocco*, 61–66.

45. Bulletin Officiel, January 17, 1983, cited in Cherkaoui, *Inventaire des Mésures*, 6.

46. The 1995 code introduced a unified investment code with homogeneous fiscal incentives for all nonagricultural activities. Incentives include exemptions for the value-added and import taxes as well as corporate profit and income tax breaks, and promotion of offshore export zones and government commitments to invest in infrastructure in order to encourage investment. International Monetary Fund, *Morocco: Selected Issues* (Washington, DC: IMF, February 1997), 10.

47. Director, Banque Marocaine du Commerce Extérieur, interview by author, Casablanca, Morocco, September 15, 1999.

48. AMITH officials, interview by author, Casablanca, Morocco, November 8, 1999.

49. The Moroccan national television channel, "2M," broadcast a documentary profiling one such entrepreneur who came from a modest, middle class family. The program presented the industrialist as an example of the new breed of "self-made men" in Morocco. Clothing firm director, interview by author, Salé, Morocco, January 25, 2000.

50. Textile firm director, interview by author, Ain Sebaa, Casablanca, October 6, 1999; textile firm director, interview by author, Casablanca, Morocco, November 26, 1999.

51. Because European producers distinguish between the two activities, with two separate professional associations representing textile and clothing manufacturers in most EU countries, AMIT decided that adding the word "clothing" would avoid confusion with its main clients. AMITH official, interview by author, Casablanca, Morocco, March 2, 2000.

52. *La Vie Economique*, March 15, 1991, 26.

53. Former AMITH official and clothing firm administrator, interview by author, Casablanca, Morocco, October 27, 1999; clothing firm director, interview by author, Marrakesh, Morocco, December 3, 1999.

54. Textile firm commercial director, interview by author, Mohammedia, Morocco, January 24, 2000.

55. Clothing firm director and former thread firm director, interview by author, Fes, Morocco, January 25, 2000.

56. Bulletin Officiel no. 4282 (December 31, 1995); clothing firm director, interview by author, Salé, Morocco, January 18, 2000; Ministry of Industry official, interview by author, Rabat, Morocco, March 29, 2000.

57. *La Vie Economique*, January 19, 1996, 3–4; Béatrice Hibou, "Les Enjeux de l'Ouverture au Maroc," Working Paper 15, Centre d'Etudes et de Recherches

Internationales, Fondation Nationale des Sciences Politiques, Paris, France, April 1996. For a detailed argument on the role of the *Campagne d'Assainissement* in inciting the CGEM to adopt a more explicitly political role in Moroccan society, see Myriam Catusse, "L'Entrée en Politique des Entrepreneurs au Maroc" (Ph.D. diss., University of Law, Economy and Science of Aix-Marseille, France, 1999).

58. *La Vie Economique*, February 16, 1996, 3.

59. *La Vie Economique*, February 16, 1996, 5–6.

60. Cloth firm administrator, interview by author, Casablanca, Morocco, November 16, 1999; clothing firm director, interview by author, Fes, Morocco, December 6, 1999.

61. Confédération Générale des Entreprises du Maroc, "Le 'Gentlemen's Agreement': Un Accord en Huit Points," *Vues economiques* 9 (1997): 225–237; *La Vie Economique*, June 28, 1996, 27.

62. Clothing firm director, interview by author, Marrakesh, Morocco, December 3, 1999. This should not suggest that all apparel manufacturers were innocent. Industrialists in all branches of the sector admit that illegal sales on the local market are rampant. The Casablanca neighborhood of Derb Ghallaf, a hub for black market sales and the favorite shopping destination for Moroccans from all income groups, is renowned for illegal sales of foreign designer clothing, much of which was assembled locally for "reexport."

63. Clothing firm administrator, interview by author, Salé, Morocco, January 25, 2000.

64. AMITH officials, interview by author, Casablanca, Morocco, November 8, 1999.

65. *La Vie Economique*, July 18, 1997, 24.

66. Textile firm director, interview by author, Casablanca, Morocco, November 26, 1999.

67. *La Vie Economique*, January 16, 1998, 26.

68. *La Vie Economique*, July 3, 1998. The Route de Mediouna is a Casablanca district where many long-standing textile producers established their factories.

69. Cloth finishing firm chairman, interview by author, Casablanca, Morocco, January 12, 2000; *La Vie Economique*, February 20, 1998, 23.

70. Clothing firm director, interview by author, Salé, Morocco, October 5, 1999; clothing firm administrator, interview by author, Tangiers, Morocco, February 16, 2000; clothing firm director, interview by author, Tangiers, February 16, 2000.

71. The *Contrat-Programme* outlined a proactive vision of business–government cooperation to boost the sector's international competitiveness. For its part, the government would reduce "indirect" production costs, notably social security payments, wages, income and other business-related taxes, transportation and energy costs, ensure access to affordable credit—a big problem for small and medium-sized clothing firms—establish a fund to finance textile firm upgrading, introduce more "flexible" labor regulations, devalue the Moroccan currency for exports, and create better equipped industrial zones where entrepreneurs could find affordable land. As part of its effort to promote sectoral cohesion, the

document specifically skirted the issue of customs duty levels on thread and cloth imports. In return, AMITH promised that its members would use the favorable growth conditions for the sector provided by the proposed government policy incentives to promote job creation on a massive scale, thereby tackling the issue of unemployment, a persistent problem facing the country as a whole. The association justified its demands by pointing to the sector's overwhelming importance in the national economy, noting that the textile and clothing industries employ 38% of the industrial labor force and account for 38% of exports, 16% of total production, and 23% of national investment. AMITH, "Stratégie de Croissance et de Compétitivité de l'Industrie du Textile-Habillement: Plan d'Action pour un Contrat-Programme (1999–2003)," Casablanca, Morocco, July 1999; AMITH officials, interview by author, Casablanca, Morocco, November 8, 1999; *L'Economiste*, July 19, 1999, 1.

72. *L'Economiste*, August 16, 1999, 4.
73. For garment exporters, one of the most effective ways to boost quality and sales rapidly would be to establish partnerships with European textile firms looking to set up overseas production units. Attracting FDI while the opportunity presented itself was paramount, compelling AMITH board members to list a series of related policy demands in their proposal to the government. Time was of the essence since crises in the global textile industry in the 1990s had touched off a new wave of European factory relocations to low-wage countries.
74. Regional labor union leader, interviews by author, Fes, Morocco, February 24, 2000 and March 6, 2000; thread firm director, interview by author, Fes, Morocco, February 25, 2000.
75. Textile firm administrator, interview by author, Casablanca, Morocco, November 16, 1999; personal communication with government minister, Rabat, Morocco, January 2000.
76. The story is further complicated by the fact that the postindependence bourgeoisie no longer confined its interests to locally oriented activities, developing holdings in export-oriented industries such as apparel production as well. As a garment subcontractor commented, "The [large-scale textile producing families] are there wherever there is money to be made" (clothing firm administrator, interview by author, Tangiers, Morocco, February 16, 2000). In the middle to late 1980s, when garment assembly subcontracting was booming, major textile industrialists branched out into clothing production. Prominent textile families such as the Tazis, Kettanis, and Lamranis launched lucrative ready-to-wear garment and knitwear export factories, hedging their holdings in the declining textile industry. The extension of traditionally dominant textile producers into the clothing industry also enabled these producers to maintain some control over AMITH's agenda and helped them to push for a compromise founded on sectoral integration.
77. A major achievement of AMITH pressure on the administration was the reduction of delivery delays due to bureaucratic import procedures for inputs such as production equipment, cloth, and thread. Previously, local customs processing

took about seven days for completion. Thanks to AMITH lobbying, processing was reduced to about six hours and further reductions with the computerization of the customs processing system were in the works. AMITH established an ongoing dialogue with the Customs Authority and Ministry of Finance, which are increasingly responsive to association demands (*Le journal*, September 11–17, 1999), 28.

78. In 1998, the administration appointed a new director of the customs authority, Abderrazak El Mossadeq, who developed good relations with the Moroccan business community and held regular meetings with CGEM and AMITH officials. Mossadeq was previously an official in the Ministry of Industry, where he oversaw major economic reforms such as price liberalization and amendments to commercial legislation (*La Nouvelle Tribune*, June 4, 1998).

79. The "industrial districts" model, most closely associated with Piore and Sabel's work on Italy, suggests that collaborative production relationships forge tight linkages among small-scale manufacturers, implying that producer networks may emerge and facilitate collective action (Michael Piore and Charles Sabel, *The Second Industrial Divide* [New York: Basic Books, 1984]). Yet the model is most applicable to high-quality "niche" industries rather than activities where price-based competition prevails. For overviews of the industrial districts literature, see John Humphrey, "Industrial Organization and Manufacturing Competitiveness in Developing Countries: An Introduction," *World Development* 23 (1995): 1–7 and "Industrial Reorganization in Developing Countries: From Models to Trajectories," in ibid., 149–162. Cawthorne critiques applications to developing countries (Pamela Cawthorne, "Of Networks and Markets: The Rise and Rise of a South Indian Town: The Example of Tiruppur's Cotton Knitwear Industry," in ibid., 43–56).

CHAPTER 9

Reconciling Privilege and Reform: Fiscal Policy in Egypt, 1991–2000

Eberhard Kienle

S
ince the late 1980s, and in particular from 1991, the government of
Egypt has implemented a program of economic reform whose declared
aim was to tackle increasingly preoccupying budgetary and external
imbalances, reduce an equally threatening level of public debt, and ensure
higher productivity and competitiveness of the economy in the long term. Like
in numerous other countries confronting similar difficulties, the reform package negotiated with the international financial institutions (IFIs) combined
macroeconomic stabilization and structural adjustment, entailing austerity
measures as well as economic liberalization. In order to rebalance the state budget and, in part, reallocate resources in ways consistent with the objectives of
structural adjustment, economic reform necessarily had to entail fiscal reform.[1]

Though not without exceptions, fiscal policy in the period of economic
reform tended to maintain and reinforce the fiscal privileges of a number of
actors and categories of actors. Sometimes these conservative effects resulted
from the selective implementation of rules and regulations, but in most cases
they were clearly intended by legislation. In terms of taxation, the privileged
included not only all those who managed to benefit from the largely discretionary methods of tax calculation and collection (subject to a degree of
arbitrariness of this sort), but they also—and indeed primarily—included the
individual and institutional earners of high incomes; in particular, earners
of high incomes from capital, as well as the owners and administrators of
companies with corporate status. Simultaneous cuts in generalized subsidies

for foods, energy, and so on, affected them like everybody else, but certainly not as much as less affluent actors. Direct taxation of the latter possibly did not increase, but higher indirect taxation hit them relatively harder. Moreover, the less affluent now tended to lose fiscal privileges in terms of targeted government expenditure that they had enjoyed earlier. This trend is exemplified, for instance, by the nonrenewal of employment contracts in the public sector; contracts that since the late 1980s had by and large become temporary contracts. Only some of the very poor were better off due to dedicated programs of poverty alleviation sponsored by the IFIs.

In the context of the present volume, the survival and reinforcement of fiscal privilege obviously raises the question whether this trend was prompted or facilitated by networks linking beneficiaries to policy makers. Without denying that such networks may have existed and that they may even have been active, my conclusions are rather cautious and indeed question the explanatory usefulness of network analysis in this case. Even if we overcome the empirical difficulty of identifying and mapping networks that do not want to be seen as such, their confirmed existence fails to inform us about the flows that take place within them and about issues such as initiative and agency. For the sake of clarity, I should add that my reservations do not apply to configurations where beneficiaries and policy makers are identical and where such identity obviously precludes us from defining them as networks.

Definitions and Limitations

The concepts of fiscal policy and reform used here are simple. They cover all sets of measures and all individual measures—but nothing more than them—that affect the budget available to the rulers. It does not matter whether the budget serves to fulfill anything like Musgrave's "basic functions of the fiscal state"—that is, the provision of public goods, distributive justice, and macroeconomic regulation.[2] My definition is not based on the uses of the budget, nor in fact on its origins, but exclusively on its management by the rulers. Though surprisingly perhaps, the distinction between private and public is irrelevant to the definition.

The explicit reference to individual measures takes into account that fiscal policy as the sum total of measures affecting revenue and expenditure cannot be reduced to more or less coherent sets of such measures that, especially if implemented regularly over a given time span, correspond to what is commonly called a "policy." As the sum total of relevant measures, fiscal policy (like any other public policy) comprises numerous individual measures that are not repeated consistently and regularly over time. Such individual measures may either reinforce or contradict the general thrust of the policy and thus also highlight the need not to confuse actual policies with policies prescribed by law.

Extending the definition beyond the state budget to the budget available to the rulers may appear to be problematic. After all, historically the *fiscus* in terms of assets of the crown is said to have been distinct from the personal assets of the emperor as an individual and from those of the empire at large (*aerarium*). The empire obviously has more recently been replaced by the state defined in Weberian terms. However, independently of whether the classic trichotomy actually existed where it was said to exist, the domination of the state by unaccountable rulers (like for instance, in Egypt) blurs the distinction between assets belonging to the former and assets belonging to the latter. Not only may the rulers in accordance with the common logic of patrimonialism determine taxes and duties payable to the state, but they might even dip into the pockets of the state in order to satisfy their own perceived needs or desires. They may also extract resources from the ruled, or allocate them to the ruled, through mechanisms that bypass institutions and structures officially declared and defined as parts of the state, for instance when they ask for commissions and kick-backs that have no basis even in the law for which they have voted by the relevant state institutions.

A major caveat is in place here in the sense that not all levies raised for the state or by state officials need to accrue to the regime. Even under patrimonial conditions, the state may have a life of its own and not all the amounts that are raised for the state serve the regime beyond the simple fact that it needs a state apparatus in order to survive. Similarly, all sorts of actors acting in the name of the state, such as ticket inspectors or policemen, may levy commissions and extra-legal fees that serve their own interests and not those of the regime.

Practically it is therefore difficult to distinguish between the budgets of the state, its agents, and the regime. Fortunately, it is not relevant for us to systematically disentangle these budgets, as our concern is not to determine who gets what and how much. We only need to be attentive to the fact that in Egypt and in numerous other countries, the actual weight of taxation and its avatars on the ruled is often higher than the amount explicitly levied in the name of and for the state.

For pragmatic reasons the following analysis focuses on only part of the revenue side of fiscal policy. We focus on taxes in the broad sense of the term, which, apart from levies officially declared as such, include levies that may be assimilated to taxation in the sense of forced extraction. In addition to "classical" sources of revenue such as indirect taxes, direct taxes, and customs tariffs we also examine two other sources that appear to be important in

Egypt, namely the bleeding of state-owned banks and funds as well as extra-legal taxation, occurring mostly on an *ad hominem* basis.

Other sources of income such as grants or receipts from sales are not discussed here. In the Egyptian case, it is important to note that the part of fiscal revenues extracted from the ruled is relatively small. Overall, officially calculated tax revenue in Egypt in the years since 1991 amounted to between 17 and 23 percent of GDP. Prior to the reforms it amounted to some 28 percent of GDP in the early 1980s, and still to some 24 percent as late as 1984.[3] Grants from abroad such as U.S. military and civil aid, royalties from the Suez Canal, and income from the sale of Egyptian oil, account for the bulk of fiscal revenues. While it is not inappropriate to label many of these sources of income as "rents," it must be clear that, strictly speaking, taxes and duties are also forms of rent.

Taxation, as a matter of course, is only one way of financing state and regime expenditure. However, as we shall see, respective privileges were not neutralized by the creation of money (or seignorage); nor were they affected by the financing of public debt that remained high even after the partial cancellation of foreign debt as part and parcel of the commitment to economic reform; public domestic debt even increased.

The Continuity of Privilege

Fiscal reform on the revenue side began with the gradual introduction and generalization of a general sales tax from early 1991. Though not a full-fledged value added tax, it substantially increased indirect taxation, except in the informal sector, which by definition largely escapes taxation. The promulgation of the "unified tax law" of 1993 (*qanun al-dariba al-muwahhada*) and later amendments in numerous but selected cases reduced direct taxation by law for individuals and businesses. However, administrative rationalization and improved collection frequently tended to neutralize these effects. Companies of corporate status continued to enjoy their former privileges to which various laws added new ones. Throughout the period, the agreements with the IFIs and the new GATT concluding the Uruguay Round entailed, and continue to entail, the gradual lowering of customs tariffs on imports. Tariffs applied to imports from the EU will further decrease and ultimately disappear once the new agreement of association governed by the principles of the Euro-Mediterranean partnership comes into force.[4]

A number of measures and developments illustrate particularly well the continuity of pre-reform privilege after the reforms. First of all, indirect taxes continued to account for some two-thirds of total tax revenue after the reforms. Tending to favor higher revenues, indirect taxation ipso facto shifted some of the new tax burden entailed by the general sales tax onto lower income brackets. Even higher sales tax rates for "luxury items" hit lower incomes and in many cases simply prevented less wealthy buyers from purchasing these items. The regressive effects of indirect taxation may only have been offset if, as sometimes suggested, earners of lower incomes relied relatively more heavily on the informal sector.

Similarly, the direct taxation of personal and corporate income remained biased in several ways, partly in law, partly in practice. Thus legislation continued to privilege higher personal incomes indirectly but substantially by granting important tax deductions for certain types of investments. Although in principle they applied even to investments on a small scale, the deductions became meaningful only if larger funds were committed. For instance, investment by individuals in corporate equity could be fully deducted from taxable income. If the amount invested was borrowed, even the interest paid was tax deductible. Similarly, there were significant advantages for lending money to corporations through corporate bonds.[5]

Reform legislation also introduced additional privileges for higher personal incomes. The maximum rates for incomes from salaries, as well as from commercial, manufacturing, and noncommercial professional activities were substantially lowered, favoring higher income brackets who consequently gained an advantage for the purchase of commodities with high income elasticity. The maximum tax rate for salaries was lowered from 45 to 32 percent, that for noncommercial professional activities (applying for instance to doctors and lawyers) from sometimes way beyond 50 to 40 percent. Although possibly neutralized by deductions, the minimum rate for salaries rose from 15 to 20 percent while the minimum tax rate of 20 percent on professional incomes was applied to incomes as low as LE 2,500.[6]

At the same time, legislation continued to privilege certain types of personal incomes from property. Thus capital gains and dividends from shares of companies enjoying tax holidays were tax-free. This was particularly relevant for large incomes from property; incomes, which in Egypt, were far higher than the highest incomes from labor. Some incomes from capital were taxed at zero-rate independently of their amount, while incomes from labor were taxed up to 32 percent. As most of the highest incomes in the country were simultaneously incomes from property, this bias in practice reinforced the bias in favor of larger incomes already discussed. The abolition of inheritance tax confirmed the same trend.

With respect to businesses, legislation continued to privilege companies of corporate status (*sharika al-amwal*, pl. *sharikat al-amwal*) including joint stock companies (*sharika(t) al-musahama*), "limited partnerships" (*sharika(t) tawsiya bil-asham*), and companies with limited responsibility (*sharika(t) dhata al-mas'uliyya al-mahduda*) that were taxed under the corporate income tax scheme. For instance, such companies enjoyed an ever-increasing array of old and new tax holidays. All new corporations with more than 50 employees were exempt from corporate income tax for an initial period of five years. The same applied to any other new corporation approved by the General Authority for Investment. In both cases, tax holidays were renewable for another five years at the discretion of the Authority.[7]

Corporations or parts thereof established in new towns such as Madinat Sadat enjoyed tax holidays for ten years and in the free zones, forever. In the economically least developed governorates of Upper Egypt, tax holidays were granted for 20 years. Other schemes applying to certain economic activities were extended by the law of 1997 to guarantee and encourage investment.[8] The differential between actual tax rates applied to corporations on the one hand and non-corporate companies on the other was substantial, such that for many of the former "tax provisions taken together should make for no tax liability under the statutes."[9]

Considering that a large part of tax from income was nonetheless paid by corporations, corporate tax may itself have been levied in increasingly non-egalitarian ways. Such inequality may reflect either discretionary discounts and arbitrary illegal surcharges, or a divide between the public and private sectors. Largely old and located outside tax holiday areas, public sector companies may have carried the main burden of taxation, only to be alleviated by new loans from public sector banks. Legislation aimed at reforming the public sector in fact subjected them to taxation (a gray area in which I would have been unable to navigate without Ulrich Wurzel's help).

However, it is also interesting to note that the share of tax revenue in total GDP decreased with fiscal and economic reform. Higher government revenues from corporate tax may therefore have been outpaced by higher corporate revenues. This is all the more likely if one considers studies of income distribution (though technically of household expenditure) that confirm the pauperization of the lower- and middle-income brackets, except for the very poor.[10]

It must be added that corporations were not only the larger companies in the country, but also that they were owned by the wealthier individuals and families. Factors such as the complexities of company law and the cumbersome and sometimes unpredictable administration of justice often discouraged small investors from investing with others in larger ventures where decision making became a collective process.[11]

In some cases, legislation was tailored to the interests of individual taxpayers. A case in point was the law to guarantee and encourage investment enacted in 1997. In the film industry, for example, it only granted tax privileges to very large companies of which there were two. One was a public sector company while the other, called "Renaissance," was controlled by one of the major families of entrepreneurs, the Sawaris.[12]

The inequalities that legislation explicitly established between various sorts of taxpayers were compounded by legal provisions that enabled the relevant government agencies—and thus the regime—to legally favor individual taxpayers on an *ad hominem* basis. The discretionary power of the Investment Authority to extend certain tax holidays beyond their initial period is only one such example.

In actual fact, tax collectors granted advantages to certain taxpayers even where the law did not grant them discretionary powers to do so. The implementation of the law indeed departed significantly from the law itself. Tax returns filed by taxpayers continued to be selectively accepted or rejected by tax collectors. Except in the case of forgery and the like, penalties remained either nonexistent or limited and indeed often negligible for large taxpayers.[13] In the case of well-connected taxpayers the amount to be paid could be officially underestimated. Conversely, in other cases it could be arbitrarily high.[14]

Privileges also continued to be granted in the area of import tariffs. Certainly, under international agreements they had to be continuously lowered. The maximum tariff dropped from 120 percent prior to 1991 to about 70 percent after 1994, but the evolution of tariffs applied to different commodities showed important differences.[15] At the same time, the number of goods covered by import bans and government approval schemes was significantly reduced, even though some bans were replaced with quality control measures. Local industries that remained better protected than others included the textile industry, which considering its large workforce, may have been protected for reasons of social stability. However, they also included car assembly plants that employed small numbers of workers, were equally uncompetitive in international comparison, but (co-)owned by important local entrepreneurs.[16]

Moreover, a clear dividing line separated the privileged from the rest when it came to the availability of credit. The lending policies of Egyptian banks remained heavily biased against small companies. The policies of public sector banks could also be detrimental to larger private businesses that did not enjoy regime patronage. This was particularly obvious in the case of the four major banks controlled by the state that hold some 70–75 percent of deposits.[17] Privileged beneficiaries included public sector companies in dire need to repay or reschedule their debts, state agencies, state officials, well-connected businessmen, and possibly members of the regime themselves. Frequently, loans without interest or collateral were simply negotiated between bank officials and their friends, for instance in the case of the famous "loan deputies" who found ways to trade their (limited) political influence against cheap money. In other cases, however, such loans were granted deliberately to regime-controlled agencies in order to stop gaps or avoid their outright financial collapse.[18] A tax on the banks themselves, this lending policy, or indeed bleeding of the banks, may at any moment turn into a form of taxation of the savings deposited in these banks, which ultimately remain a fiscal crutch for the state, the public sector, and the regime (see also contribution by Ulrich Wurzel). An instructive example is that of the publicly owned National Investment Bank that pays interest rates below the market rate to captive deposits of state pension funds, which results in the taxation without legislation of pensions.[19]

The other area where owners of capital did not necessarily enjoy fiscal privilege was that of extra-legal taxation. In its most general definition, the term may include the extraction or extortion of fees by all sorts of gatekeepers of official resources, ranging from petty administrators to former cabinet ministers acting as unavoidable facilitators for large-scale public contracts and to the regime itself. The most recent version of extra-legal taxation was the reminders to the successful that personal wealth entailed social obligations. President Mubarak himself secured a commitment from entrepreneurs to fund the construction of a considerable number of public schools. When he found out that the commitment was not translated into reality he unambiguously threatened the hesitating donors that social mobility could work both ways, downward as well as upward.[20]

Forced extraction from banks and extra-legal taxation not withstanding, those favored by the rules and practices governing the collection of taxes did not suffer from the other policies that allow rulers to feed their budgets. Under the agreements with the IFIs inflation had to be tackled, involving strict limits on the creation of money and concomitant guarantees for income from capital. At the same time, public debt was funded either via the state budget and thus through taxes levied from the less privileged, or it was funded through treasury bills yielding substantial interest, by and large purchased by the privileged and offering them an alternative to bank deposits. Even in terms of budget expenditure there is little evidence that those who paid little tax were less well served.[21]

At the time of writing the Egyptian parliament is expected to debate new legislation on the taxation of income. Under the draft law, corporate income tax would be reduced to 30 percent for all industries except petroleum companies, which would continue to be taxed at the rate of 40.55 percent. The maximum rate for self-employed professionals would be lowered to 30 percent; at the same time lower tax bands would be widened in order to apply the highest rate only to incomes more than twice as high previously.

Privilege and Rent Seeking

It is tempting to conclude on the basis of *cui bono* arguments that those who have benefited were also at the origin of the crime. In the present case, therefore, legislation and practices governing taxation would have been particularly influenced by (1) those receiving high incomes in general, (2) those receiving (high) incomes from capital, (3) those controlling or owning companies with corporate status, and (4) those able to benefit from the discretionary methods of tax calculation and collection.

From this point of view, the bias favoring corporations would most likely have been the result of private sector lobbying or pressures. However, though benefiting from the tax regime in various ways, even larger businesses have not always been happy with tax legislation. Their limited influence was clearly illustrated by the law to guarantee and encourage investment. The tax holidays granted by the law fell way short of the expectations of even the most important industries such as tourism, where major private owners of capital had been increasingly active. Thus it cannot be excluded that the regime maintained and further developed the bias in favor of corporations for its own reasons, possibly holding the view that it might contribute to the creation of jobs, or seek to cultivate the loyalty of whatever constituency.

Supposing that the tax regime was inspired by those who benefited from it, the extent of tax holidays in the film industry would have been defined by the Sawiris family in accordance with their own interests. There is, however, very little evidence of pressures emanating from the beneficiaries of the tax regime in place. There may of course have been hidden and discreet pressures, but evidence is less than scarce and insufficient to illustrate the efficacy of such pressures. The same applies to other relevant activities such as lobbying and mutual back-scratching. Ultimately, the available evidence boils down to hearsay and rumors. Often even these rumors relate to advantages obtained in areas other than fiscal policy and enable us to do no more than to infer from certain practices elsewhere that fiscal policy may have been drafted and implemented in similar ways.

Of course, nothing would have prevented the Sawiris brothers from informing the regime of their wish that their company, Renaissance, be granted special treatment. They were clearly in a position to transmit such a request, probably to the president himself. They owned and managed companies that, for instance in the field of public works and defense installations, provided services that no other company in Egypt was able to provide. With important interests in the United States, they could simply have withdrawn from Egypt, had they been treated with insufficient respect. Curtailing their business activities in Egypt or destroying their companies would have worked against the interests of the regime itself; arresting them for whatever reason would have prompted the collapse of their business run according to the recipes of "hands-on management," which made the owners indispensable.

However, in line with the earlier caveat, one may also consider that in view of the importance of the Sawiris the regime took the initiative and drafted the law in ways that would please them and convince them to further support the regime. Alternatively, the regime may have been convinced that concentration was beneficial to this industry and that for reasons of international competitiveness—Egyptian movies were an important export commodity—only a few major companies should be granted tax holidays.

Privilege and Networks

Innumerable anecdotes and rumors point to close relationships between major owners of capital and representatives of the regime, including the president and his sons. Such relationships may form networks of individuals (or other actors), or they may be part of wider such networks. However, if it is true that networks need not, and perhaps should not, be defined purely in terms of distributional intentions or outcomes, it is also true that evidence of such outcomes is not in itself evidence of direct links between the actors concerned as implied by any meaningful concept of a network. Methodologically proper analyses must not discount coincidences, accidents, or the convergence of interests without contact between their advocates.

Moreover, even ascertaining the existence of a network does not yet prove that it is the network that produces the outcomes we are analyzing. A fortiori, it does not tell us who in the network in a specific case takes the initiative or, more generally, how power is distributed between the actors concerned. This is what the authors of a major survey of approaches to network analysis refer to as the crucial difference between "the content of ties" and "the structure formed by these ties."[22] In the words of another contributor to this debate, "[w]e need to know what flows across the links, who decides on those flows in the light of what interests, and what collective or corporate action flows from the organization of links...."[23] Applied to the example of the Egyptian movie industry and indeed to Egypt at large, we would have to know whether the network(s) serve(s) rent-seeking or rent-granting strategies.

One of the few things we can say with certainty is that the Sawiris were more likely to be able to influence legislation than most other owners of capitals. The particular weight of the Sawiris as major entrepreneurs and indispensable providers of services and their privileged access to the regime put them in a position enjoyed by only a handful of capitalists in the country, including the 'Izz Mansur, Nusayr, Sawiris, 'Uthman (Osman), and Shata.

We may go a step further and rest the argument on the absence of any significant organization representing the interests of all, the majority, or a substantial part of private sector capitalists, thus preventing them from defending their interests through collective strategies. The major organizations such as the Federation of Egyptian Industries and the Chambers of Commerce included private and public sector companies. The representatives of the latter and direct government appointees always formed the majority of board members. The various organizations that more specifically catered to the needs of the private sector were established as private voluntary organizations but were also subject to intrusive forms of government control. They certainly produced studies and issued statements on issues of concern to their members. However, they never overstepped the line that separates "suggesting" from "demanding." Those of their representatives who went too far rarely survived in their positions for much longer.[24]

However, neither such arguments nor the relative weight of the Sawiris prove ipso facto that they are part of a network including major regime representatives or that they are actively networking in regime circles. Certainly, the efficacy of networks may be seen behind the fact that tax reform in particular and economic reform more generally have not at all been at the expense of individuals and families who had been major capitalists prior to the reforms. The regime and the "bourgeoisie" or the various "bourgeoisies" defined as financial, industrial, commercial, and the like, may be seen as hand in glove since the early days of *infitah*. In various specific cases such close relations could be extensively documented and the literature about corruption and patron–client relations in Egypt abounds with examples.[25] One must also admit, however, that much of the evidence presented for obvious reasons would hardly stand up in court. More importantly, there are numerous examples to the contrary which show that economically powerful individuals could find themselves in trouble. The disgrace of various business people clearly illustrates this possibility. So do the court proceedings initiated against the "loan deputies" in the late 1990s and earlier government action against Islamic banks, which not only conducted business in doubtful ways, but also threatened to become too powerful politically.

The general difficulty therefore remains to determine what may be accounted for by flows of power or information within networks, by unilateral pressures more or less discreetly exercised by business people or certain taxpayers, by advantages unilaterally granted to them by the regime, or by the simple convergence of interests between the two sides outside any sort of network.

The efficacy of networks is no more easily demonstrated on a less stringent level of proof. Certainly, members of the regime and their kin do business and socialize with (other) owners of capital. In a Bourdieuian sense, their capitals attract each other and position them close enough on the *champ social* to form what we call networks. However, other regime members are far less affluent and like their wealthier colleagues, they have often risen through the public sector, the armed forces, the police, or the trade unions. There they maintain as many friends and constituencies that in principle are no less likely to be the basis of permanent, socially embedded relationships and therefore, of networks. Considering the outcomes, relationships with or within such more modest social groups seem to be inefficient in shaping fiscal policy. If one accepts that networks are inefficient at this level, why should they be more efficient when linking the regime to the more affluent circles of society?

Privilege and External Pressures

In particular, since the agreements in 1991with the IMF and the World Bank fiscal policy has been increasingly influenced by the requirements of IFIs and international regimes to which Egypt has been a party. The general sales tax and various other pieces of tax legislation were part and parcel of the 1991 and subsequent agreements. These agreements and other international commitments were also reasons for the origin of lower customs tariffs.

How important fiscal reform was in the eyes of IFIs is illustrated, for instance, by the IMF staff report on the basis of which the Fund renewed its agreement with Egypt in 1996. The "prior actions," that is measures to be taken by Egypt as preconditions for the renewal of the agreement, included for instance "an action plan for extending the sales tax to the wholesale and retail levels in the next budget" and the reduction of various tariff rates by a number of percentage points. "Principal actions" in the domain of fiscal policy—that is actions that were part of the program itself—included detailed targets for the reduction of the budget deficit and tariff rates, as well as concrete measures to extend the sales tax to the wholesale and retail trade, and so on.[26]

The measures thus recommended or requested coincide with those actually implemented or at least initiated by the regime as described earlier. Unlike relations between the regime and private domestic capital, relations between the regime and international financial institutions and representatives of other international regimes are sufficiently documented to link policies to pressures. Undeniably, there were also networks linking, for instance, IFI officials to the government of Egypt. Some, like Yusuf Butrus-Ghali and Ahmad Galal, had themselves moved from Washington to Cairo, at least temporarily, to join the government or local think tanks. However, one may be sure that the impact of the pressures on fiscal policy did not depend on whether or not they were transmitted through such networks.

The Relative Role of Factors

In Egypt legislation pertaining to fiscal reform was primarily influenced by external pressures. In spite of delays and hesitations, the regime largely amended legislation in accordance with these pressures and may thus be considered the second most important, though largely reactive, contributor to legal change. There is no indication of other domestic actors having played a similarly effective role in redrafting relevant legislation. However, as the changes generally favored major enterprises and owners of capital, they served the interests of individuals, families, and groups that in the Egyptian context were well connected, actually or potentially. By serving their interests, these measures saved them the trouble of making their voices heard through aggressive lobbying or pressures.

Certainly, there were at least potential losers even among the well-connected wealthy. The reduction of tariffs finally hit or threatens to hit hard some industries, such as car assembly plants under foreign license operated by some of the major entrepreneurs. However, the horizontal organization of their companies that have been active in numerous other fields, as well as transition periods help to soften the impact. More importantly, they may well turn from car assemblers to general sales agents of the same brands, with regime benediction and a similar profit margin. Thus negative effects of new legal provisions may be neutralized by accompanying practices, and pre-reform winners are likely to remain post-reform winners. Such facilitation of potentially difficult transitions may well point to networks, but once again we should not discount the alternatives already referred to.

Other losers of the reform were insufficiently organized to mount opposition, or they were organized in ways that prevented them from doing so. We already discussed the relevant features of business organizations and associations. The many small traders and producers were generally not represented anywhere, except in organizations such as Chambers of Commerce, which remained under regime control. Trade unions as well were run by regime allies and clients. Where these structures failed to contain opposition, the regime could, and did, resort to outright repression.[27] No less importantly, the IFIs considered these actors to have enjoyed illegitimate privileges under the old regime, privileges that had to be cut in order to bring about successful economic reform.

Notes

1. Arvind Subramanian, "The Egyptian Stabilization Experience: An Analytical Perspective," Working Paper, no. 18 (Cairo: Egyptian Center for Economic Studies, October 1997), in particular 4–13. For a critical analysis of the reforms, cf. Dieter Weiss and Ulrich Wurzel, *The Economics and Politics of Transition to an Open Market Economy: Egypt* (Paris: Organization for Economic Cooperation and Development, Development Center, 1998).
2. Richard Musgrave, *The Theory of Public Finance* (New York: McGraw Hill, 1959).
3. Historical figures: The World Bank, *World Development Indicators on CD-ROM, 2001* (Washington, DC: 2001). In the fiscal year 1995/1996, tax revenue stood at 17% of GDP, compared to 4% in Zaire, 45% in Israel, 13–20% in ASEAN countries, and 30–40% in Western Europe. See Sahar Tohamy, "Tax Administration and Transaction Costs in Egypt," in Samiha Fawzy and Ahmad Galal, eds., *Partners for Development: New Roles for Government and Private Sector in the Middle East and North Africa* (Washington, DC: The World Bank, 1999), 159.
4. For full details of relevant tax legislation, see guides to taxation such as Jalal al-Shafi'i, *Al-mawsu'a al-daribiyya* (Cairo: 1999), which includes references to individual laws and decrees, as well as the issues of the *Jarida rasmiyya* (official gazette), where they can be found. Key new laws are laws 187/1993 (unified investment law), 227/1996 (succession), and 8/1997 (guaranteeing and encouraging investment). For an overview of tariffs, see specialized business publications such as *Business Monitor International* (annual) or the country reports for Egypt published by the Economist Intelligence Unit (quarterly and annual).
5. Mark Gersovitz, Roger H. Gordon, and Joel Slemrod, "A Report on the Egyptian Tax System," *Discussion Paper Series Middle East and North Africa*, no. 8 (Washington, DC: The World Bank, October 1993), 32–33.

6. See ibid., 54–60; law 157/1981 as amended by law 187/1993 and law 162/1997, art. 90; and al-Shafiʿi, *Al-mawsuʾa al-daribiyya*, 238, 318–319.

7. Gersovitz et al., "Report on the Egyptian Tax System," 26; Howard Handy et al., *Egypt Beyond Stabilization: Toward A Dynamic Market Economy* (Washington, DC: International Monetary Fund, 1998), 73.

8. Gersovitz et al., "Report on the Egyptian Tax System," 26; Handy et al., *Egypt Beyond Stabilization*, 73.

9. Gersovitz et al., "Report on the Egyptian Tax System," 60.

10. Eberhard Kienle, *A Grand Delusion: Democracy and Economic Reform in Egypt* (London: I.B. Tauris, 2000).

11. More generally, these factors may account for the fact observed by Gersovitz that Egyptians often do not invest in the most tax advantageous ways. See Gersovitz et al., "Report on the Egyptian Tax System," 51.

12. *Al-Ahram Weekly*, October 4, 1997, which summarizes law 8/1997; author interview with Max Rodenbeck, Cairo, September 9, 1998.

13. Gersovitz et al., "Report on the Egyptian Tax System," 58.

14. For example, see Tohamy, "Tax Administration and Transaction Costs in Egypt," 186.

15. See Handy et al., *Egypt Beyond Stabilization*, 17 and 65; The World Bank, ed., *Arab Republic of Egypt—Country Economic Memorandum, Egypt: Issues in Sustaining Economic Growth* (Washington, DC: World Bank, March 15, 1997), 66.

16. Handy et al., *Egypt Beyond Stabilization*, 65, 67 ff.; The World Bank, *Arab Republic of Egypt*, 63, 66; and Max Rodenbeck, *Egypt* (London: Business Monitor International, 1998), 67.

17. Gerard Caprio Jr. and Stijn Claessens, "The Importance of the Financial System for Development: Implications for Egypt," *ECES Distinguished Lecture Series* 6 (Cairo: 1997), 25: "...the amount of credit to the private sector lags even within the Middle East region...."

18. For example, cf. The World Bank, *Arab Republic of Egypt*, 24; Rodenbeck, *Egypt*, 111.

19. See Gouda Abdel-Khalek, "Domestic Public Debt in Egypt: Magnitude, Structure and Consequences," *Cairo Papers in Social Science* 23, no. 1 (2000).

20. *Cairo Times*, March 19, 1998. On extra-legal taxation, also see the contribution by Béatrice Hibou, chapter 6 in this volume.

21. See Abdel-Khalek, "Domestic Public Debt in Egypt."

22. Walter W. Powell and Laurel Smith-Doerr, "Networks and Economic Life," in Neil J. Smelser and Richard Swedberg, eds., *The Handbook of Economic Sociology* (Princeton, NJ: Princeton University Press; New York: Russell Sage Foundation, 1994), 371.

23. Arthur L. Stinchcombe, "Weak Structural Data," review of Mark Mizruchi and Michael Schwartz, eds., "Intercorporate Relations: The Structural Analysis of Business," *Contemporary Sociology* 19 (1990): 381, quoted from Powell and Smith-Doerr, "Networks and Economic Life," 371.

24. Kienle, *A Grand Delusion*, 40, 96–114. Due to their links with the state, these business associations are obviously quite different from those discussed in the growing literature on their importance for growth and development exemplified by Richard F. Doner and Ben Ross Schneider, "Business Associations and Economic Development: Why Some Associations Contribute More Than Others," *Business and Politics* (December 2000). For the same reasons, they are not *stricto sensu* institutions of "civil society" in the sense in which this concept is used these days.

25. For instance, see Eric Gobe, *Les hommes d'affaires égyptiens: démocratisation et secteur privé de l'Egypte de l'infitah* (Paris: Karthala, 1999); and Yahya Sadowski, *Political Vegetables: Businessmen and Bureaucrats in the Development of Egyptian Agriculture* (Washington, DC: The Brookings Institution, 1991).

26. Handy et al., *Egypt Beyond Stabilization*, 22.

27. Kienle, *A Grand Delusion*, 89–116.

About the Contributors

Melani Cammett is an Assistant Professor in the Department of Political Science at Brown University.

Jean-Pierre Cassarino is a researcher in the Department of Political Science at the European University Institute in Florence, Italy.

Bassam Haddad is an Adjunct Professor at Georgetown University and editor of the *Arab Studies Journal*, a research publication based at Georgetown and New York University.

Béatrice Hibou lectures in the political economy of reforms in developing countries at the Institut d'Etudes Politiques (IEP) in Paris.

Steven Heydemann, political scientist, is Director of the Center for Democracy and the Third Sector at Georgetown University.

Eberhard Kienle, political scientist, is Director of the Institut de recherches et d'etudes sur le monde arabe et musulman (IREMAM-CNRS) in Aix-en-Provence, France.

Reinoud Leenders is Middle East Analyst for the International Crisis Group. He is also affiliated with the American University of Beirut as an associate researcher in Political Economy.

John Sfakianakis, an historian, is currently a consultant to the World Bank. He was formerly a research and teaching fellow at Harvard University's Middle East Center.

Oliver Wils is Senior Researcher and Deputy Director of the Berghof Research Center for Constructive Conflict Management, Berlin.

Ulrich Wurzel, political economist, is currently Professor of Economics at the FHTW—Fachhochschule für Technik und Wirtschaft Berlin (University for Applied Sciences Berlin).

Bibliography

Abdel-Khalek, Gouda. "Domestic Public Debt in Egypt: Magnitude, Structure and Consequences." *Cairo Papers in Social Science* 23, no. 1 (2000).

Abdul-Nour, Ayman. "The Role of Governmental Agencies in the Shadow of Market Mechanisms" [*Dawr al-ajhiza al-hukumiyyah fi thill aaliyaat al-suq*]. Paper no. 5, Conference Series. Damascus: Economic Sciences Association, March 16, 1999.

Abdul-Nour, Khalid. "Improving the Industrial Sector" [*Ta'hil al-Qita`al-Sina`i*]. Paper no. 6, 1999 Conference Series. Damascus: Economic Sciences Association, March 23, 1999.

———. "The Private Sector in the Shadow of Protection" [*al-Qita`al-Khas fi Thill al-Himaya*]. Paper no. 13, 2000 Conference Series. Damascus: Economic Sciences Association, April 25, 2000.

Abed, George T. "Trade Liberalization and Tax Reform in the Southern Mediterranean Region." IMF Working Paper 98/49. Washington: IMF, 1998.

Abi Sa'ab, F. et al. *al-Intikhabat an-Niyabiyya al-Lubnaniyya 1996, 'Azmat ad-Dimuqratiyya fi Lubnan*. Beirut: Lebanese Center for Policy Studies, 1997.

`Adwan, C. D. " `Al-Wasta,' Bayna as-Shabab wa al-Mujtam'a." Unpublished paper delivered at Conference of Arab researchers in Amman, Jordan, 2000.

Al-Fanik, Fahid. *Barnamaj al-tashih al-iqtisadi, 1992–1998: ahdaf wa mubararat barnamaj al-in`ash wa al-tashih li-l-iqtisad al-urdunni al-muttafiq `alayha sunduq al-naqd al-duwali*. Amman: Mu'assasa Fahid al-Fanik, 1992.

Albrecht, H., P. Pawelka, and O. Schlumberger. Wirtschaftliche Liberalisierung und Regimewandel in Ägypten. *Welttrends* 16 (Autumn 1997).

Alesina, Alberto. "Political Models of Macroeconomic Policy and Fiscal Reforms." In *Voting for Reform: Democracy, Political Liberalization, and Economic Adjustment*, edited by Stephan Haggard and Steven B. Webb, 37–60. New York: Oxford University Press, 1994.

Alexeev, Michael and Jim Leitzel. "Collusion and Rent-Seeking." *Public Choice* 69 (1991).

Alston, Lee J., Thrainn Eggertsson, and Douglass C. North, eds. *Empirical Studies in Institutional Change*. New York: Cambridge University Press, 1996.

Aly, H. F. and N. Abdun-Nur. "An Appraisal of the Sixth Year Plan of Lebanon (1972–1977)." *Middle East Journal* 29, no. 2 (1975).

Amawi, Abla M. "The Consolidation of the Merchant Class in Transjordan during the Second World War." In *Village, Steppe and State: The Social Origins of Modern Jordan*, edited by Eugene L. Rogan and Tariq Tell, 162–186. London: British Academic Press, 1994.

Amin, G. A. *Egypt's Economic Predicament: A Study in the Interaction of External Pressure, Political Folly and Social Tension in Egypt, 1960–1990.* Leiden: E.J. Brill, 1995.

Amman Chamber of Industry (ACI). *Taqrir majlis al-idara li-`am 1992.* Amman: ACI, 1993.

———. *Taqrir majlis al-idara li-`am 1995.* Amman: ACI, 1996.

Amsden, Alice. *Asia's Next Giant: South Korea and Late Industrialization.* New York: Oxford University Press, 1989.

Anani, Jawad. "Adjustment and Development: The Case of Jordan." In *Adjustment Policies and Development Strategies in the Arab World*, edited by Said El-Naggar, 124–148. Washington: International Monetary Fund, 1987.

Anderson, Betty. "Jordanian Political Parties of the 1950s: Social Transformation and the Dynamic Role of Nationalist Ideology." In *The Hashemite Kingdom of Jordan, 1946–1996: Social Identities, Development Policies and State-building*, edited by Riccardo Bocco. Paris: Karthala, forthcoming.

Ansell, Christopher K. *Schism and Solidarity in Social Movements: The Politics of Labor in the French Third Republic.* New York: Cambridge University Press, 2001.

Arthur, W. Brian. "Competing Technologies, Increasing Returns, and Lock-In by Historical Events." *Economic Journal* 99 (March 1989): 116–131.

———. *Increasing Returns and Path Dependence in the Economy.* Ann Arbor, MI: University of Michigan Press, 1994.

Atallah, S. *Roadblocks to Recovery: Institutional Obstacles Facing the Private Sector in Lebanon.* Beirut: Lebanese Center for Policy Studies, 1999.

`Atalla, T. *Taqniyat at-Tazwir al-Intikhabi wa Sibul Mukafahatiha.* Beirut: Lebanese Center for Policy Studies, 1996.

Augé, Jean-Christophe. "Das jordanische Hochschulwesen zwischen staatlichem Aufbau und Privatisierung." *INAMO* 14 (1998): 14–17.

Ayad, Chédly. "Le 26.26, c'est le président Ben Ali!" *Le Soir*, August 2, 1999.

Ayman Abdul-Nour. "The Role of Governmental Agencies in the Shadow of Market Mechanisms" [*Dawr al-ajhiza al-hukumiyyah fi thill aaliyaat al-suq*]. Paper no. 5, Conference Series. Damascus: Economic Sciences Association, March 16, 1999.

Ayubi, N. N. *Over-Stating the Arab State: Politics and Society in the Middle East.* London: I.B. Taurus, 1995.

Azar, S. *La Politique de Santé au Liban depuis 1945.* Beirut: Rabieh, 1996.

Bachmann, T., A. Eickelpasch, M. Kauffeld, I. Pfeiffer, and U. Wurzel. "The InnoRegio Initiative: The Concept and First Results of the Complementary Research." *Economic Bulletin* 39, no. 1 (Berlin: DIW Berlin, 2002): 33–44.

Bachrouch, Taoufik. *Le Saint et le Prince en Tunisie*. Tunis: Faculté des Sciences Humaines et Sociales de Tunis, 1989.

Bahout, Joseph. *Les Entrepreneurs Syriens: Economie, affaires et politique*. Beirut: Cermoc, 1994.

———. "Lebanese Parliamentarism: Shadow Plays and the Death of Politics." *The Lebanon Report* (Spring 1996).

———. "Les élites parlementaires Libanaises de 1996, Etude de composition." In *La Vie Publique au Liban: Expressions et recompositions du politique*, edited by Joseph Bahout and Chawki Douayhi. Beirut: Rabieh, 1997.

Baker, Wayne E. "The Network Organization in Theory and Practice." In *Networks and Organizations: Structure, Form, and Action*, edited by Robert G. Eccles and Nitin Nohira, 400. Boston: Harvard Business School Press, 1992.

Banck, Geert A. "Network Analysis and Social Theory: Some Remarks." In *Network Analysis: Studies in Human Interaction*, edited by Jeremy Boissevain and J. Clyde Mitchell. The Hague: Mouton & Co., 1973.

Bangura, Yusuf. "Public Sector Restructuring: The Institutional and Social Effects of Fiscal, Managerial and Capacity-Building Reforms." UNRISD Occasional Paper No. 3. Geneva: UNRISD, 2000.

Banque Centrale de Tunisie. *Statistiques Financières*, no. 118 (March 1997).

Bar, Shmuel. "The Jordanian Elite: Change and Continuity." In *The Hashemites in the Modern Arab World*, edited by Asher Susser and Aryeh Shmuelewitz, 221–228. London: Frank Cass, 1995.

Barkey, Henri, ed. *The Politics of Economic Change in the Middle East*. New York: St. Martin's Press: 1992.

Batatu, Hanna. "Some Observations on the Social Roots of Syria's Ruling, Military Group and the Causes for its Dominance." *MEJ* 35 (1981).

———. "Syria's Muslim Brethren." *MERIP*, no. 110 (November–December 1982): 12–20.

———. *Syria's Peasantry, the Descendants of Its Lesser Rural Notables, and Their Politics*. Princeton, NJ: Princeton University Press, 1999.

Bates, Robert H. *Markets and States in Tropical Africa: The Political Basis of Agricultural Policies*. Berkeley: University of California Press, 1981.

Bates, Robert H. and Anne O. Krueger, eds. *Political and Economic Interactions in Economic Policy Reform*. London: Blackwell, 1993.

Bates, Robert H. et al. *Analytic Narratives*. Princeton: Princeton University Press, 1998.

Bayart, Jean-François. *L'Etat en Afrique: La politique du ventre*. Paris: Fayard, 1989.

Bayart, Jean-François, Stephen Ellis, and Béatrice Hibou. *La criminalisation de l'Etat en Afrique*. Brussels: Complexes, 1997.

Bearman, Peter. *Relations into Rhetorics: Local Elite Social Structure in Norfolk, England, 1540–1640*. New Brunswick, NJ: Rutgers University Press, 1993.

Beblawi, H. "The Rentier State in the Arab World." In *The Rentier State: Nation, State and Integration in the Arab World*, edited by H. Beblawi and G. Luciani. London, New York, and Sydney, 1987.

Beblawi, H. and Giacomo Luciani, eds. *The Rentier State: Nation, State and Integration in the Arab World*. London: Croon Helm,1987.

Becattini, G. "The Marshallian Industrial District as a Socio-Economic Notion." In *Industrial Districts and Inter-Firm Co-Operation in Italy*, edited by F. Pyke, G. Becattini, and W. Sengenberger. Geneva: International Institute for Labour Studies, 1990.

Becker, Gary. "A Theory of Competition Among Pressure Groups for Political Influence." *The Quarterly Journal of Economics* 98 (1983): 371–400.

———. "Political Competition Among Interest Groups." In *The Political Economy of Government Regulation*, edited by Jason F. Shogren. Boston: Kluwer Academic Publishers, 1989.

Bellin, Eva R. *Civil Society Emergent? State and Social Classes in Tunisia*. Ann Arbor: UMI, 1992.

———. "Tunisian Industrialists and the State." In *Tunisia: The Political Economy of Reform*, edited by I. William Zartman, 51. Boulder, CO: Lynne Rienner, 1991.

———. "The Politics of Profit in Tunisia: Utility of the Rentier Paradigm?" *World Development* 22, no. 3 (1994): 431.

Benedict, S. "Le mirage de l'Etat fort." *Esprit* (March–April 1997): 230–231.

Benhaddou, Ali. *Maroc: Les Elites du Royaume, Essai sur l'Organisation du Pouvoir au Maroc*. Paris: L'Harmattan, 1997.

Berrada, Abdelkader. "La Marocanisation de 1973: Eclairage Rétrospectif." *Economie et Socialisme* 8 (1988): 29–68.

———. "Etat et Capital Privé au Maroc 1956–1980." Ph.D. Diss., University of Mohamed V, Rabat, Morocco, November 1991.

Beyoghlow, K. A. "Lebanon's New Leaders: Militias in Politics." *Journal of South Asian and Middle Eastern Studies* 12, no. 3 (Spring 1989).

Biggart, N. W. and G. G. Hamilton. "On the Limits of a Firm-Based Theory to Explain Business Networks: The Western Bias of Neoclassical Economics." In *Networks and Organizations: Structure, Form, and Action*, edited by N. Nohria and R. G. Eccles. Boston, MA: Harvard Business School Press, 1992.

Blejer, Mario I. and Teresa Ter-Minassian, eds. *Fiscal Policy and Economic Reform: Essays in Honour of Vito Tanzi*. London: Routledge, 1997.

Boeckh, Andreas and Peter Pawelka, eds. *Staat, Markt und Rente in der internationalen Politik*. Opladen: Verlag, 1997.

Boisot, Max H. *Information Space: A Framework for Learning in Organizations, Institutions and Culture*. London: Routledge, 1995.

Bonne, E. *Vie publique, patronage et clientèle: Rafic Hariri a Saida*. Paris: CERMOC, 1995.

Bowie, Leland. *The Impact of the Protégé System in Morocco, 1880–1912*. Ohio University: Papers in International Studies, Africa Series no. 11, 1970.

Boyer, Robert and J. Rogers Hollingsworth, eds. *Contemporary Capitalism: The Embeddedness of Institutions*. New York: Cambridge University Press, 1997.

Brand, Laurie A. *Jordan's Inter-Arab Relations: The Political Economy of Alliance Making*. New York: Columbia University, 1994.

———. "The Effects of the Peace Process on Political Liberalization in Jordan." *Journal of Palestine Studies* 28, no. 2 (1999): 52–67.

Bras, J. P. "Tunisie: Ben Ali et sa classe moyenne." *Pôles* 1 (April–June 1996): 174–195.

Brass Daniel J. and David Krackhardt. "Intraorganizational Networks, the Micro Side." In *Advances in Social Networks Analysis, Research in the Social and Behavioral Sciences*, edited by Joseph Galaskiewicz and Stanley Wasserman, 207–227. London: Sage Publications, 1994.

Bromley, S. *Rethinking Middle East Politics, State Formation and Development.* Cambridge: Polity Press, 1994.

Brown, L. Carl. *The Tunisia of Ahmed Bey, 1835–1855.* Princeton, NJ: Princeton University Press, 1974.

Brücker, Herbert and Wolfgang Hillebrand. *Privatisierung in Entwicklungs- und Transformationsländern. Konzepte, Erfahrungen und Anforderungen an die Entwicklungszusammenarbeit.* Köln: Weltforum Verlag, 1997.

Brusco, S. "The Idea of the Industrial District: Its Genesis." In *Industrial Districts and Inter-Firm Co-Operation in Italy*, edited by F. Pyke, G. Becattini, and W. Sengenberger. Geneva: International Institute for Labour Studies, 1990.

Buck, Andrew, W. "Networks of Governance and Privatization: A View from Provincial Russia." In *Political Power and Social Theory*, edited by Diane E. Davis. Stanford, CT: JAI Press, 1999.

Bureau for International Narcotics and Law Enforcement Affairs. *International Narcotics Control Strategy Report.* United States Department of State, Washington, DC, March 1995.

Burt, Ronald S. *Toward a Structural Theory of Action.* New York, NY: Academic Press, 1982.

———. "Network Data from Archival Records." In *Applied Network Analysis: A Methodological Introduction*, edited by R. Burt and Michael J. Minor, 158–175. Beverly Hills, London, New Delhi: Sage Publications, 1983.

———. *Structural Holes: The Social Structure of Competition.* Cambridge, MA: Harvard University Press, 1992.

———. "The Network Entrepreneur." In *Entrepreneurs: The Social Science View*, edited by Richard Swedburg, 291. New York: Oxford University Press, 2000.

Burt, Ronald S. and Michael J. Minor, eds. *Applied Network Analysis: A Methodological Introduction.* London: Sage Publications Ltd., 1983.

Callaghy, Thomas. "Lost Between State and Market: The Politics of Economic Adjustment in Ghana, Zambia, and Nigeria." In *Economic Crisis and Policy Choice: The Politics of Adjustment in the Third World*, edited by Joan M. Nelson, 257–319. Princeton: Princeton University Press, 1990.

Camau, Michel. "Politique dans le passé, politique aujourd'hui au Maghreb." In *La greffe de l'Etat*, edited by Jean-François Bayart. Paris: Karthala, 1996.

———. "D'une République à l'autre: refondation politique et aléas de la transition libérale." *Monde arabe, Maghred-Machrek* 157 (July–September 1997): 3–16.

Caprio Jr., Gerhard and Stijn Claessens. "The Importance of the Financial System for Development: Implications for Egypt." *ECES Distinguished Lecture Series* 6 (Cairo, 1997).

Cassarino, Jean-Pierre. "The EU-Tunisian Association Agreement and Tunisia's Structural Reform Program." *The Middle East Journal* 53, no. 1 (1999): 59–74.

Catusse, Myriam. "L'Entrée en Politique des Entrepreneurs au Maroc." Ph.D. Diss., University of Law, Economy and Science of Aix-Marseille, France, 1999.

Cawthorne, Pamela. "Of Networks and Markets: The Rise and Rise of a South Indian Town: The Example of Tiruppur's Cotton Knitwear Industry." *World Development* 23 (1995): 43–56.

Central Bank of Jordan. *Special Issue on the Occasion of the Fifteenth Anniversary of the HKJ Independence: Yearly Statistical Series, 1964–1995.* Amman: CBJ, 1996.

Central Bureau of Statistics, Syria. *Statistical Abstract 1998.* See chap. 16, "National Accounts." Damascus, 1998.

Chaib, A. *L'Aventure de la liberté: essai sur le libéralisme économique au Liban.* Beirut: 1983.

———. "Les aspects économiques de Taef: une doctrine économique?" *Travaux et Jours*, no. 59 (Spring 1997).

Chammas, N. E. *L'Avenir Socio-économique du Liban en Questions: Eléments de Réponse.* Beirut: Harvard Business School Club of Lebanon, 1995.

Chang, Ha-joon. *The Political Economy of Industrial Policy.* New York: St. Martin's Press, 1994.

Chatelus, Michel. "Rentier or Producer Economy in the Middle East? The Jordanian Response." In *The Economic Development of Jordan*, edited by Adnan Badran and Bichara Khader, 204–220. London: Croom Helm, 1987.

Chaudhry, K. A. *The Price of Wealth: Economies and Institutions in the Middle East.* Ithaca: Cornell University Press, 1997.

Cherif, M. Hédi. "Document relatif à des tribus tunisiennes des débuts du XVII ème siècle." *Revue de l'Occident Musulman et de la Méditerranée*, no. 33 (January 1983): 81–82.

———. *Pouvoir et société dans la Tunisie de H'usayn Bin'Ali (1705–1740).* Tunis: Publications de l'Université de Tunis I, 1984 and 1986.

———. "Regional Development and Integration." In *Peace for Lebanon? From War to Reconstruction*, edited by D. Collings. Boulder: Reinner, 1994.

———. "Fermage (lizma) et fermiers d'impôts (lazzam) dans la Tunisie des XVII–XVIII siècles." *Etats et pouvoirs en Méditerranée, Les Cahiers de la Méditerranée.* Université de Nice, 1998.

Cherkaoui, Mouna. *Inventaire des Mésures de Politiques Economiques Prises au Maroc de Janvier 1982 à Juillet 1992.* Rabat, Morocco: Groupement de Recherche en Economie Internationale, University of Mohamed V, October 1992.

Chiha, M. *Propos d'économie libanaise.* Beirut: 1965.

Confédération Générale des Entreprises du Maroc. "Le 'Gentlemen's Agreement': Un Accord en Huit Points." *Vues économiques* 9 (1997): 225–237.

Cook, Karen S. "Network Structures From an Exchange Perspective." In *Social Structure and Network Analysis*, edited by Peter V. Marsden and Nan Lin, 195. London: Sage Publications Ltd., 1982.

Cook Karen S. and J. M. Whitmeyer. "Two Approaches to Social Structure: Exchange Theory and Network Analysis." *Annual Review of Sociology* 18 (1992): 109–127.

Cowling, K. "Privatisierung, Demokratisierung und Effizienz." In *Bedingungen ökonomischer Entwicklung in Zentralosteuropa*, edited by J. Hölscher, A. Jacobsen, H. Tomann, and H. Weisfeld, *Aspekte des wirtschaftlichen Umbruchs* 1 (Marburg: Lit., 1993).

Crouch, Colin and Wolfgang Streeck, eds. *Political Economy of Modern Capitalism: Mapping Convergence and Diversity*. London: Sage Publications, 1997.

Czichowski, Frank. *Jordanien. Internationale Migration, wirtschaftliche Entwicklung und soziale Stabilität*. Hamburg: Deutsches Orient-Institut, 1990.

Dagher, A. *L'Etat et l'économie au Liban, action gouvernementale et finances publiques de l'Indépendance à 1975*. Beirut: CERMOC, 1995.

Dakhlia, Jocelyne. *Le divan des rois*. Paris: Aubier, 1998.

Dalila, 'Arif. "The Public Sector and Its Role in Development" [*al-Qita' al-'Amm wa Dawrahu fi al-Tanmiya*]. Paper no. 3, 1986 Conference Series. Damascus: Economic Sciences Association, 1986.

———. "Syria's Economic Troubles." *Al-Sha'b* (March 1999).

———. "The General Budget Deficit and Methods for Its Treatment" [*'Ajz al-Muwazana al-'Amma wa Subul Mu'alajatihi*]. Paper no. 9, 1999 Conference Series. Damascus: Economic Sciences Association, April 20, 1999.

Dann, Uriel. *King Hussein and the Challenge of Arab Radicalism: Jordan, 1955–1967*. New York: Columbia University, 1989.

David, Paul. "Clio and the Economics of QWERTY." *American Economic Review* 75 (May 1985): 332–337.

Davis, Jeffrey, Rolando Ossowski, Thomas Richardson, and Steven Barnett. *Fiscal and Macroeconomic Impact of Privatization*. Washington, DC: International Monetary Fund, 2000.

de Dios, Emmanuel S. "Parcellized Capital and Underdevelopment: A Reinterpretation of the Specific-factors Model." *Philippine Review of Economics and Business* 30 (1993): 141–155.

Degenne, Alain and Michel Forse. *Introducing Social Networks*. London: Sage, 1999.

Dempsey, Judy. "Doubts Exist Over Benefits of Sales." *Financial Times*, March 26, 1998.

Dessouki, A. E. H. "The Public Sector in Egypt: Organization, Evolution and Strategies of Reform." In *Employment and Structural Adjustment, Egypt in the 1990s*, edited by H. Handoussa and G. Potter. Geneva and Cairo: American University in Cairo Press, 1991.

Dieterich, Renate. *Transformation oder Stagnation? Die jordanische Demokratisierungspolitik seit 1989*. Hamburg: Deutsches Orient-Institut, 1999.

DiMaggio, Paul. "Nadel's Paradox Revisited: Relational and Cultural Aspects of Organizational Structure." In *Networks and Organization: Structure, Form and*

Action, edited by Nitin Nohria and Robert G. Eccles, 118–142. Boston, MA: Harvard Business School Press, 1992.

———. "The New Institutionalism: Avenues of Collaboration." *Journal of Institutional and Theoretical Economics* 154, no. 4 (1998): 696–705.

Din Juni, `Izz al-. "Oil, the Lifeblood of Development and Industrialization in Syria: World Prices Substantially Influence Oil Exports." *al-Iqtisadiyyah* 27 (December 30, 2001).

Doner, Richard F. and Ben Ross Schneider. "Business Associations and Economic Development: Why Some Associations Contribute more than Others." *Business and Politics* (December 2000).

Dougherty, Pamela. "The Pain of Adjustment: Kerak's Bread Riots as a Response to Jordan's Continuing Economic Restructuring Programme: A General Overview." *Jordanies* 2 (1996): 95–99.

Dougherty, Pamela and Oliver Wils. "Between Public and Private: Economic Elite in Jordan." In *The Hashemite Kingdom of Jordan, 1946–1996: Social Identities, Development Policies and State-building*, edited by Riccardo Bocco. Paris: Karthala, forthcoming.

Dubar, C. and S. Nasr. *Les Classes Sociales au Liban*. Paris: Presses de la fondation nationale des sciences politiques, 1976.

Eccles, Robert G. and Nitin Nohria, eds. *Networks and Organizations: Structure, Form and Action*. Boston: Harvard Business School Press, 1992.

Economic Research Forum. *Economic Trends in the MENA Region*. Cairo: 1998.

———. *Economic Trends in the MENA Region, 2000*. Cairo: 2001.

Economist Intelligence Unit (EIU). *Syria: Country Profile, 1993, 1994, 1999, 2000, 2001*.

Ed-Din, Khayr. *Essai sur les réformes nécessaires aux Etats musulmans*. Aix-en-Provence: Edisud, 1987.

Eggertsson, Thrainn. *Economic Behavior and Institutions*. New York: Cambridge University Press, 1990.

The Eighth Regional Command Conference [*Taqaarir wa muqarraraat al-mu'tamar al qutri al-thamin*]. Damascus, 1985.

Eken, S. et al. *Economic Dislocation and Recovery in Lebanon*. Washington, DC: IMF, 1995.

El Mansour, M. *Morocco in the Reign of Mowlay Sulayman*. New York: Middle East and North African Studies Press, 1990.

El-Mikawy, Noha, Amr Hashem, Maye Kassem, Ali El-Sawi, Hafiz Abdel, and Mohamed Showman. *Institutional Reform of Economic Legislation in Egypt, ZEF— Discussion Papers on Development Policy*, no. 30 (Bonn: Center for Development Research (ZEF), 2000).

El-Sayed Said, Mohamed. "Egypt: The Dialectics of State Security and Social Decay." *Politik und Gesellschaft* 1 (Bonn, 2000): 5–18.

Elsenhans, Hartmut "Integrating Political Economy in the Comparative Study of Administration." In *Politics, Administration and Public Policy in Developing*

Countries: Examples from America, Asia and Latin America, edited by H. K. Asmeron and R. B. Jain, 16–36. Amsterdam: VU University Press, 1993.

———. *Abhängiger Kapitalismus oder bürokratische Entwicklungsgesellschaft: Versuch über den Staat in der Dritten Welt*. Frankfurt/Main: Campus, 1981. English version: *State, Class and Development*. New Delhi/London/Columbia, MO: Radiant, Sangam, South Asia Books, 1996.

El Shafei, Omar. *Workers, Trade Unions and the State in Egypt: 1984–1989*. Cairo: The American University in Cairo Press, 1995.

Emirbayer, Mustapha and Jeff Goodwin. "Network Analysis, Culture, and the Problem of Agency." *American Journal of Sociology* 99, no. 6 (1994): 1411–1454.

Emirbayer, Mustapha and Anne Mische. "What Is Agency?" *American Journal of Sociology* 103 (January 1998): 962–1023.

Erans, Peter. *Embedded Autonomy: States and Industrial Transformation*. Princeton, NJ: Princeton University Press, 1995.

———. "State Structures, Government-Business Relations, and Economic Transformation." In *Business and the State in Developing Countries*, edited by S. Maxfield and B. R. Schneider. Ithica: Cornell University Press, 1997.

Evans, Peter and John D. Stephens. "Studying Development Since the Sixties: The Emergence of a New Comparative Political Economy." *Theory and Society* 17 (1988): 713–745.

Evans, Peter, Dietrich Rueschemeyer, and Theda Skocpol, eds. *Bringing the State Back In*. Cambridge: Cambridge University Press, 1985.

Fahas, A. *Az-Zuruf al-Iqtisadiya li-al Harb al-Lubnaniya*. Beirut: Matabi, 1979.

Farrell, Henry and Jack Knight. "Trust, Institutions, and Institutional Evolution: Industrial Districts and the Social Capital Hypothesis." Unpublished paper, 2001.

Fathi, Schirin H. *Jordan: An Invented Nation? Tribe-State Dynamics and the Formation of National Identity*. Hamburg: Deutsches Orient-Institut, 1994.

Fedelino, A. "Association Agreement between Lebanon and the European Union." In *Back to the Future: Postwar Reconstruction and Stabilization in Lebanon*, edited by S. Eken and T. Helbling. Washington, DC: IMF, 1999.

Flora, Peter, Franz Kraus, and Winfried Pfenning. *State, Economy and Society in Western Europe, 1815–1975: A Data Handbook*. Frankfurt: Campus Verlag, 1983.

Freemann, Linton C. "Social Network Analysis: Definition and History." In *Encyclopedia of Psychology* 6, edited by A. E. Kazdan, 350–351. New York: Oxford University Press, 2000.

Friedman, Milton. *Capitalism and Freedom*. Chicago: The University of Chicago Press, 1962.

Friedman, Milton and Rose Friedman. *Free to Choose: A Personal Statement*. New York: Harvest, 1990.

Galal, Ahmed, Leroy Jones, Pankay Tandon, and Ongo Vogelsang. *Welfare Consequences of Selling Public Enterprises: An Empirical Analysis*. New York: Oxford University Press, 1994.

Galaskiewicz, Joseph and Mark S. Mizruchi. "Networks of Interorganizational Relations." In *Advances in Social Networks Analysis: Research in the Behavioral Sciences*, edited by Joseph Galaskiewicz and Stanley Wasserman, 230–253. London: Sage Publications, 1994.

Gambetta, Diego, ed. *Trust: Making and Breaking Cooperative Relations*. Cambridge: B. Blackwell, 1988.

Ganiage, Jean. "North Africa." In *The Cambridge History of Africa* 6, edited by Olivier and Sanderson. Cambridge: Cambridge University Press, 1985.

Gaspard, T. "The Limits of Laissez-faire: A Political Economy of Lebanon 1948–87." Ph.D. Diss., Sussex University, 1992.

Gates, C. L. *The Merchant Republic of Lebanon: Rise of An Open Economy*. London: Centre for Lebanese Studies, 1998.

Gersovitz, Mark, Roger H. Gordon, and Joel Slemrod. "A Report on the Egyptian Tax System." *Discussion Paper Series Middle East and North* Africa, no. 8. Washington, DC: The World Bank, October 1993.

Gibson, James L. "Social Networks, Civil Society, and the Prospects for Consolidating Russia's Democratic Transition." *American Journal of Political Science* 45, no. 1 (January 2001): 51–69.

Gobe, Eric. *Les hommes d'affaires égyptiens: démocratisation et secteur privé de l'Egypte de l'infitah*. Paris: Karthala, 1999.

Goldsmith, Arthur A. "Africa's Overgrown State Reconsidered: Bureaucracy and Economic Growth." *World Politics* 51 (July 1999): 520–546.

Gouffern, Louis. "Les limites d'un modèle? A propos d'*Etat et bourgeoisie en Côte d'Ivoire*." *Politique africaine*, no. 6 (May 1982).

Government of Egypt. Ministry of Economy, Research Information Sector, 1998.

Gräfe, Sebastian. *Die politische Rolle ägyptischer Privatunternehmer im Prozess wirtschaftlicher Liberalisierung der Saatgutbranche*. Magisterarbeit, Universität Leipzig, Institut für Politikwissenschaft, Leipzig, 2002.

Granovetter, Mark. "The Strength of Weak Ties." *American Journal of Sociology* 78 (1973): 1360–1380.

———. "The Strength of Weak Ties: A Network Theory Revisited." In *Social Structure and Network Analysis*, edited by Peter V. Marsden and Nan Lin, 105–130. Beverly Hills: Sage, 1982.

———. "Economic Action and Social Structure: The Problem of Embeddedness." *American Journal of Sociology* 91, no. 3 (1985): 481–510.

———. "Problems of Explanation in Economic Sociology." In *Networks and Organizations: Structure, Form, Action*, edited by Nohria Nitin and Robert G. Eccles, 25–56. Cambridge: Harvard Business School Press, 1992.

———. "Business Groups." In *The Handbook of Economic Sociology*, edited by Neil J. Smelser and Richard Swedburg, 453–475. Princeton, NJ: Princeton University Press, 1994.

Granovetter, Mark and Richard Swedberg. "Introduction." In *The Sociology of Economic Life*, edited by M. Granovetter and R. Swedberg. Colorado: Westview Press, 1992.

Guillen, Pierre. *Les Emprunts marocains, 1902–1904.* Paris: Editions Richlieu, 1971.

Haas, Marius. *Husseins Königreich: Jordaniens Stellung im Nahen Osten.* Munich: Tuduv, 1975.

Haddad, Bassam. "Change and Stasis in Syria: One Step Forward . . ." *MERIP,* no. 213 (Winter 1999).

———. "The Political Dynamics of Economic Liberalization in Populist-Authoritarian Regimes: Administrative Disintegration, Social Polarization, and Economic Stagnation in Syria, 1986–2000." Conference paper, First Mediterranean Social and Political Research Meeting, European University Institute, Florence, Italy, March 2000.

———. "Business As Usual in Syria?" *MERIP* Press Information Note 68, September 7, 2001.

Haggard, Stephan and Robert Kaufman. "Institutions and Economic Adjustment." In *The Politics of Economic Adjustment: International Constraints, Distributive Conflicts, and the State,* edited by S. Haggard and R. Kaufman, 3–37. Princeton, NJ: Princeton University Press, 1992.

———. "Economic Adjustment and the Prospects for Democracy." In *The Politics of Economic Adjustment: International Constraints, Distributive Conflicts, and the State,* edited by S. Haggard and R. Kaufman, 319–350. Princeton, NJ: Princeton University Press, 1992.

———. "The Political Economy of Authoritarian Withdrawals." In *The Political Economy of Democratic Transitions,* edited by Haggard and Kaufman. Princeton: Princeton University Press, 1995.

Haggard, Stephan and Steven B. Webb, eds. *Voting for Reform: Democracy, Political Liberalization, and Economic Adjustment.* New York, NY: Oxford University Press, 1994.

Haggard, Stephan, S. Maxfield, and B. R. Schneider. "Theories of Business and Business-State Relations." In *Business and the State in Developing Countries,* edited by S. Maxfield and B. R. Schneider. Ithaca, NY: Cornell University Press, 1997.

Hall, Peter A. and Rosemary C. R. Taylor. "Political Science and the Three New Institutionalisms." *Political Studies* 44 (1992): 936–957.

Hamdan. K. and M. ʿAql. "At-Tughma al-Maliya fi Lubnan." *At-Tariq* 4 (1979).

Hammoudi, Abdellah. *Master and Disciple: The Cultural Foundations of Moroccan Authoritarianism.* Chicago: University of Chicago Press, 1997.

al-Handasah, Dar. *A Nation-Wide Study of Quarries,* Vol. 1–2. Beirut: January 1996.

Handy, Howard and staff team. *Egypt Beyond Stabilization: Toward A Dynamic Market Economy.* Washington, DC: International Monetary Fund, 1998.

Hanf, T. *Coexistence in Wartime Lebanon: Decline of a State and Rise of a Nation.* London: I.B. Taurus, 1993.

Hardin, Russell. *One for All: The Logics of Group Conflict.* Princeton, NJ: Princeton University Press, 1995.

Harik, Judith. "The Economic and Social Factors in the Lebanese Crisis." *Journal of Arab Affairs* (April 1982).

Harik, Judith. *The Public and Social Services of the Lebanese Militias.* Oxford: Centre for Lebanese Studies, 1994.

Harik, Iliya. "Privatization: The Issue, the Prospects, and the Fears." In *Privatization and Liberalization in the Middle East,* edited by Ilya Harik and Denis J. Sullivan, 1–23. Bloomington: Indiana University Press, 1992.

———. *Economic Policy Reform in Egypt.* Gainesville, FL: University Press of Florida, 1997.

Hariri, R. *Pouvoir et Responsabilité, Coût de la paix, perspectives d'avenir.* Beirut: Arab United Press, 1999.

Harriss, John, Janet Hunter, and Colin M. Lewis, eds. *The New Institutional Economics and Third World Development.* London: Routledge, 1995.

Heimer, C. A. "Doing Your Job *and* Helping Your Friends: Universalistic Norms about Obligations to Particular Others in Networks." In *Networks and Organizations: Structure, Form, and Action,* edited by N. Nohria and R. G. Eccles. Boston, MA: Harvard Business School Press, 1992.

Helbling, T. "Postwar Reconstruction, Public Finances, and Fiscal Sustainability." In *Back to the Future: Postwar Reconstruction and Stabilization in Lebanon,* edited by S. Eken and T. Helbling. Washington, DC: IMF, 1999.

Heller, Peter, Richard Hemming, and Rupa Chakrabarti. "Macroeconomic Constraints and the Modalities of Privatization." In *Fiscal Policy and Economic Reform: Essays in Honour of Vito Tanzi,* edited by Mario I. Blejer and Teresa Ter-Minassian, 32–49. London: Routledge, 1997.

Hellman, Joel S. "Winners Take: The Politics of Partial Reform in Postcommunist Transitions." *World Politics* 50 (January 1998): 203–234.

Hénia, Abdelamid. *Le Grîd, ses rapports avec le beylick de Tunis (1676–1840).* Doctoral thesis, Université de Tunis, 1980.

Henry, Clement M. *The Mediterranean Debt Crescent: Money and Power in Algeria, Egypt, Morocco, Tunisia, and Turkey.* Gainesville FL: The University of Florida Press, 1996.

Hermann, Katja and Aufbruch von Unten. *Möglichkeiten und Grenzen von NGOs in Jordanien.* Hamburg: Lit, 2000.

Heydemann, Steven. "The Political Logic of Economic Rationality: Selective Stabilization in Syria." In *The Politics of Economic Reform in the Middle East,* edited by H. Barkey. New York: St. Martin's Press, 1992.

———. "Taxation Without Representation." In *Rules and Rights in the Middle East,* edited by Ellis Goldberg, Joel Migdal, and Resat Kasaba. Seattle, WA: University of Washington Press, 1993.

———. *Authoritarianism in Syria: Institutions and Social Conflict, 1946–1970.* Ithaca, NY: Cornell University Press, 1999.

———. "Economic Networks and the Politics of Fiscal Policy Reform in the Middle East." Unpublished paper for the Project Statement to the European University Institute, 1999.

———. "Rethinking the Politics of Economic Liberalization." Unpublished paper for Council Grant Proposal, 1999.

——. "Economic Networks and the Political Economy of Fiscal Policy Reform in the Middle East: Conceptual Starting Points and Some Preliminary Hypothesis." Unpublished paper, 1999.

Hibou, Béatrice. "Les enjeux de l'ouverture au Maroc: dissidence économique et contrôle politique." *Les Etudes du CERI*, no. 15 (April 1996).

——. *L'Afrique est-elle protectionniste? Les chemins buissonniers de la libéralisation extérieure*. Paris: Karthala, 1996.

——. "De la privatisation de l'économie à la privatisation de l'Etat." In *La privatisation des Etats*, edited by Béatrice Hibou. Paris: Karthala, Collection Recherches internationales, 1999.

——. "Tunisie, le coût d'un miracle." *Critique Internationale* 4 (June 1999): 48–56.

Hibou, Béatrice and Mohamed Tozy. "Anthropologie politique de la corruption au Maroc: fondement historique d'une prise de liberté avec le droit." *Revue Tiers Monde*, no. 161 (January–March 2002): 23–47.

Hinnebusch, Raymond A. "State Formation in a Fragmented Society." *ASQ* 4 (1982).

——. *Authoritarian Power and State Formation in Ba`thist Syria: Army, Party and Peasant*. Boulder: Westview Press, 1990.

——. "Democratization in the Middle East: The Evidence from the Syrian Case." In *Political and Economic Liberalization: Dynamics and Linkages in Comparative Perspective*, edited by Gerd Nonneman, 163–164. London: Lynne Rienner Publishers, 1996.

Hirschman, Albert O. *Exit, Voice, and Loyalty: Responses to Decline in Firms, Organizations, and States*. Cambridge, MA: Harvard University Press, 1970.

Hodgson, Geoffrey M. "Institutional Economics: Surveying the 'Old' and the 'New.'" *Metroeconomica* 44, no. 1 (1993): 1–28.

Hoekman, Bernard and Patrick Messerlin. *Harnessing Trade for Development and Growth in the Middle East*. Council on Foreign Relations, Study Group on Middle East Trade Options: 2002.

Hollingsworth, J. Rogers, Philippe C. Schmitter, and Wolfgang Streeck, eds. *Governing Capitalist Economies: Performance and Control of Economic Sectors*. Oxford: Oxford University Press, 1994.

Hopfinger, Hans and Raslan Khadour, eds. *Investment Policies in Syria [Siyasaat al-Istithmaar fi Suriyah]*. Procedures of the First Syrian-German Forum in Cooperation with the Faculty of Economy. Damascus: Damascus University, 1997.

Hopfinger, Hans and Raslan Khadour. "Development of the Transportation Sector in Syria and the Actual Investment Policy." *Middle Eastern Studies* 35, no. 3 (July 1999): 64–71.

Hopkins, Nicholas S. and Kirsten Westergaard, eds. *Directions of Change in Rural Egypt*. Cairo: American University in Cairo Press, 1998.

Horton, Brendan. *Morocco: Analysis and Reform of Economic Policy*. Washington, DC: World Bank, 1990.

Hourani, A. *La pensée arabe et l'Occident*. Paris: Naufal Europe, 1991. Second English edition, 1983.

Houssel, J. P. "L'Evolution Récente de l'Activité Industrielle à Fes." *Révue du Géographie du Maroc* 9 (1966): 78.

Hudson, Michael C. *Middle East Dilemma: The Politics and Economics of Arab Integration*. New York: Columbia University Press, 1999.

Humphrey, John. "Industrial Organization and Manufacturing Competitiveness in Developing Countries: An Introduction." *World Development* 23 (1995): 1–7.

———. "Industrial Reorganization in Developing Countries: From Models to Trajectories." *World Development* 23 (1995): 149–162.

al-Humush, Munir. *The Syrian Economy at the Turn of the Twenty-First Century* [*al-Iqtisaad al-Suri `Ala Masharif al-Qarn al-Hadi wal-`Ishrin*]. Damascus: Mashriq Maghrib Printing House, 1997.

Hutchcroft, Paul D. "Obstructive Corruption: The Politics of Privilege in the Philippines." In *Rents, Rent-Seeking and Economic Development: Theory and Evidence in Asia*, edited by Mushtaq H. Khan and K. S. Jomo. Cambridge: Cambridge University Press, 2000.

Hyden, Goren. "Governance and the Study of Politics." In *Governance and Politics in Africa*, edited by Goran Hyden and Michael Bratton. Boulder, CO: Lynne Rienner Publishers, 1992.

Ibarra, Hermina. "Structural Alignments, Individual Strategies, and Managerial Action: Elements Toward a Network Theory of Getting Things Done." In *Networks and Organizations: Structure, Form, and Action*, edited by Nitin Nohria and Robert G. Eccles, 165–188. Cambridge: Harvard Business School, 1992.

al-Imadi, Muhammad. "The Economic and Investment Policies of Syria." In *Investment Policies in Syria*, edited by Hans Hopfinger and Raslan Khadour. Damascus: University of Damascus and Central Institute for Regional Research, University of Erlangen-Nuremberg, 1997.

International Bank for Reconstruction and Development (IBRD). "The Economic Development of Jordan." Report of a Mission organized by the International Bank for Reconstruction and Development at the request of the Government of Jordan. Baltimore: John Hopkins Press, 1957.

International Monetary Fund. *Morocco: Selected Issues*. Washington, DC: IMF, February 1997.

———. *Article IV Consultation with Lebanon 2001*. Washington, DC: October 29, 2001.

International Monetary Fund/ARE 1996. Staff Report for the 1996 Article IV Consultation and Request for Stand-by Arrangement, Cairo, 1996.

Investment Development Authority of Lebanon. *Beirut Sports City Commercial Center*. Beirut: n.d.

Isma`il, Ranya. "Syria: Average Gross Domestic Product Growth Rate has not Reached 1% in 2000." *al-Hayat*, February 15, 2001.

Issawi, C. "Economic Development and Liberalism in Lebanon." *Middle East Journal* 18, no. 3 (1964).

Izmishli, Samar. "Syria: The Amount of Tax Evasion Equals Three Times the Revenues, and Weakens the Capacity of the State to Spend on Health, Education, and Services." *al-Hayat*, March 26, 2001.

Jabbur, George. *al-Fikr al-siyasi al-mu`asir fi suriya* [Contemporary Political Thought in Syria]. London: Riad al-Rayyis, 1987.

Jaidi, Larabi. *Industrie Textile et Processus d'Industrialisation au Maroc.* Rabat, Morocco: Editions de la Faculté des Sciences Juridiques, Economiques et Sociales de Rabat, Université Mohamed V, 1979, 36–37.

Al-Jam`iyyah al-Iqtisaadiyyah. Damascus: Economic Sciences Association, 1986, 1989–2001. Yearly Volumes of Conference Series.

Jansen, Dorothea. *Einführung in die Netzwerkanalyse. Grundlagen, Methoden, Anwendungen.* Opladen: Leske and Budrich,1999.

Jeune Afrique Plus, "2001: l'Odyssée de la concurrence," no. 1867–1868 (October 1996): 119.

al-Jlailati, Muhammad. "The Syrian Tax System and Avenues for Its Reform" [*al-Nizam al-Daribi al-Suri wa-Ittijahat Islahihi*]. Paper no. 7, 2000 Conference Series. Damascus: Economic Sciences Association, March 2, 1999.

Johnson, Chalmers A. *MITI and the Japanese Miracle.* Stanford: Stanford University Press, 1982.

———. "Political Institutions and Economic Performance: The Government-Business Relationship in Japan, South Korea, and Taiwan." In *The Political Economy of the New Asian Industrialism,* edited by Frederic C. Deyo. Ithaca: Cornell University Press, 1987.

Johnson, Michael. *Class & Client in Beirut: The Sunni Muslim Community and the Lebanese State 1840–1985.* London: Ithaca Press, 1986.

Jones, Leroy P. *Public Enterprise and Economic Development: The Korean Case.* Seoul, 1995.

Juha, Sh., ed. *ad-Dustur al-Lubnani, Tarikhuhu, Ta'adilatuhu, Nassuhu al-Hali 1962–1991.* Beirut: Dar al-Ilm lil-malayin, 1991.

Kahler, Miles. "Orthodoxy and Its Alternatives: Explaining Approaches to Stabilization and Adjustment." In *Economic Crisis and Policy Choice: The Politics of Adjustment in the Third World,* edited by Joan M. Nelson, 33–61. Princeton: Princeton University Press, 1990.

Kang, David C. *Crony Capitalism: Corruption and Development in South Korea and the Philippines.* Cambridge: Cambridge University Press, 2002.

Kanovsky, E. *The Economy of Jordan: The Implications of Peace in the Middle East.* Tel Aviv: University Publishing Projects, 1976.

Karam, P. D. *Exchange Rate Policies in Arab Countries: Assessment and Recommendations.* Abu Dhabi: Arab Monetary Fund, December 2001.

Kaspar, T. "Qara'at ukhra fi Iqtisad Lubnan wa mustaqbalihi." In *Beyrouth: construire, l'avenir, reconstruire le passé?* edited by N. Beyhum, A. Salam, and J. Tabet. Beirut: Dossiers de l'Urban Research Institute, 1993.

Katznelson, Ira. "Embeddedness beyond Networks: Reflections on Sociology's New Institutionalism." Unpublished draft, 1999.

Kaufman, Robert R., Carlos Bazdresch, and Blanca Hereda. "Mexico: Radical Reform in a Dominant Party System." In *The Politics of Economic Adjustment: International Constraints, Distributive Conflicts, and the State,* edited by

S. Haggard and R. Kaufman, 360–410. Princeton, NJ: Princeton University Press, 1994.

Kenbib, Mohammed. "Protection et subversion au Maroc, 1885–1912." In *Le Maroc actuel*, edited by Jean-Claude Santucci. Paris: Editions du CNRS, 1996.

Khadour, Raslan. "The Economic Effects of Administrative Corruption" [al-Athar al-iqtisadiyya lil-fasad al-idari]. Paper no. 2, 1999 Conference Series. Damascus: Economic Sciences Association, February 23, 1999.

Khan, Mushtaq H. "Rents, Efficiency and Growth." In *Rent-Seeking and Economic Development: Theory and Evidence in Asia*, edited by Mushtaq H. Khan and K. S. Jomo, 21–69. Cambridge: Cambridge University Press, 2000.

———. "Rent-Seeking as a Process." In *Rents, Rent-Seeking and Economic Development: Theory and Evidence in Asia*, edited by K. H. Khan and K. S. Jomo, 70–144. Cambridge: Cambridge University Press, 2000.

Khan, Mushtaq H. and K. S. Jomo, eds. *Rents, Rent-Seeking and Economic Development: Theory and Evidence in Asia*. Cambridge: Cambridge University Press, 2000.

el-Khazen, F. "The Making and Unmaking of Lebanon's Political Elites from Independence to Taif." *The Beirut Review*, no. 6 (Fall 1993).

———. *Lebanon's First Postwar Parliamentary Election, 1992: An Imposed Choice*. Oxford: Centre for Lebanese Studies, 1998.

———. *The Breakdown of the State in Lebanon 1967–1976*. Cambridge, MA: Harvard University Press, 2000.

al-Khouri, Riad. "Syrians account for about $6 billion of deposits in Lebanese banks alone." *Daily Star*, September 6, 2001.

Khoury, Philip. *Syria and the French Mandate: The Politics of Arab Nationalism, 1920–1945*. Princeton: Princeton University Press, 1987.

Kienle, Eberhard. "The Return of Politics? Scenarios for Syria's Second Infitah." In *Contemporary Syria: Liberalization between Cold War and Cold Peace*, edited by Eberhard Kienle. London: British Academic Press, 1994.

———, ed. *Contemporary Syria: Liberalization between Cold War and Cold Peace*. London: British Academic Press, 1994.

———. *A Grand Delusion: Democracy and Economic Reform in Egypt*. London: I.B. Tauris, 2001.

Kikeri, S., J. Nellis, and M. Shirley. *Privatization: The Lessons of Experience*. Washington, DC: World Bank, 1992.

Kilduff, M. and David Krackhardt. "Bringing the Individual Back In: A Structural-Analysis of the Internal Market for Reputation in Organization." *Academy of Management Journal* 37 (February 1994): 87–108.

Kim, Eun Mee. *Big Business, Strong State: Collusion and Conflict in South Korean Development, 1960–1990*. Albany: State University of New York Press, 1997.

Kingdom of Morocco, Ministry of Finance and Privatization. *Bulletin Officiel* no. 4627, October 5, 1998.

Kingston, Paul. "Breaking the Patterns of Mandate: Economic Nationalism and State Formation in Jordan, 1951–57." In *Village, Steppe and State: The Social Origins of*

Modern Jordan, edited by Eugene L. Rogan and Tariq Tell, 187–216. London: British Academic Press, 1994.

———. "Failing to Tip the Balance: Foreign Aid and Economic Reform in Jordan, 1958–1967." Unpublished manuscript, 1999.

Kiwan, F. "Forces politiques nouvelles, système politique ancien." In *Le Liban aujourd'hui*, edited by F. Kiwan. Paris: CNRS, 1994.

Knaupe, Henk and Ulrich Wurzel. *Aufbruch in der Wüste. Die Neuen Städte in Ägypten.* Frankfurt/Main: Peter Lang, 1995.

Knoke, David. *Political Networks: The Structural Perspective.* New York: Cambridge University Press, 1990.

———. "Networks of Elite Structure and Decision Making." In *Advances in Social Network Analysis: Research in the Social and Behavioral Sciences*, edited by Stanley Wasserman and Joseph Galaskiewicz, 274–294. California: Sage, 1994.

Knoke, David and James H. Kuklinski. *Network Analysis.* London: Sage Publications, 1982.

———. "Network Analysis: Basic Concepts." In *Markets, Hierarchies, and Networks: The Coordination of Social Life*, edited by Graham Thompson, Jennifer Frances, Rosalind Levacic, and Jeremy Mitchell, 173–182. London: Sage Publications, 1991.

Knoke, David, Franz Urban Pappi, Jeffrey Broadbent, and Yutaka Tsujinaka. *Comparing Policy Networks: Labor Politics in the U.S., Germany, and Japan.* New York, NY: Cambridge University Press, 1996.

Köndgen, Olaf. "Privatisierungspolitik in Ägypten zwischen wirtschaftlicher Notwendigkeit und politischen Widerständen." *KAS Auslandsinformationen* 1 (Sankt Augustin 1995): 27–44.

Koop, M. J. "Privatisierung und Effizienz." In J. Hölscher, A. Jacobsen, H. Tomann, and H. Weisfeld, eds., *Bedingungen ökonomischer Entwicklung in Zentralosteuropa, vol. 2: Wirtschaftliche Entwicklung und institutioneller Wandel.* Marburg: Lit., 1994.

Kornai, Janos. *The Economics of Shortage.* Oxford, Amsterdam, New York: North-Holland, 1980.

Krackhardt, David. "The Strength of Strong Ties: The Importance of Philos in Organizations." In *Networks and Organizations: Structure, Form, and Action*, edited by Nittin Nohria and Robert G. Eccles, 216–239. Boston, MA: Harvard Business School, 1992.

Kreuger, Anne, ed. *Economic Policy Reform: The Second Stage.* Chicago: University of Chicago Press, 2000.

Labaki, B. "L'économie politique du Liban indépendant, 1943–1975." In *Lebanon a History of Conflict and Consensus*, edited by D. Haffar and N. Shehadi. London: Centre for Lebanese Studies, 1988.

Lakhoua, Fayçal. "Le Processus de privatisation de l'appareil productif public en Tunisie." *Revue tunisienne d'économie*, no. 7 (1996): 144.

Layachi, Azzedine. "Economic Reform and Elusive Political Change in Morocco." In *North Africa in Transition: State, Society, and Economic Transformation in the 1990s*, edited by Yahia H. Zoubir, 43–60. Miami, FL: University Press of Florida, 1999.

Leenders, Reinoud and C. Adwan. "In Search of the State: The Politics of Corruption in Post-war Lebanon." *Mediterranean Politics* (2004, forthcoming).

Lehmbruch, Gerhard. "The Organization of Society, Administrative Strategies, and Policy Networks: Elements of a Developmental Theory of Interest Systems." In *Political Choice: Institutions, Rules, and the Limits of Rationality*, edited by Roland M. Czada and Adrienne Windhoff-Héritier, 121–158. Frankfurt/Main: Campus, 1991.

Leveau, Rémy. *Le Fellah Marocain: Défenseur du Trône*. Paris: Presses de la Fondation Nationale des Sciences Politiques, 1985.

Leri, Margaret. "Social and Unsocial Capital: A Review Essay of Robert Putnam's *Making Democracy Work*." *Politics and Society* 24, no. 1 (1996): 45–55.

———. "A State of Trust." In *Trust and Governance*, edited by Valerie Braithwaite and Margaret Levi, 77–101. New York: Russell Sage Foundation, 1998.

Lieberman, Ira W. and John Nellis, eds. *Russia: Creating Private Enterprise and Efficient Markets*. Studies of Economies in Transformation Series No. 15. Washington, DC: The World Bank, 1995.

Liebowitz, S. J. and Stephen E. Margolis. "Path Dependence, Lock-In, and History." *Journal of Law, Economics and Organization* 11 (1995): 205–226.

Lombardo, Salvatore. *Un printemps tunisien: Destins croisés d'un people et de son president*. Marseille: Editions Autres Temps, 1998.

Lorenz, Edward H. "Neither Friends nor Strangers: Informal Networks of Subcontracting in French Industry." In *Trust: Making and Breaking Cooperative Relations*, edited by Diego Gambetta, 194–210. New York: Basil Blackwell, 1988.

Luciani, Giacomo. "Allocation vs. Production States: A Theoretical Framework." In *The Rentier State: Nation, State and Integration in the Arab World*, edited by H. Beblawi and G. Luciani. London, New York, Sydney: Croon Helm, 1987.

———. "The Oil Rent, the Fiscal Crisis of the State and Democratization." In *Democracy without Democrats? The Renewal of Politics in the Muslim World*, edited by Ghassan Salamé, 130–155. London: I.B. Tauris, 1994.

Maciejewski, Edouard and Ahsan Mansur, eds. "Jordan: Strategy for Adjustment and Growth." IMF Occasional Paper 136. Washington, DC: International Monetary Fund, 1996.

Mahoney, James. "Path Dependence in Historical Sociology." *Theory and Society* 29 (August 2000): 507–548.

Maila, J. "Le Traite de Fraternité: une analyse." *Les Cahiers de l'Orient*, no. 24 (4th trimester 1991).

———. "Elections sous Influence." *Les Cahiers de l'Orient*, no. 28 (4th trimester 1992).

———. *The Document of National Understanding: A Commentary*. Oxford: Centre for Lebanese Studies, 1992.

Majlis an-nuab. *Â'dâ' majlis an-nuab (1994–1999)*. Tunis, 1994.

Makdisi, S. *Financial Policy and Economic Growth: The Lebanese Experience*. New York: Columbia University Press, 1979.

————. "Laying Claim to Beirut: Urban Narrative and Spatial Identity in the Age of Solidère." *Critical Inquiry* 23 (Spring 1997).

Malik, H. C. "Lebanon in the 1990s: Stability without Freedom?" *Global Affairs* 7, no. 1 (Winter 1992).

al-Maliki, `Abdallah. *Al-mawsu`a fi tarikh al-jihaz al-masrafi al-urdunni.* Vol. 1: *Al-bank al-markazi al-urdunni wa al-siyasa al-naqdiyya.* Amman: Al-urdunniyya li-l-tasmim wa al-taba'a, 1996.

Mansur, A. *al-Inqiliab 'ala at-Ta'if.* Beirut: Dar al-Jadid, 1993.

————. *Mawt Jumhuriya.* Beirut: Dar al-Jadid, 1994.

Manzetti, Luigi. *Privatization South American Style.* Oxford: Oxford University Press, 1999.

Manzetti, Luigi and Charles H. Blake. "Market Reforms and Corruption in Latin America: New Means for Old Ways." *Review of International Political Economy* 3, no. 4 (Winter 1996): 662–697.

March, James G. and Johan P. Olsen. *Rediscovering Institutions: The Organizational Basis of Politics.* New York: Free Press, 1989.

Marsh, David and Martin Smith. "Understanding Policy Networks: Towards a Dialectical Approach." *Political Studies* 48 (2000).

Marzouq, Nabil. "Development and Labor" [*al-Tanmiya wa al-`Ummal*]. Paper no. 17, 1998 Conference Series. Damascus: Economic Sciences Association, March 1998.

Maxfield, Sylvia and Ben Ross Schneider, eds. *Business and the State in Developing Countries.* Ithaca: Cornell University Press, 1997.

McFaul, Michael. "Russia Needs True Reform, Not Higher Taxes." *New York Times,* August 4, 1998.

Menassa, B., ed. *Constitution Libanaise, textes et Commentaires et Accord de Taef.* Beirut: Les Editions l'Orient, 1995.

Messner, Dirk. *Die Netzwerkgesellschaft. Wirtschaftliche Entwicklung und internationale Wettbewerbsfähigkeit als Probleme gesellschaftlicher Steuerung.* Köln: Weltforum Verlag, 1995.

Migdal, Joel S. "The State in Society: An Approach to Struggles for Domination." In *State Power and Social Forces: Domination and Transformation in the Third World,* edited by Joel S. Migdal, Atul Kohli, and Vivienne Shue, 12. New York: Cambridge University Press, 1994.

Milgrom, Paul and John Roberts. "Bargaining Costs, Influence Costs, and the Organization of Economic Activity." In *Perspectives on Positive Political Economy,* edited by James Alt and Kenneth Shepsle. New York: Cambridge University Press, 1990.

Moore, Pete W. "Business Associations, Politics, and Economics in Jordan." Paper presented at the annual MESA conference, Chicago, 1998.

Morrisson, Christian. *Adjustment and Equity in Morocco.* Paris: Development Centre of the Organization for Economic Co-operation and Development, 1991.

Morsy, Magali. "Présentation." In *Essai sur les réformes necessaires,* edited by Khayr ed-Din, 67. Aix-en-Provence: Edisud, 1987.

Moubayed, Sami. "EU Projects Stall in Syria." *Daily Star*, July 2, 2001.

———. "Vimpex Pulls Technicians from Syria: Working Conditions Were 'Unbelievable.'" *Daily Star*, September 17, 2001.

Mudawwar, A. *Dalil Qita' An-Naft fi Lubnan*. Beirut: al-markaz, 1996.

Musgrave, Richard. *The Theory of Public Finance*. New York: McGraw Hill, 1959.

Naba, R. *Rafic Hariri, Un homme d'affaires premier ministre*. Paris: l'Harmattan, 1999.

Nabulsi, Sa`id. "Correcting the Problems of the Labor Market" [*Tasheeh al-khalal fi suq al-`amaalah*]. Paper no. 6, Conference Series. Damascus: Economic Sciences Association, March 23, 1999.

Nasr, S. "Backdrop to Civil War: The Crisis of Lebanese Capitalism." *Middle East Report*, no. 73 (December 1978).

Nassif, N. and R. Bu Munsif. *al-Masrah wa al-Kawalis, Intikhabat 96 fi fusuliha*. Beirut: Dar an-Nahar, 1996.

Nelson, Richard. "Recent Evolutionary Theorizing about Economic Change." *Journal of Economic Literature* 33 (March 1995): 48–90.

Nelson, Richard and Sidney Winter. *An Evolutionary Theory of Economic Change*. Cambridge, MA: Harvard University Press, 1982.

Newbery, David M. "The Budgetary Impact of Privatization." In *Fiscal Policy and Economic Reform: Essays in Honour of Vito Tanzi*, edited by M. Blejer and Teresa Ter-Minassian, 9–31. London: Routledge, 1997.

Niblock, Tim. "International and Domestic Factors." In *Economic and Political Liberalization in the Middle East*, edited by Tim Niblock and Emma Murphy. London: British Academic Press, 1993.

Nohria, N. "Is a Network Perspective a Useful Way of Studying Organizations?" In *Networks and Organizations: Structure, Form, and Action*, edited by N. Nohria and R. G. Eccles. Boston, MA: Harvard Business School Press, 1992.

Nonneman, Gerd, ed. *Political and Economic Liberalization: Dynamics and Linkages in Comparative Perspective*. London: Lynne Rienner Publishers, 1996.

North, Douglass C. *Institutions, Institutional Change and Economic Performance*. New York: Cambridge University Press, 1990.

Norton, A. R. "Lebanon: With Friends like These." *Current History* 96 (January 1997): 6–12.

Nsouli, Saleh M. and Jörg Decressin. "Peace, Investment and Growth in the Middle East." *Finances et développement au Maghreb*, no. 18 (March 1996): 20.

Observatoire géopolitique des drogues. *Etat des drogues, drogue des Etats*. Paris: La Découverte, 1994.

———. *Rapport d'enquête sur les enjeux politiques, économiques et sociaux de la production et du trafic des drogues au Maroc*. Photocopy. February 1994.

———. *Géopolitique des drogues*. Paris: La Découverte, 1995.

O'Donnell, Guillermo and Philippe G. Schmitter, eds. *Transitions from Authoritarian Rule: Prospects for Democracy*. Baltimore: Johns Hopkins University Press, 1986.

O'Farell, Paul. *Privatization in Egypt: A Review of Program Development and Current Status*. Cairo, 1995.

Office of the Prime Minister. *Nata'ij Bahth al-Istiqsaa' al-Sina'I fi-l Qitaa'al-Khaas li-'Aam 1995* [*Statistical Research Results of Private Sector Industry for the Year 1995*]. Damascus: Central Bureau of Statistics, 1998.

Olson, Mancur. *The Logic of Collective Action: Public Goods and the Theory of Groups.* Cambridge, MA: Harvard University Press, 1971.

————. "Why Poor Economic Policies Must Promote Corruption: Lessons from the East for All Countries." In *Institutions and Economic Organization in the Advanced Economies*, edited by Mario Baldassarri, Luigi Paganetto, and Edmund S. Phelps, 9–51. New York: St. Martin's Press, 1998.

Onis, Ziya and Steven Webb. "Turkey: Democratization and Adjustment from Above." In *Voting for Reform: Democracy, Political Liberalisation and Economic Adjustment*, edited by S. Haggard and S. Webb. Published for the World Bank: Oxford University Press, 1994.

Ostrom, Elinor. "Rational Choice Theory and Institutional Analysis: Toward Complementarity." *American Political Science Review* 85, no. 1 (March 1991): 238–243.

Owen, R. "The Economic History of Lebanon 1943–74." In *Toward a Viable Lebanon*, edited by H. Barakat. Washington, DC: Center for Contemporary Arab Studies, Georgetown University, 1988.

————. *State, Power and Politics in the Making of the Modern Middle East.* London: Routledge, 1992.

Padgett, John F. and Christopher K. Ansell. "Robust Action and the Rise of the Medici, 1400–1434." *American Journal of Sociology* 98 (1993): 1259–1319.

Page, E. *Political Authority and Bureaucratic Power: A Comparative Analysis.* Sussex: Wheatsheaf, 1985.

Palmer, M., A. Leila, and E. Yassin. *The Egyptian Bureaucracy.* Cairo: American University in Cairo Press, 1989.

Pawelka, Peter. *Herrschaft und Entwicklung im Nahen Osten.* Heidelberg: Verlag, 1985.

————. "Die politische Ökonomie der Außenpolitik im Vorderen Orient." In *Staat, Markt und Rente in der internationalen Politik*, edited by A. Boeckh and P. Pawelka. Opladen: Verlag, 1997.

————. "Staat, Bürgertum und Rente im Vorderen Orient." *Aus Politik und Zeitgeschichte* 33 (1997): 3–11.

Pennell, Richard. "Libya and Morocco: Consensus on the Past." In *North Africa: Nation, State and Region*, edited by George Joffé, 203–220. New York: Routledge, 1993.

Perthes, Volker. "A Look at Syria's Upper Class: The Bourgeoisie and the Ba'th." *MERIP* 21 (May–June 1991).

————. "Syria's Parliamentary Elections: Remodeling Asad's Political Base." *MERIP*, no. 174 (January–February 1992).

————. "The Syrian Private Industrial and Commercial Sectors and the State." *International Journal of Middle East Studies* 24, no. 2 (May 1992): 203–230.

————. "Problems with Peace: Post-War Politics and Parliamentary Elections in Lebanon." *Orient* 33, no. 3 (September 1992).

Perthes, Volker. "The Syrian Economy in the 1980s." *MEJ* 46 (1992).

———. *Der Libanon nach dem Buergerkrieg, Vom Ta'if zum gesellschaftlichen Konsens?* Ebenhausen: Nomos Verlagsgesellschaft, 1993.

———. "Stages of Economic and Political Liberalization in Syria." In *Contemporary Syria: Liberalization Between Cold War and Cold Peace*, edited by Eberhard Kienle. New York: St. Martin's Press, 1994.

———. "The Private Sector, Economic Liberalization and the Prospects of Democratization: The Case of Syria and Some Other Arab Countries." In *Democracy without Democrats? The Renewal of Politics in the Muslim World*, edited by Ghassan Salamé. London: I.B. Tauris, 1994.

———. *The Political Economy of Syria Under Asad*. London: I.B. Tauris, 1995.

———. "Libanons Parlamentswahlen von 1996: die Akzeptanz des Faktischen." *Orient* 38, no. 2 (1997).

———. *The Political Economy of Syria under Asad*. London: I.B. Tauris, 1998.

Picard, Elizabeth. *The Demobilization of the Lebanese Militias*. Oxford: Centre for Lebanese Studies, 1999.

Pierson, Paul. "Increasing Returns, Path Dependence, and the Study of Politics." *American Political Science Review* 29 (June 2000): 251–268.

———. "Not Just What, but When: Timing and Sequence in Political Processes." *Studies in American Political Development* 14 (Spring 2000): 72–92.

Piore, Michael and Charles Sabel. *The Second Industrial Divide*. New York: Basic Books, 1984.

Piro, Timothy J. *The Political Economy of Market Reform in Jordan*. Lanham: Rowman and Littlefield, 1998.

Planel, Anne-Marie. "Etat réformateur et industrialisation au XIX siècle." *Monde arabe, Maghreb-Machrek* (July–September 1997).

Podolny, J. M. and K. L. Page. "Network Forms of Organization." *Annual Review of Sociology* 24 (1998).

Polling, Sylvia. "What Future for the Private Sector." In *Contemporary Syria: Liberalization Between Cold War and Cold Peace*, edited by Eberhard Kienle. London: I.B. Tauris, 1997.

Pool, David. "The Links between Economic and Political Liberalization." In *Economic and Political Liberalization in the Middle East*, edited by Tim Niblock and Emma Murphy. London: British Academic Press, 1993.

Posusney, Marsha. *Labor and the State in Egypt: Workers, Unions, and Economic Restructuring, 1952–1996*. New York: Columbia University Press, 1997.

Powell, Walter W. "Neither Market nor Hierarchy: Network Forms of Organization." *Research in Organizational Behavior* 12 (1990): 295–336.

Powell, Walter W. and Paul DiMaggio, eds. *The New Institutionalism in Organizational Analysis*. Chicago: University of Chicago Press, 1991.

Powell, Walter W. and Laurel Smith-Doerr. "Networks and Economic Life." In *The Handbook of Economic Sociology*, edited by Neil N. Smelser and Richard Swedberg, 368–402. Princeton, NJ: Princeton University Press, 1994.

Powell, Walter W. and Peter Brantley. "Competitive Cooperation in Biotechnology: Learning Through Networks?" In *Networks and Organizations: Structure, Form, and Action*, edited by N. Nohria and R. G. Eccles, 366–394. Boston, MA: Harvard Business School Press, 1992.

President Hafiz al-Asad's Inaugural Address, Damascus, March 13, 1999.

La Presse, "L'entreprise et l'association: ensemble pour l'avenir," May 13, 1991.

La Presse, "Esprit d'initiative, effort et don de soi pour renforcer la société civile," April 24, 1997.

Qadir al-Nayyal, Abdul, Ibrahim Ali, and 'Issam al-Sheikh Oghali. "The Informal Sector: Its State and the Requirements for Its Integration into the Formal Sector" [*Al-Qita`Ghair al-Munadham: al-Waqi`wa Mutatalibaat al-Indimaaj fi al-Iqtisaad al-Rasmi*]. Paper no. 11, 2001 Conference Series. Damascus: Economic Sciences Association, May 29, 1999.

al-Qita`al-Sina`i (Amman: Ministry of Culture and Information, 1969).

al-Raddawi, Taisir. "Policies that Provide Incentives for Investment in Syria" [*al-Siyasaat al-Muhaffitha lil-Istithmaar fi Suriyya*]. Paper no. 10, 2001 Conference Series. Damascus: Economic Sciences Association, May 22, 2001.

Randa, Taqi al-Din. "Iraqi Oil Imports Help Maintain Syria's Balance of Trade Surplus." *al-Hayat*, June 24, 2001.

Rasheed, Sadiq and David Fashole Luke. "Toward a New Development Management Paradigm." In *Development Management in Africa: Toward Dynamism, Empowerment, and Entrepreneurship*, edited by Rasheed and Fashole Luke, 4. Boulder, CO: Westview Press, 1995.

Rayes, C. "Voyage au bout de Solidère." *L'Orient-Express*, November 1996.

———. "CDR: L'Etat et son Double." *L'Orient-Express*, October 1997.

Republic of Tunisia. *Nouveau Code d'incitations à l'investissement*. API, 1994.

Rigger, Shelley. "Electoral Strategies and Political Institutions in the Republic of China on Taiwan." In *Harvard Studies on Taiwan: Papers of the Taiwan Studies Workshop* 1. Cambridge, MA: Fairbank Center for East Asian Research, 1995.

Robinson, Leonard. "Elite Cohesion, Regime Succession and Political Instability in Syria." *Middle East Policy* 5, no. 4 (January 1998).

Rodenbeck, Max. *Egypt*. London: Business Monitor International, 1998.

Rodrik, Dani. "The Rush to Free Trade in the Developing World: Why So Late? Why Now? Will It Last?" In *The Political Economy of Reform*, edited by Federico Sturzenegger and Mariano Tommasi, 209–239. Cambridge: MIT Press, 1998.

Roitman, Janet. *Fiscal Disobedience: Economic Regulation in Central Africa*. Princeton, NJ: Princeton University Press, forthcoming.

Rosenthal, Naomi, Meryl Fingrudt, Michele Ethier, Roberta Karant, and David McDonald. "Social Movements and Network analysis: A Case Study of Nineteenth-Century Women's Reform in New York State." *American Journal of Sociology* 90 (1985): 1022–1054.

Saâdi, Mohamed Saïd. *Les Groupes Financiers au Maroc*. Casablanca, Morocco: Okad, 1989.

Sadik, A. T. and A. A. Bolbol. *Mobilizing International Capital for Arab Economic Development with Special Reference to the Role of FDI.* Abu Dhabi: Arab Monetary Fund, 2000.

Sadowski, Yahya. *Political Vegetables: Businessmen and Bureaucrats in the Development of Egyptian Agriculture.* Washington, DC: The Brookings Institution, 1991.

Saif, Riad. "Exports: Between Dream and Reality" [*al-Tasdir bayna il-Hilm wa-l-waqi*']. Paper no. 13, 1999 Conference Series. Damascus: Economic Sciences Association, May 13, 1999.

Salameh, Mahmoud. "Goals-Oriented Management: Where to?" [*al-Idara bil-Ahdaf: ila Ayn?*]. Paper no. 3, 2000 Conference Series. Damascus: Economic Sciences Association, February 1, 2000.

Salzmann, Ariel. "An Ancient Régime Revisited: 'Privatization' and Political Economy in the Eighteenth Century Ottoman Empire." *Politics & Society* 21, no. 4 (December 1993): 393–423.

Sarkis, H. "Territorial Claims: Architecture and Post-War Attitudes Toward the Built Environment." In *Recovering Beirut: Urban Design and Post-War Reconstruction*, edited by S. Khalaf and P. S. Khoury. Leiden: Brill, 1993.

Sassine, F. "Is Parliament's Credibility in the Red?" *The Lebanon Report* (Spring 1996).

Satloff, Robert B. *From Abdullah to Hussein: Jordan in Transition.* Oxford: Oxford University Press, 1994.

Saxenian, Annalee. "The Role of Immigrant Entrepreneurs in New Venture Creation." In *The Entrepreneurship Dynamic: Origins of Entrepreneurship and the Evolution of Industries*, edited by Claudia Bird Schoonhoven and Elaine Romanelli, 68–108. Stanford, CA: Stanford University Press, 2001.

Sayigh, Yusif. *The Economies of the Arab World: Development Since 1945.* London: Croon Helm, 1978.

as-Sayyigh, D. *An-Nizam al-Lubnani fi Thawabitihi wa Tahawwulatihi.* Beirut: Dar an-Nahar, 2000.

Schamis, Hector E. "Distributional Coalitions and the Politics of Economic Reform in Latin America." *World Politics* 51 (January 1999): 236–268.

Scharpf, Fritz. *Games Real Actors Play: Actor-Centered Institutionalism in Policy Research.* Boulder, CO: Westview, 1997.

Schmid, Claudia. *Das Konzept des Rentier-Staates. Ein sozialwissenschaftliches Paradigma zur Analyse von Entwicklungsgesellschaften und seine Bedeutung für den Vorderen Orient.* Münster: Lit., 1991.

Schmitter, Philippe C. and Wolfgang Streeck. "Community, Market, State and Associations? The Prospective Contribution of Interest Governance to Social Order." In *Markets, Hierarchies, and Networks: The Coordination of Social Life*, edited by Graham Thompson, Jennifer Frances, Rosalind Levacic, and Jeremy Mitchell, 227–241. London: Sage Publications, 1991.

Schneider, Ben Ross and Sylvia Maxfield. "Business, the State, and Economic Performance." In *Business and the State in Developing Countries*, edited by S. Maxfield and B. R. Schneider. Ithaca: Cornell University Press, 1997.

Schneider, Ben Ross and Sylvia Maxfield, eds. *Business and the State in Developing Countries*. Ithaca, NY: Cornell University Press, 1997.

Schweitzer, Thomas. *Muster sozialer Ordnung. Netzwerkanalyse als Fundament der Sozialethnologie*. Berlin: Dietrich Reimer Verlag, 1996.

Scott, Gordon, H. "The Ideology of Laissez-Faire." In *The Classical Economists and Economic Policy*, edited by A. W. Coats. London: Muthuen, 1971.

Scott, John. *Social Network Analysis*. London: Sage Publications, 1991.

Seale, Patrick. *Asad: The Struggle for the Middle East*. London: I.B. Tauris, 1988.

Shafer, Michael. *Winners and Losers: How Sectors Shape the Developmental Prospects of States*. Ithaca, NY: Cornell University Press, 1994.

al-Shafi`i, Jalal. *Al-mawsu`a al-daribiyya*. Cairo, 1999.

Shafik, Nemat et al., eds. *Claiming the Future: Choosing Prosperity in the Middle East*. Washington, DC: The World Bank, 1995.

Shafik, Nemat, ed. *Economic Challenges Facing Middle Eastern and North African Countries: Alternative Futures*. New York: St. Martin's Press, 1998.

al-Shallah, Badr Din. *Lil-Tarikh wa-l-Thikra, Badr al-Din al-Shallah, Qissat Juhd wa `Umur* [*For History and Memory, Badr al-Din al-Shallah, A Story of Effort and Life*], 2nd edition. Damascus: Alif Baa' al-Adeeb Press, 1995.

Shams ad-Din, M. I. *Mugharat al-'Imar, bi al-Haqa'iq wa al-Arqam*. Beirut, 1999.

Shehadi, N. *The Idea of Lebanon, Economy and State in the Cenacle Libanais 1946–54*. Oxford: Centre for Lebanese Studies, 1987.

Shepsle, K. A. "*The Political Economy of State Reform: Political to the Core*." Lecture originally presented at the Seminar for State Reform, Bogota, Columbia, 1998.

Simon, Catherine. "Les appétits d'un clan." *Le Monde*, October 22, 1999.

Sines, R. "Towards an Investor-Friendly Policy Environment." In IBTCI/USAID Privatization Project, Evaluation Services Contract, Quarterly Review. Cairo, January 1–March 31, 1998.

Skaffe, Phillipe. *Ali Baba and the Forty Thieves: The Myth and the Reality (Tracing the roots of Corruption in the Arab Personality)*. Paper presented at the International Anti-Corruption Conference in Prague, 2001.

Solnick, Steven L. *Stealing the State: Control and Collapse in Soviet Institutions*. Cambridge: Harvard University Press, 1998.

Springborg, Robert. *Mubarak's Egypt: Fragmentation of the Political Order*. Boulder, CO: Westview Press, 1989.

Stark, David and Bruszt Laszlo. *Post-Socialist Pathways: Transforming Politics and Property in East Central Europe*. Cambridge: Cambridge University Press, 1998.

Statistical Abstract 1990, 1998, 1999, and 2000. Damascus: Central Bureau of Statistics.

Stinchcombe, Arthur L. "Weak Structural Data." Review of "Intercorporate Relations: The Structural Analysis of Business," edited by Mark Mizruchi and Michael Schwartz. *Contemporary Sociology* 19 (1990): 380–382.

Subramanian, Arvind. "The Egyptian Stabilization Experience: An Analytical Perspective." Working Paper no. 18. Cairo: Egyptian Center for Economic Studies, October 1997.

Sukkar, Nabil. "The Crisis of 1986 and Syria's Plan for Reform." In *Contemporary Syria: Liberalization Between Cold War and Cold Peace*, edited by Eberhard Kienle. London: I.B. Taurus, 1997.

Sulayman, Taqi ad-Din et al. *Al-Qada' al-Lubnani, Bina' wa Tatwir al-Mu'assasat*. Beirut: LCPS, 1999.

Suleiman, Ezra N. and John Waterbury. *The Political Economy of Public Sector Reform and Privatization*. Boulder: Westview Press, 1990.

Sullivan, Denis and Ilia Harik, eds. *Privatization and Liberalization in the Middle East*. Bloomington: Indiana University Press, 1992.

Susser, Asher. *On Both Banks of the Jordan: A Political Biography of Wasfi Al Tall*. London: Frank Cass, 1994.

Tell, Tariq. "Les origines sociales de la glasnost jordanienne." In *Moyen-Orient: Migrations, démocratisation et médiations*, edited by R. Bocco and M. R. Djalili. Paris/Geneva: PFUF/IUEHEI, 1994.

Thelen, Kathleen. "Historical Institutionalism in Comparative Politics." *Annual Review of Political Science* 2 (1999): 369–404.

———. "Timing and Temporality in the Analysis of Institutional Evolution and Change." *Studies in American Political Development* 14 (Spring 2000): 101–108.

Thelen, Kathleen and Sven Steinmo. "Historical Institutionalism in Comparative Politics." In *Structuring Politics: Historical Institutionalism in Comparative Analysis*, edited by Sven Steinmo, Kathleen Thelen, and Frank Longstreth, 1–32. New York: Cambridge University Press, 1995.

Thompson, Graham, Jennifer Frances, Rosalind Levacic, and Jeremy Mitchell, eds. *Markets, Hierarchies, and Networks: The Coordination of Social Life*. London: Sage Publications, 1991.

Tohamy, Sahar. "Tax Administration and Transaction Costs in Egypt." In *Partners for Development: New Roles for Government and Private Sector in the Middle East and North Africa*, edited by Samiha Fawzy and Ahmad Galal. Washington, DC: The World Bank, 1999.

Trabulsi, F. "At-Takawun at-Tabaqi li as-Sulta as-Siyasiya ba'd al-Harb." *Ab'ad*, no. 6 (May 1997).

———. *Sallat bi-la Wasl, Michel Chiha wa al-Idiyulujiya al-Lubnani*. Beirut: al-Nashr, 1999.

United States Embassy, Tunis, Tunisia. "Foreign Investment in Tunisia: Incentives under the New Code." *Middle East Executive Reports* 17, no. 9 (1994): 19–21.

Union Tunisienne de l'Industrie, du Commerce et de l'Artisanat (UTICA). *La mise à niveau de l'entreprise*. Tunis: UTICA, 1995.

Valensi, Lucette. *Fellahs tunisiens: L'économie rurale et la vie des campagnes aux 18 et 19 emes siècles*. Paris: Mouton, 1977.

Vickers, John and George Yarrow. *Privatization: An Economic Analysis*. Cambridge, MA: MIT Press, 1998.

Vitalis, Robert. *When Capitalists Collide: Business Conflict and the End of Empire in Egypt*. Berkeley, CA: University of California Press, 1999.

Wade, Robert. "East Asia's Economic Success: Conflicting Perspectives, Partial Insights, Shaky Evidence." *World Politics* 44 (January 1992): 270–320.

Wahba, Mourad Magdi. *The Role of the State in the Egyptian Economy: 1945–1981.* Reading: Ithaca Press, 1994.

Wakim, N. *Al-Ayadi as-Sawd.* Beirut: al-Nashr, 1998.

Wallerstein, Immanuel. "The Bourgeois(ie) as Concept and Reality." *New Left Review* 167 (January–February 1988): 91–106.

Wassermann, Stanley and K. Faust. *Social Network Analysis: Methods and Applications.* New York: Cambridge University Press, 1994.

Wasserman, Stanley and Joseph Galaskiewicz. "Introduction: Advances in the Social and Behavioral Sciences from Social Network Analysis." In *Advances in Social Network Analysis: Research in the Social and Behavioral Sciences*, edited by S. Wasserman and J. Galaskiewicz. California: Sage, 1994.

Wasserman, Stanley and Joseph Galaskiewicz, eds. *Advances in Social Network Analysis: Research in the Social and Behavioral Sciences.* California: Sage, 1994.

Waterbury, John. *The Commander of the Faithful: The Moroccan Political Elite, A Study of Segmented Politics.* London: Weidenfeld and Nicholson, 1970.

———. "Tribalism, Trade and Politics: The Transformation of the Swasa of Morocco." In *Arabs and Berbers*, edited by Ernest Gellner and Charles Micaud, 231–257. London: Duckworth, 1972.

———. "Endemic and Planned Corruption in a Monarchical Regime." *World Politics* 25 (July 1973): 534–555.

———. *The Egypt of Nasser and Sadat: The Political Economy of Two Regimes.* Princeton, NJ: Princeton University Press, 1983.

———. "The Heart of the Matter? Public Enterprise and the Adjustment Process." In *The Politics of Economic Adjustment*, edited by Haggard and Kaufman. Washington, DC: Overseas Development Council, 1989.

———. "The Political Management of Economic Adjustment and Reform." In *Fragile Coalitions: The Politics of Economic Adjustment*, edited by Joan M. Nelson, 39–56. Washington, DC: Overseas Development Institute, 1989.

———. "Twilight of the State Bourgeoisie." *IJMES* 23 (1991).

———. *Exposed to Innumerable Delusions.* New York: Cambridge University Press, 1993.

Weber, M. *Economy and Society: An Outline of Interpretive Sociology.* Berkeley/Los Angeles/London: University of California Press, 1978.

Weiss, Dieter. *Wirtschaftliche Entwicklungsplanung in der VAR (Ägypten)—Analyse und Kritik.* Cologne and Opladen: Verlag, 1964.

———. "Institutionelle Aspekte der Selbstblockierung von Reformpolitiken: Fallstudie Ägypten." *Konjunkturpolitik* 1 (1992).

Weiss, Dieter and Ulrich Wurzel. *The Economics and Politics of Transition to an Open Market Economy: Egypt.* Paris: OECD Development Centre, 1998.

Wellman, Barry. "Structural analysis: From Method and Metaphor to Theory and Substance." In *Social Structures: A Network Approach*, edited by Barry Wellman and Stephen D. Berkowitz, 19–61. Cambridge: Cambridge University Press, 1988.

Wellman, Barry and S. D. Berkowitz, eds. *Social Structures: A Network Approach.* Cambridge: Cambridge University Press, 1988.

Wetter, J. "Public Investment Planning and Progress." In *Back to the Future: Postwar Reconstruction and Stabilization in Lebanon,* edited by S. Eken and T. Helbling. Washington, DC: IMF, 1999.

White, Harrison. *Identity and Control: A Structural Theory of Social Action.* Princeton, NJ: Princeton University Press, 1992.

Williams, Robert J. "The New Politics of Corruption." *Third World Quarterly* 20, no. 3 (1999): 487–489.

Williamson, Oliver E. *Markets and Hierarchies: Analysis and Antitrust Implications.* New York: Free Press, 1975.

———. "Calculativeness, Trust, and Economic Organization." In *Journal of Law and Economics* 36 (April 1993): 453–502.

———. *The Mechanisms of Governance.* New York: Oxford University Press, 1996.

Willke, Helmut. *Systemtheorie III: Steuerungstheorie.* Stuttgart/Jena: Gustav Fischer Verlag, 1995.

Wils, Oliver. "Foreign Aid Since 1989 and Its Impact on Jordan's Political Economy: Some Research Questions." *Jordanies* 5/6 (June–December 1998): 100–120.

———. "Private Sector Monopolies and Economic Reform in (Post) Rentier States: The Case of Jordan." *Asien Afrika Lateinamerika* 28, no. 4 (2000): 365–397.

———. *Wirtschaftseliten und Reform in Jordanien: Zur Relevanz von Unternehmer-Bürokraten-Netzwerken in Entwicklungsprozessen.* Hamburg: Deutsches Orient-Institut, 2003.

Wilson, Rodney. "The Role of Commercial Banking in the Jordanian Economy." In *The Economic Development of Jordan,* edited by Adnan Badran and Bichara Khader, 45–61. London: Croom Helm, 1987.

World Bank. Arab Republic of Egypt, Technical Assistance Project for Privatization and Enterprise and Banking Sector Reforms, 1992.

———. *Bureaucrats in Business: The Economics and Politics of Government Ownership.* Washington, DC: 1995.

———. *Lebanon Private Sector Assessment.* Washington, DC: November 1995.

———. *Growing Faster, Finding Jobs: Choices for Morocco.* Washington, DC: World Bank, 1996.

———. *From Plan to Market: World Development Report 1996.* Washington, DC: World Bank, 1996.

———. *Arab Republic of Egypt—Country Economic Memorandum, Egypt: Issues in Sustaining Economic Growth.* Washington, DC: World Bank, March 15, 1997.

———. *The State in a Changing World: World Development Report 1997.* Washington, DC: World Bank, 1997.

———. *Knowledge for Development: World Development Report 1998/99.* Washington, DC: World Bank, 1999.

World Bank and International Finance Corporation. *Privatization: Principles and Practice.* Washington, DC: 1995.

World Development Report, 1996: From Plan to Market. New York: Oxford University Press, 1996.

Wurzel, Ulrich G. "Structural Adjustment in Egypt: Announcements and Implementation of the Privatization Program 1990–1996." *Asien, Afrika, Lateinamerika* 27, no. 2 (1999).

———. *Ägyptische Privatisierungspolitik 1990 bis 1998. Geber-Nehmer-Konflikte, ökonomische Strukturreformen, geostrategische Renten und politische Herrschaftssicherung.* Hamburg, Münster: Lit., 2000.

Wurzel, Ulrich G. and Henk Knaupe. *Entwicklung der Entlastungsstadt Tenth of Ramadan in Ägypten: Erfolge und Fehlschläge in Industrie, Wohnungswesen und Infrastruktur.* Münster: Lit., 1996.

Yachoui, E. *Restructuration et croissance de l'économie Libanaise.* Beirut: Librairie du Liban, 1983.

Young, M. D. "Misreading the Signs: Parliament and the Second Republic." *The Lebanon Report* (Spring 1996).

Zaalouk, Malak. *Power, Class, and Foreign Capital in Egypt: The Rise of the New Bourgeoisie.* London: Zed Press, 1989.

Zaki, Moheb. *Egyptian Business Elites: Their Visions and Investment Behaviour.* Cairo: Ibn Khaldoun Center, 1999.

Zamiti, Khalil. "Le fonds de solidarité nationale: pour une approche sociologique du politique." *Annuaire de l'Afrique du Nord* 35 (1996): 705–712.

Zartman, I. William. "King Hassan's New Morocco." In *The Political Economy of Morocco,* edited by I. W. Zartman, 1–33. New York: Praeger, 1987.

———. "The State on a Tightrope: Institutionalization and Negotiation." In *North Africa: Development and Reform in a Changing Global Economy,* edited by D. Vandevalle, 229–241. London: Macmillan, 1996.

Zghal, Riadh. "Le Développement participatoire: Participation et monde du travail en Tunisie." In *Stratégies de privatisation: comparaison Maghreb-Europe,* edited by Driss Guerraoui and Xavier Richet, 210. L'Harmattan/Casablanca/Paris: Les Editions Toubkal, 1995.

al-Zuhairi, Bashir. "Improving the Banking System in Syria to Satisfy the Needs of Economic Development" [*Ta'hil al-Nithaam al-Masrifi fi Suriyya li-Talbiyat Ihtiyajaat al-Tanmiya al-Iqtisaadiyya*]. Paper no. 3, 1999 Conference Series. Damascus: Economic Sciences Association, March 2, 1999.

Zysman, John. *Governments, Markets and Growth.* Ithaca: Cornell University Press, 1983.

———. "Dynamic Diversity: Institutions and Economic Development in Advanced Countries." In *The Political Economy of Diversity: Evolutionary Perspectives of Economic Order and Disorder,* edited by Robert Delorme and Kurt Dopfer, 126–146. Hants, UK: Edward Elgar, 1994.

Index